Going Local?
Linking and Integrating Second-Home Owners with the Community's Economy

Polish Studies in Economics

Edited by Ryszard Kokoszczyński

Volume 9

PETER LANG

Adam Czarnecki

Going Local? Linking and Integrating Second-Home Owners with the Community's Economy

A Comparative Study between Finnish and Polish Second-Home Owners

PETER LANG

Bibliographic Information published by the Deutsche Nationalbibliothek
The Deutsche Nationalbibliothek lists this publication in the Deutsche Nationalbibliografie; detailed bibliographic data is available in the internet at http://dnb.d-nb.de.

Cover Design:
© Olaf Gloeckler, Atelier Platen, Friedberg

This publication was financially supported by the Institute of Rural and Agricultural Development of the Polish Academy of Sciences.

ISSN 2191-8848
ISBN 978-3-631-72901-4 (Print)
E-ISBN 978-3-631-72902-1 (E-PDF)
E-ISBN 978-3-631-72903-8 (EPUB)
E-ISBN 978-3-631-72904-5 (MOBI)
DOI 10.3726/b11462

PL Academic Research is an Imprint of Peter Lang GmbH.

Peter Lang – Berlin · Bern · Bruxelles · New York · Oxford · Warszawa · Wien

This publication has been peer reviewed.

www.peterlang.com

Table of contents

Tables, maps and figures in this book

Tables

Figures

Maps

Abstract

Numerous rural communities in Europe have been facing dramatic outmigration, depopulation and the distortion of socio-demographic structures. At the same time, despite their difficulties they have become increasingly attractive places of residence and leisure for urban migrants, including seasonal incomers as second-home owners. Thus, from the rural viewpoint, the crucial question arises of whether the second-home phenomenon can be a factor that helps to mitigate these negative effects in the countryside and therefore contributes to its resilience and vitality by creating substantial demand for local goods and services. This comparative study (of Finland and Poland) aims to examine the strength and complexity of economic links between second-home owners and locals as well as the level of integration of second-home owners into the local economy. The concept of a "determinants-performance-impact" triad was applied in order to take a possibly complex and comprehensive approach to the entire logical process of the drivers, preconditions, consumption practices and spending, and their effect on the local economy. As a result, the strong integration and considerable (albeit internally differentiated) impact of second-home owners' consumption on the local community was confirmed in terms of income growth, while less significant in terms of job creation. A complex pattern of local consumption drivers and preconditions was reconstructed, revealing the decisive role of household income/wealth. In addition, the distinctiveness of seasonal compared to regular spending, usefulness of the individual and family life-cycles as well as the owner's life-course perspective in exploring the temporal shift in consumption and the significance of informal purchasing were confirmed.

Key words: second homes, second-home owners, consumer behaviour, spending patterns, local purchasing, local economy, rural areas, Finland, Poland

Preface

The rise in wealth along with growing free-time resources and more popular flexible lifestyles in recent decades have largely stimulated the search, mainly among urban dwellers, for new forms of recreation and leisure to compensate for the pressures and inconveniences of urban life (namely stress, rush, environmental pollution, crime, etc.). Despite second homes – often identified as holiday – , summer – , vacation homes – not being a new phenomenon, they are very common in the Nordic countries (e.g. Finland), while their popularity has been gradually increasing in other, "transitional" countries (e.g. in Poland). What is more, changing spatial/localisation patterns of second homes all over Europe have been confirmed. Today second homes are no longer geographically limited to metropolitan zones and tourism-based communities (coastal, lake districts, mountains), but have tended to concentrate even in less attractive leisure destinations – traditional rural areas or even those with declining agriculture. This changing pattern has been driven by the improved accessibility to more remote, peripheral areas as well as by the generational change, in which farms and properties are inherited by the descendants of their former owners and then converted into secondary residences. Consequently, the once largely concentrated second-home phenomenon has become more widespread in rural areas.

On the other hand, it is precisely these areas, based on a traditional, monoculture economy (agriculture and forestry), that are usually considered as problem areas, with various negative phenomena and processes associated with depopulation, ageing, "brain drain", limited financial resources and low attractiveness for investors and new residents. Since the 1990s, these areas have attracted considerable attention from researchers, NGOs and policy- and decision-makers (mostly with regard to the search for new directions and development opportunities) who often highlighted the significance of job creation, increasing incomes and rural (economic) diversification in order to strengthen local communities and counter depopulation and other negative trends.

This comparative work (Finland-Poland) aims to assess the significance of the second-home phenomenon for the rural economy through an examination of the level of integration and exploration of economic relationships between second-home owners and local people. Since the economic impact is highly dependent upon second-home owners' consumption patterns, and these in turn are dependent on consumer-behaviour drivers and other preconditions, this study has attempted to take a wider look at second-home owners' local economic performance and has followed the logical sequence of cause-effect relations in order to better understand the mechanisms and the extent to which various consumer preconditions are reflected in particular actions and local effects. The "determinants-performance-impact" triad approach consequently provided an opportunity to fully and comprehensively address the research problem.

This six-part monograph is entirely dedicated to the economic aspect of the second-home phenomenon in the context of rural development. Its basic design is anchored in a factor-performance-impact triad of the second-home owners'/users' consumption behaviour. Chapter 1 outlines the broader (quantitative) context for the study, focusing on contemporary transformations in the European countryside with an emphasis on its stable and distinctive element, i.e. second homes, in an attempt to justify the selection of countries to be compared with regard to their similarities and differences in this respect. The main research idea, including the research objectives, hypothesis, methodology, data sources and the selection of case-study communities, is presented in chapter 2. Chapter 3 presents a broad theoretical framework of this research. It outlines the theories, concepts and findings of previous research in the field, i.e. socio-cultural, economic, psychological and other supplementary factors, preconditions and drivers of consumption behaviour, recognition of economic links and expenditure patterns demonstrated by second-home owners locally, as well as the visitors' economic integration and an assessment of their impact on the local economy. Chapter 4 is dedicated to research outcomes and interpretations, including factors of local consumption, second-home owners' economic performance (comprising basic data on the size and structure of the commodity bundle, consumer typology, income elasticity, Engel's curves, individual and family life-cycles and the informal economy) and their impact on the local economy. The research results are discussed in chapter 5, with reference to relevant scientific literature, while some broad conclusions are drawn and demonstrated in chapter 6. The book ends with a list of references.

Acknowledgements

This work was supported by the Polish Ministry of Science and Higher Education under the grant "The significance of second homes in the development of rural areas" [N N114 122935] at the Institute of Rural and Agricultural Development, Polish Academy of Sciences in Warsaw (2008–2011), the postdoctoral project "Second homes: chance or threat for rural economy?" at the Karelian Institute, University of Eastern Finland in Joensuu (2012–2014), the international project "Homes beyond homes: Multiple dwelling and everyday living in leisure spaces" (HOBO) [Project No 255424] supported by Academy of Finland (2012–2015) and the postdoctoral grant "Second homes as a potential for the Local Economic Development (LED)" supported by the Finnish Foundation for Municipal Development, KAKS (2015–2017).

This book would not have been written without the help and efforts from many people contributing to my study at various stages of the whole research process. First, I am very grateful to my book reviewers, C. Michael Hall, Kati Pitkänen and Jerzy Wilkin, for their insight and valuable comments that helped me improve the quality of this text. Special thanks go to Kati Pitkänen for numerous questions and suggestions on how to properly interpret the data for Finland, and also for her earlier contribution to the conceptualisation of the research idea and to the design of the survey. Second, since the starting point for the comparative study was the Polish survey, let me take this opportunity to thank Krystian Heffner, who supported me throughout the entire research and writing process. Third, seeing that the Finnish part of the study was, for various reasons, more demanding, it would not have been successfully concluded without the involvement of people I worked with in Finland, especially Maarit Sireni, Lea Kervinen (Karelian Institute, University of Eastern Finland) and Manu Rantanen (Ruralia Institute, University of Helsinki), who helped me in so many ways and contributed their time and expertise to my research project.

The release of this book was financially supported by the Foundation for the Development of Polish Agriculture.

fdpa

Foundation for the Development of Polish Agriculture

Fundacja na Rzecz Rozwoju Polskiego Rolnictwa

1. Background

In the introductory section of this monograph, a wider macro-scale background for the research problem undertaken in the study is summarised. It provides grounds for building-up the theoretical framework and conducting a further analysis. The emphasis is on the rural transformations in the post-war era from the European viewpoint and the present study traces back the most fundamental socio-economic changes and tendencies observed over several past decades in the European rural space. Adopting a historical perspective, this study also presents different development/rural change trajectories observable for a long time in two systems greatly distinctive in political and economic terms – capitalism (Finland) and socialism (Poland). The following section is an attempt to justify the selection of both countries to be compared with regard to second-home owners' consumption behaviour and its implications for rural communities. The idea of choosing these countries is supported by, on the one hand, contrasting characteristics between Finland and Poland based on country-scale population and economic performance, while on the other, by potential similarities recognised in ongoing social and economic processes in the countryside (Map 1.1). Then, a brief outline of the second home phenomenon and its growing scale and apparently changing localisation pattern in a more statistical and geographical terms is provided. It precedes the general rationale to formulate research objectives and undertake the whole study.

Map 1.1 Surveyed countries and their location in Europe

Source: Own study.

1.1 European rural areas in transition: towards post-productivist and multifunctional countryside

The European countryside has always been subject to change, but the changes, as seen by the scientific community over recent decades, have been far-reaching and dramatic (Murdoch & Marsden 1994; Muilu & Rusanen 2004; Slee 2005; Perkins 2006; Halamska 2011). In essence, there has been a functional and structural transformation in terms of population, work and policies on a previously unknown scale. The post-war-period productivist/Fordist paradigm, which saw agriculture and other primary industries (e.g. forestry) as a key function and a dominant rural economic activity, has changed radically since the 1990s (Hardill, Graham & Kofman 2001). As a result of increasing pressures and the negative health and environmental effects of large-scale, high-investment farming, the formerly critical focus on food production and provision (as the main role of agriculture) has shifted from the question of volume to that of quality. Thus, the commercial model of agriculture, often characterised by pesticide use, global market orientation and competitiveness, has largely been contested by researchers, which was apparently reflected in recent policies (at that time) (Wilson & Rigg 2003, 2007; Almstedt 2013). As a result, these rising environmental and social concerns have become a causative force for a shift in the development paradigm from a productive to a post-productive countryside (Evans, Morris & Winter 2002). Hence 'the simple equation between the rural economy and the agricultural sector has been undermined' (Allanson & Whitby 1996, p. 1), thus being no longer valid and explanatory, so there has been a shift in thinking, ideology and the perception of what the countryside should be and for whom.

Agricultural decline (in terms of income and employment) has been accompanied by the matching processes of urban residents' increasingly profound exploration and growing interest in the more distant countryside (often motivated by the tiring disadvantages of urban living, such as crime, pollution, noise, traffic, stress, rush, anonymity, overpopulation), with the countryside seen more as a place of consumption, as can be seen for instance by second-home owners (Flognfeldt 2002; Gallent 2014). This has given rise to a new development paradigm of a post-productive and consumption countryside, which has been widely criticised for various reasons (Wilson 2001; Wilson & Rigg 2003; Mather, Hill & Nijnik 2006). These new incomers and society in general have begun to value environmental goods (services, leisure, recreation opportunities) over the basic commodity provision – food supply. So the growing interest in rural areas on the part of external actors, considerably fuelled by attitudes and perceptions of a rural idyll (Halfacree 1997; Boyle & Halfacree 1998; Dirksmeier 2008; Vepsäläinen & Pitkänen 2010), has fuelled an even more intense and widespread shift towards a post-productive (consumption) countryside. However, it seems that in such circumstances – agricultural decline and depopulation – these mostly urban interests in consuming the rural were only a 'natural' response, or taking the opportunity to consume and exploit the countryside that was provided by negative, macroeconomic processes – depopulation, emigration, land abandonment. Thus, the shift from a productive to post-productive consumption countryside has far-reaching effects on the functions of agriculture and the rural areas, with an increased emphasis on functions other than productive. As Marsden and Sonino (2008) stated, in this paradigm, the focal point has shifted from the logics of scale and specialisation of farms (as a critical local resource) towards local environmental protection and natural amenity enhancement. One driver of this is not only industrial capital but the rising factor of urban and ex-urban residents. This group is highly motivated by residential, recreational and leisure goals, which are seen as purely consumption-driven. Thus, nature is here considered mainly as a landscape value (consumption good). In the post-productive paradigm, agriculture, which has lost its original socio-economic importance, can be considered from a multifunctional perspective – albeit very narrowly – mostly in terms of land-use. Other functions and features of agriculture are also production, aesthetic, ecological and social, but rather from the perspective of external stakeholders.

As some have argued (Wilkin 2011), agriculture has always been multifunctional, although in the past multifunctionality was directed inward, i.e. particularly towards farm household members, since it provided not only food but also everyday articles. In the post-productive paradigm, multifunctionality is addressed outwards to satisfy the various needs of external urban stakeholders, who treat the rural and agriculture as a consumption good essential in the context of landscape conservation and land use. Since external demand is highly concentrated in leisure, it means that second-home tourism has become an example or even a product of the post-productive countryside (Vepsäläinen & Pitkänen 2010). However, Finnish researchers have argued that it is different in Finland, taking into account the long history and commonness of second homes even at the time of principally more agri-food production models of the rural economy. Here it seems that second homes are not a product of a post-productivist, consumption countryside, although they contribute to this paradigm or/and take advantage of such a rural change towards a more dynamic and widespread development (favourable conditions). As researchers have pointed out, drivers behind the creation of meanings and notions of the rural include a popular discourse in the media that is highly influential in terms of how the countryside is understood. Interestingly, as stressed in some works, several Common Agricultural Policy (CAP) reforms have introduced policy instruments supporting environmental and landscape conservation, and these have also had a great impact both in terms of the actual use of the rural space and the use of local resources by incomers. So in addition to this, the discourse has been initiated and developed outside of the countryside, as it is based in and takes account of an urban viewpoint, needs and interests. Often considered a rural idyll myth, although widely contested by many (Emmery 2009; Vepsäläinen & Pitkänen 2010; Frisvoll 2014), such idyllic representations are an important incentive for potential second-home owners as well as traditional tourists, visitors and future permanent residents (retirement migrants) (Vepsäläinen & Pitkänen 2010). They frequently construct a bucolic image of the countryside that has nothing in common with its actual state after the process of agricultural industrialisation and rural modernisation (Woods 2005). This image often represents a countryside that no longer exists – if it ever did. Based on an illusion it consequently contributes to a demand for a countryside that does not exist, and thus promotes individual or collective policies aimed at restoring the old order or preserving its relics. This often conflicts with local people's preferences and ideas with regard to the place in which they live. What is more, preserving the traditional countryside for second-home owners and other ex-urban population groups contradicts the modernisation of the rural economy as a critical resource of wealth, well-being and improved living conditions. In light of this, whose interest should prevail? That of the locals or that of the rest of society? Hence, an inherent attribute of the rural idyll is its high 'conflicto-geneity', not only in terms of land-use and local resource consumption but also with regard to contradictory visions of the rural's future and the management of the countryside.

Previous studies have shown that second-home owners (similarly to permanent urban immigrants to rural areas) are a powerful group, although they do not have the right to vote in local elections (of the second-home municipality) and with large concentrations of second homes/leisure areas they are a major influence on local-authority decision-making. This applies not only to local, individual conflicts but also affects large groups within the rural community. On the other hand, the emphasis on agriculture's non-productive functions is not necessarily out of keeping local people's views and interests, especially if compensated financially by CAP or other such measures. This could be even seen as a stimulus to the demand for rural goods and services, even if it is based on an idyllic conception on the part of urban residents. The supply of sometimes not-too-obvious goods and services related to the ecosystem, environment, landscape, aesthetic and social spheres may contribute to rural incomes and more broadly to rural resilience, vitality, livelihood (including supplying various goods and services, such as recreational, construction and maintenance, to second-home owners). This can thus also be treated as a reaction to certain negative processes that have been occurring in the countryside for decades. In Finland, the continuous emigration from rural to urban areas has considerably eroded rural areas socially and demographically, leading to depopulation and the distortion of local socio-demographic structures. The effects include an ageing population, a brain drain and worsening economic prospects (decrease of entrepreneurial initiatives due to age and intellectual shortages), impoverishment (falling living standards due to restructuring/centralisation of public services, lower financial resources, capital potential to invest etc.). These processes have been ongoing since the post-war period and now the consequences are clearly leading to polarisation and growing inequalities between metropolitan and rural areas. In Poland, in the 1990s, the return of many part-time manufacturing workers to agriculture with few new employment opportunities for them made the rural economy and labour market unviable. Nowadays, it seems that in both countries such a functional and political shift should be seen as an action towards stopping the outflow of the rural population to urban areas. In other words, these are to retain the population of the countryside by finding employment opportunities there (locally) or in nearby small towns here considered as 'traditional' local labour markets for rural people. The latter, however, remains problematic due to the change in the economic base, especially in small mono-industrial and mining urban centres that are suffering economically and socially as much as rural communities in transition.

In light of this, finding a balance between the excessive demand for local resources (in some regions) as a far-reaching threat to the future of these areas, and the provision of sufficient income and employment such as the postulated (rural and agricultural) multifunctionality embedded strongly in diversity, can be developed most comprehensively by taking account of the interests of various groups in a sustainable development paradigm.

1.2 Contrasting contexts? Rationale for the Finnish-Polish comparison

What is the rationale behind comparing these two countries with regard to rural change and the second-home phenomenon? At first glance, it seems that Finland

and Poland differ from each other significantly in many aspects, which makes it hard to find potential similarities. In fact, there is much evidence to support this view in relation, for example, to population size, density and distribution, land-use, economic structure, wealth levels, the role of the welfare state, society structure and formation, well-being and lifestyles, (long-term) institutions and culture (see Table 1.2.1). What is more, the second-home phenomenon, the focal point of this study, also varies considerably between the two countries in terms of its scale, commonness, drivers, origins and sometimes usage. All the differences, or at least the large-scale ones affecting the whole society, stem from distinctive historical backgrounds, geopolitics, traditions and environmental or physical conditions. As a result, even the differentiating elements mentioned above are in some cases directly or indirectly important or even decisive for the course of rural change, second-home ownership and usage and the links between them. Thus, the emphasis was first and foremost on potential similarities, as they provide suitable grounds for comparison, revealing, for example, various or common trajectories within rural change or in second-home integration with the local economy. Moreover, it should be remembered that these countries are both members of the European Union and as such they are covered by relevant EU policies and regulations in various aspects, e.g. CAP and regional policies.

Table 1.2.1 Finnish-Polish comparison – basic socio-economic indicators

<table>
<tr><td colspan="7">Country size and rural areas, 2015</td></tr>
<tr><td></td><td colspan="3">Total (km²)</td><td colspan="3">Proportion of rural areas (%)</td></tr>
<tr><td>Finland</td><td colspan="3">338,424</td><td colspan="3"></td></tr>
<tr><td>Poland</td><td colspan="3">312,679</td><td colspan="3">93.1</td></tr>
<tr><td colspan="7">Population, 2015 (1)</td></tr>
<tr><td></td><td colspan="3">Total</td><td colspan="2">Density (per km²)</td><td>Proportion of rural population (%)</td></tr>
<tr><td>Finland</td><td colspan="3">5,489,821</td><td colspan="2">18.1</td><td>29.5</td></tr>
<tr><td>Poland</td><td colspan="3">38,437,239</td><td colspan="2">122.9</td><td>39.7</td></tr>
<tr><td colspan="7">Population, 2015 (2)</td></tr>
<tr><td></td><td>Live births</td><td>Deaths</td><td>Natural change</td><td>Net migration</td><td colspan="2">Total change between 1 January 2014 and 2015</td></tr>
<tr><td>Finland</td><td>57.2</td><td>52.2</td><td>5.0</td><td>15.4</td><td colspan="2">20.5</td></tr>
<tr><td>Poland</td><td>375.2</td><td>376.5</td><td>-1.3</td><td>-10.9</td><td colspan="2">-12.2</td></tr>
</table>

Employment, 2014						
	Employment rate (% population aged 20–64)	Activity rate, %	Unemployment rate (% labour force)	Youth unemployment rate (% labour force 15–24)	Long-term unemployment rate (% labour force)	At-risk-of-poverty or exclusion (% of total population)
Finland	73.1%	75.4%	8.7%	20.5%	1.9%	17.3%
Poland	66.5%	67.9%	9.0%	23.9%	3.8%	24.7%

GDP, 2014				
	Current prices, million EUR	Current prices, million PPS	EUR per capita	PPS, EU-28=100, EUR per capita
Finland	205,474	166,457	37,600	111
Poland	410,990	717,452	10,700	68

Human Development Index, HDI, 2015	
Finland	0.883
Poland	0.843

Investment, 2013, % share of GDP		
	Business investment	Household investment
Finland	10.6%	6.4%
Poland	10.1%	4.6%

Consumption expenditure of households, 2014		
	As a proportion of GDP (%)	Per capita (euro)
Finland	59.2%	6,400
Poland	52.6%	19,600

Gross value added at basic prices, 2013, % share of total gross value added (1)					
	Agriculture, forestry & fishing	Manufacturing	Construction	Distributive trades, transport, accommoda-tion and food services	Information and communication
Finland	2.8%	18.7%	6.8%	17.0%	5.2%
Poland	3.8%	24.7%	6.5%	27.3%	3.5%

Gross value added at basic prices, 2013, % share of total gross value added (2)					
	Financial and insurance activities	Real estate activities	Professional, scientific, technical, administrative and support services	Public administration, defence, education, human health and social work	Arts, entertainment and recreation; other services (1)
Finland	2.5%	13.1%	8.5%	22.2%	3.3%
Poland	4.3%	5.9%	7.2%	13.7%	3.1%

Source: CSO, Statistics Finland, Eurostat, OECD 2013a, 2013b, 2014, 2015.

Despite significant differences in structures, institutions and culture, there are surprisingly many similarities in processes, tendencies and their effects (albeit mostly of a negative character) occurring in the countryside in both countries. These similarities include a decline in the primary sector (in agriculture and forestry), its declining position in national economies (Figure 1.2.1) and its diminishing role as an income and employment opportunity for rural people, 'deagrarianisation' (a shift from agriculture and forestry towards manufacturing and service-related activities; see Figure 1.2.2), increasing unemployment (partly hidden), selective rural emigration to large cities and metropolitan regions, depopulation, the 'brain drain', impoverishment (or relatively weak income growth at best) and human and intellectual capital erosion in the local community.

Figure 1.2.1 Value added in agriculture and service sector as percentage of GDP in Finland and Poland (1975–2015), %

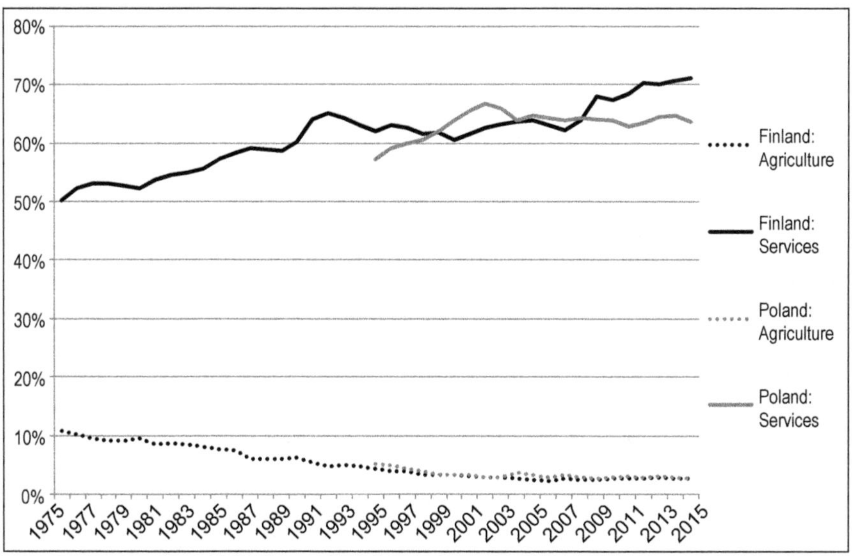

Source: World Bank 2016.

Added to this are falling fertility rates, ageing populations, a rising demographic dependency ratio, the weakening of economic prospects due to decreasing intellectual, innovative and entrepreneurial potential, a fall in local people's financial resources, lower tax revenues to local council budgets and the resulting cuts in public services. These are the main tendencies in the rural areas of both countries, obviously showing a general trend.

Figure 1.2.2 Employment in agriculture and service sector (percentage of total employment) in Finland and Poland (1980–2014), %

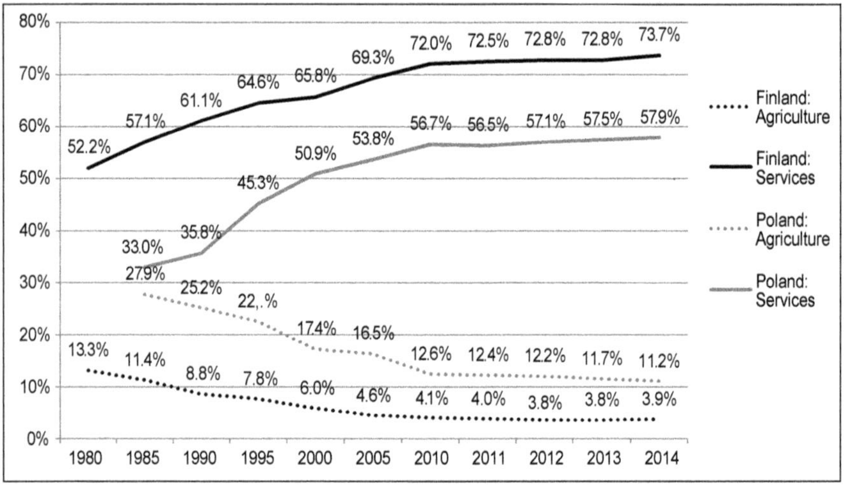

Source: World Bank 2015.

Here rural also includes small urban centres that for decades were an important local labour market for the rural non-farming population, although functionally and economically closely associated with agriculture and forestry as local service centres (processing manufactures and input and auxiliary service suppliers). Especially those in rural heartland areas have been losing their service functions due to globalisation, transport developments and poor competitiveness. However, apart from struggling rural communities suffering from depopulation and its socio-demographic effects, there are also successful communities that have found new development directions, or are implementing innovative ideas making it possible to diminish or stop the negative trend and retain the demographic potential at levels necessary for a viable and prosperous community. This happens for rural communities with a strong multifunctional economic base, often located in peri-urban communities (Rusko and Sipoo in Finland,

Nadarzyn and Stepnica in Poland) and established tourism-based communities (Eckerö in Finland, Rewal and Mielno in Poland), or specialised-economy municipalities (e.g. some mining communities: Kleszczów), or even those with innovative, although contested, employment concepts (Paltamo in Finland). However, most of the countryside is facing major existential problems and this is true for both countries (see Table 1.2.2). Thus, although there are many clear differences in preconditions and structures, there are obvious, long-standing similarities in the background to the countryside, manifesting in rural change that is going mostly in the same direction. Given the background differences as well as similar processes of change, although with a two-to-three-decade time lag in Poland compared to Finland, the focus on the second-home phenomenon is here treated as an attempt to examine its capacity to provide an alternative to the mostly negative effects of rural change.

Table 1.2.2 Finnish-Polish comparison – socio-economic situation in rural regions

Old-age population in rural regions, 2012				
	Share of people aged 65+		Old-age people dependency ratio (65+/15–64)	
Finland		19.5%		30.6%
Poland		13.5%		19.1%
Economically active population, people aged 25 and over, 2011				
	Intermediate regions		Predominantly rural regions	
Finland		30.3%		38.3%
Poland		37.2%		32.9%
Employment rate, people aged 20–64, 2011				
	Intermediate regions		Predominantly rural regions	
Finland		72.5%		70.7%
Poland		63.0%		65.0%
Unemployment rate, people aged 25 or more, 2011				
	Intermediate regions		Predominantly rural regions	
Finland		7.0%		6.5%
Poland		8.6%		8.6%
Employment in rural regions, 2009, % of total employment				
	Primary sector	Manufacturing	Construction	Services
Finland	8.5%	18.8%	7.5%	65.2%
Poland	27.0%	21.1%	7.4%	44.5%

Gross value added in rural regions, 2010, % of total value added

	Primary sector	Manufacturing	Construction	Services
Finland	5.6%	24.2%	7.4%	62.8%
Poland	8.5%	26.9%	8.3%	56.3%

Other gainful on-farm activities for agricultural holdings, 2010

	Share of holdings with other gainful activities	Tourism, 100%=holdings with other gainful activities	Processing farm production	Renewable energy production	Forestry work	Wood processing	Contractual work	Handicrafts
Finland	26.5%	9.7%	6.9%	5.9%	6.4%	2.5%	0.3%	58.6%
Poland	3.3%	8.8%	13.7%	1.1%	1.9%	1.3%	12.3%	18.9%

Standard output of agricultural holdings from other gainful on-farm activities, 2010

	10–50% of turnover from other gainful activities	>50% of turnover from other gainful activities
Finland	8.9%	3.8%
Poland	2.3%	2.0%

Source: Eurostat 2009, 2010, 2011, 2012.

It is worthwhile to combine these issues, as despite the similarities in rural processes, there are significant differences with regard to second homes (as discussed above) in terms of origins, scale, distribution and usage. As there is a temporal shift in rural change, namely counter-urbanisation in favour of Finland, one may treat what happens there as a model or future target for potential analogies in Poland. Thus, on the basis of the Finnish countryside, including second homes, one may predict a similar scenario for Poland and, crucially for the study, answer the question of the potential role of second homes in tackling current rural problems when they become a widespread feature of the countryside. Therefore, we can see a potential perspective of what may happen in Poland in the future and to what extent second homes can be a remedy providing an alternative source of income and employment for the rural population, thus contributing to the livelihood, resilience and vitality of the countryside.

Despite significant differences in many aspects, mentioned above, the rural change that has occurred in Finland since the 1960s and since the 1990s in Poland is driven by and consists of many analogous processes giving rise to similar effects.

A. Post-war and contemporary emigration from rural to urban areas has led to gradual (in Finland very dynamic) urbanisation, as the urbanisation index in Finland increased from 30% in 1950 to almost 70% in 2014 and from 32% in 1946 to 60% in 2014. Despite largely similar general tendencies, the main difference is that in Finland the tendency is consistently rising (with some periods of dynamic and some of weak growth) whereas in Poland, after a steady increase up to the 2000s (with a peak of 61.7% in late 1990s), there has been a relatively small but constant decrease, now reaching 60.3%. Since this difference is largely dependent upon the definition of the rural used in public statistics, these changes in population trends can be explained by introducing various categories of the urban and the rural. In Finland, the positive trend has been observed in all urban categories (i.e. inner and outer urban areas) as well as for peri-urban zones, although the highest was recorded for inner-urban areas (from 23.5% to 26.2% in the period 1990–2014) while the decrease held for all urban areas, and even areas adjacent to urban areas. For Poland, although the population of rural administrative areas has been growing consistently, an increase has in fact been noted only in the immediate surroundings of regional cities (from 4.6% to 5.9% in years 1997–2014), that is highly urbanised areas, although administratively still rural (so the trend can be misleading and does not reflect the actual situation). This was the only type of a 'growing' area, since 'purely' urban areas have been gradually losing their population (61.9% to 60.3% in same period) and other rural areas (there is no distinction between rural heartland and remote rural areas in Polish public statistics) have maintained their population at the same level (33.6%-33.7%).

However, some studies have shown a dramatic depopulation in most of remote areas (eastern border communities and regional fringes in central and eastern Poland). Thus, to sum up, the population has remained stable in rural heartland areas while remote areas have become increasingly abandoned. Hence, while in Finland the main direction of permanent migration is to urban areas, which is leaving the countryside increasingly depopulated, in Poland, the main direction is into suburban zones (Lisowski 2005, 2007), with the population leaking out of urban areas but remaining stable in the rural ones. This to some extent matches seasonal, leisure migration tendencies of second-home owners, who in Finland prefer to have their cottages located far from their primary homes – in rural heartlands and sparsely populated, remote rural areas – while their counterparts in Poland also tend to locate them in peri-urban or more distant locations (albeit more naturally appealing), as secondary residences are being pushed out by new permanent residents (ex-urban dwellers).

B. The long-term intense emigration from rural areas to large cities and suburbs is a key-driver of many negative socio-demographic and economic processes in the countryside in both countries. As people leave rural areas mostly for economic reasons (in search of suitable employment), it is the most mobile members of rural society who decide to leave, i.e. young, relatively well-educated and skilled people. Hence, the human resource and intellectual capital critical for the future of those areas are drained out, dramatically worsening development perspectives. Emigration leads to progressive depopulation, especially of more peripheral communities, being a direct factor in further erosion of the socio-demographic and economic base. A further consequence is the distortion of demographic structures, reflected in an ageing population, brain drain and, consequently, weak economic prospects for both individuals and local councils, whose income from taxation to the local budget is still decreasing, thus undermining funding for local public services. This is an increasing burden for local authorities, affecting local people's well-being.

As a result, the shortage in public services acts as a further push factor for those left in the countryside, contributing to further depopulation, and in this case affecting older people and not only younger and promising residents. These processes have been observed in both countries, but the most recent depopulation trend has been clearly stronger in itself as well as in its negative effects in Finland, given its nationwide scale and increasing dynamics. In Poland, it is more limited to remote areas while in Finland it is most visible in peripheries but has been gradually spreading into rural heartland areas, central villages and even areas adjacent to urban centres. The ageing process has been affecting both societies to a large extent since the post-war baby-boomers have been gradually retiring.

1.3 Second homes as an ever-growing phenomenon: key-drivers, scale and spatial patterns in Finland and Poland

Second homes are not a new phenomenon and some researchers have traced its manifestations back even to the distant past. Thus, there were summer residences of wealthy patricians in the Roman Empire (Dijst *et al.* 2005), royal summer residences in the Chinese Empire (Wang 2006), gardens and villas belonging to nobles and wealthy residents of Beijing in the feudal era (Yang 2001), holiday palaces in the countryside built by wealthy representatives of a feudal class (Tress 2002 as cited in: Nouza, Ólafsdóttir & Müller 2013), or even fortified houses outside the settlements in rural areas in the Middle Ages under episcopal ownership in Normandy (Cassett 1999). In most European countries, the possession of a summer residence or second home was initially reserved for the wealthiest and highest social class (Higley 1995), but up until World War II and the 1950s second-home ownership gradually broadened to include the upper-middle classes (Clout 1969). In the following decades, the most dynamic growth of second-home ownership was observed not only in capitalist countries (Grano 1952; Nordell & Rydberg 1959; Coppock 1977) but also in the socialist bloc, e.g. in Czechoslovakia, Hungary and Poland (Kowalczyk 1994; Csordás 1999; Vágner, Müller & Fialová 2011). This was partly due to several universal factors and macroeconomic processes independent of ideologies and partly due to some new preconditions specific to each of the politico-economic systems.

The key drivers of leisure-oriented second-home ownership were most often increases in wealth (middle and lower classes) and free-time resources, an increase in spatial mobility, improvements in transport giving increased access to more remote locations, the development of leisure property-related legislation, changing socio-demographic structures (ageing and increasing life expectancy) as well as personal motivations, changing lifestyles, consumption patterns and fashions (Patmore 1970; Coppock 1977; Matczak 1986; Kauppinen 1991; Hardill, Graham & Kofman 2001; Hall & Müller 2004). The latter group, widely considered as socio-cultural factors, were very important for Finns as well as other Nordic societies, in which second-home ownership is strongly entrenched in culture (Tuulentie 2006; Giambelluca *et al.* 2014), even perceived as a national cultural heritage (Hall, Müller & Saarinen 2009) or a common way of life (Tress 2002). Thus, in those societies, the economic conditions (wealth and social class) are becoming less and less significant, and second-home ownership crosses the social/wealth divide and involves middle- and even low-income earners as well. It was completely different for Poles, for whom (until the above-mentioned generational change in the 1990s-2000s) the main factor was income status. It is still a very important driver for the second-home movement, especially for those buying homes in famous tourist locations (coast, lakeside), although, since the generational change, the inheritance of rural houses and land and their conversion into second homes especially in typically rural locations has become an equally important precondition. Thus, owning a second home in Poland is to a lesser extent connected with specific lifestyle and cultural preconditions (which is the case in Finland); additionally, the economic factor has been gradually losing its importance (at least in certain locations) in favour of demographic factors, thus enabling more people (although mainly with rural roots) to have their own second home and becoming a more common form of leisure in Poland.

Since the two countries in this study represent (historically) different economic development models, here they can be treated as their exemplifications with regard to the second-home phenomenon or leisure and tourism even in a broader sense. Although one may consider summer rural/forest residences of medieval Polish kings as the origin of the second-home phenomenon in Poland, most researchers place its beginnings in the 19th century and the first decades of the 20th century, referring to summer houses of rich factory-owners outside the city during the industrial revolution in Poland (Pardała 2015), or residences as a common element of garden-city concepts pursued in many European countries in the early 20th century (Baranowska 2007). Basically the same has been identified by researchers in Finland (Tuulentie 2006). In both countries, at that time, the major group of owners were wealthy members of the upper class, the aristocracy, factory-owners etc. Regardless of the later development trajectories, which historically evolved differently, the turning point for both countries came in the 1960s and 1970s, when the most dynamic growth in secondary residences was observed, although to a clearly lesser extent in Poland.

Interestingly, the same macroeconomic processes were at work in both countries at that time, such as dynamic industrialisation (and structural change in agriculture in Finland (Hiltunen & Rehunen 2014)) and high demand for a rather unskilled labour force, which consequently induced rural emigration of post-war baby boomers and resulted in rapid urbanisation (here considered as the growing size of cities). However, in Finland, this massive population outflow towards cities and urbanised areas left behind vast areas of land attractive for leisure purposes, especially in more remote locations (Hiltunen & Rehunen 2014), thus prompting the location of second homes there and changing the functions of the countryside in the short term. In Poland, in contrast, the outflow of baby boomers did not cause any serious changes in rural areas at the time or even until the 1990s. Despite a heavy emigration to cities – a kind of a 'natural' trend towards rural restructuring – no such changes took place, since agriculture remained dominant in the countryside. The emigrants' parents or siblings did not sell the land but still used it for farming, and the immigrants' resources were far too limited to purchase or build property, since their prime concerns were with living in the city, where housing shortages were permanent throughout the socialist era. In light of this, it is worth noting that although the same important factors appeared at the same time, the effects were felt immediately (in the short term) in Finland, while in Poland there was a gradual shift – mostly to the 1990s – in taking advantage of these causative processes. In other words, as many consider second homes to be an example of counter-urbanisation (Buller & Hoggart 1994; McIntyre, Williams & McHugh 2006; Halfacree 2008, 2012; Adamiak, Pitkänen & Lehtonen 2016), one can say that, although the key drivers occurred approximately at the same time, counter-urbanisation itself began some two to three decades earlier in Finland than it did in Poland. Thus, there is a shift not only in scale but in spatial tendencies.

While even in the 1980s the main tendency in Poland was for the concentration of secondary residences within weekend tourism zones, i.e. near large cities (Matczak 1986; Dziegieć 1987; Kowalczyk 1994, 1995), there was a gradual rather than a radical shift in the 1990s and especially in the 2000s, when second homes increasingly began to be located in more remote areas. This was first because, compared to Warsaw, Łódź and other large cities, the main tourism regions – the coast, mountains and lake districts – are on the country's borders. Secondly, an overlapping concurrent process has been observed since the 2000s, whereby after several decades urban people started to move into the more remote, traditional countryside (less attractive compared to the main tourism regions but more attractive because of the belief in the rural idyll). Thus, interestingly, despite the origins of the counter-urbanisation process going back to the 1960s-1970s, counter-urbanisation itself did not become evident until the 2000s. This was partly due to the same mechanism observed at that time in Finland – but now happening in Poland, under a capitalist market economy, with surpluses of cheap, abandoned rural land in remote locations as economic drivers, and with a construction boom (in the first decade of the 2000s) and with the first visible increase in peoples' wealth after the transition. This increase made it possible to build new properties or convert former permanent homes into secondary residences. This tendency partly overlapped with a kind of a generational change that enhanced the counter-urbanisation and rural gentrification process, i.e. delayed the consumption of the countryside by former migrants to cities from periods of the dynamic emigration in the 1970s. Since post-war baby boomers who were rural emigrants in the 1960s-1970s are now retirees, they are returning to their birthplace properties inherited from their parents, who in the meantime passed away. Thus, in contrast to Finnish second-home owners, they have barely been consuming the countryside through second home locations since the 2000s. Therefore, the two tendencies have overlapped.

In Finland, one needs to bear in mind that secondary residences, often small wooden cottages, have traditionally been located on lakesides near the permanent home (Vuoristo 2002; Tuulentie 2006), and this is still a strong tendency today (see Map 1.3.1), although there have been certain geographical changes, with remote rural areas and rural heartlands gradually becoming the most attractive second-home/leisure destinations (Statistics Finland 2010). This tendency has been observed in more remote locations such as in Lapland, which was an area of rapid growth in secondary residences just in the 1970s and 1980s (Tuulentie 2006). This growth confirms the main difference in geographical location and second home ownership between Poland and Finland, in that in the latter, favourable economic factors (cheap land due to depopulation) prompted second-home movement almost immediately, and in the former, it happened 20–30 years later – which was the shift in the counter-urbanisation tendencies in both countries (Map 1.3.2 & Figure 1.3.1).

Finland has been one of the world leaders in second-home ownership since 2013, when there were almost 498,700, of which 405,000 were owned by private persons (at the time in Sweden, the top country in this ranking, the figure was 570,257 (Statistics Sweden 2014)). In Finland, the number of holiday homes has doubled over the past 33 years, with the highest increase in 1980s, while during the 2000s it slowed significantly, partly due to the economic crisis of 2008 (Laitamäki & Järvinen 2013). However, it is expected that the popularity of such a form of leisure will be growing in Finland, reaching 560,000 cottages by the year 2025 (Perrels & Berghäll 2010 as cited in: Pitkänen & Puhakka 2012). In 2012, more than a quarter of Finnish households owned a secondary residence (Statistics Finland 2013) while one in two had access to one through their relatives or friends (approx. 3 million out of a population of 5.3 million) (Statistics Finland 2010). If one positions second homes within total housing resources, in Finland in 2013, they accounted for approx. 19.2%, which is very high by international comparisons. There has been a slight decrease since 2000 (19.6% to 19.2%), showing stagnation in the second housing market, especially compared to the 1980s, when growth was at its highest (from 14.1% to 18.1%) (Statistics Finland 2014).

Map 1.3.1 Secondary residences per km² in Finland (2013)

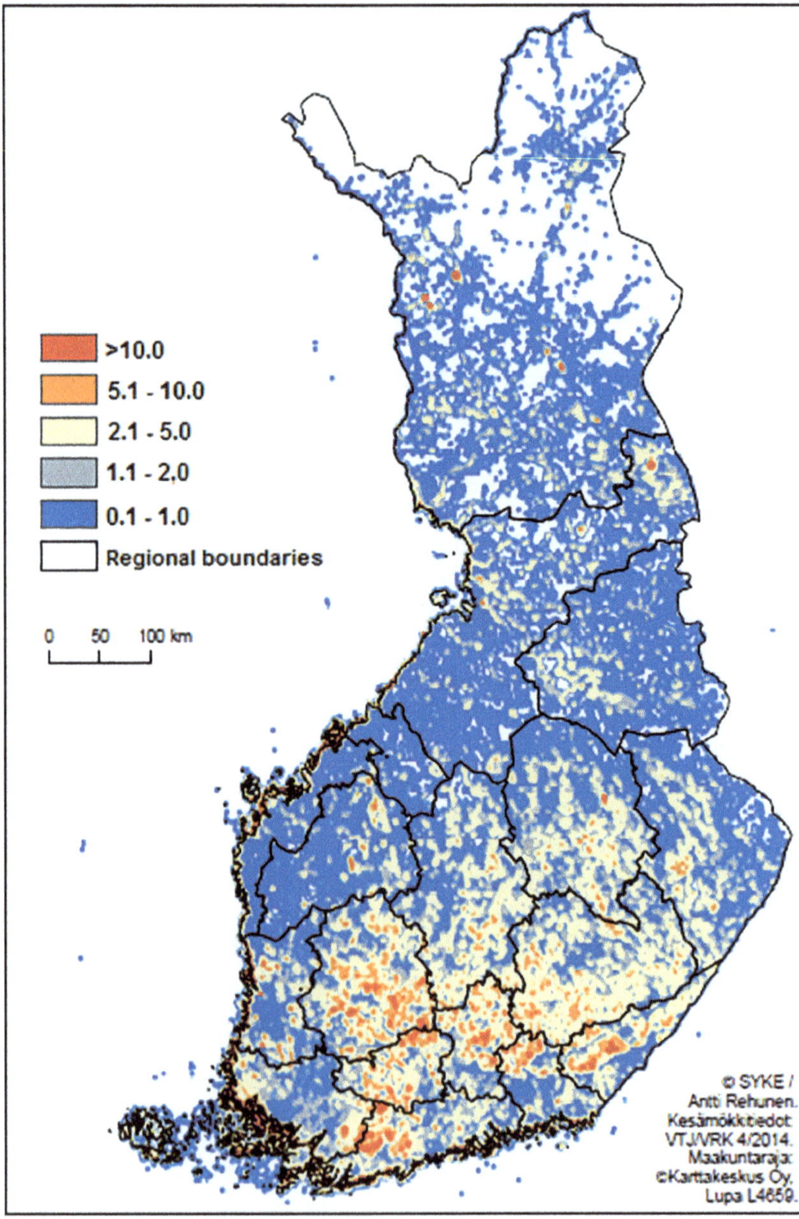

Source: Finnish Environment Institute (SYKE), 2014.

Comparing the scale of this phenomenon to the situation in Poland, there is a significant disproportion in favour of Finland, as in the 2002 National Housing Census (the most recent source of data on this phenomenon) only 201,500 second homes were owned by private persons. However, the very strict definition used at that time makes it necessary to consider this phenomenon narrowly, as it excluded all lightly built wooden cottages, without foundations and not weatherproofed. Thus, the number was certainly an underestimate, as it meant that only 2.1% of the total housing resources in Poland were secondary residences. Here, the absence of or the poor quality of Polish public statistics on secondary residences should be underlined, since the popularity of second-home ownership can be only assessed by data from representative surveys conducted by Polish statistical services as well as other research institutes. Based on these data sources, in 2013, 4.3% of households owned a secondary residence while 12.4% owned a so-called recreational plot. The recreational plot is a statistical category widely used by public statistics and other institutions and in fact means a cottage. The former category is reserved only for 'real' second homes (in contrast to wooden cottages) that have foundations and were constructed according to building codes and permits (Czarnecki & Frenkel 2015). Thus, one may consider the proportion of recreational plots to be the proper value and indicator of the popularity of second homes in Poland, which is half the level of Finland, although the tendency is positive and still growing.

Map 1.3.2 Second-home dynamics in Finland, % (1970–2013)

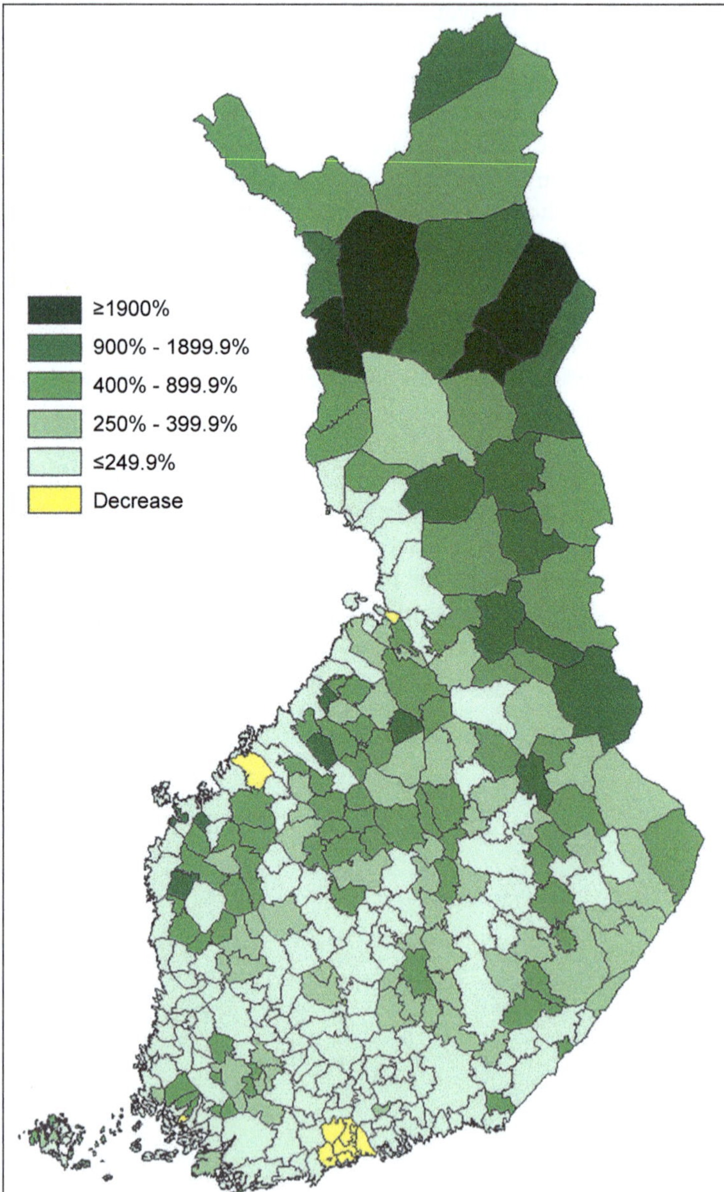

Source: Statistics Finland, 2014.

With regard to the changing pattern of the second-home ownership in Finland, various researchers have already identified its main factors and preconditions – those that are relevant historically and those that have recently appeared and are rapidly gaining in importance (Statistics Finland 2010; Hiltunen *et al.* 2013; Hiltunen & Rehunen 2014). The main historical but still valid factor is a decline in agriculture and other primary industries, inducing outmigration from rural areas and a consequent depopulation. These negative population tendencies are in turn reflected in the increasing areas of abandoned land at competitive prices, which has been an unquestionable incentive for potential second-home owners. As mentioned above, this factor was already crucial in the 1970s, but with the growing urbanisation of the Finnish society, partly due to rural emigration, these negative economic and consequently demographic tendencies have still significantly shaped the rural-urban relations. Hence, this is a long-term factor boosting the opportunity for potential new second-home owners to own and find a proper location. However, such an opportunity is moderated by another important factor that is land and property prices. Those have been constantly increasing in Finland over past decades to the point that the value of a second-home property at an attractive location at a shoreline front is far higher than of other types of rural property (*Maanmittauslaitos*, NLS 2015). Thus, during the past decades, second homes have increasingly become a luxury item. Factors that have also been identified include natural environmental amenities such as the length of the shoreline (as a crucial explanatory factor) (Hiltunen & Rehunen 2014). This means that the longer the shoreline, the greater the possibility for direct access to the lake, river or sea. Hence, the highest concentration of secondary residences is in the Finnish Lakeland and on the coast. Such highly regarded natural values have also affected the distribution or changing localisation pattern towards the north of Finland (Lapland). Although this tendency (a growing interest and number of holiday homes there) is not new, since it appeared in the 1970s and increased later, it has become a principal explanation for current geographic trends (over past 40 years, the dynamics were the highest there). Lapland, like other remote locations, has been increasingly re-settled by second home owners, also due to its growing accessibility (Kauppila 2010) – more flights to the north but also a developing road network and an improvement in road quality (Map 1.3.2). The accessibility factor has greatly contributed to changing the traditional location pattern of second homes, although many holiday homes are still located within the daily and weekend zone of the permanent home, i.e. in suburban and peri-urban zones of large and medium urban centres, but also in the hinterland of small towns. Thus, the change is the greatest in the north while the density remains the highest in southern Finland, which is where most large urban centres with the majority of second home owners are located. According to researchers, rural roots and inheritance are another important influencing factor (Pitkänen 2008; Heffner & Czarnecki 2011), as in fact people with rural origins have tended to build their second homes or convert their parents' home into holiday homes in their places of origin (for psychological but also economic reasons – as the land was cheaper or even free of charge). This was especially true when it was inherited, which meant there was no free choice of location.

Figure 1.3.1 Changing location pattern of second homes in Finland: Growth in the number of secondary residences in various types of area in Finland, 1995–2009=100%, 1995=100%, %

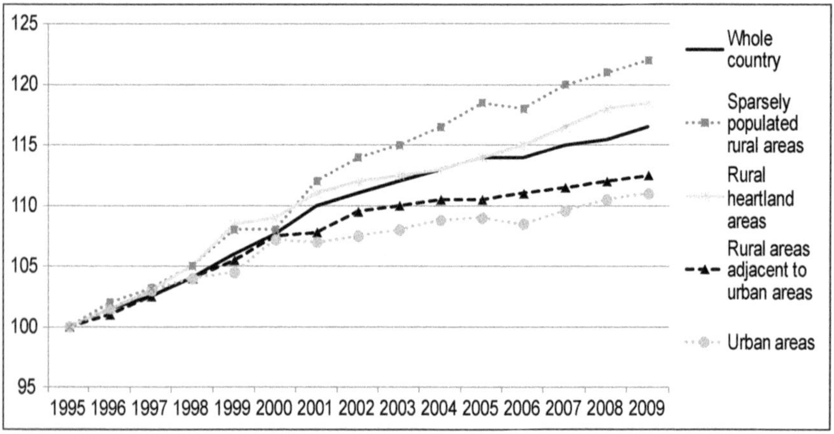

Source: Statistics Finland, 2010.

In a more topographic approach, unlike other (non-Nordic) countries, Finnish cottages are usually located outside villages and settlements and have no clear settlement structure (Hiltunen & Rehunen 2014). Thus, they are more dispersed in forest surroundings along the mosaic of natural waters (Pitkänen 2008), with only 14% of cottages located in villages (Vepsäläinen & Rehunen 2009). This dispersal is to some extent explained by the traditional search for isolation (Hiltunen 2007; Pitkänen 2008; Vepsäläinen & Pitkänen 2010) but also probably by more practical issues such as direct access to the water/lake/river and the feeling of independence. Additionally, the large scale of the second-home phenomenon along with its specific spatial pattern reflect in the relation of the number of summer to permanent homes at the local/municipal level (see Map 1.3.3). In 2012, there was the prevalence of secondary over permanent residences in 18% of Finnish municipalities and among them the highest proportion of those units in total housing resources was observed in the coastal municipality of Kustavi (660%) (Statistics Finland 2013). These numbers certainly show the potential of second homes in terms of local social and economic development and, at the same time, the great challenge with regard to local spatial, strategic planning and sustainable use of local resources.

Map 1.3.3 Relation of secondary residences to permanent homes in Finland (2013)

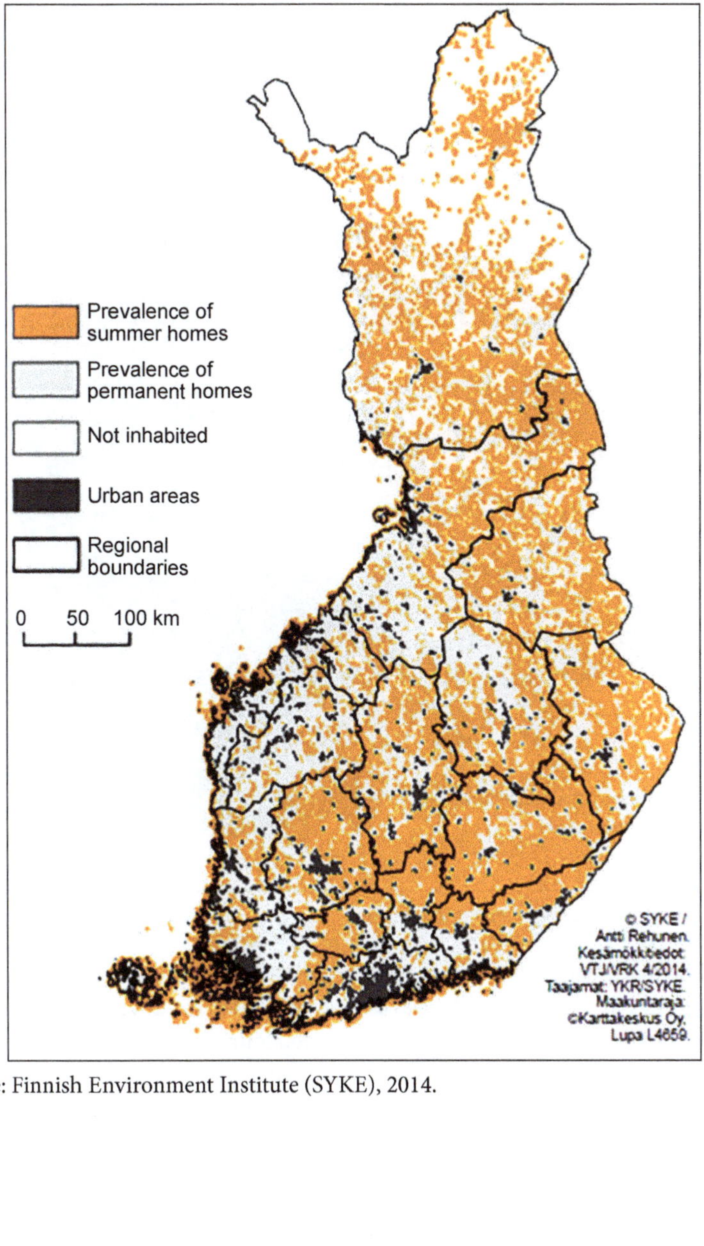

Source: Finnish Environment Institute (SYKE), 2014.

In Poland, a previous study has revealed a significantly diverse picture, with 62.5% of secondary residences being located in villages (with neighbouring permanent homes) and 30.5% creating separate agglomerations of cottages, while only 7% were isolated or dispersed (Heffner & Czarnecki 2011). This can partly be explained by a considerably higher average urbanisation level and population density in Poland.

The restrictive definition of second homes in public statistics in Poland, excluding typical summer cottages, not only affects the understanding of the second-home phenomenon there but also its spatial distribution (Map 1.3.4).

Map 1.3.4 Secondary residences in Poland (2002)

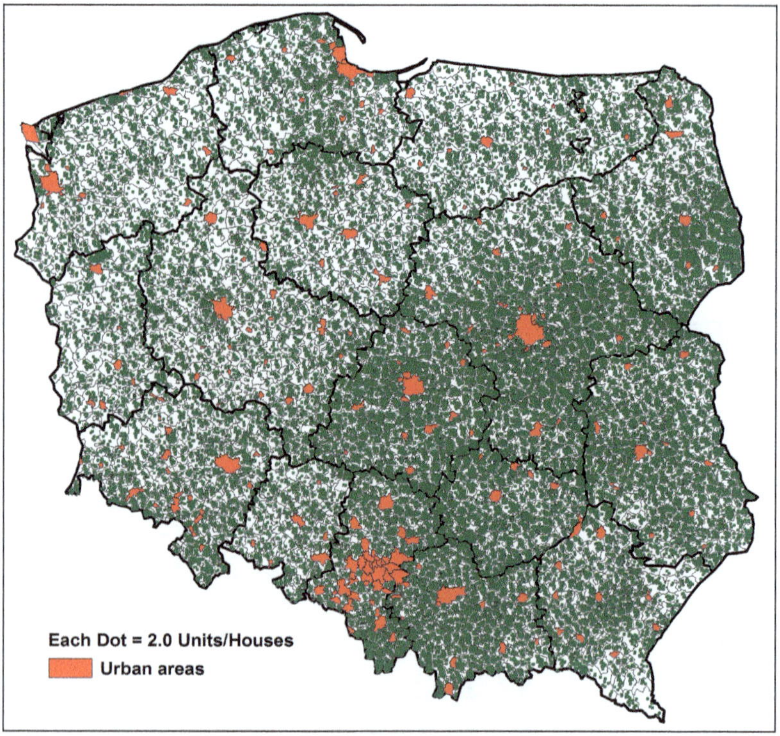

Source: National Housing Census 2002, CSO.

According to Müller, Hall & Keen (2004) and Hall (2014), in general, purpose-built second homes (in Poland mainly seen as typical wooden summer cottages) are concentrated largely in traditional or highly regarded tourism regions such as the Baltic coastal zone, lake districts or mountain regions. This spatial pattern is not confirmed by data from public statistics, since here, the distribution of second homes does not fit the locations of tourism areas. This mismatch may be explained by a population change since the distributions of second homes and depopulated areas overlap to a large extent (Map 1.3.4 & 1.3.5). This latter tendency is due to the restricted definition that excludes typical summer cottages but (according to the definition) includes recreational buildings with construction permits, i.e. in most cases abandoned farm buildings or residences converted into second homes. Thus, still according to the above-mentioned researchers, such forms of secondary residence are most common in peripheral locations, often with a highly attractive landscape but with net migration loss. Since there are no recent data on the current overall number of secondary residences, this map (from 2002) provides the only picture of the distribution of second homes so far, with a qualification that it is based on the restricted definition and is thus only partial. Although even the data from public statistics do not provide a complete picture of the phenomenon, the initial conclusion is that second homes are a common element of the Polish countryside, as they can be found in every community, albeit with wide variations in their distribution (Heffner 2011b).

Map 1.3.5 Population change, % (1995–2013)

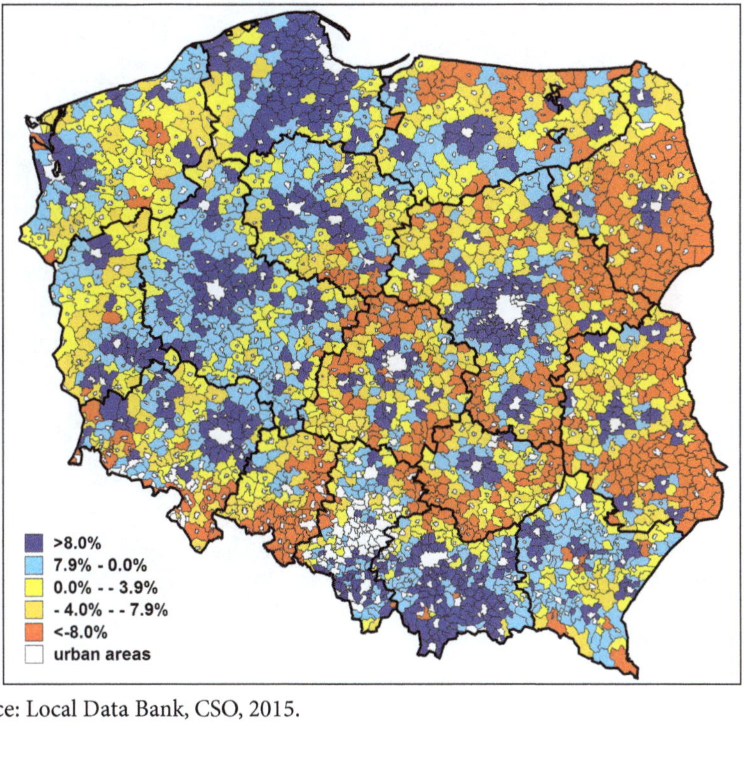

Source: Local Data Bank, CSO, 2015.

Map 1.3.6 shows the concentration of second homes based on their proportion in total housing resources. It is useful in identifying the factors influencing second-home location. One of the crucial factors was linked to well-developed tourism measured by a synthetic index based on natural and anthropogenic amenities, accommodation services, employment in the tourism sector and tourist numbers (Derek 2008). Thus, the most famous, well-established tourist localities, on the coast, in lake districts and mountain resorts, had major concentrations of secondary residences. Another recently increasingly important factor is the high level of natural amenities as well as high-quality natural environment and landscape (mainly clean and unspoilt areas) but with weak or at most moderately developed tourism in terms of tourist interest and pressure. The above-mentioned characteristics apply mostly to areas within large forests, landscape parks or around national parks, especially those outside the above-mentioned famous tourism regions.

Map 1.3.6 Percentage of secondary residences in total housing resources, % (2002)

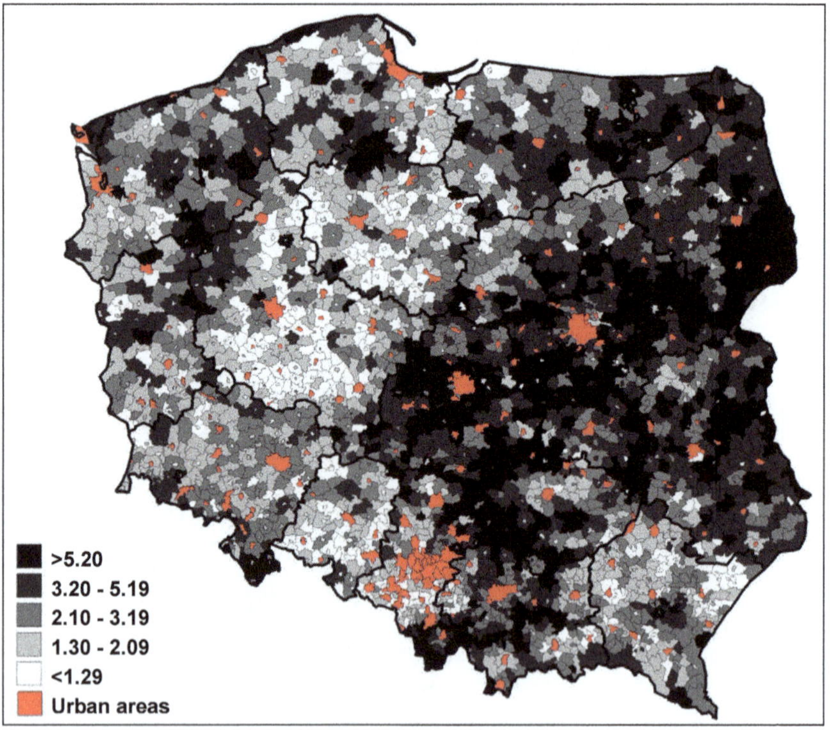

Source: National Housing Census 2002, CSO 2003.

Proximity to a large city and at the same time an efficient transport system enabling short travel times to a second home was also very important. Second-home owners are usually permanent residents of large urban centres, which has encouraged the concentration of secondary residences in suburban and peri-urban areas of Warsaw, Łódź, Cracow, Rzeszów, Lublin and Poznań, proving the importance of the proximity of the weekend zone. Furthermore, as mentioned above, the definition used in public statistics favours converted second homes, which is why depopulation and deagrarianisation are so clearly seen as key-drivers. They have both been determining the location of holiday homes for several decades. The impact of this factor has been strongly felt in particular in eastern Poland (in the Podlasie and Lubelskie regions) and in central Poland (in the Mazovia, Świętokrzyskie and Łódzkie regions) – the main emigration areas during the socialist era and later. The result is a growing number of abandoned farmhouses and related farm buildings. The large supply of empty buildings and vast areas of disused agricultural land has created an essential opportunity to build a new second home or convert abandoned buildings. Thus, attractiveness to tourism (natural beauty), proximity to large cities or conurbations and depopulation are the main factors in shaping second-home location and spatial tendencies. In many areas, these factors combine, and their influence thus overlaps and to some extent is mutually reinforcing (synergy) (Heffner 2011b), as for instance the peri-urban north-eastern zone of Warsaw with its high-quality natural amenities.

On the other hand, there are several characteristics that can be seen as major obstacles to the location of second homes. First, one should mention well-developed agriculture (large-scale commercial farming), which is evident in particular in rural regions that have achieved success during the recent structural changes resulting from the system transformation and accession to the EU, including the capitalisation on the CAP. Hence, there is a very low number and low density of second homes in such regions, i.e. Kujawy, Wielkopolska and the Opole region. The direct effect of these changes has been the maintenance of the agricultural character of these regions (through diversification and growth supported by the CAP). In addition, typical agricultural areas with large-scale farming are usually not very attractive for leisure and tourism. Obviously, the degradation of the natural environment and landscape have significantly hindered the second-home development in major mining areas (coal, brown coal, copper and sulphur mines) as well as in the immediate surroundings of the highly industrialised towns and cities of Upper Silesia (with dense concentrations of coal mines and foundries).

Despite the shortage of public data providing an up-to-date picture of the distribution of second homes in Poland, i.e. the overall number of secondary residences (units), the latest public statistics (surprisingly) at least partly reveal the actual situation by giving data on recently constructed secondary residences (from the period 2008–2015). The new data come after almost 15 years of a lack of statistics on this subject: these are the most recent and, in fact, the only data on current trends in holiday homes (and leisure) and are also useful for the comparison with trends observed in Finland.

These data confirm that the current trend in the location of second homes has been slightly changing recently and gives priority to high-quality natural amenities and unspoilt landscapes, although located outside well-known crowded tourism regions, i.e. especially in communities in lake districts that have not been particularly popular among tourists and visitors (Map 1.3.7). Of course, some well-established tourism communities on the coast and in lake districts are still important and attractive for second-home owners. However, an increase is not as significant as in places yet to be fully discovered by tourists.

Map 1.3.7 Newly-built secondary residences (new unoccupied homes/absolute values) (2008–2015)

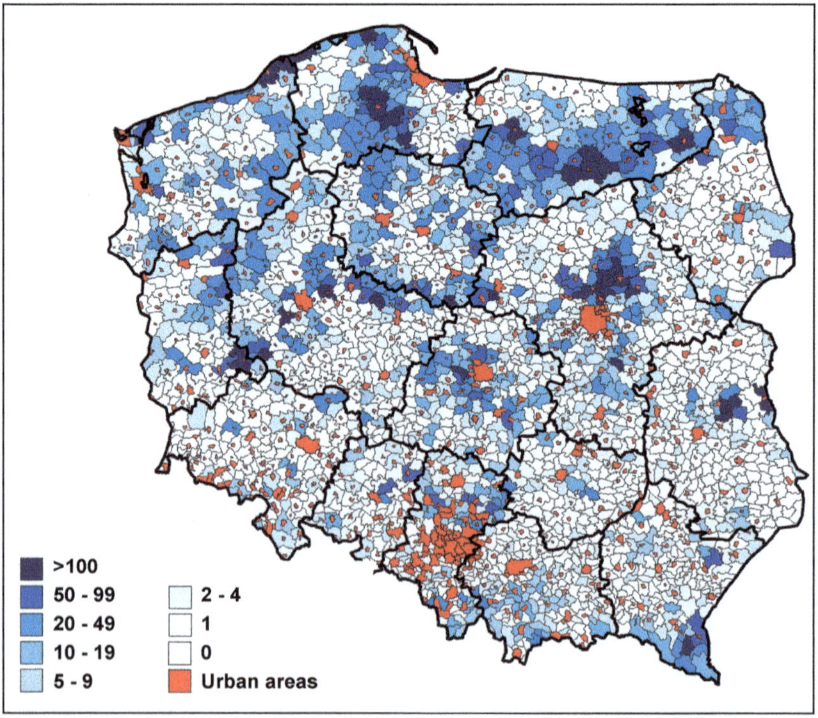

Source: Local Data Bank, CSO, 2015.

The accessibility factor is still of great importance, as most of the growing second-home localities are still within the periurban zone of large urban centres (Warsaw, Tri-city and Łódź). This significance is particularly clear in the case of the Łódzkie region, which is relatively unattractive for tourism and leisure from the point of view of natural amenities (so there are no other factors that might modify the influence of the proximity to cities). Here, new, purpose-built second homes are almost entirely located in the area around the regional capital, Łódź. Furthermore, the decline in agriculture along with depopulation cannot be established as the most important factors here, as it rather seems that their impact is the strongest when combined with natural amenities. The same holds true for the combined influence of depopulation and the relative proximity to large cities, as interestingly the influence of the former is itself higher in central (with two main cities – Warsaw and Łódź) than in eastern Poland, which is generally less easily accessible. To sum up, this picture confirms the main factors identified on the basis of the data from the 2002 Census, but at the same time it shows some new trends, first and foremost those related to natural amenities. It confirms a growing interest in purchasing land and constructing secondary residences in traditionally rural areas as well as in more remote ones (along the eastern border, Ziemia Lubuska and Bieszczady). It seems that new second-home owners appreciate the availability of relatively cheap land but still with a high natural value (albeit not already consumed by tourism and the leisure sector) and at the same time they take into account the shorter travel distance, as they often tend to spend their weekends there. This accessibility is constantly changing and the average radius is growing as the transport system and consequently car access has been gradually improving, including in more remote areas. It also seems that, similarly to Finnish second-home owners, the new generation of their Polish counterparts seeks a kind of isolation, but unlike Finns they do so in a broader context, avoiding well-established tourism regions (but still contributing to more densely built localities/villages) while Finns exercise their desires in a more topographical context of maintaining their distance from their neighbours.

1.4 Rationale

As shown above, although aspects of the European countryside vary greatly between countries and regions, for several decades there have been two intertwining socio-economic macro-scale tendencies. On the one hand, there is the decline of the primary sector (agriculture and forestry), its decreasing role as a source of income and labour for rural people, resulting in emigration, depopulation, the distortion of rural socio-demographic structures and worsening economic prospects and living conditions. On the other hand, there has been a large influx of former urban residents to the countryside, including seasonal residents as second-home owners, who, following the post-productive spatial pattern, have recently significantly shifted from suburban and traditional tourism-based areas towards the rural heartlands, the 'deep' countryside and more remote rural areas.

In light of the above, there is a need to examine whether and to what extent second homes can positively influence the rural economy through their income and employment contribution. Furthermore, in order to make a more precise assessment, it is necessary to follow the entire sequence, starting from factors and preconditions influencing second-home owner's consumer behaviour, his/her local economic performance (local purchasing) as recorded in expenditure practices and spending patterns as well as the effects on the community's economy.

2. Research design

2.1 Scope of the study

Similarly to other social phenomena, second homes are of a highly complex and multifaceted nature. These elementary attributes are clearly evident when second homes are anchored in the context of rural development, which is basically the topic of this study. A variety of local circumstances determining second housing growth, diversity and spatial pattern, a multitude of relationships with the rural space itself as well as with its distinct resources, institutions and residents, and, additionally, an array of impacts and implications resulting from second homes for the local community prove its multi-aspect character starting from spatial, environmental, through political, demographic to economic dimension. Given the complex nature of this phenomenon and its apparent indirect influence on consumer behaviour, it should be noted, however, that the extent of this exploratory research was purposefully and exclusively limited to the economic aspect. Thus, here, the scope of the study – an economic aspect of the second home functioning – was delimited by second-home owners' consumer behaviour factors, patterns and impacts on the community's economy in terms of income and employment. Although not explored deeply, other non-economic aspects were taken into account as explanatory variables in the course of determining drivers underlying the scale, frequency and structure of local purchasing among second-home owners.

2.2 Main purpose

With a brief reference to the rationale for the study (see section 1.4), for several decades two intertwining macro-scale socio-economic processes have been observed in European rural areas, albeit highly differentiated in various aspects between countries and regions. On the one hand, there has been the decline of the primary sector (agriculture and forestry), with its decreasing role as a source of income and labour for rural people, resulting in long-term, intense and selective outmigration, depopulation and the distortion of rural socio-demographic structures as well as in worsening economic prospects and living conditions. On the other hand, there has been a large influx of ex-urban residents to the countryside, including seasonal residents as second-home owners. This influx has recently shifted significantly from suburban and traditional tourism-based areas towards rural heartlands, the 'deep' countryside and more remote rural areas following the post-productive spatial pattern.

In light of the above, there is a need to search for new development and alternative income opportunities for rural populations, to build up 'new' communities resilient to external changes and to keep the countryside vital, liveable and prosperous from a long-term perspective. At the same time, second-home owners have increasingly become an important social group in the countryside due to the vast flows of people, their large and diverse demand for local resources, as well as their powerful status influencing local decision-making processes.

Hence, the main issue is to examine the strength and complexity of economic relationships between second-home owners and the locals (farmers, business owners and other individuals) or in a broad sense to explore supply-and-demand linkages and assess their role in developing more sustainable, resilient and vibrant rural communities. Given the above, the main purpose of this study is to determine how deeply Finnish and Polish second-home owners are integrated into the community's economy, what the key drivers of their consumer behaviour are, and consequently, what is the impact of second-home owners' spending on the local community (mostly in economic terms).

2.3 Research objectives

The study is designed to address the following research objectives, structured according to the triad (DETERMINANTS-PERFORMANCE-IMPACT) approach, i.e. determinants of local consumer behaviour, consumers' local economic performance (spending) and the impact of consumer spending on the local economy.

DETERMINANTS

Obj1: To reveal the key factors and preconditions (e.g. respondents' socio-demographics, incomes, trip-related variables, lifestyles, destination characteristics etc.) that influence:

- the evidence-based occurrence of local purchasing by second-home owners,
- the level of local spending (economic flows),
- the commodity bundle provided locally,
- local 'informal' purchasing.

Obj2: To identify the main obstacles in second-home owners' willingness and propensity to make local purchases; in other words, to identify possible points of expenditure leakages from the local economy.

PERFORMANCE

Obj3: To identify and evaluate economic relationships between second home owners and the local community (businesses, farms and individuals) in terms of:

- scale – here considered as the number of actors involved (i.e. second-home owners purchasing locally);
- monetary value, i.e. money spent by second-home owners;
- the object of transactions, e.g. agricultural produce, everyday articles, building materials, services, etc.;
- the character of supply channels, i.e. 'formal', in which goods and services are provided by local businesses (including farms), and 'informal' – by local residents.

Obj4: To recognise the dynamics of second-home owners' local consumption patterns (changes in size and structure of demand) with regard to:

- different income levels (by examination of income elasticity of demand as well as of Engel's law and curves for various goods and services purchased locally by second-home owners);
- subsequent phases in the family life-cycle and the owner's life-course.

Obj5: To build a typology of second-home owners' local consumption patterns (a consumer typology).

Obj6: To measure the scale and assess the importance of 'informal' local purchasing by second-home owners.

IMPACT

Obj7: To assess the economic impact of the second-home owners' spending on the local community in terms of:

- scale, i.e. number of local actors involved (local product and service suppliers),
- economic value, i.e. the amount of money earned through the provision of goods and services to second-home owners;

– scope, by identifying local economic sectors that benefit most from second-home tourism, e.g. retail of foodstuffs, retail of building materials, construction services, garden and maintenance services, etc.

Obj8: To assess the significance of the second-home phenomenon for the local community in non-economic terms based on residents' opinions.

2.4 Hypotheses

As discussed in sections 1.2 and 1.3, besides certain similarities recognised mainly in general demographic trends occurring in the rural space of Finland and Poland (i.e. depopulation, ageing, rural out-migration), there is a strong evidence base about both countries as contrasting contexts of second-home functioning. The vast array of differences observed through development indicators reflects a distinctive cultural, social, economic and geographic backdrop for comparison at the macro-scale/national level. Beside the diversity in traditions and customs, in society organisation and policy framework, variations in economic performance of businesses and households, yet in organisation of retail trade system and public service sector, there are also clear differences in direct regard to the second-home phenomenon and related aspects – its origins, quantity, spatial distribution, usage patterns and intensity, leisure activities, daily practices and even relevant policies and regulations.

In light of the above, the following introductory thesis named *Consumption convergence* is stated:

Consumption convergence: In spite of contrasting cultural, social and economic contexts as well as sharp differences in second home functioning, Finnish and Polish second-home owners are becoming similar in terms of consumer behaviour. That said, the possession and utilisation of the second home has strong convergence/unifying ability that resembles individuals' local consumption.

The introductory umbrella thesis statement encompasses a bunch of specific hypotheses. The set of those, by reflecting the research objectives and the state-of-the-art as presented in chapter 3, *Theoretical framework: key theories, concepts and literature overview*, was formulated and structured according to the *determinants-performance-impact* triad approach. It furnishes an advantage of more complex and integrated sequential path to the analysis that consequently provides the author with more definite and comprehensive understanding of the multiple process of second-home owners' consumption in rural locations.

DETERMINANTS

- **Household wealth vs. accessibility H_1:** Second-home owners' household income, as a crucial explanatory factor of consumer behaviour, declines in importance in favour of trip-related variables, namely the distance between permanent and secondary residence (Keynes 1964; Bohlin 1982; Müller 2002a; Nicolau & Más 2005; Pouta, Neuvonen & Sievänen 2006; Zalega 2012; Czarnecki 2014; Dybczak, Tóth & Voňka 2014).
- **Urban influence H_2:** Having an urban status predetermines second-home owners to purchase goods and services locally (Węgleński 1992; Cowell & Green 1994; Lehto *et al.* 2004; Laesser & Crouch 2006; Hawk 2013; Pitkänen, Adamiak & Halseth 2014).
- **Social amenities H_3:** Second-home owners are more likely to purchase locally and spend larger amounts of money in municipalities where the distance to local shops and services is short (Mathieson & Wall 1982; Alward, Workman, & Maki 1992; Paajanen 1994; Rinne & Saastamoinen 2005; Heffner & Czarnecki 2015).

PERFORMANCE

- **Income effect H_4:** Engel's laws for food, home fees/charges and luxury products prove to apply here in the same way as they do for regular household spending (Deaton, Ruiz-Castillo & Thomas 1985; Zalega 2012; Ilmakunnas 2014).
- **Commodity bundle H_5:** The proportion of basic commodities and home-related expenses in total local expenditure is equal for regular and seasonal (second-home) consumption (Statistics Finland 2013; CSO 2015).
- **Family life-cycle and life-course perspective H_6:** Spending levels for local produce decrease while the commodity bundle becomes less diverse with subsequent family life-cycle stages and the owner's life-course (Gourinchas & Parker 1997; Antonides & van Raaij 1998; Müller & Hall 2004; Hall 2005; Paris 2010; Lundmark & Marjavaara 2013; Rantanen 2014).
- **Demand for informal purchasing H_7:** Informal purchasing is less common among Finnish than Polish second-home owners (Smuga *et al.* 2005; Rădan-Gorska 2013; Schneider & Williams 2013; Łapiński, Peterlik & Wyżnikiewicz 2015; Din *et al.* 2016).
- **Logic of informal purchasing H_8:** Formal economy's failure, in terms of spatial accessibility and product availability, prompts second-home owners to make use of informal distribution channels (Sassen 1998; Williams & Martínez-Pérez 2014; Williams & Horodnic 2016).

IMPACT

- **Income creation H_9:** The contribution of second homes to local household income rise proves its significance as an important/main source of income (Hoogendoorn, Mellet & Visser 2007; Velvin *et al.* 2013; Oliveira, Roca & Roca 2015).
- **Jobs creation H_{10}:** The contribution of second homes to local labour market proves its significance as a job-maintaining rather than job-creation factor (Luloff *et al.* 1994; Marcouiller 1997; Gallent, Mace & Tewdwr-Jones 2002; Müller 2002a; Wallace *et al.* 2005).
- **Developmental impact H_{11}:** Second-home tourism, in the local people's opinions, is less significant in strictly economic terms (income and source of employment) but more appreciated in broad developmental terms (infrastructure and service provision) for the local community (Velvin *et al.* 2013; Oliveira, Roca & Roca 2015).

2.5 Methodology

Data collection techniques

Since the study comprised a quantitative part (mostly as a backdrop to the survey itself) and a qualitative part, this is reflected in the character of the data and sources of information. For the quantitative background concerning the number of secondary residences and their spatial distribution, the data were provided by public statistics: the database is the 2002 National Population and Housing Census, the Local Data Bank (BDL) 2008–2015 by the Central Statistical Office (CSO 2002, 2008–2015) and current statistics provided by Statistics Finland for the period 1970–2014. The information for Finland was supplemented by the GIS data on the number and location of secondary residences in 2013 and 2014 from the Population Information System provided by the Population Register Centre (*Väestörekisterikeskus*, VRK).

The qualitative data for Poland were collected from direct interviews with second-home owners and local people, while for Finland this was done entirely by the postal survey. The direct interviews in Poland were carried out in 20 selected municipalities (see section 2.6) in the early autumn of 2009. In total, 398 interviews with second-home owners and 200 interviews with local people were completed, which gave respectively 20 and 10 direct interviews in each of the municipalities surveyed. It is particularly important for the research aim – economic links – that the interviewed second-home owners' cottages were in the same locations (villages) where the locals surveyed lived permanently. However, the sample of second-home owners comprised only individuals whose permanent residence was outside the second-home municipality; the same applied to the Finnish study.

The Finnish postal survey was conducted in the autumn of 2013 and included questionnaires mailed out to 1,000 second-home owners whose cottages were located in 20 selected municipalities (see section 2.6) and to 500 local residents from the same municipalities. The sample prepared by the Population Register Centre (VRK) included respondents from both groups who were adults but not over 80 years of age. Here, the response rate was very high and for second-home owners accounted for 46.7% while for local residents it stood at 31.2%. It should be also noted that in the Finnish and Polish studies, apart from local people, the respondents were solely the owners or co-owners of second homes, excluding those who rented or leased a cottage. Despite the fact that the Finnish law since 2000 has made foreigners eligible for real-estate purchases (incl. summer homes; Lipkina 2013), in the survey, only second homes owned by Finnish citizens were taken into account. The same rule was applied to the Polish survey in the course of drawing the sample of second-home owners; here, however, the regulations are not as favourable as they are in Finland and a specific permission issued by the Ministry of the Interior and Administration is needed in the case of acquiring agricultural land, forest or a second home by a foreigner (Dz. U. z 2012 r., poz. 729; Dz. U. z 2014 r. poz. 1380).

The data obtained from the survey covered some topics crucial for the study, i.e. economic relationships between second-home owners and local people (farmers, business owners and other rural residents) in terms of the amount of local spending and the object of transaction. It also covered local people's views of the impact of second homes on the local community as well as additional but relevant data on the respondents' socio-demographics, secondary residence characteristics, daily practices and the utilisation of the second home etc. (see Appendix for questionnaires).

Data analysis methods

A range of statistical methods were applied to the study in order to fulfil the research objectives. First, the classification trees (also known as the decision-tree learning method) were used as a powerful method to identify factors influencing local purchasing by second-home owners. The classification tree is one of the techniques often used in data mining, which was here applied to build a predictive qualitative model, since it makes it possible to make suppositions on the possible qualitative outcome, i.e. whether these types of transactions occur or not. Such a classification tree is a graphic model resulting from the partition of the entire dataset into homogenous sub-sets based on dependent variable values. A partition is a multi-stage procedure that at each step may use a different independent variable in order to distinguish the most homogenous sub-sets (Łapczyński 2003). This method has many advantages – first and foremost, its clear and visible graphic presentation, which is quite simple to analyse, interpret and understand. There are no limitations concerning particular statistical distributions of variables; lack of data is acceptable, as well as atypical observations; the model can be validated by using a statistical test, and the recurrent use of independent variables in different parts of the tree makes it possible to reveal the context and interrelationships between variables (Łapczyński 2003).

Second, non-parametric statistical tests such as U Mann-Whitney and Kruskal-Wallis H tests were applied in order to identify factors determining the revenues obtained by locals from providing second-home owners with various goods and services (i.e. flows of capital to the local economy).

Third, cluster analysis, as one of the most commonly used tools in data mining and for pattern recognition in multivariate statistical methods, was employed to create a typology of consumer patterns based on the structure of the local commodity bundle. It is a widely known technique that makes it easy to group observed objects into clusters based on their similarities in a wide range of characteristics and observations (Romesburg 2004).

Fourth, as for basic econometric methods, Engel's curves were used first to examine the dynamics of real local expenditures and the proportion of the household budgets spent on various types of local goods (basic, luxury and housing) as a result of a change in household income, and second, to compare these expenditures with regular household expenditures. Income elasticity of demand was then measured as a percentage change in the quantity of various local goods and services resulting from a second-home owner's household income dynamics. Each of these methods was used to measure second-home owners' local spending performance.

Fifth, in order to measure the impact of second-home owners' spending on the local economy, a basic estimator of the total second-home owner spending in the area (including the number of second-home owners and the average spending per visitor) was used (Stynes 1997, 1999) to provide more details on whether and how much income second-home tourism generates for rural households, farms and other rural businesses. The value obtained was related to the reference base, i.e. the average rural household income.

Finally, a forward stepwise regression analysis was applied to the study in order to learn more about the preconditions for providing goods and services to second-home owners and distinguish some crucial characteristics of local sellers.

2.6 Terms and definitions

The problems of inconsistent terms and the lack of a single, universal definition of second homes have been raised on numerous occasions in international scientific discourse (Hall & Müller 2004, 2012; Paris 2009; Mazón, Huete, & Mantecón 2010), e.g. in the context of barriers to international comparisons. Similarly, a lack of consensus is apparent in the concepts and definitions used by the statistical services of different countries. As regards terminology, the situation seems fully justified, considering that many countries have their own widely used national terms, most often using those that are popular, traditional or originate from official terminology for the phenomenon in question, e.g. referring to 'summer home' ('dom letniskowy' in Poland, 'kesämökki' in Finland), 'cottage' (mökki in Finland), or 'recreational plot' ('działka rekreacyjna' or simply 'działka' in Poland (CSO 2006, 2010)). Since there is a variety of specific types of holiday/summer home within a country, statistical services may use a very broad term to cover all categories in order to look at the size of the phenomenon precisely. This is how it works in Finland, where secondary residences and their numerous variations (Pitkänen & Vepsäläinen 2008) are considered in public statistics as one category – free-time residences, i.e. 'recreational buildings constructed permanently on the site of their location or residential buildings that are used as holiday dwellings, excluding holiday cottages for business purposes, buildings in holiday villages and allotment garden cottages' (Statistics Finland 2014).

Whatever national terms we apply, however, the universal nature of the second home phenomenon obliges researchers and statisticians to use international equivalents. The internationalisation of terminology and statistical categories is also an effect of joint institutions' (e.g. Eurostat) regulating the supply of consistent data needed to set up a common comparable platform to analyse various global phenomena. Because of this, the notion of a 'second home' is generally considered as the most universal term (Pitkänen & Vepsäläinen, 2008, p. 2), and consequently, appears increasingly often in statistics and legislation.

In Poland, the categories of 'second home' and 'second dwelling' were introduced into the 2002 Census and in 2004 into Polish legislation on the acquisition of agricultural and forest properties as well as second homes. As the definition stands, based on the official definition, a 'second home' is a property (not a self-contained apartment or flat) designated for leisure and recreational purposes that is not the owner's permanent place of residence. The owner makes their own decision as to whether the property will be used as a 'primary' (permanent) or 'secondary residence'. In the case of a 'primary residence' – as opposed to the 'secondary residence' – it must be proved to the authorities that it is habitable and the owner can live there (Dziennik Ustaw, 2004, p. 11714, 11717–11718).

However, there were certain discrepancies between the above-mentioned definition and those commonly used by Polish statistical services, e.g. in the 2002 national housing census, which is so far the only source of data on the total number of secondary residences. In the 2002 Census, a very restrictive understanding of the residence category was applied, including second homes in the 'building' and 'dwelling' sections.

In the 'building' section, second homes were included in the category of (temporary) recreational buildings. This included structures whose construction required a residential building construction permit, whose main purpose is a temporary residence (e.g. during holidays and weekends), as well as buildings which were previously used as permanent residences but are currently designated for temporary use.

In the 'dwelling' section, for occupied dwellings, second homes were recognised as those used only on a temporary or seasonal basis (when they are called 'temporarily occupied dwellings'). Meanwhile, for unoccupied units (a structure registered during the census in which no one lives permanently or temporarily), the reason for not being occupied was determined. Second homes were included in the subcategory of dwellings designated for temporary (seasonal) stays ('second homes' or literally 'second flats'). Both recognitions in practice excluded many 'typical summer cottages' that did not require a construction permit ('light' wooden houses) or had been built illegally.

Despite the fact that countries and public institutions lack consistency in defining 'second home' in their legislation and statistics, one can distinguish certain common features that these definitions present as the main attributes, features and distinctions of second homes, such as:

- use (temporary, seasonal, occasional, for weekends and holidays),
- purpose (recreation, leisure),
- users (owner, his/her family),

- location (rural areas, countryside, outside urban areas, outside permanent residence),
- appearance (detached dwelling), and
- ownership (private, of a household or a single family).

In this study, these are considered as crucial and universal attributes and constituents of second homes, since they are applicable to both countries surveyed.

2.7 Municipalities surveyed: criteria and selection

The qualitative part of the study (the survey) was conducted in 20 municipalities in Poland and 20 municipalities in Finland (i.e. in units of the same territorial level – LAU2 (local administrative units), the former NUTS5 level according to the Eurostat definition). The selection of municipalities surveyed was multi-criteria, taking into account the following: first, the (highest) percentage of secondary residences in the total housing resources, which was reflected in the highest concentration of the second-home phenomenon (based on the data from the National Population and Housing Census 2002 for Poland and from current statistics provided by Statistics Finland); second, the different functional type of the municipality, i.e. highly agricultural, predominantly agricultural, tourism-based, mixed and suburban (based on the most popular functional typology of rural municipalities in Poland (Bański 2009), and by using simple indicators such as the percentage of those employed in the primary sector, in the tourism industry and the urbanisation index for the Finnish survey based on public data provided by Statistics Finland); and third, the location of the survey unit in one of the main landscape zones (coastal, lowlands and mountains in Poland, coastal, Finnish Lakeland and Lapland in Finland). Since the proportion of secondary residences in the total number of household-dwelling units was the main criterion for municipalities selection, this, in effect, was reflected in a different number of units surveyed representing subsequent functional and landscape categories.

Map 2.7.1 Surveyed municipalities in Finland against landscape and functional background; Percentage of secondary residences in total housing resources

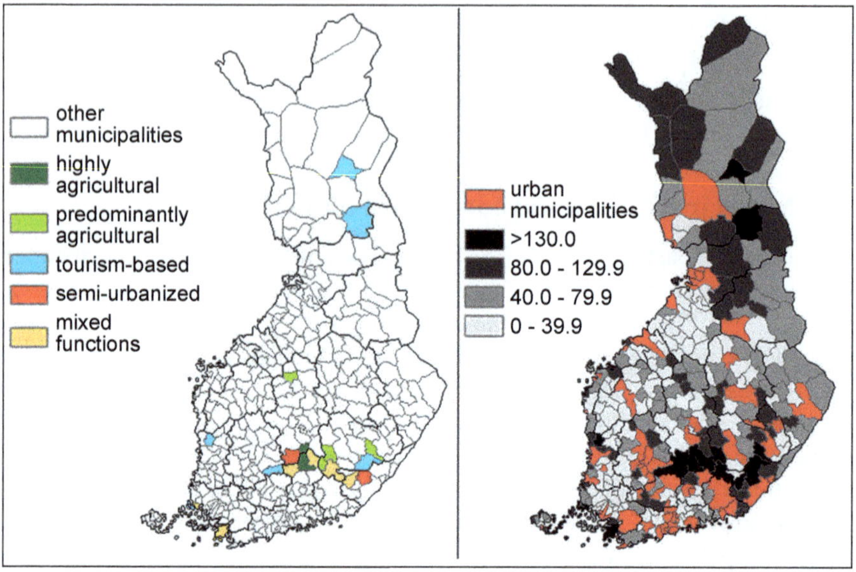

Source: Statistics Finland 2013.

In Finland, nine of them were rural and eleven were semi-urban (including small towns with the population not exceeding 5,000 inhabitants). Twenty Finnish rural municipalities were selected: Hartola, Hirvensalmi, Kivijärvi, Kuhmoinen, Luhanka, Mäntyharju, Padasjoki, Pertunmaa, Puumala, Pälkäne, Savitaipale, Sulkava, Sysmä and Taipalsaari (as representatives of the Finnish Lakeland), Pelkosenniemi and Posio (as Lapland municipalities) and Kemiönsaari, Kustavi, Siikainen and Taivassalo (as coastal municipalities) (see Map 2.7.1).

Map 2.7.2 Surveyed municipalities in Poland against landscape and functional background; Percentage of secondary residences in total housing resources

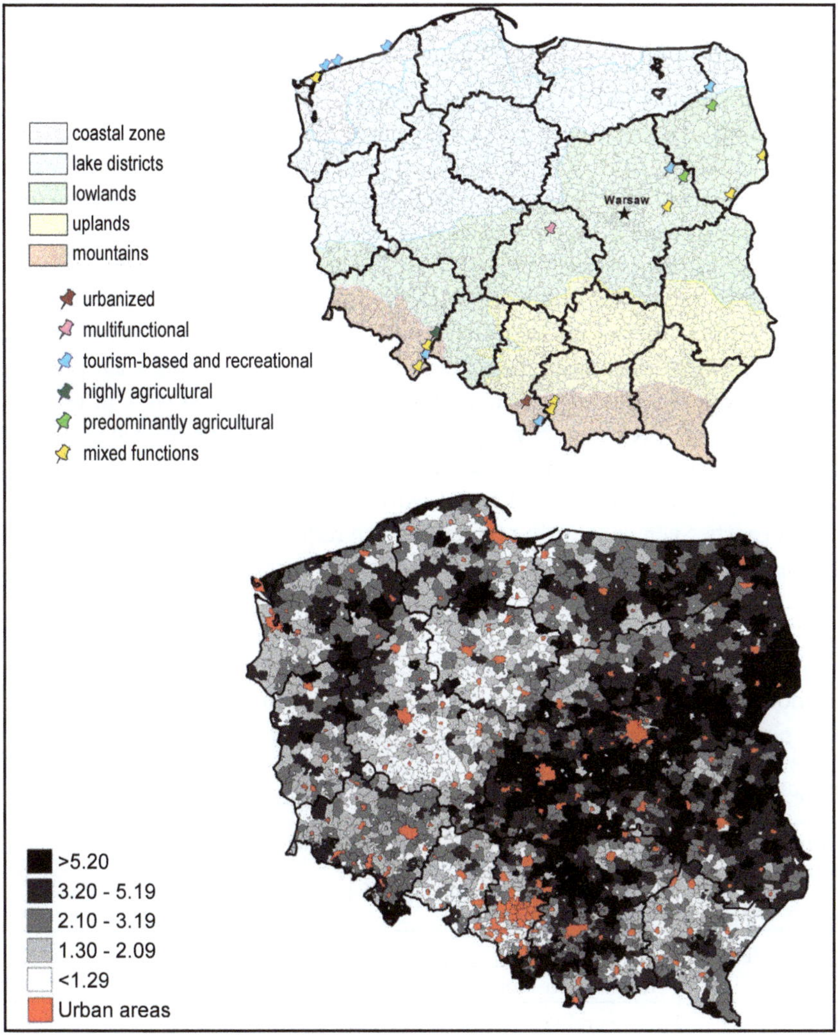

Source: CSO 2002, Bański 2009, Kondracki 2002.

As a result, 20 municipalities were selected for the Polish survey, i.e. Brenna, Koszarawa, Lądek-Zdrój, Międzylesie, Stryszawa, Ujsoły, Ziębice and Złoty Stok (from mountains and foothills), Brok, Goniądz, Kałuszyn, Kosów Lacki, Mielnik,

Narewka, Rajgród and Zgierz (from lowlands in central and eastern Poland), and Dziwnów, Mielno, Rewal and Wolin (coastal municipalities) (see Map 2.7.2)).

2.8 Sample characteristics

A basic description of the sample is given below as an important point of reference and a useful complementary part with regard to further more advanced and focused empirical analysis. It comprises second-home owners' socio-demographics, their conduct while at the cottage as well as secondary residence simple characteristics and its location in geographical and functional contexts.

Among the second-home owners surveyed, there was the prevalence of male over female owners, albeit clearly more asymmetric for Finns than for Poles (see Fig. 2.8.1). There were important contrasting characteristics between both nations surveyed with regard to the respondents' age (by economic age groups). Although the majority of owners in both countries surveyed were in working non-mobile age/pre-retirement age, the extreme age groups were significantly diverse in terms of frequencies, with a considerable proportion of the post-working age among Finns and 1/3 of working mobile age among their Polish counterparts. Such contrasting structures also reflected in the following associated attributes, i.e. household size as well as the respondent's education level and economic activity. As a result of diverse age structures, one may observe families in different life-phases – more often single (more likely during widowhood) and two-people households (empty nesting households) for Finns, while the domination of two-people households (pre-childhood period) and three to four people households (young families with children) among Poles.

Table 2.8.1 Second-home owners' socio-demographic characteristics, %

Attribute		Finns	Poles
Gender	Female	34.0%	46.1%
	Male	66.0%	53.9%
Age groups*	Working mobile	5.4%	31.0%
	Working non-mobile	49.1%	48.3%
	Post-working	45.5%	20.7%
Household size	Single	14.1%	9.5%
	Two people	66.2%	36.7%
	Three-four people	15.8%	48.5%
	Five and more people	3.9%	5.3%

Attribute		Finns	Poles
Permanent residence	Capital city (Helsinki; Warsaw)	14.1%	16.6%
	Other large cities (≥100.000)	24.0%	50.8%
	Medium-sized towns.1 (50.000–99.999)	14.8%	6.8%
	Medium-sized towns.2 (20.000–49.999)	17.1%	8.8%
	Small towns and villages (<20.000)	30.0%	15.0%
	Abroad	0.0%	2.0%
Education	Primary/elementary school	13.4%	2.0%
	Vocational school, training course	19.9%	8.9%
	High school	33.9%	40.1%
	University, polytechnics	32.8%	49.0%
Economic activity	Business owner	13.1%	29.5%
	Senior executive, specialist	15.5%	15.8%
	Lower white-collar	9.2%	11.6%
	Manual worker	8.2%	8.7%
	Unemployed	0.9%	2.6%
	Retired	51.6%	27.1%
	Housewife	0.9%	1.3%
	Other	0.6%	3.4%
Economic sector	Agriculture, forestry, fishing	2.3%	2.0%
	Manufacturing and construction	27.1%	21.4%
	Trade and services	70.6%	76.6%
Commuting to work	Yes	39.5%	18.1%
	No	60.5%	81.9%
Net monthly household income	Very high (≥7,501€ / ≥10,001 PLN)	10.1%	7.1%
	High (5,001–7,500€ / 5,001–10,000 PLN)	22.4%	17.7%
	Average (2,501–5,000€ / 3,001–5,000 PLN)	45.6%	35.4%
	Low (1,251–2,500€ / 1,501–3,000 PLN)	18.4%	30.5%
	Very low (≤1,250€ / ≤1,500 PLN)	3.5%	9.3%

Attribute		Finns	Poles
Rural origins	Yes	60.9%	11.6%
	No	39.1%	88.4%

* Finns: 'working mobile' 18–44, 'working non-mobile' 45–64, 'post-working' 65+; Poles: 'working mobile' 18–44, 'working non-mobile' males 45–64, females 45–59, 'post-working' males 65+, females 60+.

Source: Own study.

Then, consequently, the owner's age in a more indirect way reveals itself in more favourable education characteristics for Poles (with the vast majority of respondents having obtained high-school diploma and/or having graduated from a university/university of technology). Despite the fact that the higher education levels were also frequent for Finns, there was, at the same time, a noticeable percentage of those having only elementary education or who had undertaken a vocational school/training. Furthermore, age structures partly reflected in the respondent's economic activity, especially in the prevalence of retired people in Finland and a higher proportion of business owners in Poland (over twice as many as in the case of Finns). Interestingly, the age differentiation did not reflect in household income structures, since there was a more favourable asymmetry towards wealthy households for Finns while for Poles, conversely, the tendency was towards poorer families. The urbanisation index of the country was proved by the respondent's permanent place of living – for Finns, it was more often medium-sized, small towns and rural areas while more urban status (often in the capital city and other large cities) was observed for Polish second-home owners. An additional attribute was considered: namely, the respondent's rural origins were in keeping with a popular view present in the literature with regard to prevailing rural society in Finland, with the domination of second-home owners with rural roots setting them apart from Poles, among whom such a feature is relatively unusual.

Purchasing a property was the most frequent way of coming into possession of a cottage for both nations. However, Finns were more likely to build (by themselves) a cottage on an inherited piece of land, while Poles were more inclined to build it on an acquired plot. For Finns, unlike for Poles, it was also more frequent to inherit a property, entirely or partly (combined with partly acquisition), which is in line with the previously mentioned common rural origins for Finnish cottagers. The average length of ownership was 19.2 years (with the median of 18 years) for Finns, while for Poles, this period was considerably shorter, standing at 11.9 years (with the median of 10 years), which still reflected Polish second-home owners' young age structure. Hence, there was the prevalence of 1–10-year home ownership for Poles over Finns, while there was a predominance of 20–50-year home ownership for Finns over Poles.

Apart from the owner's close family, also friends (especially for Poles) and other relatives were among other cottage users. Renting out the cottage was very rare among both populations surveyed. It was even observed that Polish second-home owners spent a few weeks more at the cottage (15.8 weeks, with the median of 13) yearly while for their Finnish counterparts it was 11.3 weeks, with the median of 9 weeks, which may also have a clear impact on the size and structure of local expenditures. In addition to the length of stay, a shift is also observed with regard to seasonality of the second-home stay. While the summer season is the most popular among second-home owners to stay at the cottage, May June and July are the most crowded months among Finns. The abovementioned shift is made by Polish owners, who tend to stay longer during August, which, however, is less popular among Finns, mainly due to the beginning of the autumn semester in schools and worsening weather conditions as compared to earlier summer months. Then, in terms of the distribution of stays and visits, another shift is noticeable, which for Finnish second-home owners is mirrored in more frequent and shorter visits – reflecting in low rates of standard deviation – while among Poles it shows in less frequent visits (often limited to the summer season with no other visits outside that period) but longer stays encompassing one or two summer months – reflecting in high standard deviation values. Additionally, a large population of Finnish second-home owners (mainly those in pre-retirement and retirement age) stated that the length of stay at the cottage was apparently getting longer compared to the past year while for the majority of Poles it remained stable. Then, one third of Polish respondents declared an intention of moving permanently to the second home in the future, while for Finns only 18% did; at the same time, those who rejected that idea accounted for almost 70% for Finns and almost 43% for Poles.

The average size of the secondary residence was significantly larger for Finns than for Poles – 85.5 sq. m and 77.5 sq. m respectively. Additionally, the majority of the second housing stock was between 50 to 100 sq. m large both for Finns and Poles, but there were more smaller houses (up to 50 sq. m) in Poland (1/4 of all the homes surveyed) and approximately equivalent proportion of larger residences (over 100 sq. m) in both countries. In terms of home-equipment, nearly all of the residences surveyed had electricity, but there were noticeable differences as regards heating, water supply and wastewater disposal. Only 2/3rds of holiday homes in Poland were winterised whereas in Finland this proportion accounted for over 90%. Then, only every tenth cottage was provided with water service by the supply network in Finland while in Poland, this was the case for every second one (with approximately similar percentage of those having well or fresh water – 40–47%). The wastewater disposal was provided by one's own septic tank (more than 50% in both cases), albeit in less than 25% of homes surveyed in Finland and Poland a wastewater disposal network was connected. Furthermore, Polish summer homes were better equipped than Finnish ones because relatively more of them had a kitchen, bath/shower/WC and garage, while more Finnish residences had terraces and fireplaces. Then, they were similarly equipped with TV and fridge, but only 1/5 of Finns had a washing machine, which was more common in Polish homes (2/3), probably due to the needs resulting from a relatively long uninterrupted (on average) length of stay at the second home over the year.

A relatively low urbanisation index along with the domination of traditionally dispersed settlements in the countryside reflected in the prevailing second-home built environment in Finland, i.e. the vast majority of residences (almost 75%) were located in dispersed settlements, while the rest of them were situated in central villages, leisure/second-home areas and a marginal proportion in tourism resorts; no homes were located in towns. Conversely, in Poland, the structure was much more complex and differentiated. Second homes occurred mainly in villages and tourism resorts, but were also located in scattered settlements, (planned) second-home areas and also small urban centres. Then, second homes were located in municipalities of various functional types, with the prevalence of mixed functions in Finland while mixed and tourism-based municipalities dominated in Poland. The distribution of types among municipalities surveyed was more even in Finland and more polarised in Poland, with only relatively small proportions of highly agricultural, predominantly agricultural and semi-urban territorial units.

There was the prevalence of female-respondents over male in the sample of local people surveyed in both countries (see Fig 2.8.2). More than 80% of Finnish respondents were in pre-retirement and retirement age while over 40% of Poles were in working mobile age, which altogether is in line with the second-home owners' age structure. Then, this situation was indirectly observable also in the distribution of other socio-demographic features, i.e. household size, which was significantly larger for Poles (the domination of 3–4 people households) than for Finns (the prevalence of 2-people units). There was additionally a relatively large proportion of single families among Finns while almost every fourth household surveyed in Poland comprised 5 or even more members. As a consequence of diverse age structures, there were relatively more less-educated respondents in Finland and more well-educated in Poland, although differences in this regard were not that strong as in the case of second-home owners. Interestingly, age and education did not reflect that clearly in the structure of economic activities undertaken by local people. Although there was a clear prevalence of business owners (mostly farmers) in Poland, in terms of paid work, the proportions of individuals working as specialists, managers, senior executives and also low white collar employees were higher among Finns than among Poles, for whom jobs as manual workers were more common. The above mentioned domination of elderly people was reflected in a considerable percentage of retired people in Finland. Additionally, for working people in Finland, it was twice more common to commute to work outside the municipality of permanent residence than in Poland. In terms of the household financial situation, most of Finnish locals obtained average incomes while for Poles these were mainly low and very low thresholds. However, it has to be mentioned that only four income groups were applied in the Polish study as opposed to five categories for second-home owners.

Table 2.8.2 Local people's socio-demographic characteristics, %

Attribute		**Finns**	**Poles**
Gender	Female	58.1%	62.4%
	Male	41.9%	37.6%
Age groups*	Working mobile	16,8%	42.3%
	Working non-mobile	52.9%	36.0%
	Post-working	30.3%	21.7%
Household size	Single	19.2%	10.4%
	Two people	59.6%	22.0%
	Three-four people	14.1%	45.1%
	Five and more people	7.1%	22.5%
Education	Primary/elementary school	28.4%	20.9%
	Vocational school, training course	29.7%	25.1%
	High school	27.7%	39.7%
	University, polytechnics	14.2%	14.3%
Economic activity	Business owner	15.0%	34.3%
	Senior executive, specialist	6.5%	6.1%
	Lower white-collar	11.1%	5.8%
	Manual worker	13.1%	16.4%
	Unemployed	7.2%	4.2%
	Retired	44.4%	24.0%
	Housewife	1.3%	3.1%
	Other	1.3%	6.1%

Attribute		Finns	Poles
Commuting to work	Yes	43.3%	21.8%
	No	56.7%	78.2%
Net monthly household income**	Very high (≥7,501€ / ≥5,001 PLN)	6.0%	10.4%
	High (5,001–7,500€ / 3,001–5,000 PLN)	9.3%	22.0%
	Average (2,501–5,000€)	43.3%	–
	Low (1,251–2,500€ / 1,501–3,000 PLN)	27.3%	45.1%
	Very low (≤1,250€ / ≤1,500 PLN)	14.0%	22.5%
Length of ownership/ residence	≤9y	18.8%	12.1%
	10–19y	14.9%	11.8%
	20–29y	13.0%	19.8%
	30–39y	15.6%	16.0%
	40–49y	15.6%	16.3%
	≥50y	22.1%	24.0%
Place of living (settlement type)	Small town	0.7%	15.9%
	Central village	67.9%	18.7%
	Other settlement	31.4%	65.5%

* Finns: 'working mobile' 18–44, 'working non-mobile' 45–64, 'post-working' 65+; Poles: 'working mobile' 18–44, 'working non-mobile' males 45–64, females 45–59, 'post-working' males 65+, females 60+.

** For Polish respondents only four income categories were applied: 'very high', 'high', 'low' and 'very low'.

Source: Own study.

Finnish locals lived permanently mainly in central villages, which played an important role of local service centres for the surrounding area while only 1/3 lived in other, i.e. mainly scattered settlements. For Poles, it was also significantly diverse, seeing that the majority (2/3) lived in small villages, and the rest was evenly distributed among small urban centres and central villages.

3. Theoretical framework: key theories, concepts and literature overview

Throughout this chapter, a number of primarily microeconomic theories and concepts are presented, following the order *determinants-performance-impact* of the consumer (second-home owner) behaviour in rural locations. Obviously, the sequence is rather arbitrary than strict since, due to the contextual character and often intense interplay between its components, it is problematic and even impractical in some cases to separate determinants and factors from consumption tendencies and potential areas of impacts. The structure of the chapter seems to be quite complex as it consists of several levels/sub-chapters, which, however, reflect the current state-of-the-art and generally acknowledged classifications of the consumer behaviour drivers (merged into broader categories: social, demographic, cultural, economic, psychological and other/additional), consumption tendencies and consumption-related theories as well as the concepts that build a solid foundation for anchoring the spending pattern analysis and for attempting to interpret research findings in terms of impacts and implications for local economies and more generally – rural communities.

This section comprises a selection of theories which, in the author's onion, are the most relevant and have a great explanatory value on the following: what induces second-home owners to be local customers; how they perform in terms of consumption in a rural, leisure destination; what and how much they purchase and how much they spend locally; and finally, what their contribution to the community's economy is. Importantly, the decision about what concepts to take into account while constructing the theoretical framework was highly influenced by the fact that rural economy is not and cannot be conceptualised nor approached by applying any specific distinctive theory, but rather by employing various concepts and constructs. Hence, this study refers to theories of microeconomics, consumer behaviour, tourism, development economics, but also ideas concerning agriculture as an economic and non-economic function as well as its marketable and non-marketable products.

Importantly, when considered in the context of mobility, second homes are often seen at the cross-section of tourism and migration (Bell & Ward 2000; Williams & Hall 2000; Hall & Williams 2002; Müller 2002b). Here, despite being contested, the 'permanency' of the move can provide a firm ground for positioning second homes on the tourism-migration continuum (Müller 2002b). As previous research has shown, second homes represent the entire mobility spectrum (Müller

2002b) from short-term (weekend) to long-term/seasonal stays extending beyond summer holidays. Thus, the exact position on the continuum based on 'permanency' (despite other relevant features such as place attachment, for instance) may vary considerably. Consequently, with regard to this study's focusing on consumer behaviour and its implications for the local economy, it seems rational to make an assumption that the position on the tourism-migration continuum in terms of 'permanency' reflects in second-home owner's spending by combining diverse 'proportions' of distinctive regular (everyday) and leisure spending patterns. Thus, operating on the premise that regular and leisure consumption are critical to recognise second-home owners' economic conduct in rural locations, this chapter utilises and integrates the state-of-the-art in (general) consumer behaviour and second-home research.

3.1 Factors and preconditions influencing second-home owners' spending patterns (DETERMINANTS)

Consumer behaviour and spending patterns are formed and modified by a wide variety of factors and preconditions, which are classified differently in economic and sociological literature (Wilson & Gilligan 2005; Foglio 2008; Hudson 2008; Armstrong *et al.* 2009; Rudnicki 2010; Zalega 2012). The typologies used usually follow the 'problem' approach, revolving around economic, psychological, socio-demographic, biological, cultural (socio-cultural) and geographic factors (Wilson & Gilligan 2005; Hudson 2008; Armstrong *et al.* 2009), or abide by divisions according to the subject of consumption and its context/circumstances, thus relating to consumers' (individual, internal, endogenous) and background (external, exogenous) determinants (Kieżel 1995; Foglio 2008). As traditional classifications do not include specific factors and influences relevant to explaining consumption by second-home owners (e.g. relational/trip-related characteristics and destination-related factors), or only include them too narrowly, these factors were taken into consideration in this section in order to supplement the factors typical of regular household spending.

3.1.1 Demographic and socio-cultural factors

Many researchers have stressed the great importance of households' socio-demographic characteristics in shaping consumer behaviour and spending (Lazear & Michael 1988; Bylok 2005), although it needs to be underlined that they have referred to the head of the household's socio-demographics rather than to all household members. Second-home/tourism studies usually take the owner's socio-demographic characteristics and/or the household size and family composition as the main reference points. These category factors usually include gender, age, the phase in the family life cycle, household size and composition as well as the location of the household (permanent residence in terms of urbanisation level or just an urban/rural status). As previous research has revealed, consumer's gender and age can make a difference in the course of explaining tourist's spending patterns on site (Bowie & Buttle 2004). The purchaser's age is especially considered a significant distinguishable variable across new forms of tourism, as is the notion of lifestyle (Agarwal & Yochum 2000). Here, the family life-cycle and the owner's life-course can be very useful as an explanatory theory, as has been proved in Finnish (Rantanen 2014) and other foreign studies (Downward & Lumsdon 2000; Jang *et al.* 2004; Pouta, Neuvonen & Sievänen 2006) which focus on demand for local services among second-home owners, and demonstrate significant explanatory power for differences in expenditure patterns.

Furthermore, according to some researchers, the varied purchasing of certain products such as clothing, cosmetics, books and tourism products can be explained (to some extent) by gender (Linehan 2008; Heitmann 2011). However, others have stressed that gender is not a significant consumer-spending determinant in relation to tourism products (Agarwal & Yochum 2000; Henthorne 2000; Jang *et al.* 2004; Wang & Davidson 2010), with the exception of Thrane (2002), who argues that males spend more than females, especially on luxury goods (Ackerman, Griskevicius, & Li 2011). In general, this factor influences spending patterns and preferences as well as the decision-making process and the forms of communication, since men and women make purchasing decisions in completely different ways. For men, the decision-making process is linear while for women it is much more complex and detailed – a spiral path (Prasad 2012) – since women tend to search for ideal solutions, thus demanding more and more precise information and using a wider range of data sources on the product. In addition, women appreciate personal contact, obtaining opinions about the product from staff, opinion leaders/experts and friends, while men focus on impersonal data sources (leaflets, catalogues etc.).

Where second homes are concerned, the need for personal contacts may induce more purchases by women (including informal transactions, usually made directly from individuals such as farmers and other rural residents or at local summer markets). Women may then choose specific brands and high-end products, tending to find ideal solutions and thus spending more than men would, although we should remember that in some rural locations female consumers may neglect such preferences, given the limited availability of certain products and brands.

An age-related factor – a phase in the family life cycle – is found extremely influential, through a decision-making process, in shaping consumer behaviour and household spending patterns (Rich & Jain 1968; Hawks & Ackerman 1990; Du & Kamakura 2006). Despite numerous categorisations in the family life-cycle, a few universal stages can be identified and structured according to the household head's life stage progression, although also other relevant variables must be taken into consideration, such as marital status, the presence or absence of children and children's age. As systematised by Solomon (2006) for the youth phase, up to 35 years of age, the following variants can be determined: 1. Bachelor I (one adult in a household), 2. Young married (with no children), 3. Full nest I (young married couple with a child), and 4. Full nest II (young couple with children). Furthermore, for the middle-age stage (35–64 years old), 1. Bachelor II (one adult in a household), 2. Childless couple, 3. Delayed full nest, and 4. Full nest III can be distinguished. Finally, for the elderly stage (over 65 years of age), the following are usually recognised: 1. Bachelor III, 2. Older couple, 3. Empty nest (a married couple with no children living with them), 4. Solitary survivor (widowhood stage). However, this more traditional approach has been undermined by sub-stages and family types that were not taken into account for this concept, e.g. second marriages involving children from previous marriages, single parent households or single family units existing throughout the whole cycle. Hence, modern family life-cycles are clearly more complex and convoluted, encompassing more distinctive family units/variants (Murphey & Staples 1979; Bojanic 1992, 2011).

Given that a family or often a household is commonly recognised as a consumption unit and usually comprises more than one person, purchasing decisions are made within the group of its members; the family life-cycle thus plays an important role in understanding the consumer behaviour being shaped by more demographic factors (age): household size and its structure. In general, consumers have different needs and preferences (different priorities in the hierarchy of needs) according to the various stages of family life (Wagner & Sherman 1983; Wright 2006; Kotler & Keller 2015) and as one approaches the next stage of the family life-cycle, new products and services are demanded (Gourinchas & Parker 1997). That is why the life-cycle factor is crucial in order to segment the market demographically (Neal, Quester & Hawkins 2004). For instance, while for young, single adults' typical spending is on clothing, entertainment and processed food products, for young (married) couples with children it is basically children's clothing, baby care accessories, medical expenses, insurance as well as larger homes and home appliances (Antonides & van Raaij 1998). Then, conversely, for the middle-aged people with older children at home (full nest stage II), there is a clear shift in consumption which sees more spending allocated to child education, personal electronic items, holidays and family size packages. In the empty-nest stage (when children leave home), expenses are more on luxuries, travel, hobbies and home improvement (not to mention the shifts/changes in daily/regular household consumption in terms of demand size and commodity bundle), being a result of money and asset accumulation (Antonides & van Raaij 1998).

In the context of second-home owners, the life-cycle factor may be important in explaining the ownership of holiday homes since, unlike second-home use, ownership is more associated with the (potential) consumer's age and his/her stage in the family life cycle, often considered as a manifestation of retirement migration (Cosenza & Davis 1981; Breuer 2005; Stewart & Stynes 2006). Ownership takes place at a certain stage, usually in older middle-age or even old-age, although sometimes, when financial conditions are favourable, it may happen even earlier – for young couples with (or without) children.

Here, the concept of family life-cycle has a greater explanatory value by referring to the owner's/consumer's personal (professional) life cycle and the consumer life-cycle hypothesis of Modigliani and Ando (1957), which is in fact an economic theory, albeit with strong explicit associations with the consumer's age and life-cycle stage. The aforesaid concepts tend to explain a variety of second-home owners' strategies and trajectories within each phase of the second-home ownership. This explanatory power matters because, first and foremost, coming into possession of a second home and also its further use and spending on it are affected by additional factors underpinning these theories – the owner's life course (Müller & Hall 2004; Paris 2010), his/her stage of professional career, the phase in the family life cycle (Hall 2005) and obviously household income/wealth (Belsky, Di & McCue 2006; Brunetti & Torricelli 2014).

Besides the basic demographic personal attributes such as gender and age, the educational level is generally of great importance in shaping consumer behaviour (Schiffman, Hansen & Kanuk 2008). This factor basically works in a dual manner, since a higher education level is more indirectly reflected in higher incomes (the productivity of labour rises with education), thus increasing consumer purchasing power and expanding and diversifying his/her potential commodity bundle. A household with more educated members also has greater access to knowledge, facts and ideas, a greater facility to assimilate and evaluate new pieces of information as well as an increased ability to make use of them efficiently (Becker 1965). This is reflected in more rational (efficient) consumer choices but at the same time in a greater awareness of market diversity, deeper knowledge of product features (advantages and disadvantages) and effects (Solomon 2006). In general, the education level stimulates (greater) needs and creates opportunities to satisfy them through higher incomes and awareness. As a result, the structure of the commodity bundle changes and for well-educated second-home owners it may mean a large proportion of infrequent goods (leisure and luxury accessories, home appliances) and services (use of recreation facilities) and, as a result of greater awareness, even more appreciation for local organic food products (from local summer markets). Following Becker's formulation of household activities (Becker 1965; Michael & Becker 1973; Michael 1975), a household consisting of well-educated members is more efficient in some activities and thus a greater volume of some commodities may be 'produced'/consumed with a given amount of time and money. For example, if the education improves consumer knowledge and awareness in leisure (active, healthy and diverse ways of spending free time), this commodity – relaxation, recreation – related to leisure will be relatively cheaper than another. What is particularly important is that this mechanism will be acting as an incentive in shifting consumption to a relatively cheap activity (Michael 1975). Consequently, considerable changes in consumption and spending patterns may occur, thus inducing (greater) demand for the possession of a holiday home as well as for sport and recreation activities in the course of spending time at a second home. Consequently, with an education level reflected in a more efficient stay at a secondary residence, it will mean that the same amount of a commodity – relaxation, recreation – is purchased by a household each day for less time and money. So in general, Becker saw education as a key indicator expressing the influence of, in his opinion, a crucial factor, i.e. knowledge, in a more formal way. The required knowledge of how to combine basic commodities' characteristics into more complex qualities that satisfy consumer needs was here a critical ability. In fact, it does not matter if such knowledge was certified (through formal education from institutions) or was gained in some other way (self-education, experience) since it could be equally and efficiently used to meet consumer needs and expectations. However, at the level of quantification/operationalisation, it is more useful if the knowledge is ordered into formal categories that are easier to obtain and describe than self-education, for instance.

Furthermore, according to some researchers, job position (and economic activity) as an education-related factor may be important in shaping consumer behaviour and spending patterns (Cage 1989; Uusitalo 1980; Bihagen 1999; Schiffman, Hansen & Kanuk 2008), although others have cast doubt on this relationship (Houthakker & Taylor 1970). As with education level, job position may have an indirect impact – usually through higher incomes, as the position in the labour market hierarchy rises, or between employed and unemployed people (Lázaro,

Molto & Sanchez 2000) – as well as a direct impact – since it gives rise to special needs resulting from the occupation (e.g. executive managers vs. farm workers) as well as social roles and status and consequently lifestyles and motivations. In the context of second-home owners' spending, a Polish study showed that manual workers spent a higher proportion of their local expenditure on food products than entrepreneurs and senior managers did, while for the latter group, the proportion spent on construction and infrequent services (catering, cultural and health-related) was considerably higher than for manual workers and lower white-collar workers (Czarnecki 2014).

Urban status has also been considered as an important independent variable influencing consumer behaviour (Cowell & Green 1994; Lázaro, Molto & Sanchez 2000; Katz-Gerro & Talmud 2005; Turczak & Zwiech 2013). Some of the consumer's socio-demographics (education, wealth, economic activity, occupation, job position and first and foremost social class) may be echoed in his/her origins, which here are considered as the urban status (metropolitan, middle-sized, small town) or the rural status, which basically means his/her permanent residence (Lehto *et al.* 2004; Laesser & Crouch 2006). Thus, permanent residence may be treated as a universal variable. However, there are slightly contrasting considerations of differences and similarities between urban and rural populations. According to some researchers, urban residents differ significantly from rural people with regard to lifestyles and social status as well as motivations, preferences, attitudes and beliefs towards certain products and services as well as places of purchase and channels of distribution (CSO 2013, 2015; Hawk 2013; Turczak-Zwiech 2013). This view has been, however, the subject of much critique, in view of how efficiently macro-scale processes, such as urbanisation and modernisation, have shortened the distance between both social groups in various aspects – education, work, incomes, lifestyles etc. and made each of those less socially and economically homogenous than they ever were before (Fuguitt, Brown & Beale 1989; Węgleński 1992; Pitkänen, Adamiak & Halseth 2014).

As for second-home owners, who are mostly urban residents, local purchasing and spending patterns may be influenced by higher incomes (higher than average in the countryside) but at the same time by rural roots or specific motivations towards more natural, rural products, and they will be thus purchasing local food products using local catering services etc. Their needs and preferences may be highly influenced by a wide range of products available on the urban market, which in some rural locations must be limited (rather in Poland than in Finland, due to specific distribution channels). Thus, purchasing basic commodities takes place locally and more sophisticated products are bought at the permanent residence, restricting consumer needs to whatever can be obtained from local retailers and services.

There is no doubt that household size (number of members and the number of children as a separate category, in this case second-home users) is an influential factor in the levels of demand and spending (Thrane 2002; Nicolau and Más 2005). This is because the increasing size of the household is not only reflected in growing needs and demand but also in growing disposable income (adult members/those bringing income to the household), and thus in an increasing purchasing power (Cage 1989; Bobonis 2009; Czech 2012). As mentioned above, having children can be of great importance to explaining the structure of household spending (Labrecque & Ricard 2001; Dikčius *et al.* 2014). In tourism studies (measuring tourism spending), the total number of travellers (considered as the total number of household travels) has been found to be positively related to the total or daily expenditure (Agarwal & Yochum 1999; Dávila *et al.* 1999; Lee 2001) while negatively related to the total expenditure per person (Taylor, Fletcher & Clabaugh 1993; Wang & Davidson 2010). In contrast to Agarwal & Yochum (1999), who found that a greater number of children has a negative impact on the total expenditure, Wang *et al.* (2006), Lee (2001), and Nicolau and Más (2005) did not find children's impact to be significant. Instead, the composition that is the number of adults in the travelling party was found to be positively related to the total expenditure (Wang *et al.* 2006). Jang *et al.* (2004) argued that the total spending was affected not by the number of adults in the group, but rather by whether the traveller had companions or not.

Culture

At first glance, it seems that culture influences people's lives in an invisible way which is difficult to determine. This becomes more evident when compared with other groups that are culturally preconditioned such as nations/subcultures (Samli 1995; Wiśniewska 2005; Savani, Markus & Conner 2008; Durmay, Çelik & Oruc 2011). This is why culture is so important in this comparative study, as it has implications in different behaviours and spending patterns of Polish and Finnish consumers.

As defined by Szczepański (1970), culture is 'all the products of human activity, tangible and intangible values as well as recognised, objectified practices accepted in any communities/societies and transferred to other communities and the next generations.' (Szczepański 1970, p. 78). Thanks to the formation of norms and standards of behaviour, it becomes a universal system of conduct regulation, which, however, is subject to social evolution (Światowy 2006, p. 115).

The influence of culture on consumer behaviour can be seen in different purchasing habits, preferences and practices, as well as in different ways of promoting products (Rudnicki 2012). Tradition and inclination have a crucial impact on purchasing routines in the case of basic commodities and everyday-use products (Bryła 2013; Briones Alonso 2015). These factors are widely reflected in the national/regional cuisines, nutritional patterns and diets (Song *et al.* 2005; Fanzo *et al.* 2013), e.g. in a high proportion of milk and dairy products in the diet of all age groups in Finland and other Nordic countries (FAO 2010; LUKE 2013), and a still large proportion of potatoes in the Polish diet (although gradually decreasing since the 1960s) (FAO 2008).

Thus, culture may influence second-home owners consumer behaviour in a more indirect but considerable way that can consequently reflect in a variety of spending patterns among subcultures – revealing differentiations between Poles and Finns but also regionally within these groups (Kuśmierczyk 2002; Similä *et al.* 2005; Lähteenoja *et al.* 2007; Utzig 2013). This difference is manifested in the demand for various goods, which, along with their availability and quality, creates a basic precondition for satisfying it either locally or externally.

Interestingly, culture may be an important determinant of the frequency and place of purchase, since e.g. food in Poland is very often purchased daily and urban residents used to get it (raw fruit, vegetables and grain) from farmers' markets (CBOS 2013; Cyran 2013; Urban & Michałowska 2013), so for second-home owners this preference may be reflected in purchasing food and agricultural produce directly from farmers in rural locations. Although this tendency has nowadays been modified by people's largely buying such goods from hypermarkets, supermarkets and discount stores (not only in urban areas), for more aware consumers, this spending pattern may even stimulate their need to search for more natural, local products, thus raising their motivation for local and direct purchasing. Direct purchasing gives the consumer the opportunity to learn more about products and finally to socialise and initiate social contacts that can be of great importance for some types of people, e.g. for open-minded and actively participating second-home owners. On the other hand, despite seeing economic potential in direct sales of food products to individual customers, in Finland, local farmers are highly aware of specific obstacles to efficiently use such distribution channels – these obstacles include increasing formal requirements concerning food quality and sanitation, regulations, competition of imported commodities and specific types of agricultural produce that make direct transactions less possible, e.g. dairy products (Puupponen *et al.* 2015; Rizzo 2016).

Social class and reference group

Some researchers have argued that some standard socio-demographic measures only partially explain the variations in consumption patterns, one of the main reasons being the character of the middle class, which is a broad and diverse economic group (Shaw & Williams 2004). Thus, in order to be more precise, the social and reference groups are often included in the course of assessing the consumer-behaviour determinants, e.g. with regard to tourism (Moutinho 1987; Fratu 2011).

The Oxford Dictionary describes a social group as a number of individuals associated or aggregated together to a greater or lesser degree, either because they share certain features, such as class, ethnicity, etc., or because they are bound together by patterns of interaction (Simpson & Weiner 1989). There are various types (depending on e.g. size, make-up, characteristics) of social groups, such as family, friendship, informal/formal, shopping, consumer-action and work groups (Tyagi & Kumar 2004). As some researchers have argued, those social groups can be seen as social communication networks. Thus, they may be more influential on consumer spending patterns through informal, word-of-mouth communication (based on social validation, credibility and possibly pressure to conform) than mass advertising (O'Shaughnessy 2012). This influence is exerted basically because a social group has some particular characteristics whose foundations are more complex and durable than some marketing campaigns. These characteristics include: 1. a relatively stable spatial integration, 2. a sense of attachment/community and identity, 3. mutual interdependency of its members (cooperation, division of work), 4. similar cultural attributes and the acceptance of the common value patterns, 5. sharing the same position with regard to the division of economic goods, hierarchy of power and prestige (Rudnicki 2012, p. 116).

Through personal relationships with others in the group, members of a particular social group will seek to adjust their spending patterns to its ideal consumption pattern. This pattern is shaped by the group's habits, preferences and tastes regarding specific products, brands, shopping patterns, frequency and size of purchases, places of purchase and distribution channels, the acceptance of new products and sources of information (Rudnicki 2012). This influence can be seen, for example, among consumers who strongly identify as more environmentally concerned, as a result of which they have more positive opinions and knowledge of organic brands (Ahmad & Thyagaraj 2015).

For second-home owners, their origins, under the assumption that they usually come from a certain middle class stratum (Selwood 2006; Paris 2010), may lead to acquiring the property and following the spending pattern typical of middle-class second-home owners, which may mean expenditure on specific home equipment, building materials, specific location, leisure activities, etc.

Furthermore, the reference group to which a consumer aspires, with which a consumer identifies and whose norms he/she accepts (Rudnicki 2010) may have an impact on their behaviour, since it functions as a source of information and model of attitudes, values and desires to which consumer behaviour and his/her social status is compared. The reference group influences consumer behaviour through its opinions and suggestions during purchasing decisions or related to the choice of the brand. Usually, consumers have three main reference groups: the associative group (to which they currently belong), the aspirational reference group (to which they aspire) and the dissociative group (which they want to leave/reject).

Reference groups may influence consumer purchasing decisions through their impact on the level of consumption aspirations, thus inducing consumer satisfaction or dissatisfaction with what he/she has gained, and showing consumer patterns related to how to spend free time, preferred place of purchase etc. (Hurrelmann 1996; Cooper *et al.* 2008). Reference groups play a major role in promoting certain brands (as this attracts attention which is visible to all), and this role, in general, is much greater in the case of luxury goods than in the case of basic commodities (Bearden & Etzel 1982).

Many consumer transactions are made under reference-group pressure, since consumers tend to purchase products which are wanted, accepted or envied by others, or just because they have learnt more about the product (Bywalec & Rudnicki, 2002; Rudnicki 2012). This relationship to the reference group leads to the shifting down phenomenon, which means that products formerly reserved for certain social groups higher in the social hierarchy are becoming common and more widespread among the lower social groups, as for instance secondary residences/holiday homes and such homes in prestige or famous tourism locations (Czapiński & Panek 2013). In this context, growing access to luxury goods may also mean the imitation of lifestyles and ways of spending free time at a second home (e.g. more active/sporting), thus influencing actual spending patterns and purchases of the necessary accessories.

3.1.2 Economic factors

In this study, the economic factors influencing second-home owners' spending patterns have been considered only at the micro-scale, i.e. referring to the household-unit level, which is a crucial explanatory approach for the research topic. According to many researchers, the economic factors determining consumer behaviour and expenditure patterns can be divided into two main categories: internal (endogenous) – consumer-dependent – and external (exogenous) – not dependent upon the household (Kolny 2004; Rudnicki 2012; Zalega 2012). In the context of second-home owners'/users' purchases, in the first category, the focus is usually on personal and household (disposable and discretionary) income, savings and leisure time, as well as on the size, type and level of equipment with durable goods of the permanent and secondary residences (fixed household assets). The other category includes product price levels, changes in prices and price comparisons, supply site, the type of a product (goods/services) acquired as well as distribution channels and places of purchase.

Disposable/discretionary household income and savings

In general, consumer income is widely considered to be a central factor determining consumer behaviour and household spending (Cage 1989; Bae 1992; Lehto *et al.* 2004; Mehmetoglu 2007). Researchers usually use personal income (Armah & Teensma 2012) or household income to measure its impact on consumer spending (Smallwood & Blaylock 1982; Cai, Hong, & Morrison 1995; Rausch, Metcalf & Reilly 2011) although it seems more appropriate to use household income in such a context, since most purchasing decisions and expenditures are made within the household and for its common purposes (Lancaster 1975; Baker, Graham & Harker 1998; Vermeulen 2002), including the time spent at a second home. Household income includes all forms of income such as salaries, wages, retirement income, all types of social benefits, allowances, dividends, profits from property ownership and leasing, compensation for damages and injuries, donations, gambling winnings, prizes, awards and others (ILO 2003; CSO 2011; OECD 2013a).

To be more precise, monthly or annual disposable or discretionary income in total or per capita (household member) is particularly applicable to consumer studies (Gąsiorowski & Kuszewski 2004; CSO 2013). Disposable income is all household members' personal after-tax income (OECD 2013b), while discretionary income is the disposable after-tax income less all payments for current bills, including rent or mortgage, property and inheritance tax, donations, alimony, child support and losses resulting from fortuitous, identifiable and insurable events (Landefeldt *et al.* 2010; Russell, Watson & McGuinnity 2013). In analysing second-home owners' consumption behaviour, it seems more justified and rational to use disposable household income, since some current bills are strictly secondary-residence-related expenses such as (leisure) property tax.

In economics, the relationship between disposable income and consumer expenditure is widely known as the propensity to consume, identified by Keynes (1964) and described as a specific psychic/mental attribute of society explaining this relationship. The average propensity to consume is the proportion of disposable income which the individual spends on consumption, while the marginal propensity is the proportion of additional income that an individual consumes. With regard to consumer spending induced by second-home ownership (i.e. expenditures on both holiday home-related commodities and taxes), the average and marginal propensity to consume may differ significantly between owners and non-owners as well as among the owners, i.e. their households and among specific types of products purchased. This propensity can be measured and explained by demand income elasticity (see section 3.2.2).

As the higher (highly-rated) needs grow with an increase in household income, this relationship is particularly important for second-home ownership and usage, since it may make it possible to reveal needs such as experiences enriching self-esteem and self-actualisation through hobbies, travel, interests etc. (see: Solomon 2006), and obviously through second homes. Hence, rising incomes may reveal the need to own a secondary residence/holiday home and a constant need for leisure and relaxation that is decisive for its (frequent) usage and potential development (equipment). These needs are highly conditioned by the free-choice fund, which is identified as the part of household disposable income left after basic needs have been satisfied (Zalega 2012).[1] To understand the importance of the household surplus/free-choice fund in the creation and satisfaction of highly rated leisure activities, one has to refer to the Polish nationwide survey on tourism consumption, which revealed the avoidance of travel spending as the first need to be cut from the household commodity bundle in reaction to the anticipation of lower income, and the rapid fall in consumer expenditure on tourism resulting from lower incomes (Rudnicki 2010).

Apart from influencing higher expenditure, an increased household income also changes the structure of the commodity bundle purchased by households. This relationship has been noticed and described by several researchers (Lipsey, Steiner & Purvis 1987; Dybczak, Tóth & Voňka 2014). In this context, what is known as Engel's three laws and curves have been of great importance in analysing and explaining consumer needs for tourism, e.g. adventure tourism (Löt-

---

1 Basic needs in this case do not include those related to second homes, since they are not as natural as everyday household consumption but occur only when the owner/user stays at the second home.

ter, Geldenhuys & Potgeiter 2013) and leisure activities, e.g. outdoor recreation (Boman *et al.* 2013), while in this study, they were employed in order to learn more about the structure of second-home owners' local purchases (see section 3.2.1).

The house/flat, its fixtures and fittings

Household wealth, as an economic factor influencing consumer behaviour, is often identified through fixed assets such as a house/flat owned by a household, including its physical standard – size (utility space and number of rooms), layout, building materials used, technical condition and its fixtures and fittings – media/networks and durable goods, facilities and utilities (Panek 2000). All these constitute the spatial-material framework of the household, forming a specific home infrastructure for consumption (Wątorski 1987, p. 14–15). Hence, a house/flat can be seen as the space where everyday family functions, tasks and actions (including preparing and consuming meals, sleeping, socialising, educating, relaxation and recreation) are carried out and where basic needs are fulfilled, thus enabling higher needs to develop as well as fixed assets to be collected (at home) (Kusińska 2009; Zalega 2008, 2012). In this study, the site where all of the above are realised is the permanent home as well as the secondary residence (holiday/summer home), which permits their users to satisfy highly rated leisure needs.

Interestingly, the additional but important function of a home and its fixtures and fittings is that they contribute to maintaining a certain comfort of life and reduce the negative impact of any periodic fall in current income on the satisfaction of household members' needs (Zalega 2012). Under the assumption that a secondary residence/holiday home is a type of equipment (as it is listed in some nationwide household surveys, e.g. CSO 2006, 2010), such a function may be crucial for some households in maintaining and (fully) meeting their recreational needs in a situation where they cannot afford traditional tourism.

In addition, a higher level of furnishing with various types of durable goods (home utilities and accessories, electronic appliances and devices satisfying the needs related to home entertainment, education and recreation as well as mobility 'items' enabling to move in geographical space (Sikorska 1988)) may have a considerably positive impact on leisure and the ways of spending free time, including the place (home/second home or other locations) where such needs are satisfied (Zalega 2012). The importance of such determinants has been widely analysed in verifying the compensation theory (Dijst & Vermuelen 1999; Strandell & Hall 2015), assuming the influence of the permanent home (size and quality) and its built environment on the willingness to compensate for insufficient conditions through second-home ownership as well as on the appearance, characteristics and built environment of the secondary residence. Most studies have found a positive correlation in this respect (Dijst & Vermeulen 1999; Skak 2004; Módenes & López-Colás 2007), although some have considered these factors to be insignificant (Wippler 1968; Norris & Winston 2010).

Besides the impact on second-home ownership, the permanent home and its furnishings may influence the importance and the use of the holiday home. These impacts can be seen particularly when the equipment in a permanent home grows and it thus plays a more important role as a 'place of consumption of art', as a substitute for the cinema, theatre, opera or concerts, as well as a place of education and recreation (Pronovost 2007).

Furthermore, as with the permanent home, the secondary residence/holiday home with its own characteristics may have a significant explanatory power in the context of analysing second home owners'/users' consumption behaviour and spending patterns (including local purchasing). This is particularly apparent in the analysis of the demand for local construction or renovation services, maintenance services or building materials, since a larger house usually needs more and more frequent maintenance work (and thus expenditure). Consequently, such needs may be met by the owner's buying chemicals and cleaning agents (locally) or by a local or non-local cleaning company. Here, the theory of the product life-cycle, where the product is a second home, combined with individual and family life-cycle concepts, may be helpful in understanding such consumption patterns (see section 3.2.3). Having a kitchen at a second home may give rise to expenses related to basic food products, as food can be prepared at home, while no kitchen may mean more eating-out expenses, e.g. local restaurants or take-aways.

A wooden cottage of a light construction, i.e. without foundations, may limit the length of stay and various leisure-time activities, thus making local spending patterns more selective (the prevalence of expenditure on services than on goods), but not necessarily limited in terms of the amount of spending described above based on the kitchen issue. Having a winterised secondary residence may indirectly but significantly and positively influence the use of retail and other local services, thus contributing to local spending through an increase in the total length of stay. Constant improvement of technical conditions of the house apparently reveals itself in a relatively new construction pattern for second homes in Finland – a shift from simple wooden cottages towards large, well-equipped villas (Pitkänen & Vepsäläinen 2008; Nieminen 2010). This change, along with existing already-equipped converted second homes, provides owners with solid grounds for longer stays and more frequent visits over the year, also outside the summer season. In addition, the possession of tools and DIY equipment may lower the impact on the local service sector (maintenance, renovations, construction) at least to some extent, and this effect is very often enhanced by the owner's attitude to spending time doing minor works by themselves (Bourdonnec 2010).

Leisure time

There are many contradictory theories, concepts and interpretations concerning the definition and distinctions of leisure time (Rojek 2000) and the trade-off between work and leisure (Veal 2006, 2009a; Douglas & Morris 2007), its origins and preconditions (Veal 2009b), and its links to consumption (Cieloch, Kuczyński & Rogoziński 1992; Roberts 1999; Cahuc & Zylberberg 2004; Stebbins 2009). Nevertheless, leisure time can basically be considered to relate to time outside of obligations (including work) and the satisfaction of basic physiological needs that can be freely disposed of and used for rest, entertainment and self-improvement (Zawadzka & Ferenz 1998), or, as Jung (1987) has stressed, free time is a sociological category, one of three main social times besides the working time and obligation time.

In addition, the main attribute of the second-home phenomenon is that it is basically for leisure purposes. Here, leisure time has been included in the category of economic factors influencing consumer (second-home owner) behaviour mainly due to the strong connection and interplay between income, work and consumption. As Zalega (2012) has pointed out: 1. free time is a normal good, since the demand for it grows as household/personal income grows; 2. a consumer with a certain time for work makes decisions related to free time; 3. workers work longer hours in response to an increase in wage rates – if the employer is offering a higher price for labour, the worker is prepared to offer more of it (substitution effect); 4. with a higher wage rate, the worker can secure the same income level by working fewer hours (income effect) (Owen 1969 as cited in: Veal 2006, p. 143).

As Veal (2006) stressed, such a work-leisure trade-off is nowadays the most important element in leisure studies, clearly being a quintessentially economic issue. This is crucial for the free-time a household has at its disposal and its distribution over the total time span, and at the same time for its financial situation (resulting from higher or lower incomes). The former are strictly linked to the length of stay at a second-home as a constituent and foundation for decisions such as whether to visit (or stay at home, visit friends or go on a weekend trip organised by a travel agent), when (now, next weekend or in the summer), for how long (a day, a weekend or the entire summer season) and if so, how to spend the time (stay there all the time or travel around in the neighbourhood, visit places, eat out or cook for oneself, do minor repairs at home or take part in local summer events etc.). Such decisions are likewise decisive for (second-home owner) consumer behaviour, the demand for goods and services, the amount of spending (including local purchasing) and finally the contribution of the latter two elements to the local economy.

Type of a product acquired

Obviously, consumer behaviour and expenditure patterns depend significantly upon the type of a product purchased, with the notion of a product in economic terms being widely considered as 'everything that can be found on the market, attract the attention, be acquired, utilised and consumed satisfying one's desire or need' (Kotler 1994, p. 400). Thus, an item, service, idea, place etc. can be found by consumers as products to purchase (Rudnicki 2012).

Every product on the market has its own basic and additional functions. The former are expressed by the actual attributes of a product and determine whether and to what extent the consumer needs are fulfilled. The latter reflect interdependencies between a product and consumer, including the convenience of use, aesthetics and particularly quality (Kuś 2011), thus determining its utility to the consumer. In fact, additional functions may be equally or even more important for the consumer than the basic functions, depending on the type of a product, consumer needs, attitudes and motivations and social status (Jolibert *et al.* 2012). The significance of additional functions can be also seen in the case of second-home purchases. Besides satisfying a basic need – providing a secondary, temporary or seasonal place to live – some additional functions related to size, furnishings, design, building materials, topographic situation and the distance from the permanent home, tourist facilities, shops and services may be crucial in choosing the location and deciding to buy something.

Researchers use a range of different classifications for products. Some look at, on the basis of the frequency of purchase, whether products are purchased often, periodically and episodically (Rudnicki 2012). Others classify them according to the character, distinguishing between everyday products, selectable and luxury products (Mruk & Rutkowski 1994), while some use specific criteria such as sales volume, average annual growth rate, the utilisation of key resources and return on investment (Fluitman 1973) or use categories based on public-institution regulations (UN 1998; OECD 2011a). In the second-home research analysing the spending patterns of German owners in Sweden, Müller (1999) proposed a distinction between everyday articles, building materials, construction services, maintenance services, infrequent goods and infrequent services. The most valuable feature of this typology is that it reflects the actual (predominant) and universal structure of second-home owners' expenditures, thus emphasising the core products and services that are technically and physically related to the home itself, such as building materials and construction and maintenance services, since these often play an important role in such seasonal residents' spending.

The type of a product can be crucial for second-home owners' consumer behaviour and spending patterns (local and non-local purchasing) in two respects: its availability on the local market (supply side) and its quality. The availability of certain products and brands on the urban (permanent residence) and rural markets (second-home location) may differ quite significantly even within one region, and this disproportion may be reflected in the owners' spending patterns. In particular conditions, some specific products can only be obtained on urban markets, which may lead to an increase in second-home related purchase in the permanent place of residence or to the acquisition of potential substitutes available locally. Others, such as raw agricultural produce, can be bought mostly in rural communities, which may largely contribute to local purchasing. The question of availability (along with price levels) can be crucial in shifting spending patterns towards substitutive and complementary products, thus having an impact on multiple goods and consequently reflecting in the amount and structure of purchase. Thus, if something is unavailable on the rural market, it induces no local purchases for that product and (probably) for complementary goods, since we may expect, in terms of economic rationality, that they will be purchased together in the permanent place of residence prior to the visit or on the way to a second home. Then, if the product is unavailable on the rural market, its substitute can be purchased there (if it is available) but having information about it may allow the consumer to provide themselves with the first one they wanted before the trip to a second home. The range and availability of products are heavily influenced by the country's supply network and system. In Finland, for example, the retail market system provides access to the same products at the same prices throughout the country, thus having a neutral/positive influence on second-home owners' local spending patterns. On the other hand, the evidence from Poland suggests that products supplied by small local retailers and service companies can be sometimes of a poor quality (resulting from low equipment levels, the owners' weak management and professional qualifications) and come at greatly uncompetitive prices compared to those provided by large, city-based international companies (Smolarek & Dzieńdziora 2010; Cyrek 2013; Bański 2015). Some particular products, however, may be regional/local, meaning they can only be bought locally (special food products, gifts, souvenirs etc).

Prices, price changes and price comparisons

Price is one of the most important factors shaping consumption behaviour through its direct influence on consumer's purchasing decisions (Devine & Marion 1979; Chang & Wildt 1994; Bywalec 2007), although the latest research in the field has called this into question, pointing out the decreasing knowledge of prices among consumers as a result of the growing wealth of societies, the dramatically increasing range of goods and services available, and the information chaos that provides too much for most people's memory to handle (Dziekański 2012).

In general, relations between the product price and the demand for it are described by Marshall's demand law, according to which a fall in prices results in an increase in demand and vice-versa (Marshall 1920), although, in fact, this interrelation is largely dependent upon the type of products purchased. It may vary depending on whether there are (many) substitutes or not, whether it is a basic or luxury good, whether the price is relatively high (at a reference period) or whether the product makes up a high or low proportion of household expenditure. This relationship can be measured using price elasticity of demand.

In the context of second-home consumption patterns and spending, it is somewhat natural for the consumer to compare prices between the products needed that are available on the rural market (where the second home is located) and on other accessible markets (permanent residence, neighbouring communities and on the way to a second home). In some countries (Poland), prices of the same products may vary significantly between locations (regions, rural-urban dichotomy) (Rudnicki 2012), due to regional preconditions as well as different supply systems resulting in varied competitiveness between suppliers (small family shops and large chain supermarkets, small family or one-person service companies vs. large nationwide companies). These differences may affect second-home owners spending patterns, including their local performance. While everyday articles can be purchased at convenient prices in urban supermarkets before one travels to a second home, others, such as 'organic', fresh food products, construction and maintenance services, can be less expensive at rural destinations.

Another important issue is that product prices may change over time and space, e.g. with relatively high prices, especially for everyday products, in the peak summer season in typical tourist localities (on the coast), and relatively low prices in typical rural regions and outside the summer season and winter holidays (Commons & Page 2001). Second-home owners consumption patterns are usually heavily influenced by elevated prices in the summer season: some owners try to avoid high local expenses and use products bought prior to the visit to a second home (Heffner & Czarnecki 2011). For relatively poor second-home owners, very high prices in the summer season (when they do not buy products outside the local market) are much more likely to influence the structure of their commodity bundle through higher prices of food and basic commodities (Giffen commodities). On the other hand, the household's vulnerability to price changes (rises), especially for basic/food products, decreases with greater income and wealth (Sabates-Wheeler *et al.* 2008). Hence, for second-home owners (often affluent people), it may only have a limited influence on their (non-) local purchasing.

For luxury goods, such as a second home itself, a price increase may result in greater demand (known as the Veblen paradox), explained by the demonstration effect based on the willingness to stand out by purchasing such products. Possessing a second home provides the owner with exclusiveness and higher prices make the product even more luxurious, and even act as a stimulus for the purchase. This paradox in some cases may explain the periodic growth of demand and purchasing of holiday homes at certain locations.

As described in the previous section, price changes may be of great importance in second-home owners' spending patterns (amount and structure of spending) since they impact on demand and the purchasing of substitutions and complementary goods. When the price of certain goods falls, the substitutive effect comes into play, which means a higher demand for these goods and at the same time a fall in the demand for their substitutes. The role of this effect is visible when a consumer makes a purchasing decision by comparing substitute goods and taking into account utility values and prices. This may lead to a second-home owner's rational purchasing of cheaper products available at the permanent place of residence or looking for high quality with higher prices.

Distribution channels and places of purchase

The individual consumer or household's choice of distribution channel is highly dependent upon four factors: their general attitude towards shopping, the planning of a purchase and the expenditure by the consumer, the shop's attributes and the perception of such attributes. More specifically, the consumer's attitude to the place of purchase can be determined by a type of a product, prices, the quality and range of goods, staff, locality, the convenience of purchase (working hours, layout, available parking), settling of complaints, special offers, advertising and reputation, crowds and the ambience of the shop (Rudnicki 2012, p. 140).

In general, the consumer/second-home owner can easily use both direct and indirect channels of distribution of goods and services. As some researchers have stressed, direct distribution is the shortest way from the producer to the consumer and has many advantages both for the consumer and the supplier, including the minimum misinformation, additional knowledge about the product, often cheaper prices and no transportation costs (Aguglia & Salvioni 2010; Pinchot 2014). As some studies have found, for second-home owners, this form of provision is important when purchasing agricultural produce, raw materials, food products (including simply processed ones) and maintenance and construction/renovation services (Ryan *et al.* 1999; Heffner & Czarnecki 2015). In the leisure/tourism sector, direct channels of distribution predominate, which stems from the fact that these services can only be consumed during the process of their production i.e. *in situ* (Rudnicki 2010).

In deciding where to source goods and services, the location of the retailer or service provider with regard to the holiday-home location is evidently as important for second-home owners as it is for regular tourists (Hathaway & Hughes 2000; Timothy 2005; Heffner & Czarnecki 2011). Particularly in remote locations, more dispersed settlements and rural areas far from urban centres (in general in the traditional countryside, where most second homes are concentrated (Jaakson 1986; Gallent & Tewdwr-Jones 2000)), accessibility – the distance, time and cost of travelling – is of great importance in shaping consumer behaviour and spending patterns (Müller 1999, 2002b). Lack of shops in the village or the surrounding area forces second-home owners to purchase products in their permanent place of residence or on the way to a secondary residence. If this is not possible (when the distance is too great for frequent visits), it is necessary to search for other retailers even in neighbouring municipalities (especially when the distance is shorter than to the nearest shops in the second-home municipality). The proximity to shops and the ease of travelling to the nearest shop may result in frequent and repeated purchases, while long distances or infrastructure difficulties in reaching it (bad road conditions) produce the opposite result (i.e. avoiding local purchases and looking for another service provider). This spending pattern can be basically explained by a general consumer attitude to minimising the cost of shopping as expressed in monetary value and the time spent on it and in the energy proportional to the time taken. For some consumers, all of these can be efficiently reduced when retailers and service providers are concentrated in one area, thus fostering the cluster effect and satisfying consumer needs (time- and money-saving solution) by the policy of cheap prices by hypermarkets, supermarkets and shopping malls (Eppli & Benjamin 1994; Deželan 2001; Konishi 2005). On the other hand, everyday articles (including foodstuffs) are usually bought near home, because for basic commodities saving time is more important than money for many consumers. Infrequent purchases are then often made far from the second-home location as they tend to be concentrated in large villages or nearby small towns. Here, the inconveniences related to distance can be compensated by the attributes of certain shops, such as a special atmosphere, a wide range of offers or just specific product features unavailable closer to home (Short 1996; Rudnicki 2012).

3.1.3 Psychological factors

Motivations and needs

As Światowy (2006) stressed, motivation is usually employed to inspire consumers to specific actions, since it plays an important regulatory role. It induces relevant actions, sets the desired direction and retains necessary operations until the goal has been accomplished (Moorman 1990; Jachnis 2007). Hence, motivation is a unique group of processes that intervene in consumer behaviour between stimulus and response (Cătoiu & Teodorescu 1997 as cited in: Mahika 2011). Such an array of constituent processes is grounded in the basic physiological and socio-psychological needs and desires of all human beings (Cassidy 2005).

Even though leisure purposes are a fundamental attribute in the definition of a second home, it turns out that the typology of motivators in tourism (Swarbrooke & Horner 2005) has a limited explanatory potential on second-home owners' consumer behaviour. The authors distinguished several motivating factors concerning taking a vacation and taking a particular vacation to a specific destination at a particular time. However, second-home owners do not have the full freedom in choosing the leisure destination (as some of them inherited the second home and the overwhelming majority return to their secondary residence each year, not having the choice of changing their second-home location every year), so the typology is applicable to the study only to a very limited extent.

In these circumstances, despite the criticism of Maslow's most popular theory of human motivation as a consequence of a hierarchy of needs (1943), in the context of tourist motivation studies (Witt & Wright 1992; Schiffman, Kanuk & Hansen 2008), this is in fact a more useful framework for identifying consumer needs compared to a typology of motivators in tourism. This is an even more efficient tool if it is supplemented by the Travel Career Ladder (TCL) developed by Pearce (1982, 1988), which links the changes in the individual's travel motivation with travel experience. While positioning second-home ownership within the hierarchy of needs and needs-based motivations, this phenomenon can definitely be considered as a response to the highest needs related to self-esteem and self-actualisation, enriching experiences through satisfying aspects such as hobbies, travelling, interests etc. (see: Solomon 1996) and/or sometimes as a response to social needs including social status and prestige, since having a secondary residence is often a symbol of wealth in Central-Eastern European societies and at least to some extent meets these needs (Czapiński & Panek 2014). The second-home phenomenon is not a tourism issue alone but rather a more complex matter, placed somewhere on the tourism/seasonal-permanent mobility continuum. The owners/users spend time at a secondary residence (even several months a year), and thus the full range of needs may be demanded, including those of physiological character, security and belonging as well as those identified by P. Pearce – relaxation, stimulation, relationships, self-esteem and development and fulfilment. From the perspective of the local community (including businesses), it is crucial whether and to what extent such needs will be fulfilled locally by using local resources and engaging local firms. Since there are no studies linking second-home owners' consumer motivations with local purchasing, it is useful to refer to some tourism studies or to consumer studies (household spending patterns) or to place the present study somewhere in the middle on the shopping-recreational shopping continuum. Boedeker's (1997) distinction between these two forms of shopping may be of help, as the place on the continuum and its associated features are highly determined by the length of stay at a second home (Martinez-Garcia & Raya 2008; Barros & Machado 2010), the distance between the primary and secondary residence and attitudes and the main reason for spending time there. In addition, some tourism studies have stressed that the local attractors encouraged tourists to the destination, but the motives for visiting did not have an impact on local spending (Downward & Lumsdon 2000, 2003). There is a bulk of literature concerning specific types of tourism or specific (local) products in the process. For instance, to identify the preconditions of food/culinary tourism (tourists' purchases of local food products), the concept of four categories of motivation has been applied: physical, cultural, interpersonal and status and prestige (McIntosch, Goeldner & Ritchie 1995). This classification was discussed and developed in further studies referring to questions of more detailed needs and motivations, such as tastes, the knowledge of different cultures, authentic experience, social relationships, health concerns, self-esteem, recognition and the desire to attract others' attention (Fields 2002; Kim, Eves & Scarles 2009). Similarly, researchers have examined the motivation issue with regard to tourist purchases of souvenirs and gifts (Kim & Littrell 2001; Gordon 1986; Littrell *et al.* 1994; Swanson 2004 as cited in: Wilkins 2009). The motivations behind tourist purchases in a tourism destination have been studied in the context of diaspora tourism and nostalgic goods relating to cultural identity, memory, tradition, religion, social bonds (Newland & Taylor 2010) and the motivation for genealogical research by tourists (Gergelyova 2007). Obviously, this topic has been very important for shopping tourism research, with the attempt to explain it through the push-pull model

(Kinley, Josiam & Kim 2003) or using theories of utilitarian and hedonistic consumer motivations (described below) (Hawkins, Best & Coney 2001; Suhartano, Ruhadi & Triyuni 2015). According to Yazdani (2007), prestige, economic, self-esteem and nostalgia/vanity are among the main motivations for tourist shopping.

Before referring to the principal types of consumer motivation, it should be stressed that according to Johnston & Conroy (2008) the shopper is no longer synonymous with the purchaser, since, referring to Tauber's (1972) study, people often have different motives for shopping, from role-playing and self-gratification to seeking social experiences outside home (Johnston & Conroy 2008, p. 381).

Several types of consumer motivation may have a great explanatory value and be crucial to learning more about second-home owners' consumer behaviour and spending patterns (including local purchasing). First, within the utilitarian motivation, the purpose of shopping is an attempt to achieve practical objectives, convenience and benefit, and thus it is treated as a necessary chore (Jachnis 2007). Therefore, utilitarian values make the process of purchasing more rational (Batra & Ahtola 1991) and efficient (Babin, Darden & Griffin 1994). Hence, with regard to second-home owners' (local) economic performance, this type of motivation may for instance mean the absence of or limited local purchasing when it is easier (organisationally, time- and money-saving-wise) to satisfy basic needs at a permanent place of residence in easily accessible large stores and supermarkets with a wide variety of products than in small, less accessible local shops. Then, there is the hedonistic type of motivation, which has been described as the facets of behaviour that relate to the multisensory, fantasy, and emotive aspects of consumption (Holbrook & Hirschman 1982). As an opposite to utilitarian consumption it has a more subjective and less rational background, and thus, from the point of view of the local economy (goods and service providers), may apparently be more important and beneficial, since some of the rationale concerning accessibility, prices, quality, utility and variety may be contradicted by actual consumer choices. This irrationality of consumption can be seen in some second-home owners' expenditure patterns, described in the empirical section of this book, defined by a high demand for various types of local goods and services. The behavioural freedom emphasised by reactance theory (Mowen 1995), based on a free choice of brands, products and services by the consumer, may also be useful in learning more about second-home owners' local consumption. Reactance is a consumer reaction whereby the freedom of consumption is at risk due to external social pressure to purchase certain products or from impersonal obstacles resulting from insufficient supply or a rise in prices (Jachnis 2007). Hence, for instance, too limited availability of desired local products may result in people's spending pattern changing, with their avoiding local grocers in favour of shops at their permanent place of residence or in neighbouring municipalities. One could find such relationships and the potential for explaining second-home owners' spending patterns and local purchasing also in other theories, such as the Optimum Stimulation Levels theory (Steenkamp & Baumgartner 1992) or Prospect Theory (Kahnemann & Twersky 1979, Tversky & Kahneman 1992).

Emotions

According to a growing number of researchers, emotions are one of the psychological factors that play a particular or even central role in shaping consumer's behaviour, as they are an inherent feature in the decision-making process of choosing from a variety of goods and services, their volume, qualities, utilities and prices. They also influence people's (non-economic) abilities and the propensity to purchase goods and services and consequently their satisfaction (Hawkins, Best & Coney 2001; Consoli 2009; Lee, Lee & Choi 2011). Izard (1977) and Plutchik (1980) have argued that there are several basic emotions, such as acceptance, anger, contempt, disgust, distress, fear, guilt, interest, joy, shame, surprise and trust, with positive or negative connotations. Thus, they may significantly determine people's conduct in economic terms, giving them positive energy or weakening their ability to make rational decisions about their daily habits, including consumer behaviour (Ackerman *et al.* 2009; Hwang & Lee 2015).

Although the links between emotions and second-home owners' consumption patterns (and particularly physical location where money is spent) have not been examined so far, these relationships have been increasingly examined in tourism and leisure studies (Bowen & Clarke 2009; Cohen, Prayag & Moital 2014), e.g. regarding decisions on holidays (White & Scandale 2005), purchasing tourist or leisure services (Chuang 2007), connecting between tourist destinations and associated emotions (Hosany & Gilbert 2009; Lee & Jeong 2009), linking emotions with the involvement in tourist activities (Santos, Ramos & Almeida 2014), or examining emotions resulting from the tourist experience (McIntosh & Siggs 2005). Here, undoubtedly, we can imagine that for instance emotions such as joy/sadness and their wider and longer-lasting consequences may have impacted the owner's decisions as to whether to visit a second home, when and for how long, alone or with family etc., and that such factors may indirectly influence second-home owner spending patterns.

Furthermore, the direct influence of bad experiences with local retailers and service providers may induce negative emotions, causing the owner to avoid purchasing locally. On the other hand, the trust in local people along with an interest in trying out new products from local grocers may be of great importance in shaping the willingness and propensity to purchase locally and to intentionally avoid shopping in the permanent place of residence prior to the trip to a second home.

Attachment to place

Tourism researchers have found that the attachment to a place, personal involvement and destination image are the antecedents of consumer (destination) loyalty (Hernández *et al.* 2007; Yuksel, Yuksel & Bilim 2010; Toyama & Yamada 2012; Souza & Simões 2014), although they are mediated by consumer satisfaction (Brocato 2006; Prayag & Ryan 2012). Thus, the attachment to a place can be considered as one of the important factors directly and indirectly shaping leisure behaviour and spending patterns by influencing the consumer's choice of places of purchase (Williams *et al.* 1992; Soutar & Sweeney 2001; Ryan 2009) and consequently the choice of products (Park & McInnis 2006; Ujang & Dola 2007; Ujang 2010).

Attachment to a place is in general defined as a strong, long-lasting affective and identity bond between a person and a place (Hummon 1992; Low & Altman 1992; Hernández *et al.* 2007), which develops regardless of the objective qualities of the place (Debenedetti & Oppewal 2009). It is highly dependent upon individual experiences and emotions (Morgan 2010; Scannell & Gifford 2010) and largely anchored in consumers' attitudes (Jorgensen & Stedman 2001; Stedman 2002), thus being a multidimensional rather than a simple cause-effect relationship (Lewicka 2011). Since it influences consumer satisfaction, place attachment affects commitment and destination loyalty (Sousa & Simões 2014), in contrast to the brand attachment and loyalty, as it focuses on 'where to shop' rather than 'what product (brand) to buy' (Ryan 2009). However, it should be stressed that the choice of the place of purchase directly affects the range of products available (so in effect it influences product choices), which is more likely to happen in remote, rural locations.

Researchers views on the meaning of place attachment are consistent. They point out that people's bestowing meaning on physical dimensions of places is the first necessary condition to establishing and developing interpersonal or social relationships, which together leads to strong attachment to a place (Sherry 1998; Kleinc & Baker 2004; Brocato, Baker & Voorhees 2015). In summary, place attachment has three main components: a physical basis, a social dimension (Hidalgo & Hernandez 2002; Brocato 2006) and the 'affective' components (Kyle, Graefe & Manning 2005; Nielsen 2014). Importantly, the physical dimension of a place – a concept foundation – can be considered as a geographical locale or resource (Stedman 2002), thus relating to the notion of a sense of place that is strictly associated with the specialness, distinctiveness or authenticity of a place (Graham, Mason & Newman 2009).

Furthermore, despite these components, the construct of place attachment has been described as having two distinct dimensions: place identity, which refers to a symbolic or affective attachment to a place, and place dependence, which refers to a functional attachment to a place (Gross & Brown 2008 as cited in: Nielsen 2014). The latter is an individual's evaluation of the environment in terms of its functionality in satisfying unfulfilled needs (Backlund & Williams 2003 as cited in: Brocato, Baker & Voorhees 2015). Hence, it has a more direct impact on consumption patterns and expenditures, e.g. on fees and spending preferences (Kyle, Absher & Graefe 2003). In terms of local purchasing, place dependency may be translated into local dependency (pull forces), when the local conditions (cost and time accessibility, products availability and prices etc.) are favourable to attracting and maintaining consumers and competitive with other locations, or into local independence (push forces), when such local conditions are weak, thus forcing consumers to search for other, more convenient places for their purchases.

From the perspectives of second-home owners and local economy, the main issue to be examined in this context is whether and to what extent place attachment informs decision-making processes on purchasing local goods and services and, in addition, if and how it affects destination loyalty in terms of purchasing. Although the question of place attachment has also been examined by researchers in the context of second homes (Stedman 2006; Kelly & Hosking 2008), they have mainly emphasised the choice of cottage location (McIntyre & Pavlovich 2006), its preconditions among second-home owners (Kaltenborn 1997), including the intensity and frequency of use of a recreational dwelling (Pitkänen, Puhakka & Sawatzky 2011) and also the role of place attachment in second-home owners' attitudes to the rural and associated daily practices at a second home (Mottiar & Quinn 2003). Hence, not much attention has been paid to the possible influence of place attachment on the purchasing decision-making process and the destination loyalty in terms of consuming local goods and services. In the context of local economy (size and structure of flows), considering the role of place attachment would be even more necessary, given that through shared experiences places can evoke common meanings (Pretty, Chipuer & Bramston 2003) and as such may induce collective consumer behaviour (Brocato, Baker & Voorhees 2015).

We can assume that the length of stay is one of the most important predictors of place attachment (Hernández *et al.* 2007), that some holiday homes are inherited

(Hiltunen & Rehunen 2014), and that the owners have roots in the location and relatives living in the same neighbourhood (Pitkänen 2008; Flemsæter 2009) or have previous leisure experiences at the place (Giuliani 1991). Consequently, we may expect that indirect but individual (more or less significant) place attachment may influence daily purchasing decisions of a person staying at a second home, thus enhancing local purchasing. Further, bearing in mind that individuals have a strong attachment to a place and they wish to protect it (Budruk, Thomas & Tyrell 2009; Scannell & Gifford 2010), one can suppose that such consumers will be more economically ethnocentric, preferring local shops and services and following such a consumption pattern despite certain occasional unfavourable conditions (an uncompetitive and inaccessible local market). Then, as some have argued, place attachment also plays a crucial role in engaging new consumers, since the strength of place attachment moderated by consumer satisfaction induces positive word-of-mouth (ambassadorial attitudes (Ryan 2009)) and lower switching intentions (Brocato, Baker & Voorhees 2015), thus contributing to the local economic ethnocentrism.

Learning and memory

Learning is a process that draws upon acquiring and collecting experiences and new knowledge, which in effect leads to permanent changes in (consumer) behaviour or makes it possible to modify previous habits and activities (Zalega 2012). Regardless of whether we consider learning in the narrower or broader sense – solely as a conscious and intentional or including simultaneous involuntary processes (Witt 2001) – what is the most important for consumer behaviour and expenditure patterns is that learning is a key to activating adaptive mechanisms adjusting consumer behaviour (in favour of the consumer) to certain objective conditions (external factors), and as such is a critical factor of change (Mutombo & Bauler 2009). As stressed by Moorthy, Ratchford & Talukdar (1997), learning is essential to individual consumer behaviour since during the process consumers develop information search strategies that reflect the trade-off between the perceived benefits and the cost of the search (cited in: Mills & Lowe 2013, p. 16). What is more, long-term memory allows people to register, store, update, reorganise and repeatedly recall information gained from learning, associations and all the types of sensual impressions crucial for repeating actions, and thus largely contributes to consumer habits (Block & Williams 2007; Zalega 2012).

As regards cognitive learning theories, they emphasise the individual as a problem-solving entity who actively uses information from their surroundings to master their environment (Schiffman, Kanuk & Hansen 2008), which in the context of consumer behaviour means making rational decisions and fulfilling needs and expectations according to one's tastes and utilities. On the other hand, behavioural theory shows that learning can be treated as a way of inducing certain specific changes in (consumer) behaviour, shaping one's reactions to external events (Solomon, Bamossy & Askegaard 1999). For consumption patterns and local purchasing it may mean that opportunities and obstacles to meeting one's needs and expectations resulting from certain objective circumstances can trigger and promote actions and strategies that can be advantageous or disadvantageous for the local economy. For example, a first visit to a second home with no grocers in the area determines shopping in the permanent place of residence and no local purchases in the future. Here, learning helps consumers to avoid supply problems and can be treated as a critical condition to the adaptation to a new situation. Comparing the prices, assortment and quality of goods and services between places of provision is a way of learning to make more rational and satisfactory decisions as to where to buy such products (Mills 2002). Interestingly, the construct of the 'savvy' or 'knowing' consumer as the concept contradictory to the 'sucker' is in fact based on learning, which makes a consumer more conscious and resistant to manipulation by large corporations and the mass media, with the consumer reclaiming their own sense of identity (Paterson 2006). Here, in some cases, it may mean that consumers (second-home owners) will be more keen to reject sales chains' offers (usually based on high volumes and cheap prices) in favour of a more local, 'natural' or 'niche' and more truthful offer provided directly by local producers, e.g. farmers. In addition, learning may influence consumption patterns more indirectly, given that one can learn from family, friends or media which products or brands to choose/avoid because of taste, health impacts, access, prices and utility (Baker, Graham & Harker 1998; Block & Williams 2007; Funk 2008; Schiffman, Kanuk & Hansen 2008). If they are needed during the stay at a secondary residence, these products may or may not be accessible (physically, economically) in a village/surrounding area, and thus long-lasting learning may indirectly but strongly determine second-home owners' local purchasing and spending patterns. Finally, since the advantages for (tourism) marketing resulting from cognitive learning are widely used nowadays (Peter & Olson 2010), including in advertising and promotional activities (Chiou, Wan & Lee 2008) or even simple signs (road signs) (Batkoska & Koseska 2012), they may be of great importance for local goods and service suppliers to firmly link their activities with second-home owners' demand, as some report a lack of information on this (Steinmetz 2010; Heffner & Czarnecki 2011).

3.1.4 Additional factors

Destination-related factors

Besides the socio-demographic and cultural factors, holiday-home location characteristics/destination-related factors (Mathieson & Wall 1982; Paajanen 1994; Rinne & Saastamoinen 2005) also have a considerable impact on second-home owner's consumption behaviour and expenditure patterns on various territorial scales: a village/locality, municipality/community, neighbourhood, immediate and further surroundings, leisure-time area/zone etc. The significance of such factors was confirmed by Ross (1994, p. 6), according to whom the demand demonstrated locally is 'a function of characteristics and attributes of the tourism destinations, their attractions, prices and the effectiveness of the market of the destination'. In the context of second-home owners' economic performance, the attributes of tourism destinations may be widely considered as factors determining service accessibility, which is dependent on the level (number and concentration, spatial distribution) of basic services and facilities (grocery stores, specialty shops, businesses, recreation facilities) and the location of a village (a second-home location) with regard to towns and cities or local growth/service centres (Wall 1997; Heffner & Czarnecki 2015) or the degree of diversification of the economy (Khan, Chou & Wong 1990; Alward, Workman, & Maki 1992). In reference to one of previous Polish studies on second homes, questions of (spatial- and time) accessibility and service infrastructure are reflected in destination-related synthetic measures such as municipality size (number of permanent residents and secondary residences), functional type and urban/rural status (Heffner & Czarnecki 2015). Destination-related factors have revealed positive relationships between the scale of local purchasing among second-home owners (proportion of actors involved), the amount of local spending and spending patterns in general in municipalities well-equipped with basic services, which usually means urban ones with a strong tourist function. In addition, in leisure areas with a high concentration of vacation homes, there was a relatively high demand for maintenance services provided locally. There was a greater demand for some specific products such as local agricultural produce (dairy products, vegetables and fruits) in highly or predominantly agricultural communities (from the functional viewpoint), thus underlining the importance of the accessibility of food producers (Heffner & Czarnecki 2011; Czarnecki 2014). At the same time, many researchers have stressed the low local purchasing in suburban municipalities due to the proximity of a large and diversified urban market nearby (Szkup 2003), and thus usually a short distance between primary and secondary residences (see more in section: *Relational and trip-related factors*).

The dominant economic function of a destination may be useful in clarifying the impact on local purchasing through product prices, since in traditional tourism localities there is a significant increase in prices of various goods (ranging from basic foodstuffs to luxury leisure/sports accessories), especially in the peak season and then a rapid fall outside the summer/winter period (Commons & Page 2001; Bizzari & Querini 2006; Vanhove 2012). Additionally, the quality and diversity of leisure activities available at a destination, resulting both from the market effectiveness and the environmental and functional characteristics of the destination, may induce different consumer behaviour and spending patterns. The well-recognised and marketed visitors' needs and motivations may be reflected by a wide range of activities supported locally, since the levels of expenditure are associated with certain tourist activities at the destination (Laesser & Crouch 2006; Pouta, Neuvonen & Sievänen 2006; Mehmetoglu 2007). Despite the fact that less commodified goods and services requiring higher financial, personal and logistical effort induce higher local expenditures than highly commodified ones (Laesser & Crouch 2006), the second-home phenomenon, given its specificity (relatively longer stays or frequent visits), may differ, as foodstuffs and basic commodities account for a large proportion of local purchases (Czarnecki & Heffner 2008; Pammer *et al.* 2008; Brida, Osti & Santifaller 2011).

Marketing expenditure and effectiveness are considered to be particularly important for consumer spending at a destination (Song *et al.* 2012), and this is reflected in the supportive actions jointly undertaken by local authorities, businesses, associations and other public bodies in brand, image and value creation (Palmer & Bejou 1995; Flagestad & Hope 2001; Wang & Pizam 2011). In the context of second-home owners' local purchasing, the effectiveness of the market may be crucial to learning, recognition, linking with and strengthening their demand for local goods and service providers, thus increasing their incomes and, in general, contributing to the local economic growth and development. Such effects can be achieved through various marketing activities, promotions or organising local events that allow people (consumers and suppliers) to trade directly.

Relational and trip-related factors

Besides the importance of destination-related characteristics, second-home owners' consumer behaviour and expenditure patterns (local purchasing) are influenced by trip-related factors or relational characteristics strictly relating to the distance between the primary/permanent and secondary residence (Wang & Davidson 2010). According to numerous studies on the economic impact of second homes, such a distance (whether measured as a physical distance or by time) is the most important factor shaping local purchasing by second-home owners (Bohlin 1982; Czarnecki 2014; Marjavaara 2008; Müller 2002b; Müller, Hall & Keen 2004; Nordin 1993, 2011), which is particularly evident in the course of analysing the purchases of goods. Distance may be considered as the most important and universal factor (across various socio-demographic categories, geographical locations, purchased products and countries/nations) determining local expenditures by second-home owners. Shorter distances influence local purchasing in a fairly negative way as most of second-home owners buy food and basic commodities in their permanent location and bring it all to their cottages. Longer distances, on the other hand, make second-home owners more keen to buy local products (Chhabra, Sills & Rea 2002; Nicolau & Más 2005; Pouta, Neuvonen & Sievänen 2006; Thrane 2002). This relationship is closely associated with the number of visits and the length of stay at a secondary residence since shorter distances are usually reflected in more frequent visits (more equally distributed over the year) but for relatively short periods (one-day, weekend, public holidays), while longer distances are connected with fewer visits (even one per year) but for a relatively long time (e.g. the entire summer season). Thus, first, the latter pattern creates the demand for infrequent goods and services, and second, if one bears in mind the limited physical possibilities to stock up with goods for a long stay in advance, basic commodities and foodstuffs brought from outside the municipality are insufficient and so will be sourced locally.

Since most second-home owners worldwide are urban residents, the influence of distance is even greater because it means significantly greater access to urban markets (often at more favourable prices, product quality and range) (Cyrek 2013). The relationship between one's urban status and local purchasing is not that clearly visible or even non-existent for some services, given that in certain conditions (in an easily accessible place, near home), products are usually easily acquired by second-home owners themselves, so they are selected and paid for directly by the purchaser/owner. For second-home-related services (construction, renovation, maintenance) that have to be done on site, if they are not purchased locally but in the owner's permanent place of residence, it always means that the company chosen has to commute to the place of work (the second home), which is usually reflected in higher costs, longer hours and maybe additional organisational complications. Hence, for most second-home owners, economically and organisationally, it makes more sense to use local service providers.

In addition, factors frequently used to examine tourists' expenditure patterns such as the length of stay (measured by the number of nights spent at a tourist location) or the number of visits can be of great importance to learning more about the grounds for purchasing decisions and the level of spending (Kozak

2001; Mottiar 2006; Anderson 2011). The length of stay in particular has positive implications for visitors' spending and consequently for the local economy (Agarwal & Yochum 1999; Thrane 2002; Downward & Lumsdon 2003; Nicolau & Más 2005; Pouta, Neuvonen & Sievänen 2006), but a negative impact on daily tourist expenditure (Taylor, Fletcher & Clabaugh 1993; Mehmetoglu 2007). This is obviously related to the constant need to meet basic needs such as foodstuffs and everyday articles and the growing need (along with the period of stay) to satisfy needs and expectations that come high up in the hierarchy (e.g. for infrequent goods and services). The number of visits to a secondary residence during the year has diverse implications and connotations, since numerous visits are possible when the distance between the permanent home and the holiday home is relatively short, but (as mentioned above) this means that local spending is rare and the levels are low.

Certain means of transport allow second-home owners to manage disadvantageous expenditure patterns, as they buy products at their permanent residence or on the way to a second home. This happens usually when they travel by car rather than train, long-distance coach or bike, which is an obvious result of the physical ability to transport commodities (Velvin *et al.* 2013). Here, it works similarly to how it works for a traditional tourist bringing food products from their permanent place of residence in order to avoid high tourist prices in the peak season (Kachniewska 2011).

Nevertheless, the specific, leisure-oriented, second-home purpose of travel, e.g. leisure or work, may also be important in assessing the impact on consumer behaviour and its local economic effect (Wang & Davidson 2010). The leisure purpose may induce the demand for various local goods and services (especially highly rated ones – infrequent services strictly related to leisure time) while work purposes may limit the owner's need to some basic commodities. Then, the multiple-dwelling phenomenon, with one person owning two and more residences, can be observed in most affluent societies (Steinicke, Čede & Cirasuolo 2011) and obviously has an influence on local spending, as the leisure time needs to be split into shorter periods between locations, thus having a more dispersed but individually lower impact on the local economy.

3.2 Second-home owners' spending patterns (PERFORMANCE)

In this section, the most fundamental theories and concepts are briefly presented, i.e. those relevant to the benefits of second-home owners' local spending. Also, the amount and structure of locally sourced commodity bundle are explained.

3.2.1 Engel's laws and curves

In general, economic growth, here exemplified at the micro-scale by the rise of household income, is a leading force shifting consumer behaviour and spending patterns (Deaton, Ruiz-Castillo & Thomas 1985; Ilmakunnas 2014). As is commonly argued, structural changes in the commodity bundle purchased by households are best explained by F. Engel's three laws and curves, one of the most robust empirical findings in economics (Foellmi & Zweimüller 2008). These laws are sometimes supplemented by Engel's extended first law, known as the Engel-Schwabe-Wright law, associated with service provision (Inglot-Brzęk 2010).

According to Engel's first law, the share of consumption expenditure on food declines with an increasing household income, although the absolute spending on food continues to grow. This is due to the expenses on food growing slower than the rise in income, and it means that the relative change in demand for food products is proportionally lower than the relative change in household income. The coefficient of income elasticity of demand, therefore, varies between 0 and 1 (inelastic demand) (see Fig. 3.2.1.1).

Figure 3.2.1.1 Engel's curves for food products, housing and luxury goods, %

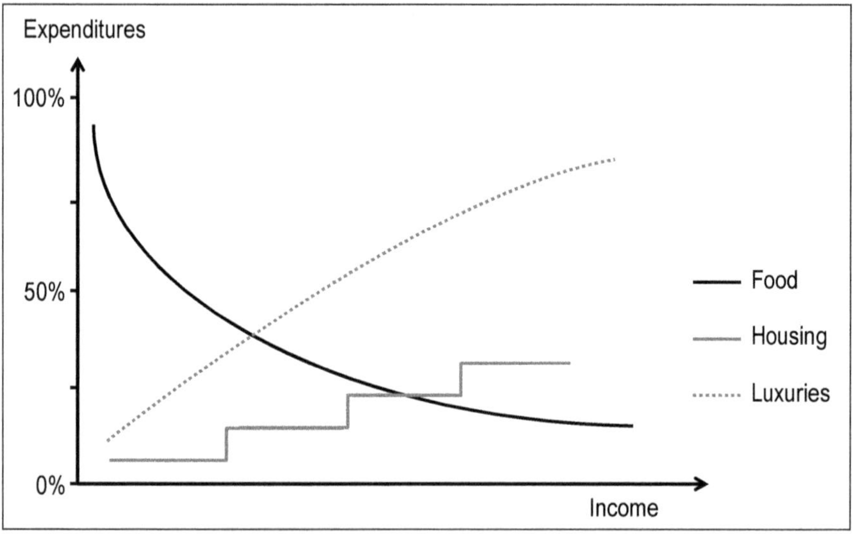

Source: Zalega, T. (2012). *Konsumpcja: Determinanty, teorie i modele*. Polskie Wydawnictwo Ekonomiczne: Warsaw.

Engel's second law refers to the relationship between household income and household expenditures on housing (rent and utilities, such as electricity, water and gas etc.) and according to his observations, as the household income rises, home maintenance costs increase dramatically. This means that relative changes in income and such expenditures are proportional and so the income elasticity of demand coefficient equals 1. This positive correlation can be supplemented by Schwabe's theorem that the lower the income, the larger the proportion incurred by rent (Philipson 1937 as cited in: Zalega 2012).

Engel's third law (and its extension by the Engel-Schwabe-Wright law) concerns luxury goods in the commodity bundle as influenced by a rise in household income. This shows that as household income rises, so does the proportion of expenditure on luxury goods. Thus, the relative change in demand for such commodities is higher than the relative change in income, so it is reflected in a value of the coefficient of income elasticity of demand higher than 1 (elastic demand). However, whether and in what ways luxury and normal goods are perceived by consumers may differ quite significantly (Christodoulides, Michaelidou & Li 2008). For developed countries (wealthy households), some luxury goods may be seen as a normal, while for some underdeveloped societies, even certain normal goods (home accessories) may be considered luxuries (Vickers & Renand 2003; Rudnicki 2010).

Engel's curves, as a graphic presentation of the relationships between household income and various types of commodities (described above), are often extended by the Törnquist demand function: it confirms that there is the core of household expenditure, and the remaining part is evenly distributed over other groups of commodities. This latter part comprises luxuries and relative luxuries (as opposed to necessities) and can be purchased when a household attains a certain income threshold (Deaton 1986). Törnquist demand function is very useful for identifying various types of goods as well as foe indicating the hierarchy of urgency and measuring the levels of saturation with subsequent goods.

In the context of second homes, no studies have focused strictly on their owners' commodity bundle to an extent that would enable researchers to examine how Engel's laws apply to them, even though it is expected that they could reveal slightly different relationships between household income and its expenditure than in typical cases, i.e. regular spending.

However, in this regard, first it is important to properly categorize household expenditures. First, since having a secondary residence (for leisure and self-esteem purposes) can be treated entirely as a higher-hierarchy need, it is classified as a luxury good (the home/property itself and/or the use of second homes including various expenses). On the other hand, utilising a second home with all the activities it involves results in second-home-related spending on various goods and services for basic home maintenance as well as luxury goods (food products, everyday articles, building materials and infrequent goods and services etc.). Thus, the expenditures related to a second home can be treated entirely as one category – a luxury commodity (regardless of their composition) – or can be broken down into various types of goods according to the categorisation of a typical (permanent) commodity bundle. In this study, both approaches are equally important, as they give us a broad possibility to precisely explain and understand consumption patterns and mechanisms as well as to verify traditional theories relevant to household consumption patterns in typical conditions of the permanent residence.

As consumption patterns have not so far been studied in the context of second homes, it seems that the conventional rules may not explain (or only partially explain) consumer performance in such circumstances. Here, second-home owners' spending patterns and consumer behaviour are only a fraction of their everyday life's regular consumption pattern. This means first that their partial character in spatial terms – relocation in geographical space and spending – occurred only on site (in the second-home location), even though this does not necessarily comprise all second-home related purchases (as some are made outside the location of a second home). Second, there is the partial character in time – consumption behaviour limited by a certain time activity (only during the stay at a second home), even though some second-home related purchases may be incurred outside of that (before or after the trip, in other markets). Third, this is seen in terms of needs reflected in the structure of commodity bundle, as consumers tend to satisfy a specific leisure-related demand under particular conditions, shifting towards leisure-oriented goods and services.

3.2.2 Income elasticity of demand

Disposable household income, as mentioned above in the discussion of the economic determinants of consumption patterns, is critical in shaping the size and structure of household expenditure (Riihelä, Vaittinen & Vanne 2011; Kasprzyk & Leszczyńska 2012). This influence, also mentioned previously, is in general explained by Marshall's law on the rise in consumer spending along with household income (Marshall 1920). In reality, however, their formation is largely modified by several other factors, including the type of a product (good/service) on which a household incurs expenses. Thus, a detailed relationship between the relative income change and the relative change in spending on various goods within the commodity bundle can be measured precisely by the income elasticity of demand index (Ferguson & Gould 1975).

In general, there is a low demand elasticity for basic commodities because income growth is reflected in a relatively lower rise in expenditures on such goods, and luxury goods are usually highly elastic commodities, since such expenditure rises dynamically and relatively faster than income growth. It is also worth noting that there is a time lag in changes in spending patterns, which stems from an income change as a result of (previous) consumption habits and lifestyles, such as for example excessive consumption as a 'lagging' effect of a previously unsatisfied demand (Woroniecka-Leciejewicz & Terwińska 2008). Consequently, decisions on home purchase can be delayed, but also choices behind new home-related commodities as well as the place of purchase (local/non-local) may shift over time.

In the context of second-home owners' spending patterns, the issues to be examined and explained are whether and to what extent the income elasticity of demand for various types of goods and services (expenditures related to second homes) is in line with the typical elasticity for regular household spending or traditional tourist spending. Also, there is a question of how the splitting of expenditure between two properties affects the owners' interest and demand in purchasing various products, and consequently, whether and to what extent it can be explained by traditional theories and laws.

With regard to a second home as a luxury good, there are many similarities to tourism products, which is more important given that there have so far been no studies of second-home owners' expenditures with regard to the income elasticity of demand. However, this topic has been examined in the field of tourism studies (Mak 2004; Dwyer & Forsyth 2010; Niezgoda *et al.* 2012), which is thus a reference point for considering second homes as an entirely luxury good. Income elasticity of demand has been examined by many researchers, who have considered day-trips, domestic travel and short-haul international travel as being perceived as normal by travellers, rather than as luxury goods (Downward & Lumsdon 2000; Leones, Colby & Crandall 1998; Lehto *et al.* 2004).

As some studies have found, in general, the demand for tourism products increases with a household income growth (Hsieh, Lang & O'Leary 1997; Stabler, Papatheodorou & Sinclair 2009), which confirms that the demand for tourism is income elastic and follows the rule for luxury goods. However, apart from the fact that tourism income elasticities differ over time (Morley 1998), there are some tourist segments such as business trips and VFR travel in which demand is relatively less income-elastic than for instance international travel (Croes & Vanegas Sr 2005; Muñoz 2007) or leisure tourism (Bull 1995; Holloway 2012). This may therefore mean that second-home tourism (apart from expenses related to the property purchase) is also less income-elastic, since this specific form of tourism does not generate the accommodation costs seen in typical tourist spending patterns, also because short (day) visits do not necessarily result in any serious expenses apart from food and transport. The latter is the most likely for second-home owners, as other studies have found that household income is insignificant for day trips, which results in a low elasticity of demand (Downward & Lumsdon 2000; Leones, Colby & Crandall 1998).

With regard to income elasticity for various goods and services that tourists purchase in Australian tourism destinations, some works have shown that entertainment (here considered as infrequent services) is the most income-elastic (with a coefficient of 1.4), followed by transport (1.15), and then income-elastic shopping (0.8) (here part of everyday articles, non-food) and food products (0.7) (Divisekera & Nguyen 2014). This means there is an increase in the allocation of visitors' spending on the first two commodities (seen by tourists as luxury goods) while it is less than proportionately stable for the latter two, as a result of a growth in household budgets (seen as basic commodities). It has been also suggested that for some commodities (everyday-use articles and entertainment) income elasticity varies spatially (regionally), while for transport and food it is more or less equal (Divisekera & Nguyen 2014). This was partially confirmed and partly contradicted by a subsequent study on income elasticity of foreign tourists in Northern Ireland, with the emphasis on the influence of their countries of origin on spending at the destination (Divisekera & Deegan 2010). Depending on the countries of origin, commodities such as shopping (everyday articles and infrequent goods) were treated as luxuries by British visitors and as basic commodities by mainland Europe and the rest of the world. On the other hand, commodities such as entertainment and sightseeing were seen as basic goods by the British and as luxuries by tourists from North America and the rest of the world (Divisekera & Deegan 2010).

As Honkanen & Mustonen (2007) have found, for the wealthiest consumers, the income elasticity for tourism products is lower than for slightly less wealthy people, which confirms that the demand for 'luxury' goods (tourism products) does not change proportionately with the rise of income but grows gradually for the highest groups of consumers. Furthermore, Wang & Lee (2011) have pointed out that for tourist expenditures on infrequent services (catering, eating out) income elasticity is greater than for basic food from shops and grocers, since the growth in household budgets allows people to spend more on catering.

Another important issue to be considered when assessing income elasticity of demand for leisure property is the type of income. As stressed by researchers, 'household income is thought of in two ways: current income, which is a highly transitory measurement of earnings in a single year, and permanent income, which is a long-term concept of what household income will be into the future' (Belsky, Di & McCue 2006, p. 4). The general view is that the former is likely to be the most appropriate, showing considerably higher elasticity indices compared to current income elasticities (Polinsky & Ellwood 1979; Goodman & Kawai 1982). It has also been observed that incidental income such as credits and loans is the crucial factor even more than other external financial support (more significant than income itself) in shaping holiday home purchases by Poles (Wyrębek 2010). However, as the focus of this study is on regular annual consumer spending, the elasticities were confirmed by using current annual income.

The impact of household asset values and changes in them (here, possession or purchase of a second home) can affect the size, but even more interestingly the structure of spending. For instance, when crediting the construction/purchase of a second home, it is not only wealthy households that are more likely to incur a large proportion of expenditures on repaying the loan, which may limit their regular consumption both at the permanent place of residence and at the second home (shorter stays and visits, import of products from outside etc.). A similar situation may occur in poorer households that have increased their household assets through the inheritance of a second home. And here, at least several scenarios and various (non)usage strategies are possible to follow: 1. a rationalised one, in which an increase in wealth, in the form of a secondary residence, entails higher maintenance costs. This, along with the desire to keep the house for various purposes (e.g. family, ambition etc.) may result in the shifting of some costs (for basic commodities and maintenance) from the permanent place of residence to the second home location through extended stays, or it may even reflect in specific housing adjustments towards a new smaller/cheaper permanent dwelling enabling the owners to maintain their second home; 2. cost-effective, in which the expenses are as low as possible, just enough to provide basic maintenance (paying local fees, taxes, utilities) that would be the lightest burden on the new owner's household budget (but at the same time meaning little or no actual use of the home) – this can last until there is a rise in income. Otherwise, scenarios 3 or 4 are possible; 3. minimalistic, when the maintenance costs are covered for example by renting out the holiday home; or 4. rejection, when the maintenance costs are so high that they cannot be covered in the long run, and thus, the second home is sold to cover basic needs.

On the other hand, in the case of wealthy households, an increase in household wealth (level of assets through e.g. buying a house) may result in the transfer of a large part of regular household expenditures to second-home-related ones, including those incurred locally, through extended stays, frequent visits, active leisure time activities locally, additional lifestyle changes/leisure, family visits, further equipping of a second home, etc. Thus, a shift in the purpose and size of expenditures is possible (growing flows on second-home-related purposes and decreasing flows for permanent-home-related expenses), as well as spatial shifts from expenditures incurred in the permanent place of residence to those at a second-home (local purchasing). But these expenditures do not necessarily have to overlap, as the shifts may be not proportional. In any case, it is possible that the rise in income in such households will act as a stimulus for further expenditures of a higher order.

3.2.3 Consumption theories

Although there are many microeconomic consumption theories and concepts that have a significant explanatory value for consumer behaviour (cardinal and ordinal utility, consumer surplus or revealed preferences), these would be of limited relevance to this study, as there are no empirical data on which to base their explanatory value. Instead, three other theories have been selected as a foundation to interpret second-home owners' consumer behaviour (described briefly below), although they will also not be verified empirically for the same reasons as those mentioned above. The major advantage of Lancaster's characteristics and Becker's theory is that, in the author's opinion, they are very useful tools to better understand a "specific" second-home owners' consumer behaviour, thus contributing to the analysis mainly descriptively rather than in a purely mathematical way.

The Lancaster Characteristics Model

Regardless of the critique over its very limited applicability to real life situations, the unjustified rejection of variations in consumer preferences and valuations of different characteristic combinations with different end-uses (Bowbrick 2014) or the exclusion of variety driven consumer behaviour (Wierenga 1984), the New Economic Theory of Consumer Behaviour (or of consumer demand), widely known as the Lancaster Characteristics Model (Lancaster 1966, 1971, 1975, 1979), is still considered an important development (Wierenga 1984) and one of the most influential theories regarding consumer behaviour in the field of economics and marketing (Backhouse & Middleton 2000; Bianchi 2006; de Vries 2008).

This theory stems from what at the time was a new assumption, that instead of the traditional consumption theories, seeing goods as direct objects of utility, the utility is derived from the properties of the goods (Lancaster 1966, p. 133). Furthermore, Lancaster referred to the substitution of goods, arguing that since each good has many different characteristics which can be shared by other goods/services, goods may be replaced by others with the same desirable characteristics. Another important suggestion was that a combination of two goods may possess characteristics different from the two of them consumed separately (Lancaster 1966).

What does this theory make distinctive and significant forsecond-home owner behaviour as a consumer? First, as stressed by researchers (Bae 1992), it derives from the substitution of goods that are seen as alternative sources of desired characteristics. This sort of substitution provides an opportunity for the consumer to make a free choice from among goods and services according to his/her preferences (and budget constraints). Under these conditions, a service may be chosen instead of a combination of goods, and thus 'a purchased service provides benefits to aid in time allocation' (Bae 1992, p. 20). Hence, it may at least partly explain the second-home owners' preference (or consumption pattern) for purchasing some local services, such as renovation, maintenance or catering services, instead of doing this work themselves (Rantanen & Hyyryläinen 2012; Marcouiller, Gartner & Chraca 2013; Oliveira, Roca & Roca 2015). Some seasonal residents are likely to treat these as a chore and time burden, especially related to special conditions (recreational purpose and limited length of stay).

Second, given that the combination of goods provides more different (valuable) characteristics than one good (here a service), it may be seen as a reason for some second-home owners doing this work themselves or with the help of neighbours and relatives, thus obtaining possible additional characteristics (e.g. learning, experience or social characteristics) to those originally gained, i.e. housing and aesthetic ones in the case of renovation services, for example.

Third, the benefits in time allocation resulting from the characteristics of goods are still an important distinction for consumer choice regarding a place of purchase. Assuming that one of the goods' characteristics is their availability (a large amount and a wide variety) and accessibility in space, time and cost, these will act as the main stimuli behind a second-home owner's preference to purchase products (rather than services) outside the second home location. This is usually done in the permanent residence (urban area) in a shopping mall or supermarket before the trip to a second home, i.e. where the time- (and often money-) saving considerations may apply. Thus, these goods will not be purchased in scattered and inaccessible locations with a poor range and low quality of products, unlike it often happens in rural areas (e.g. in Poland).

The fourth factor is strictly related to the previous one and supported by Lancaster's (1966) distinction between 'primitive' and 'sophisticated' consumption economies. For less developed or underdeveloped economies, there are fewer goods than characteristics, and for the more developed ones there are more goods than characteristics, so the consumer is guaranteed any combination of characteristics he/she desires, subject only to household budget constraints. This dichotomy can be translated, although in a highly generalised manner, into the division into the local/rural and urban market in terms of a product availability, which seems crucial in this relational spatial context (rural-urban) with regard to second-home owners' consumption patterns. Since possible combinations of characteristics are more likely to apply on a well-supplied market, which is usually urban, this is basically why some second-home owners tend to avoid buying locally. However, it is possible that the perceived utility of goods available in these two distinct locations is not just a result of variety but of brand and quality diversity and loyalty.

Fifth, as similar goods may have different distinctive characteristics, the origins of local or regional food products may affect purchasing preferences. Considering freshness, original recipes, traditional species and often organic characteristics as distinctive properties of local foodstuffs available mainly on the local markets, these appealing qualities are apparently decisive for many second-home owners' local consumption patterns.

Becker's theory (Theory of Time Allocation and New Home Economics)

The role of time and its allocation within the household activities and consumption is the focal point and common issue for Lancaster's Characteristics Model and Becker's Theory of Time Allocation (1965) as well as his New Home Economics (Michael & Becker 1973). As a result, both Becker's contributions are of great relevance to the consumption study of second-home owners, though one has to bear in mind that leisure as an opposition – albeit increasingly less sharp – to working time is the main constituent of and an intrinsic characteristic of the second-home phenomenon worldwide (Kowalczyk 1995; Paris 2010; Gallent 2014). Another advantage of Becker's (1965; Michael & Becker 1973) scientific input in this context was that he has developed a concept of a 'household production function', explaining households' consumption mechanisms with regard to their time resource and income. In addition, his recognition of households as 'decision centres' of labour supply, consumption and leisure instead of individuals (Becker 1965, 1981) was a valuable contribution to explaining the consumption and decision-making process.

With the Theory of Time Allocation, Becker (1965) attempted to build a theoretical basis of household consumption choice that regarded the costs of time on an equal footing with the costs of market goods, also taking non-working uses of time, which was then a novelty, into account (along with Long's (1958) & Mincer's work (1962)) and comparing this to traditional demand theories (Heckman 2014;

Chiappori & Lewbel 2015). As there are different types of goods with different prices, according to this approach, by analogy, there are different types of time use generating different costs, e.g. working days with hourly pay and/or weekends and holidays with shadow prices as non-marketable goods (Michael & Becker 1973). The above assumption was crucial for the entire 'household production function' concept, since each household attempts to maximise its utility, and its various needs can be satisfied through the 'commodities' (e.g. nutrition, good health, relaxation etc.) yielded by corresponding household production activity (e.g. eating, convalescing, visiting a second home, etc.) as a result of a combination of consumption goods (capital/income) and time allocation (labour) within the household (Michael 1975). Obviously, these resources are of limited availability: time only affords 24 hours per day and capital is a subject of household budget constraints (incomes and non-income earnings). In this framework, a household uses its time directly – by producing commodities – and indirectly, by selling its members the time to get to the marketplace and during purchasing goods and services on the market (Michael 1975, p. 237). Although it has 'only' an indirect impact on purchasing behaviour and spending patterns, that influence is pervasive and overwhelming, since it concerns all the possible commodities that a household desires and all the necessary market goods and services that its members decide to acquire.

From the perspective of second-home research, the crucial thing is that in general the 'household production function' works as a trade-off between time and money/income (Becker 1965), i.e. working and non-working time allocations that have a direct influence on the production of commodities such as – in this context the most important ones – leisure, relaxation, recreation, good health, well-being etc. and related production activities, here second-home ownership and use (both physical and temporal terms (length of stay)) along with the abundance of leisure activities. Thus, in a broad sense, time allocation in leisure activities and its trade-off with (paid) working time creates the foundations for spending time at a second home and not for other purposes. In a stricter sense, time allocation on various second-home-related commodities (and production) then requires the purchase of necessary goods and services locally and non-locally.

In spite of the general difficulties in categorising human activities as leisure activities (e.g. work on the house, minor renovations and maintenance), in Becker's concept, such a categorisation is both unnecessary and irrelevant (Chiappori & Lewbel 2015). This is because the provision of commodities always requires employing time and goods/services, although in different proportions (also in economic terms) and different combinations (e.g. meals prepared at home and takeaways or eating out). So for Becker, the only economically relevant features of any type of consumption or leisure activity are its associated foregone earnings and contributions to utility (Chiappori & Lewbel 2015, p. 3).

Becker's contribution to the New Home Economics is relevant here since it focuses on the mechanisms of consumer choices within the household. Such decisions are not made individually but collectively for the whole household. What is more, consumption choices are in fact decisions on time and income allocation within the household and are determined by bargaining among its members, with outcomes that may therefore depend on the determinants of the bargaining power of each household member (known as distribution factors) (Becker 1974 as cited in: Chiappori & Lewbel 2015, p. 2). The choices in question are more complex given that the cost of leisure time differs from the cost of working time, with the influence on the decision-making process and bargaining among household members reflected in goods and services market provision (Tribe 2015). Thus, the specific trade-off between time and capital allocation agreed by household members is reflected in the collective (within a household) consumer behaviour and consumption pattern (including the size and structure of expenditures and the place of purchase). If the household decides to procure a commodity called leisure, it procures spatial and economic footprints as their members shift a certain amount of time and expenditures from everyday consumption to leisure, relocating a part of consumption from the permanent home and at the same time procuring specific commodities that are strictly second-home related (leisure-related) and that can be obtained only by the interaction with the local economy.

3.2.4 Consumption tendencies

Informal economy/purchasing

The Research Institute of Market Economy has found that in 2015 the shadow economy (including illegal activities, hidden operations (mostly in terms of understating turnover in legal enterprises) and informal operations (mostly unregistered work)) made up 19.2% of Polish GDP (Łapiński, Peterlik & Wyżnikiewicz 2015). However, according to their estimates, only a quarter of the GDP generated by the shadow economy came from unregistered work. This phenomenon is much larger than in Finland (13% in 2013) or other Nordic countries (Denmark 13%, Norway 14%, Sweden 14% in 2013) (Schneider & Williams 2013), which are highly developed economically and have stricter tax systems. Since locals occasionally supply second-home owners with food products and simple work without registration, it is necessary to consider this issue in the study.

One of informal economy's inherent characteristics can be the heterogeneity of its forms and mechanisms (De Miras 1990; Losby *et al.* 2002; Bottazzi 2003), thus creating certain definition problems, especially in international comparisons (Ishengoma & Kappel 2006; Schneider & Williams 2013). Such heterogeneity is reflected in a wide range of concepts used to describe this socio-economic phenomenon internationally – the illegal, irregular, unofficial, undeclared, hidden, invisible, parallel, subterranean, black, shadow, marginal, second, curb or broadly considered non-observed economy (Losby *et al.* 2002; Gutiérrez-Romero 2010). In light of such a wide variety of concepts, informal economy is a more generic and comprehensive term (Bottazzi 2003), used most commonly in scientific literature. In general, informal economy contributes to the country's economy, but the activities are informal in terms of registration, tax payments, operating licences, conditions of employment or regulations (Becker 2004).

According to Bottazzi (2003), informal economy comprises three main elements: irregular economy (including unregistered economy and unrevealed economy), informal economy (including domestic work, mutual help, do-it-yourself, self-consumption), and criminal, strictly illegal economy (see Figure 3.2.4.1). The activities of unregistered, irregular economy are carried out by officially registered enterprises but at least partly circumventing fiscal regulations in order to hide some of the profits. Then, unrevealed irregular economy is entirely based on activities producing and/or selling the same goods and services as those provided by officially registered enterprises to the people (Bottazzi 2003). In the context of second-home owners' and local people's economic performance as well as their mutual relations, examples of unrevealed irregular economy along with informal economy are particularly relevant to this study as they can be identified and quantified on the basis of the available data.

In economic terms, informal economy is largely based on cash transactions (Feige 1979; Schoepfle, Perez-Lopez & Griego 1992; Losby *et al.* 2002), and thus its character makes it possible to precisely measure the flow and assess its significance for national economy. However, informal economy is also manifested through forms of barter (Losby *et al.* 2002), considered by G. Bottazzi as various combinations of mutual assistance within an already informal economy, e.g. product for product, product for service (or vice-versa) or service for service (Carlin *et al.* 2000). These relationships may be even more common between second-home owners and local people than within the local population as a whole. This is because in some cases they can be seen as a confrontation of two different worlds (urban versus rural) with different technical, financial and influence capabilities, varied needs and motivations, unequal access to some goods/services and differing knowledge and credentials.

Consequently, for a more efficient and accurate understanding of the relationships between second-home owners and the locals in informal economy, both cash and non-cash exchanges need to be taken into account (Levitan & Feldman 1991). This view is shared by Pahl (1984), a sociologist and anthropologist rather than an economist, and it is even more relevant for this study, since informal economy is considered more broadly as a household strategy (this refers to determinants, individual preferences and consumption performance of a household). Here, equally importantly, it is a source of community cohesion, directly related to social bonds and community development, and thus has more to itself than just an economic aspect (Losby *et al.* 2002).

Figure 3.2.4.1 Informal economy and second-home owners

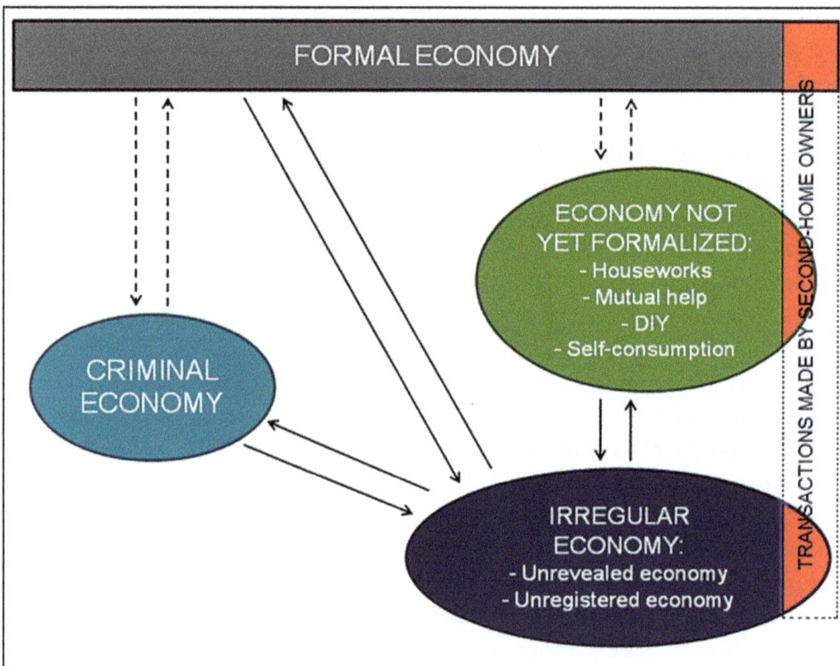

Source: Based on Botazzi, G. (2003). Sull'economia informale: Temi e problemi di ricerca. In: F. Lazzari & A. Merler (Eds.), *La sociologia delle solidarietá: Scritti di onore di Giuliano Giorio*, (pp. 353–366). Franco Angeli: Milano.

In fact, 'close ties to neighbours, friends and family members often play a role in the existence of informal work activities' (Losby *et al.* 2002, p. 15), and thus, they are preconditions for the establishment of such relationships. These in turn (if they bring satisfaction and have wider positive repercussions) may foster social capital, as is the case with local food systems integrating consumers (mostly tourists and visitors) into the local community (Dougherty, Brown & Green 2013). This more general (social) effect is indeed possible, given that informal economy is responsive to family or community needs rather than to purely economic benefits, which is reflected in the nature of personal ties between actors defined by essentially non-economic norms and institutions (Gaughan & Fermand 1987 as cited in: Losby *et al.* 2002). The importance of social needs in informal economy is confirmed by a Polish study which revealed that informal purchasing by second-home owners was highly influenced by their social ties with local people (only with locals rather than contacts with other groups) and by their having relatives living at the location of a second home (Heffner & Czarnecki 2015).

Moreover, informal transactions happen more often in the countryside (Schneider & Williams 2013), and thus, they may be even a consolidating force, at least to some extent determining the level of social integration and community viability, especially if they respond to some families/communities crisis situations (Losby, Kingslow & Else 2003). Thus, they are 'natural' reactions in the rural community in the form of barter or just mutual assistance of neighbours and friends. On the other hand, with regard to services and products provided by locals to others (seasonal residents, tourists, second-home owners, visitors, people passing through), cash transactions can be more evident and frequent. In this case, it may mean that economic value is a leading motivation unless these consumers are treated as a familiar part of the community (neighbour, friend, former resident etc.).

At the same time, economic value can be seen as a crucial factor in choosing the way of doing business (formal or informal), given that such a decision can be a rational evaluation of the relative costs and benefits of entering existing legal systems (De Soto 1989, p. 185). This is how it works in Poland in the case of basic service providers (acting under seasonality and low local demand), since calculations including economic burdens such as taxes, social and health insurance, permits and certificates (in some professions) may in turn be a justification to cease or to not initiate an activity within the formal system (Łapiński, Peterlik & Wyżnikiewicz 2015). Informal economy generally originates in unemployment and poverty (Marcelli, Pastor & Joassart 1999) and in some countries (in Poland in the 1990s), these socio-economic problems are more visible and difficult to tackle in rural areas (on the one hand because of their specific origins, e.g. high unemployment, generations of unemployed in post-state-farm communities, and on the other hand because of no or limited possibilities – lack of economic opportunities, low level of intellectual capital, low local demand for goods and services etc.) (Halamska 2001). Hence, informal economy has a dual spatial character – stronger in the countryside than in cities, resulting from disparities and inequalities including varied public support. Thus, it is not necessarily viewed negatively but rather with ambivalence and in some less developed communities it is treated as a common practice that everyone is aware of. As a result, it may operate as a lively background for efficient word-of-mouth marketing, spreading information about a 'good' builder, cleaner, etc. also among second-home owners.

Besides Bottazzi's distinction (2003) and various other classifications, the typology of informal economy based on the context of work proposed by the International Labour Organisation (ILO 2002) is very useful for this study. It distinguishes two categories: people working for someone else (doing primary or extra work which is paid but not taxed) and self-employed people who do sporadic/seasonal odd jobs, provide services and products (using bartering for services) besides their own official business (Losby *et al.* 2002; ILO 2002). For the former context, such situations may often appear in the relationships established by second-home owners, e.g. by engaging construction/renovation or maintenance/cleaning companies that employ a large number of workers who are not always officially registered and are thus untaxed and have no social security benefits (Łapiński, Peterlik & Wyżnikiewicz 2015). This may be a common practice in particular in tourism localities in the summer season with regard to leisure/tourist housing construction (Smuga *et al.* 2005). Furthermore, with reference to the previous studies, in some countries, especially in rural communities, such sporadic/seasonal work is done by retirees (Ogloblin & Brock 2006) or even the disabled (depending on the degree of disability and type of work) (ILO 2014). In Poland, such people provide second-home owners with agricultural produce (even if, due to the small area, they have never been farmers) and with basic services such as maintenance or security (Czarnecki 2014; Heffner & Czarnecki 2015). Although their main source of income is a retirement pension or disability benefit, their work is unregistered and untaxed, and hence is treated as a part of informal economy. Informal economy is quite widespread in the tourism sector (Smuga *et al.* 2005; Nowak, Herbuś & Szczerbowski 2012), although it usually covers accommodation/services (Din *et al.* 2016; Rădan-Gorska 2013) and thus does not apply in the context of second homes unless they are rented out to people by using the same rules.

However, besides illegal economy, there are some other exclusions from informal economy that do not have such negative connotations. Direct purchases of agricultural produce as well as raw and processed food products are particularly relevant for this study and thus should be explained. Here, a direct purchase means one conducted directly from individuals, including farmers; but since farmers are business owners – in fact the owners of an officially registered and taxed enterprise (farm) – the transactions are not considered as a part of informal economy. In most European countries (e.g. in Poland), tax regulations allow farmers to sell a certain amount (Dziennik Ustaw 1997, 1998, 2015) of their produce (milk, eggs, fruit, vegetables etc.) directly (including to individual consumers), regardless of whether they are purchased on the farm or from a market (still directly from the farmer). A farmer does not have to register this retail activity as long as it is below a certain sales volume. This exemption does not apply to agricultural produce suppliers who are not farmers (with an agricultural area of less than 1 hectare) or to retired farmers. Thus, if they sell their products, such transactions are part of informal economy. Another issue concerns processed agricultural products, which farmers were not allowed to sell directly to individuals until 2015. New regulations (Dziennik Ustaw 2015) have since 1 January 2016 allowed farmers to engage in such retail activities, but still to a limited extent and in accordance with food safety standards. In Finland, individuals are allowed to sell 5 kg of fish a day (without tax) under the so-called 'subsistence fishing' (*Kotitarvekalastus*).

Prosumption and natural consumption

Some gardening work or even small-scale farming is very common for second-home owners, often being treated not as a necessary evil and a task that has to be done but as a traditional and popular way of spending time at a holiday home (Jarlöv 1999; Müller 2002a; Hiltunen 2007; Pitkänen, Adamiak & Halseth 2014) – a pleasurable pastime that gives personal enjoyment and satisfaction to the hobbyist/owner and even improves his/her self-esteem.

Besides being a hobby, this, however, may be seen, at least to some extent, as a manifestation of one of the present-day trends in consumption – the so-called prosumption (or at least natural consumption). The term stems from 'professional'/'production' and 'consumption', and has been introduced in order to describe a situation in which goods and services are created by the same people who will ultimately use them (Tapscott & Williams 2006). Such a scenario was first suggested by McLuhan & Nevitt (1972, p. 4) but the term 'prosumption' was introduced by Toffler (1980) as a prediction of the future blurring and merging of the roles of the producer and the consumer (shifting a part of production onto the consumer under the DIY rule (Zalega 2012)). In economic terms, prosumption consists in value creation actions undertaken by a consumer to create a product (good or service) that he or she will ultimately use (Szymusiak 2015), so it means the creation of a product for personal consumption.

According to Toffler (1980), prosumption is an attribute of a 'third wave' society following the 'first wave' (agricultural/farming society) and 'second wave' (industrial society), although such a system was also typical of the first wave, when a farmer/manufacturer was also a consumer of their own production. This is basically the same as what is called 'natural' consumption, i.e. the consumption of goods produced by a consumer within his/her household (foodstuffs, repairs) for his/her own purposes. But the main difference between them is that the latter is not self-sufficient (as a farmer was in the first wave) but cooperates with a producer, enabling them to actively contribute to the market (Szul 2013). Thus, such a cooperation results in a prosumptive lifestyle in which consumers become producers – through designing or modifying products according to their needs and preferences (Toffler 1980).

In addition, Toffler (1980) makes a distinction between the consumer in the first wave, primarily expecting economic profits from prosumption (incomes, savings), and the third wave consumer, expecting social and ecologic benefits. Thus, referring to second-home owners as well as their activities and daily practices at a holiday home including spending patterns, it seems that they combine the first and third waves of prosumption. Since hobby farming, DIY, small renovations, repairs and maintenance are a common part of second-home owners' leisure-time activities (Müller 1999; Bevan & Rhodes 2005; Kankaanranta 2011, Pitkänen, Adamiak & Halseth 2014) and are created within the household, they should rather be considered as 'natural consumption', which has more in common with the 'first wave' prosumption, although the owners are definitely not self-sufficient and do such activities only for certain periods of the year (i.e. when they are staying at the second home). As in the 'first wave', the motivations for prosumptive actions are (probably) purely economic. On the other hand, even small-scale farming may be ecologically motivated (own, organic agricultural produce) and lifestyle-motivated (like most of second-home owners' activities) (satisfying more than basic needs) and thus not strictly economically oriented, so in ideological terms, it would exemplify the third-wave prosumption. This is more likely, as some researchers have pointed out that the blurring/'de-differentiating' of the categories of work and leisure, or entwining work and leisure activities (Tuorila 2006), which is increasingly frequent among second-home owners (Hiltunen 2004; Stewart & Stynes 2006), is a driving force for prosumption (Bywalec & Rudnicki 2002). Given such preconditions, in this context, a second home can be seen as an ideal arena for prosumption. Its specific lifestyle can be a manifestation of the activity of a prosumer, who tries to satisfy his/her basic as well as self-esteem needs and leisure, ecological (organic products – not using pesticides and synthetic fertilisers while retaining biodiversity, enhancing soil fertility etc.) and social motivations (renovating the home, renewing a road together with relatives and neighbours and then utilising it).

Local purchasing as a form of consumer ethnocentrism

Local purchasing is also a deliberate action or a consumer strategy (Williams 2002) and at the same time an increasingly common consumption trend observed mainly in developed countries (Hess 2009; Obach 2015). This type of consumer behaviour is emblematic especially among more aware, better-informed and active consumers, given that in the globalised and highly-complex economic environment the strategy requires excellent flows of information and explicit actions. For most researchers, local purchasing commonly relates to food products (agricultural produce, raw and processed food) as it has much in common with a 'local food' concept (Amilien 2005) or generally basic commodity acquisition (Balázs 2012; Schmit, Jablonsky & Mansury 2013). However, in fact, it covers the whole range of the commodity bundle, including all goods and services (Kurland, McCaffrey & Hill 2012).

As one may expect, researchers have seen such consumer strategies mainly as an intentional reaction to the ongoing globalisation of the market, with local products being displaced by more competitive outside sources (Wanninayake 2014). Consequently, such consumer actions may assumedly support and strengthen the local/national economy, but also reduce negative externalities of globalisation – protecting the natural environment by cutting transportation costs (Holmes *et al.* 2015) and preventing further layoffs as a result of decreasing market share and demand for local products (King & Ilacqua 2014; Holmes *et al.* 2015). In addition, for some other researchers, the need/willingness to save the local economy manifested through deliberate local spending may also occur during economic crises (Prazić, Devcić & Jergović 2014). Such a consumer behaviour may be enhanced by certain habits and daily practices, e.g. 'brand' or specific 'product' loyalty, thus naturally and automatically prompting consumers to choose from within a limited range, i.e. local products or from certain locations.

Regardless of the reasons behind it, such an attitude has a lot in common with ethnocentrism, better described in this context as consumption localism (Kurland, McCaffrey & Hill 2012). In general, it is defined as a basic attitude expressing the belief that one's own ethnic group or culture is superior to others, and that one's cultural standards can be applied universally (Hooghe 2008, p. 1). According to Sztompka (2002), it can be used to judge other groups, often leading to resentment and even hostility. In terms of consumer behaviour, ethnocentrism (also called consumer patriotism or economic patriotism) is a consumer attitude of preferring domestic, regional or local products, i.e. produced by local companies or using local resources (including a local workforce) or those under local brands, over products from the outside (Shimp 1984; Shimp & Sharma 1987). It results in overrating domestic products and in depreciating imported ones (Szromnik 1998), although the former is usually more emphasised than the latter (Watson & Wright 2000; Cheng & Zhen 2004). Given the foundations of ethnocentrism, it has been widely argued that this model of consumption has little in common with economic rationality or even functionality (of purchased products) as it is driven by other motivations, here a moral obligation or a duty related to national ideology (Figiel 2004).

What is important in consumer ethnocentrism in the context of local purchasing is its diverse range of territorial preferences, including those concerning local goods, services and brands. Thus, in its local dimension, it may explicitly support or strengthen the community's economy. Moreover, previous research has shown that the influence of local purchasing on a community's economy is relatively stronger and broader by inducing a local multiplier effect, since local companies are more keen to reinvest the money locally through inputs from local suppliers. Hence, the financial leakages are shifted in time and money remains in the local economic system for a longer time (Kurland, McCaffrey & Hill 2012). In addition, increased local purchasing leads to higher tax revenues for the municipal budget and consequently to greater funding for local public services and facilities.

Consumer ethnocentrism may increase second-home owners' local purchases both indirectly – through consumption preferences for specific (local) products, services or brands only available in certain locations – or directly – through preferences for the place of purchase or a distribution channel (e.g., directly from a farmer or in the marketplace rather than in a supermarket). Thus, it is not necessarily the product choice but the choice of the place of purchase that may be decisive for a second-home owner's potential contribution to the local economy.

Furthermore, the strength of consumer ethnocentrism may vary (moderate to aggressive) and be selective, i.e. concerning certain goods, services or brands, and thus influencing local purchasing differently in a situation in which there is limited availability and a poor range of local products, e.g. in suburban communities outside the peak season. A previous comparative Polish-Finnish study of elderly consumer preferences (over 55 years of age) has found that it was mainly Finns who took the place of origin of a food product into consideration when making consumer choices (Człapka-Matyasik, Fejfer & Homan-Helenius 2014). Moreover, Finnish and international research has shown that the ethnocentric attitude manifested itself among Finns mainly through their perception of the country of origin as a product quality relatively strongly compared to neighbouring and other countries (Auruskeviciene, Vianelli & Reardon 2012). In general, Finns are expected to be more ethnocentric in consumption terms than Poles, since ethnocentrism is popular in countries with strong and appreciated economies (Szulce 2013, p. 35), and this is without a doubt the case in Finland. At the same time, as another study has shown, the propensity of Polish individual consumers to buy domestic food products is not very high (40%) (Angowski & Lipowski 2014). In Poland, this preference is often reduced by availability, accessibility, price competitiveness and quality-related issues, thus being only partly reflected in evidence-based purchasing tendencies and generally remaining stable at a moderate level over recent decades (Falkowski, Rożnowski & Witkowski 1996; Szromnik & Wolanin-Jarosz 2013).

3.3 Second-home owners' local purchasing and its importance for the local economy (IMPACT)

3.3.1 Second homes and local economic development (LED)

As far as it concerns local economic impacts and/or the role of the second-home phenomenon for local economic development (LED), three fundamental and well-developed existing research lines can be distinguished: implications for the size and structure of local financial resources, i.e. 1. the rise and diversification of income for households and enterprises, including farms (Hoogendoorn, Mellet & Visser 2007; Velvin *et al.* 2013; Oliveira, Roca & Roca 2015), and for municipal budgets due to property tax revenues and local payments (Tewdwr-Jones, Gallent & Mace 2002; Bonilla & Mordt 2008; Heffner & Czarnecki 2015); 2. implications for the local labour market, i.e. the generation of new jobs (Mazón 2007; Guisan & Aguayo 2010; Scanlon, Sagor & Whitehead 2014); and 3. implications for the local infrastructure, i.e. through accessibility and quality improvements for entrepreneurs and residents (Müller 1999; Leppänen 2003; Matteucci, Lund-Durlacher & Beyer 2008), which indirectly determines local people's well-being and local economic development.

The widespread view among tourism and rural researchers dealing with this subject is that second homes provide a meaningful boost to rural economies (Newby 1988; Leppänen 2003; Tamer *et al.* 2006). The creation of new jobs for local people, mainly in retail, personal and housing-related services (Sikorska-

Wolak 2007), a rise in the incomes of local entrepreneurs, farmers and their families (Nielsen *et al.* 2009), a contribution to local municipal budgets through the tax payments (Rebollo & Baidal 2003; Torres & Domínguez-Menchero 2006) as well as a gradual improvement of the local infrastructure (Nordin 1993, 2011; Müller 1999; Tamer *et al.* 2006) are the most frequently mentioned positive aspects of this impact. This consideration is based on the significant though varied influence of second homes on local economic development during the consecutive stages of the second-home ownership cycle. Economic relations between second-home owners and the rural population (including local officials) are established as early as the initial phase – when the property, land and/or dwelling is purchased, leased or newly built. The new owners pay to buy or lease the property, and thus, the first links (flows of goods and financial resources) between the main stakeholders involved are initiated. Relations develop further at later stages, when the home has been built or converted into a second home, renovated, furnished and then when the owners contribute the necessary local payments, for example taxes, to the rural councils' budgets and when they use services provided by the local community, such as retailing, transport, recreation, gastronomy, health and security services (Hoogendoorn, Mellet & Visser 2005). Additionally, research conducted in the US has shown that second homes, particularly at the initial phase of their life cycles, generate substantial private expenditures, which are usually made locally and as a result support local businesses (mainly construction, equipment and furnishing services). At the next stage, the type and size of expenditures change, since the money is mostly spent on retail, gastronomy and other everyday services (Powers & Cooper 1976).

The marked predominance of individual leisure pursuits and a relatively high percentage of second homes in the community may have a favourable impact on the amount of capital resources of the local municipal and household budgets (through higher incomes). In addition, since the economic links between second-home owners and local people are usually long-term (except for purchasing the land or the house), they may be significantly valuable or even critical with regard to the financial stability of local and household budgets. Hence, this kind of high-quality resource is particularly welcome in light of future perspectives and opportunities of rural development as well as contemporary challenges resulting from macro-scale processes and structural changes, i.e. globalisation, technological change, a decline in agriculture and other primary industries, unemployment, 'selective' depopulation and ageing, etc.

The idea of the positive influence of second-home tourism on the creation of new employment in construction and services has been raised by researchers as often as it has been called into question. The opponents, who regard its importance for local labour market as overrated, usually point out a relatively low number of new occupations, their seasonal and part-time character, employment insecurity and low wages in comparison to jobs generated by other industries (Blank 1989; Gallent, Mace & Tewdwr-Jones 2002; Luloff *et al.* 1994; Marcouiller 1997; Wallace *et al.* 2005). For this reason, part-time workers such as co-owners or family members involved in running the business should be included in possible detailed estimates of the economic impact of second homes. Research in Sweden and Germany has found that, because of their specific nature, second homes stimulate the development of only certain forms of economic activity – not industries driven by the traditional tourist sectors, such as accommodation, transport, gastronomy, recreation services and the likes. Businesses that benefit most from second-home tourism are those supplying fittings and fixtures, building materials, foodstuffs and various everyday articles. However, second-home owners are more likely to spend less on renovations and modernisations than permanent residents or people intending to retire to their holiday properties (Coleman 1982; Wallace *et al.* 2005). According to Müller (2002b), second-home owners in Sweden and Germany spend as much on shopping as the locals, thus contributing not so much to the creation of new jobs as maintaining the existing ones.

Furthermore, there are different opinions as to the nature and strength of economic relations between second-home owners/users and local enterprises (mainly grocers) in the case of suburban and peri-urban locations. On the basis of the research carried out in the 1990s in the area around Cracow, sales of foodstuffs and products at local shops can be considered to be one of the main additional opportunities for local people to raise their incomes, with 84% of second-home owners saying they buy food locally (Gaś 1996/7). On the other hand, a study in Poland at the beginning of the 2000s revealed a low level of such links in the vicinity of another large city, Łódź, where a relatively high percentage of respondents buy everyday articles in the city, their permanent residence, before going to their second homes (Szkup 2003). A possible reason is that many second homes are far from the village centre, where most retail outlets are concentrated or, which seems to be more common and important, that products available in urban markets are usually cheaper, better quality and more varied. Another reason why people buy everyday articles before the trip to their second homes may be that prices in local shops rise sharply in the holiday season, especially in areas attractive for tourism (Norris & Winston 2009). Given these practices and tendencies, in this case, the impact of second homes as a driver of employment and growth for local businesses (or local economy in general) is significantly weaker, since newcomers/seasonal residents spend too little to enable the local economy to develop to provide them with goods and services needed (or become a business environment for the tourism of second homes). Furthermore, these kinds of second-home owners' expenditure patterns surely affect the level of local economic integration, and consequently, the "rural community considered as a social organism becomes a place where various external needs are met, although it is not involved with the process (flows of goods, services and capital). What is more, there is no stable transfer of financial resources from urban/external to rural areas, hence rural community as an economic organism at least [does] not benefit, but rather incurs obvious and measurable losses" (Bukraba-Rylska 1991, p. 78).

Research into the impact of second homes on the financial resources of permanent residents in rural communities also has to take into account the ownership status of such properties and the length of stay during the year, since second homes are not only used by their owners and their families but are also rented out. This obviously does not generate direct income for the local population but for the second-home owners from outside the rural community, who in this case should be treated as outside investors (Mika 1997).

The improvement of the infrastructure is mentioned as one of the most beneficial influences of second homes on the local community (Tamer *et al.* 2006; Heffner & Czarnecki 2011). An increase in the number and concentration of second homes translates directly into seasonal residents' increased demand for basic facilities, which at the same time contributes to improved access to them for the local population. In communities with a significant concentration of second homes, their owners, although as non-permanent residents they usually have no voting rights in local elections (except in Canada, for instance) but pay taxes and other local duties, often constitute a force powerful enough in the process of local development. Hence, they are able, at least to some extent, to influence some strategic decisions to be made by local authorities, e.g. concerning local investment priorities in the infrastructure or promoting local authorities' activity and creativity in applying for external funding or focusing on certain policy areas (crucial for second-home owners) (Heffner & Czarnecki 2011).

However, expanding utility networks (electricity, water, sewage, gas, roads and central-heating systems) as well as basic services (including transport, healthcare and security) poses serious risks to the sustainability of local budgets, because of the greater concentration of second homes and higher expenditure by local self-governments, not only on building but in particular on maintaining public services and networks, with demand for these rising sharply during holidays and weekends. This problem has frequently been raised in the literature (McKenzie, Martin & Paris 2008; Romita 2010). International researchers' opinions suggest that second-home owners generate high public costs associated with providing access to public services and basic facilities, but they do not consume the two types of traditional tourist products which are of key importance – accommodation and gastronomy services. It is these services that are taxed and contribute considerably to the local budget (Torres & Domínguez-Menchero 2006), and hence some local businesses based on selling to visitors do not benefit as much from second-home tourism as they do from traditional tourism. Obviously, in most countries, second-home owners are compelled to pay property tax and possibly other local fees to the local council budget. However, this cannot be a suitably efficient instrument to refund municipal expenditures on infrastructure, facilities and public services either due to too low tax levels, ineffective tax collection system or residence registration failure, in the case when the second home and consequently municipal infrastructure are used year-round/permanently while the taxes, except the property tax, are paid to the formally permanent place of living (that happens in many suburban municipalities in Poland).

Public costs are particularly high in remote rural areas, where there is no local town planning and the relevant regulations are not respected either by investors (second home owners) or the representatives of local authorities or other relevant bodies. Thus, new, abandoned second homes appear in areas far from the densely built-up areas outside the existing settlement of permanent residences or even outside clusters of second homes settlements. Investments usually turn out to be economically and environmentally unjustified, not only because they are carried out to meet the needs of people who do not stay in the area for more than a few weeks a year (Norris & Winston 2007). For deserted and more scattered residences, the owners express the need to provide them at least with some basic infrastructure, and this usually requires more financial resources to build and maintain kilometres of networks than in denser localities (Crowley 2006; Stephenson *et al.* 2001).

An important problem associated with this issue is the need to balance the local budget, also ensuring a steady income outside the holiday season, when revenues drop while the local infrastructure still has to be maintained. It has therefore been proposed that second-home owners should be taxed (Preissing *et al.* 1996; Frost & Lawrence 2006) or should refund the infrastructure costs of local municipal budgets (FitzGerald 2005).

3.3.2 Second homes and multifunctional rural development (functional diversification)

As mentioned in the rationale section, many rural areas in both countries have faced negative tendencies and a number of serious social and economic problems. Some of these have been market-driven (in the short run) while most are structural (in the long term), resulting from macro-scale processes, of which the most crucial for the countryside was a decline in the primary sector – agriculture in Poland (Musiał 2007; Wojewodzic 2014) and agriculture and forestry in Finland (Nivalainen 2003; Hetemäki & Hänninen 2009; Lehtonen, Tykkyläinen & Voutilainen 2012). As a mostly monocultural rural economy is not resilient but more vulnerable to external forces and changes (Bogdanov & Vasiljević 2011; Siciliano 2012) that threaten social and economic cohesion (Raczyk & Majkowska 2015), such macro-level tendencies have produced many negative effects. These effects are reflected in the rise in (hidden) unemployment, poverty, declining living standards, economic emigration and depopulation and thus distortion of demographic structures (ageing and brain drain) (Naukkarinen, Rusanen & Colpaert 1993; Vihinen, Tapio-Biström & Voutilainen 2005; Stanny 2012; Hörnström, Perjo & Johnsen 2015).

In this context, it needs to be stressed that, generally, diversified economic structures are more resistant and less vulnerable to external economic shocks (crisis, mega events) and political transitions periods (as in Poland in the 1990s) and thus better able to recover afterwards. At the same time, as Imbs & Wacziarg (2003) have argued, less specialisation and greater diversification of economies reflects in their wealth. However, in terms of economic growth, more diversified economies are less effective and efficient than specialised economies in 'boom' periods (Gill *et al.* 2014). Thus, for sustainable economic development (not growth), it is more desirable to diversify the structures of rural/local economies but at the same time to make their composition more locally interdependent rather than dependent on external agents. Here, enhancing and strengthening local links (integration) is more reliable and beneficial in the long term than relying on external bonds (global contacts), which are more profitable in the short run and thus, more economically efficient in contributing to economic growth.

The diversification of rural economy is the core element of the concept of rural multifunctional development (sometimes called rural multifunctionality) (Skawińska 1994; Czarnecki 2009). This concept has its origins in Britain in the 1980s (Kłodziński 1996; Allanson & Whitby 1996) and relates to rural economic diversification developed by policy-makers to tackle the negative trends observed in the countryside at that time, such as recession and unemployment broadly considered as the 'rural crisis' of late 1980s and early 1990s (EC 1988; Cloke 1989; Cox, Lowe & Winter 1989). It was further developed by Polish rural researchers seeking an alternative development concept for rural areas in the initial period of socio-economic transition in the country in the early 1990s, seeking a remedy for the dramatic socio-economic decline (Heffner 2000, 2011a; Wilkin 2008).

The multifunctional development of rural areas can be considered in the most general terms as a strategy to diversify the local economy by initiating and developing non-agricultural economic activities (Kłodziński 1992, 1997). To be more precise, multifunctional rural development cannot be understood in a very narrow way as a job-creation process, since it is a wide-ranging term drawing upon local community development, entrepreneurship, strategic planning, infrastructure improvement and diversification of farming activity (Kłodziński 1997, p. 41), thus including determinants and necessary preconditions and on the other hand economy- and society-wide effects (e.g. modernisation of agricultural sector and community well-being). It should be underlined that in the process of diversification (inclusion of any new activities) of a rural economy, primary functions (agriculture and forestry) must still remain as stable constituents and not be excluded from the rural economy, as this would lead to economic urbanisation rather than rural multifunctionality.

In addition to its rationale and justifications, the main long-term purpose of making economic monoculture more differentiated is the improvement in rural people's working and living conditions, or in a broader sense the creation of new socio-economic structures with the predominance of service-sector employment, or in other words restoring the vitality and viability of rural areas. As a result of economic diversification, the attractiveness of rural areas, either for permanent inhabitants (preventing further depopulation) and for new, potential second home owners (in order to attract them as new, at least temporary, inhabitants), increases, thus preserving the areas' viability (Kłodziński 1999; Adamowicz & Zwolińska-Ligaj 2009).

Given the above, the question arises of how second-home tourism can contribute to the rural/local economic diversification and thus indirectly help to alleviate ongoing negative processes in the countryside and strengthen local communities. As many studies have shown, through their considerable demand for a variety of local goods and services (subject to budget constraints, market competition, seasonality and disadvantageous consumption patterns), second-home owners may create favourable market conditions for local businesses (including farms and households) to sell local products and thus become (formal and informal) suppliers to second-home owners/users (Adamiak 2012; Rehunen *et al.* 2012).

Second-home owners/users do not consume an important part of local services, i.e. accommodation services, but instead they need building and maintenance services that are unusual for traditional visitors. Thus, depending on the size of demand (the number and concentration of second homes in the community, and their owners' consumption behaviour), they may generate an opportunity for new economic activity and in a broader sense contribute to the diversification of the local economy. In this context, the level of demand is crucial, as it ensures the economic rationality of running a business, its economic performance and possible profits. As the demand for local products and services is highly dependent on many interrelated factors, this may mean that the demand may induce only seasonal or one-time activities, or only for some specific activities/industries.

Another problematic issue is rural multifunctionality, as this is often neglected by researchers in the field. Is this the multifunctionality of rural people (i.e. pluriactivity of individuals)? Is it the multifunctionality of a household (i.e. the occupational pattern of its members regardless of the location of their jobs)? Is it the multifunctionality of a village (a structure of jobs/workplaces within a settlement regardless of workers' permanent place of residence)? Is the multifunctionality a function of the rural/local labour market structure (Jurek 1996)? In light of previous research that has stressed the strong linkages between functional diversification and restoring the viability of rural areas, entrepreneurship and sustainable utilisation of local (labour) resources, it proves to be the last of these. In other words, it means that the actual rural multifunctional development can be recognised only by using the economic and non-economic resources of the local workforce. In detail, it implies the engagement of local labour in initiating and developing new economic activities (entrepreneurship) on site, i.e. strictly in their location (village/municipality). Otherwise, it is just a manifestation of subsequent phases of urbanisation (in its economic aspect) or socio-economic changes that do not contribute to the local economy. Thus, in more technical terms, it means that outside enterprises that supply second-home owners do not contribute to the concept of multifunctionality, as the owner is not based in the locality (and possibly transfers profits out of the community). The same situation concerns local business owners who hire outside labour or who serve second home owners informally (without registration and official contracts).

3.3.3 Second homes and multifunctional agriculture

The multifunctional agriculture concept has been widely employed in social and political debate on contemporary rural change and the future of farming activity since the late 1980s (Marsden & Sonnino 2008; Jean-Vasile 2013). It sees technical advance in the industrialisation of agriculture and in the growing environmental concerns about its side effects (Roep & Oostindie 2005; Andersson & Lehtola 2009). As defined by OECD (2000), the 'multifunctional agriculture' concept stresses that agriculture produces multiple commodity and non-commodity outputs, taking into account the fact that some of the non-commodity outputs may exhibit the characteristics of externalities or public goods, where markets for these goods function poorly or are non-existent. Thus, apart from its traditional productive functions (food and fibre production), agriculture as an activity with a non-productive function supplies society with important non-commodity outputs. These can be classified in various ways, the most popular of which was proposed by Dutch researchers van der Ploeg & Roep (2003). They categorised agricultural services and functions as: white (ensuring food security and food safety), green (managing land resources, creating habitats for wildlife fauna and flora, protecting animal welfare and sustaining biodiversity), blue (water resources management, water quality improvement, flood prevention, production of water and wind energy) and yellow (sustaining and enriching the cultural traditions and identities of villages and regions, developing farm-based tourism and hunting) (van der Ploeg & Roep 2003).

What is important and underlined in the definition of multifunctional agriculture is that both functions are usually interconnected. This means that it is not possible to provide society with non-commodity outputs without producing commodity outputs or in other words without conducting regular farming activity (Van Huylenbroeck 2003; Le Cotty & Voituriez 2003). Thus, agriculture must exist and be engaged in production in order to enable society to make use of its many beneficial non-productive functions (Wilkin 2010, p. 30).

In light of the above, it can be said that agriculture has always been multifunctional (Swagemakers 2003; Mettepenningen *et al.* 2011) despite the subsequent stages of its development. However, one has to be aware that many non-commodity outputs are side-effects (or externalities) of the production function, which means that their costs and benefits are not reflected in the market price of agricultural goods and services, thus constituting a source of market failure (Hediger & Lehmann 2003). Such externalities have various characteristics: positive or negative, intended or unintended, complementary or conflicting, valued in existing markets or not (marketable and non-marketable goods and services) (OECD 2001). Although they are intuitively associated with the natural environment, in fact they also comprise non-commodity outputs that are also valuable for socio-cultural and economic aspects of rural life (Ollikainen & Lankoski 2005; Miškolci 2008). For instance, while intensive commercial farming accelerated by technological and agronomic progress may result in growing air, water and soil pollution and a labour surplus, at the same time small-scale family (subsistence) farming may help to maintain biodiversity, prevent environmental deterioration, ensure jobs for rural people and enhance cultural identity, rural folk traditions and patrimony (Wilkin 2010).

Many non-commodity outputs generated by agriculture have the characteristics of a public good. Consequently, with reference to the theory of public choice, their provision to society is decided by the relevant institutions and political actors in reaction to so-called market failure (Wilkin 2010), which means that they are supplied without any monetary compensation (OECD 2008, 2011b). Since the market cannot supply society with sufficient public goods (positive effects) nor cope satisfactorily with the negative side-effects (EC 1997), this under- or over-provision resulting from market failure is addressed by state policies and regulations (state aid). In the EU Common Agricultural Policy, such goals can be met for instance by agri-environmental schemes or through the Less-Favoured Area Support Scheme (LFASS) or other instruments that support biodiversity, water conditions, energy security, food safety, local identity or rural cultural heritage.

Furthermore, it has been argued that multifunctional agriculture and broadly considered rural multifunctionality may assume different forms depending upon the development paradigm, economic system and physical scale on which it is regarded (Wilson 2007). As Marsden & Sonnino have argued (2008), in the agro-industrial paradigm, multifunctionality is considered very narrowly as limited to the pluriactivity of farm household members, who combine agricultural and non-agricultural incomes in order to survive in difficult market conditions. Thus, here multifunctionality is restricted not only in its concept but also in its spatial aspect, using a farm-based approach to the micro-scale – a farm/household unit. In the post-productive consumption paradigm, the focus shifts from a farm- to a land-based approach, in which the growing and varied interest in consuming the countryside, rural space or just farmland is observed from the perspective of industrial capital but also of urban and ex-urban residents. Hence, farmland becomes an object of consumption accelerated by different consumer needs and motivations, and thus its various functions (productive and non-productive) are emphasised by the farmland diversification approach instead of the very limited farm-based approach. And finally, in the sustainable development paradigm, multifunctional agriculture 'acquires its most comprehensive meaning and displays its highest integrative development potential' (Marsden & Sonnino 2008, p. 423). As this paradigm integrates farms and agricultural land, it shifts towards a more complex although still local approach emphasising interrelationships and interdependencies between its constituents. By refocusing on the productive function of agriculture (which induces various non-commodity outputs) it underlines its role in building up sustainable communities through ensuring jobs, maintaining local identity, cultural heritage and providing ecosystem services, thus demonstrating its significance not only for rural communities (adding to rural household incomes) but also for society as a whole.

Following most rural sociologists and human geographers, taking second-home owners' origins, dwelling strategies, everyday life practices, expenditure, land-use and free-time spending patterns into account, the second-home phenomenon is a manifestation of counter-urbanisation trends and an exemplification of the 'post-productive' and 'consumption countryside' (Buller & Hoggart 1994; Hoogendoorn 2010; Halfacree 2012). In this context, in which the countryside is treated mostly as a space of consumption by second-home owners, agriculture is losing its importance as an economic function in favour of natural amenities and the (rural, not necessarily agricultural) landscape, here considered as a consumption good (Marsden & Sonnino 2008). Therefore, this paradigm is basically a perspective of second-home owners (mostly urban residents following the urban consumption model) as well as of their motivations and consumption preferences. Thus, here, the countryside is an object of consumption satisfying the needs of seasonal residents (Burchardt 2002; Burton & Wilson 2006; Horáková 2010).

Although commodity outputs are still important for second-home owners' daily practices, they may not necessarily be provided by local farmers and local food-product suppliers but by their outside counterparts. Consequently, the local demand expressed by second-home owners is focused on land, space and the natural environment (non-commodity outputs). However, the interest of second home owners in utilising local resources can in turn be dangerous, given the often intense, excessive and unsustainable consumption of local resources on the one hand and the weakening possibilities for provision with non-commodity outputs resulting from the displacement of agricultural activity by leisure and tourism functions on the other (especially in areas with a high concentration of secondary residences and tourism). Hence, in this context, under undue and unbalanced consumption(ism), agricultural multifunctionality has a very limited potential to develop, owing to the focus of second-home owners' demand for land, which first deprives farming of its critical resources and then does not include other non-productive functions, e.g. social or cultural.

It is far more beneficial for both sides if an attempt is made to combine and anchor multifunctional agriculture and second homes into the sustainable development paradigm in order to keep the countryside vital, liveable and prosperous (with continuing farming activity), although mutual benefits are possible here. This means, on the one hand, a more diversified demand from second-home owners both for commodity and non-commodity outputs provided by agriculture, and at the same time less excessive and more sustained in terms of demanded volume and (negative) influences of daily practices, consumer behaviour and the ways of spending free time on the supply side (production activity). On the other hand, it is a matter of a fact that agriculture may contribute widely to rural people's living conditions in economic terms but also most probably to that of seasonal residents, which results in rising residential property values in the surrounding area (Garrod & Willis 1992; Irwin 2002) or in rising prices for rural accommodation (Vanslembrouck, Van Huylenbroeck & Van Meensel 2005). Existing agriculture provides a range of basic commodities (food products) but also non-commodity outputs such as ecosystem services, preventing soil erosion, water retention and quality, maintaining specific and appealing landscapes that are appreciated by many etc., which may significantly affect living conditions, second-home owners' activities and the general utility level (satisfaction) of being a second-home owner and spending time at a particular location. It is therefore all the more important that previous research has shown that declining agriculture has a range of negative impacts on rural landscape and ecological systems (MacDonald *et al.* 2000), thus leading to worsening living conditions at a second home and a decrease in the satisfaction in using the residence.

It seems that in light of current changes in spatial patterns of second homes in Europe there are some specific locations (less attractive than tourism or leisure destinations), such as formerly agricultural regions or rural heartland areas or deep rural zones, with a moderate number of secondary residences in which a potential symbiosis between the two is possible, as the rural multifunctionality provides the highest integrative potential. A number of positive interrelationships may be established in such areas, such as a natural tendency to link small-scale farming activity and moderate but highly diversified demand for local resources, commodity and non-commodity goods and services. This is more likely to happen when second-home owners have rural roots, share the local/rural identity and develop small-scale farming themselves, thus contributing to the maintenance of the agricultural activity or at least keeping the farmland in good agricultural and environmental condition. Thus, second-home owners have become increasingly influential actors in the countryside, who may considerably contribute to the fulfilment of the rural and agricultural multifunctionality concept (Gómez-Limón, Vera-Toscano & Rico-González 2012).

3.3.4 Second homes, local food production systems and short supply chains

As many researchers have argued, in contrast to large-scale commercial farming, local and alternative food production systems are often embedded in tourism and leisure (Vittersø & Amilien 2011; Sidali, Kastenholz & Bianchi 2013; Høst 2014). They have become increasingly important for tourists and seasonal residents (second-home owners) for two major reasons: the economic, aesthetic and utility benefits of the proximity of local food producers to consumers (Hall & Gössling 2013; Tanasă 2014), and the specific, unique, geographically limited and usually traditional food products on offer (Torres 2002; Kim, Eves & Scarles 2009; Sims 2009). These two main issues, which are considered in rural/food studies basically as a short-supply chains/re-localisation and the origins of food, are worth exploring in more detail in the context of second homes.

Local food production systems are situated within the broadly seen alternative agri-food networks (AFNs or AAFNs), which in their various forms include farmers' markets, farm shops, food cooperatives, organic agriculture and foods with a geographical indication of origin (Renting, Marsden & Banks 2003; Forssell & Lankoski 2014). All activities within AFNs are commonly perceived as a response to the growing environmental and social concerns resulting from large-scale farming (the agri-industrial model) and conventional food distribution (Scrinis 2007; Friedland 2008; Maye & Kirwan 2010). As other researchers have pointed out, local systems are at the same time an alternative to the ongoing globalisation and Europeanisation processes that increasingly produce uniform and standardised food products, blurring intercultural differences and thus providing more homogenous and/or hybrid consumption (Jokinen, Järvelä & Puupponen 2009; Zalega 2012).

In general, the concept of local food can be considered from two perspectives – first, attributive, which refers to the origin of food and its unique and distinctive characteristics linked to a specific location and consequently to tradition and cultural identity (Sireni 2006); and second, relational, which is more a process than a feature and is aimed at re-arranging the distribution of food products by shortening the distance between the producer and the consumer, which is beneficial for both sides (Barrantes 2004). The former is more anchored in a specific place and based on socio-cultural values while the latter is more about the changing position in the food-supply network by re-establishing distribution connections and exchange relations (Bowen & Mutersbaugh 2014). As one may expect, these approaches are not equivalent. Food products (in the former case) may be supplied through traditional distribution channels, not necessarily reducing the distance between the producer and the consumer, and thus not contributing so much to the local economy (where it was produced) but conventionally to intermediaries such as wholesale, retail and transport companies, creating a certain economic loss (inefficiency) for consumers. From the latter perspective, it is more likely that such local food networks will be beneficial for both sides. For producers, they may reduce distribution and transport costs, and thus, increase their profit margins (and re-invest to the quality improvement). In a wider context, they may benefit the local economy, as a result of taxation and contribution to the local labour market, and finally also the consumer, who gets a local product at favourable prices (since there are no extra costs for intermediaries). Moreover, this is an opportunity for various rural producers and not only those who provide unique (certified) local or regional products.

What then is the role of second-home owners in contributing to the local food production systems? First, with regard to re-connections between food producers and consumers and the creation of shorter supply chains, it is always easier for farmers from areas around large cities and urban regions to reduce the supply chain and sell agricultural produce directly to consumers on the urban market (as the transport costs and arrangements are relatively low and uncomplicated). In addition, in the other direction, it is also not difficult for urban consumers to visit surrounding rural areas and buy from farmers' markets, farm shops, local food cooperatives etc. It is more complex and problematic for more distant and peripheral rural regions in which distribution channels are more fragmented and spatially limited, transport costs are high and intermediary units are more likely to appear and take the advantage of location downsides. In these locations, second-home owners, with their large and diversified (although seasonal) demand for local food products, may act as the nearest 'natural' consumers, thus creating short supply chains with no intermediaries. As previous research shows, second-home owners are very keen to buy directly from farmers (Czarnecki 2014), either from the farm or from a farmers' market, and as a result, they re-arrange distribution channels from conventional to alternative (here local) models. This confirms that certain changes in economic relationships may happen naturally without any regulations or supporting policies. Second, social ties, proximity, interpersonal relations and the trust between the consumer and the producer have been identified as critical resources for establishing well-functioning local food production systems (Heffner & Czarnecki 2015). It means resocialising food by ensuring direct contacts between the producer and the consumer (Kirwan 2004), which consequently form the basis of the food's value and meaning (Marsden, Banks & Bristow 2000). At the same time, many second-home owners declare their rural roots and also the fact that they have friends and relatives in the village of their second home (Czarnecki 2014). This partly shows their local embeddedness, but also reveals an established network of social relations and trust with the locals, especially with regard to the popularity of informal transactions mostly based on direct purchasing. Second-home owners are therefore particularly important in the light of their large contribution to local food production systems, which takes place naturally, without the need for institutional support or incentives.

Regardless of the approach, local food products in general are produced with local resources. Thus, in terms of the sustainability of rural systems, it makes even more sense for such resources to be collectively managed within the community, as is the case with rural food markets controlled by the locals (Moreno & van der Ploeg 2011).

3.3.5 Second homes and social enterprises/cooperatives

There is an alternative, although widespread, view that second-home tourism has little beneficial impact on the local economy, with its seasonality (Wallace *et al.* 2005) and disadvantageous consumption patterns (Bohlin 1982; Czarnecki 2014) resulting in rather meagre household and business incomes. Since the economic gains from serving second-home owners are moderate to marginal, and thus cannot form a primary source of income, it seems that in such unfavourable circumstances the focus should be first on broader socio-economic rather than strictly economic effects. Secondly, it should be on the community-owned form of organisation rather than regular (privately owned) enterprise, as in this situation the latter is economically unviable, being unable to produce sufficient returns for its stakeholders and owners (Teasdale 2009; Barraket & Anderson 2010). Whereas renowned tourist regions attract both traditional and second-home tourists, and thus have a great income and development potential for local businesses, in less attractive leisure destinations –traditional rural areas, remote localities – it seems more rational to build on social enterprises that could supply visitors with local goods and services (Osborne 1998; Farmer, Steinerowski & Jack 2008).

Despite the inherent diversity of organisational forms of social enterprise (association or cooperative, for profit or non-profit) (Duniam & Eversole 2013), in general their main feature is the reinvestment of profits for social purposes in the business or the community (Lewis, Hunt & Carson 2006). Social enterprise combines 'traditional resources of non-profit organisations (donations and voluntary participation), commercial revenue (originating both from public and private customers and founders), and business activity' (Borzaga & Solari 2001, p. 333). Hence, it is positioned 'at the crossroads of market, public policies and civil society' (Nyssens 2006; Huotari 2008) and committed to achieving a specific social purpose (Mair & Noboa 2003) that can be considered as a pro-community or community-development action. As pointed out by Pättiniemi (2006, p. 23), social enterprises may play slightly different roles in, on the one hand, welfare states (e.g. in Finland), in which they supplement the existing welfare system by providing opportunities to those less able to participate in working life or by providing citizens with the means to effectively influence the social services they need, and, on the other hand, in countries with less developed welfare systems, in which they are important elements of welfare provision. However, it does not change the fact that in certain cases they may be a critical resource or a vehicle for meeting both individual (e.g. long-term disabled and unemployed people) and collective goals (i.e. community development).

As regards social objectives, such enterprises contribute, for example, to combating social exclusion (socially integrating poorly qualified, disabled, long-term unemployed people, social aid recipients as well as young people and isolated individuals and helping them into the labour market (Burchardt, Le Grand & Piachaud 2002; Pättiniemi 2006; Fraisse 2008)). Alternatively, they supply social and community care services (Borzaga & Defourny 2001; Evers 2001) emphasising the 'high quality but low costs products and services' and resulting in 'real opportunities for their workers and the whole community' (Lewis, Hunt & Carson 2006). Thus, to sum up, the positive implications of a social enterprise for the local community fall into three broad contexts: the delivery of (basic) services in deprived communities abandoned by the private sector; 2. The provision of employment opportunities, either directly or through training, work experience and matching local people to jobs (which is the focal point of the Finnish consideration of a 'social enterprise' (Jumppanen *et al.* 2013)); and 3. economic development, by creating more enterprising communities and attracting new people to business (HM Treasury 1999, Cabinet Office of the Third Sector 2006 as cited in: Teasdale 2009, p. 2).

What is advantageous in the context of linking the supply side on the part of rural/local communities and the demand side driven by second-home owners needs is that social enterprises act in various economic sectors (services, distribution, retailing, construction, real estate, manufacturing, food production as well as art, media and culture (Kernot & McNeill 2011; O'Connor *et al.* 2012) and serve customers by delivering numerous products. Hence, the more diverse the local offer, the more opportunities there will be for members of social enterprises for economic and non-economic benefits, satisfying more needs for second-home owners and consequently ensuring stronger ties with the local community. With regard to the main impact areas of social enterprises, an area of mutual benefit for both sides should be underlined. While the local demand of second-home owners is (at least partly) met, the profits from the transaction are redistributed among the members of the social enterprise. This, therefore, contributes to their household incomes and purchasing power, and possibly to the variety of the local economic multipliers effects (see e.g. Stryjakiewicz 2005, 2007), or the profits are reinvested in the business, thus contributing to the maintenance of economic sectors that would otherwise no longer supply local residents with public services (e.g. health, recreation, social, cultural and real-estate services).

Many have argued that this organisational form of enterprise is the most rational in the countryside, in remote areas or at least non-urban locations, given various specific and relevant characteristics of the rural community. These characteristics include a greater propensity to engage in social rather than commercial entrepreneurship (Williams 2007), trust and active civic participation (Dale & Onyx 2005 as cited in: Farmer, Steinerowski & Jack 2008), and a sense of belonging to a community, mutual support, self-reliance and self-help (Black & Hughes 2001). Consequently, social enterprises in various different sectors apparently have exceptional opportunities to develop successfully, especially given the more suitable social and location preconditions. However, from the perspective of some post-communist European countries (e.g. Poland), this positive view of a strong rural community must be qualified, since throughout the socialist era those 'natural' traditional social bonds within the rural community (including individuals, farmers, local authorities, institutions and businesses) were being constantly dismantled. Since the political transition period in the 1990s, these social ties have been gradually restored, although the process is still ongoing and has taken longer than expected. This has obviously affected the formation of various local social and economic initiatives, including social enterprises. On the other hand, as some Polish researchers have argued, social enterprises can be a response to the social costs of transition, including mass unemployment and impoverishment and the expanding gap in living standards caused by the reduction of the public welfare system (Leś 2008). Despite the challenging circumstances, linking customers to local goods and service providers and enhancing these relationships may in some cases not be that problematic, as second-home owners reveal social characteristics that are traditionally attributed to rural society. Many of them have rural roots, close friendships and kinship relations with the locals, thus justifying their high local participation, place attachment, interest in local issues, and socially and economically they constitute an integral part of the community.

However, seeing that a large majority of second-home owners worldwide are urban residents, it seems that they can demand more professional and higher quality goods and services, so their consumer satisfaction and utility level might not be satisfied by rural social enterprises. Nevertheless, a previous Polish study has shown that a considerable proportion of second-home owners use informal services even for serious construction or renovation work (Czarnecki 2014; Heffner & Czarnecki 2015). Thus, it is more likely that for those who informally hire locals who are not always professionals, quality is losing its importance in the face of favourable prices that are usually lower than the official market price. With all these arguments in mind, it seems that there are potential synergies between second homes and social enterprises that can provide a promising direction of development for local/rural communities.

4. Research findings

The economic relationship between visitors and the host community is a core issue for impact assessment. The emphasis on the scale, character, economic value and the object of trade between second-home owners/users and local people was of key importance to understanding their implications for the local economy and thus to meeting the research objectives.

As previous works have shown (mostly in economic impact studies), the role of tourism in developing a local economy can be considered from both perspectives – tourists themselves and the receiving region (Müller 1999). However, anyone attempting to make such an assessment needs to be aware of limitations and obstacles to either of these approaches. Measuring the impact through local community (individuals' and entrepreneurs') revenues often presents difficulties in extracting the income received by a particular group of tourists (here: second-home owners) from the total income (Müller 1999). It is especially challenging to make such calculations for well-known, established tourist destinations and resorts that attract numerous visitors in the peak season and have a more diverse make-up of tourists and the ownership of tourist operators (with mixed local and external investment capital), employing complex distribution channels and supply chains (with many intermediate links) and engaging service suppliers from many more businesses representing various economic sectors.

Obviously, certain limitations and confusions have also arisen in the course of making impact assessments from the tourist/consumer perspective, although those disadvantages are of a different nature. Here, difficulties usually result from the method of data collection, since the details required, such as the level of spending, object and sometimes place of purchase, are provided by respondents retrospectively, usually over a longer period unless the expenditures have been reported continuously in the respondent's diaries.

Other obstacles to depicting a true image of the impact are to grasp consumer expenditure/local people's sales through informal distribution channels, i.e. goods and services offered by individuals unofficially, without registering and taxation. As in the case of service providers, these are illegal operations that exemplify the shadow economy; they are often not reported by respondents, thus leading to the underestimation of the overall impact on the community's economy. However, given the character of informal economic relationships, such information is more likely to be gained from tourists/second-home owners than from locals with the first responsibility for offering them.

Despite the limitations and obstacles resulting from both approaches, these are the most trustworthy methods of the reconstruction of consumption patterns (although still involving unreliable human memory). Note, however, that the purpose of the study is only to estimate the scale of local transactions made by second-home owners in order to facilitate a more or less generalised impact assessment. Hence, in this work, economic relationships were analysed and evaluated from two key perspectives: second-home owners/users, i.e. due to their relatively reliable and valuable reporting on local expenditures, as well as the local community's representatives, so that it facilitated an assessment of the economic and non-economic impact of second-home phenomenon on the local people's wealth and well-being.

This chapter's structure has reflected the sequence of research objective and hypotheses. The first section was thus entirely dedicated to one-time spending incurred by second-home owners on site, i.e. mostly purchases of land and property. The second section referred to annual/recurrent expenditures and the main factors influencing the level of local spending. The third part was structured chronologically according to the second-home ownership cycle, drawing upon the nature of economic relationships. Hence, it starts with the description of creating one's own leisure living space (constructing, expanding or renovating a house) – purchasing building materials and construction/renovation services, and ends with the description of the state of being a second-home owner (using a house) – purchasing foodstuffs, everyday articles and infrequent goods as well as maintenance and infrequent services. It also included basic data on spending as well as factors behind second-home owners' spending patterns within subsequent categories of goods and services. The following section presented a typology of common consumption patterns based on the make-up of the second-home owners' commodity bundle. The dynamics of second-home owners' demand for local goods and services and changes in the commodity bundle depending on the purchasers' income were then examined by making use of income elasticity of demand and Engel's curves. Consequently, the dynamics of changing expenditure patterns with regard to the ongoing phases of the second-home ownership cycle were investigated. Next, the analysis of the scale and role of informal channels of distribution in supplying second-home owners with local goods and services was presented. Finally, the impact of the second-home phenomenon on the local economy in terms of revenues/flows of money and potential jobs and in non-economic aspects (well-being-related) was assessed and the most beneficial industries and groups of individuals and their characteristics were identified.

4.1 Second-home owners' local consumption patterns: factors and spending

4.1.1 Non-annual/one-off expenses

Since the focus of this study is on recurrent local spending by second-home owners, one-off expenses, namely acquiring the land, house or property are here treated as a distinctive category. The other reason why this is a separate type of purchase is that unlike recurrent transactions, here considered as annual operations (over past 12 months), these occurred at different times, some even in the 1960s. The data on land/property purchases were collected solely for Polish second-home owners, thus making this part of the analysis not comparable with the data set for Finns[2]. In addition, the obstacle was to gather relevant data from respondents, since they were somewhat reluctant to reveal such information, especially to report specific amounts of spending, which is not particularly unusual in Polish society, which regards it as provident to keep such data private. Thus, those who did not report the amount of spending, along with those who inherited secondary residence, have significantly reduced the size of the sample from 398 to 247 respondents.

As mentioned above, the first purchases (of land or property) among the owners surveyed were made in the late 1960s, while the peak occurred in the 2000s (53.4% of total purchases reported in the survey), which is basically in line with nationwide trends observed in the housing market (including seasonal/summer residences) in the second part of the 2000s until the effects of the economic crisis emerged with a certain time lag in Poland. To be more consistent with the level of expenditure, given political circumstances, i.e. the transition from centrally planned socialist economy to capitalist market economy at the turn of the 1990s and the accompanying monetary devaluation and hyperinflation resulting in the

2 The data on land and property prices in Finland is collected and analysed by the National Land Survey of Finland (*Maanmittauslaitos*, NLS) through the Official Purchase Price Register. According to the most recent report on that issue, "the median price of a summer home with a shoreline in a planned area (master plan area or detailed shore plan) was at €109,000 while outside planned zones with a shoreline – at €80,300 and of a summer home on a dry land – at €45,000 in the first half of 2014" (NLS 2014). Then, the sumer home shore plots located in the region Päijät-Häme in the Finnish Lakeland (encompassing some of the municipalities surveyed in this study, i.e. Hartola, Padasjoki and Sysmä) were considered as the most expensive in the whole country (median price – €168,000) while those located in sparsely populated areas – the cheapest ones (median price of €25,000) (NLS 2014).

re-denomination of the Polish currency in 1995, the purchases which occurred earlier than 1995 were not taken in consideration when calculating and analysing changing prices on the housing market.

The prices varied significantly, but they were highly dependent upon the object of transaction. As far as land purchases were concerned (with no successive expenses related to the house construction), the amount of spending ranged individually from PLN 800 to PLN 300,000 with the mean value at PLN 38,199 (€9,183) and the median value at PLN 24,000 (€5,769). When adjusted to constant prices with the use of the annual price index of consumer goods and services provided by the Central Statistical Office, these values ranged from PLN 1,208 to PLN 453,122 (from €290 to €108,923 according to the average exchange rate for September 2009) while the mean value was at PLN 49,659 (€11,937) and the median value at PLN 33,468 (€8,045). Obviously, the price declared by the respondents was associated with the size of the piece of land acquired, and its equipment with basic infrastructure (such as electricity, water supply etc.), location (in more or less attractive destinations, i.e. region, municipality and topographic situation) and the size of supply with available land. However, given that the data on plot size/area were categorised on the ordinal scale, it was not possible to perform a dynamic analysis of land prices changes over time (1995–2009). Nevertheless, by using tau-Kendall test, it was possible to identify a coastal location (as opposed to a mountain area), tourism-based (as opposed to mixed function) communities and typical tourism resorts (in opposition to 'rural heartland' areas) as the highly stimulating land-price factors. In addition, it was observed that the land price increased with the size of the municipality (number of permanent residents), being the highest in small towns, while the lowest in remote locations away from central villages and/or agglomerations of holidays homes.

The amount of spending was also calculated for property purchase (land + house), for which individual spending levels varied considerably, from PLN 5,000 to PLN 3,000,000, with the mean value of PLN 225,580 (€54,225) and the median value of PLN 105,000 (€25,240). The adjusted values for the 2009 prices were calculated still on the basis of the annual price index of consumer goods and services and accounted from PLN 6,059 to PLN 4,262,970 (from €1,456 to €1,024,752), with the mean of PLN 282,629 (€67,939) and the median of PLN 118,937 (€28,588). Similarly to land purchases, property prices were affected by the landscape type, i.e. the most attractive and favourable location of the property on the Baltic coast clearly reflected in the highest prices. On the other hand, property values were negatively associated with the location of holiday homes in the lowlands (of central and eastern Poland) and in mountain areas as less attractive leisure destinations. This was proved by the community-function type, since the prices were relatively low in highly and predominantly agricultural communities (largely depopulated and thus having land/property surplus to be used for other, e.g. leisure purposes) and of mixed functions, while they were very high in well-known/established tourism-based communities. Additionally, property prices were relatively low in 'rural heartland' areas, while the highest in tourist resorts and, to a lesser extent, in second-home agglomerations/leisure zones. Interestingly, however, denser settlements such as villages were highly rated economically and probably more desirable due to better infrastructure and easy access to public services (which affected the higher prices) rather than isolated locations/scattered settlements.

4.1.2 Annual/recurrent expenses

According to the survey data, the vast majority of the respondents – 92.3% of Finns and 93.3% of Poles – reported purchasing goods and/or services locally, i.e. at the second home location, which actually meant at least one purchase over the 12 months covered by the study. For the Finnish consumers, local expenditure totalled €1,423,413, ranging individually from €6 to €34,150. The mean per buyer was €3,305 whilst the median was much lower – €1,935 – showing the prevalence of a relatively low local monetary expenditure. For Poles, the total spending amounted to PLN 2,186,822 (€525,678) and varied from PLN 40 to PLN 122,200 (€10 to €29,375) with the mean of PLN 8,030 (€1,930, at the archive exchange rate at the time the survey was carried out, i.e. €1 = PLN 4.16 in September 2009) and the median value – PLN 3,600 (€865).

Obviously, the exchange rate conversion is purely illustrative and does not allow direct comparisons. Given the different economic preconditions/situation in both countries, along with different social, demographic and economic characteristics of populations based on the income level, purchasing power, prices of goods and services to some technical conditions concerning the survey samples and case-study selection, there is no substantive/content-related justification for comparisons of this kind, as the compilation is no more than indicative.

Comparability of the populations studied (Poland-Finland, social and occupational groups, functional types etc.) was provided by the application of relative measures, both on local spending levels (annual spending on different goods and services per person/household member) and on the structure of local spending (the share of spending on six predefined types of goods and services in the overall local spending by second-home owners, again per household member). Household-budget researchers frequently raise the issue of economies of scale, i.e. in this case how the size of a household (the number of members) affects the overall spending level as well as the structure of spending, with some household expenses remaining constant (e.g. charges for some home-related expenses) (Czech 2012). In accordance with the researchers' suggestions, this was levelled out with the help of double weightings. These involved the OECD scale of equivalence in the 70/50 formula, a method which assumes that the first adult has the value of 1, the next adult of 0.7, and a child of 0.5. This technique makes it possible to preserve the above-mentioned data comparability.

The average individual local household spending by second-home owners was €1,978.50 for Finns and PLN 3,149.60 (€757.10) for Poles. Further comparisons of local spending according to significant characteristics of the respondents, their leisure practices, second homes and their locations are easier to perform if we assume the average level to be 1.00. However, it is worth noting that at the start that this indicator will vary less among Finns than Poles, since it is expressed in EUR for the former and in PLN for the latter (where, due to a relative weakness of the currency, the spending ranges are greater). The point here, however, is not to compare the two countries but rather to compare the descriptive categories (independent variables) explaining the diversity/similarity of spending levels, and to seek analogies in the correlations between spending and the above-mentioned key characteristics.

The analysis focused exclusively on statistically significant correlations (by using non-parametric Mann-Whitney U and Kruskal-Wallis tests). In the table one asterisk marks those with the significance of 0.05 and two asterisks those with greater significance (Table 4.1.2.1). The respondents' ages significantly differentiated the values of local spending among Poles, where the indicator was 1.14 for the youngest group (of mobile working age) and 0.79 for the oldest. The area of variation between the two extreme groups was as much as PLN 1,093, or 35% of the average. Next comes the origin (place of permanent residence) for Finns, with the highest indicator value of 1.54 in Helsinki and the lowest of 0.78 in small towns, and the range of up to as much as €1,500, which accounts for up to 75% of the average spending. This correlation was strong in all the categories of the study's urban-rural continuum – spending grew with a rising urban status, which yet again indicates better salaries among urban, especially big-city dwellers compared to the rest of the country. Such an unequivocal correlation was not found among Poles, but one can definitely point to Polish people living permanently abroad (not a large group, and one not included in the Finnish study) as those with the highest average local spending.

Similarly, the respondents' education had a greater impact on expenditure differentiation among Finns than among Poles. The spending indicator was 1.20 for the best-educated group and 0.64 among those with elementary education. At the same time, the degree of variation was €1,110, while the average spending of the latter group was just over half that of the university-educated group. Among Poles, spending was higher in the working group (1.06), especially among entrepreneurs and higher-level specialists and executive managers, than in the non-working group (0.95). Among Finns, where more detailed categories of professional activity were used, it was higher mainly among people with a higher professional status: entrepreneurs, specialists, civil servants and higher-level white-collar workers (1.30–0.96). It was the lowest among the unemployed (0.06), and in the working group – among manual labourers, it was even lower than among retirees. Interestingly, Finnish second-home owners showed no disproportion between the working and non-working groups, which can be partly explained by the lower variability when spending levels are expressed in EUR, but also by smaller disparities in income between working people and retirees (who were the clear majority among second-home owners) in Finland compared to the situation in Poland.

Table 4.1.2.1 Finnish and Polish second-home owners' local spending against selected breakdowns

	Finns	Poles		Finns	Poles
Respondent's age	**2.669**	***-1.865**	**Second home size**	****38.049**	****34.184**
Working mobile	1.00	1.14	≤49.9 sq. m	0.67	0.43
Working non-mobile	1.01	1.00	50–99.9 sq. m	0.86	0.96
Post-working	0.98	0.79	100–149.9 sq. m	1.23	0.93
Respondent's permanent place of living	****32.009**	**13.634**	≥150 sq. m	1.78	2.33
Helsinki / Warsaw	1.54	0.97	**Second home equipment** [b]	***24.119**	****16.940**
Other large cities (≥100,000)	1.05	0.91	0	0.61	0.82
Medium-sized towns.1 (50,000–99,999)	0.92	1.57	1	0.64	0.46
Medium-sized towns.2 (20,000–49,999)	0.78	0.62	2	0.99	1.03
Small towns and villages (<20,000)	0.85	1.19	3	1.32	1.09

	Finns	Poles		Finns	Poles
Respondent's education	****19.333**	****17.092**	**Distance to health centre**	****4.128**	**-1.09**
Primary/elementary school	0.64	1.30	≤15 km	1.17	1.16
Vocational school or vocational training course	0.66	0.89	>15 km	0.84	0.83
High school	1.14	0.86	**Distance to pharmacy**	****4.257**	****-3.289**
University/polytechnics	1.20	1.13	≤15 km	1.14	1.11
Respondent's economic activity	**-1.732**	***21.492**	>15 km	0.85	0.87
Working	1.00	1.06	**Distance to grocery**	****3.440**	**-0.383**
Non-working	1.00	0.95	≤15 km	1.09	0.98
Net monthly household income	****35.222**	****37.284**	>15 km	0.83	1.16
≥7,501€ / ≥10,001 PLN	1.44	2.57	**Distance to specialty shop**	****-2.670**	**-1.675**
5,001–7,500€ / 5,001–10,000 PLN	1.26	1.21	≤15 km	1.11	1.00
2,501–5 000€ / 3,001–5,000 PLN	0.91	0.89	>15 km	0.93	1.00
1,251–2,500€ / 1,501–3,000 PLN	0.79	0.82	**Distance to restaurant**	****4.342**	****-5.775**
≤1,250€ / ≤1,500 PLN	0.36	0.52	≤15 km	1.16	1.26
Respondent's rural roots	***-2.383**	***2.483**	>15 km	0.81	0.68
Yes	0.88	0.45	**Leisure activities: Cooking** [c]	****3.075**	–
No	1.17	1.07	Yes	1.70	–
Functional region	**0.034**	****19.407**	No	0.68	–
Finnish Lakeland / Lowlands (Central & Eastern Poland)	1.00	0.60	**Leisure activities: Renovating/DIY** [c]	****-2.134**	****-3.030**

	Finns	Poles		Finns	Poles
Coastal (+Siikainen) / Coastal (Northern Poland)	1.01	1.22	Yes	1.39	2.24
Lapland / Mountains (Southern Poland)	1.02	1.29	No	0.98	0.86
Tourism resort [a]	**-0.921**	**-2.917	**Total number of leisure activities**	*33.999**	**12.626**
Yes	0.71	1.36	0	0.43	0.81
No	1.00	0.95	1 (1–4)	0.64	0.93
Leisure/summer homes area [a]	**-0.084**	*-2.368**	2 (5–6)	0.94	1.03
Yes	1.40	0.56	3 (7–9)	1.06	1.16
No	0.96	1.19	4 (>10)	1.34	0.61
Length of ownership	*11.825**	**4.820**	**Social activity. Total**	**28.904	*-2.465
≤4y	1.23	1.41	Yes	1.29	1.11
5–9y	1.03	1.06	No	0.88	0.94
10–19y	1.14	0.86	**Social activity. Local markets, local events**	**-3.018	**-0.502**
20–29y	0.95	0.81	Yes	1.35	1.55
≥30y	0.74	0.86	No	0.93	0.94
Localisation factors: Municipality of birth	*-1.771	**2.043	**Social activity. Other (NGOs, meetings etc.)**	**-2.841	**-2.146
Yes	1.07	0.08	Yes	1.54	1.24
No	0.98	1.06	No	0.90	0.97
Localisation factors: Inheritance	**0.454**	**2.598	**SH usage over past 3 years**	*16.976	**35.520
Yes	0.49	0.77	Increased (a lot + slightly)	1.10	1.50
No	1.02	1.04	Remained stable	1.01	0.71

	Finns	Poles		Finns	Poles
Length of stay: Nights spent	****64.731**	****29.494**	Decreased (a lot + slightly)	0.70	0.70
0	0.40	4.50	I cannot say	0.70	0.81
≤29	0.47	0.80	**Plans to use SH as permanent in the future**	****22.877**	****20.075**
30–59	0.77	0.42	Yes (+ probably yes)	1.19	1.82
60–89	0.94	0.58	No	0.92	0.68
90–149	1.43	1.18	I cannot say	1.04	0.73
≥150	1.67	1.54			
Travel distance	****36,367**	****17,244**			
≤49 km	0.64	1.08			
50–99.9 km	0.87	0.80			
100–199.9 km	1.21	0.83			
200–499.9 km	1.09	1.59			
≥500 km	0.77	1.74			

[a] Types of prevailing built environment in the second-home location: 'Urban area/town', 'Central village or village', 'Sparsely populated rural area', 'Tourism resort', 'Leisure/summer home area', 'Island'.
[b] Number of second-home equipment listed in the questionnaire form: TV, refrigerator and washing machine.
[c] Various activities undertaken ('Yes') or not ('No') by the owners while staying at a second home, i.e. sports, cooking, visiting friends, sauna, reading, renovating/DIY etc.
Source: Own study.

Moreover, household income was one of the most important factors affecting local spending among second-home owners in both populations considered. To generalise, the higher the income, the higher the local spending level, with a very large variation, from 1.44 for the wealthiest to 0.36 for the least affluent Finns, and from 2.57 to 0.52 respectively for Poles. The variation was especially wide among Poles, at PLN 6,465 (2,148 among Finns) and was equal to four times the average spending for the poorest group. Hence, in both populations, income contributed to the greatest disproportions in local spending levels.

Variables describing family ties to the village where the second home was located, and also those associated with the way the owners came to acquire their second home, which was often related to such ties, had a perceptible impact on local spending. To generalise, rural roots, the second-home locality being the respondent's place of birth, relatives and friends currently living in the second-home village/municipality and above all inheriting the second home had a negative effect on the level of spending on local goods and services – for Finns it was 0.87 to 1.15 for those who had purchased their second home, and for Poles – from 0.40 to as much as 1.96 for those who had purchased the land and built their second home. First of all, building a home is likely to contribute significantly to increased spending (also locally), while inheriting a home in most cases largely precludes such a necessity and thus does not contribute to raising the overall level of spending. In addition, as the analysis outcomes showed, inheriting coupled with the rural background and having relatives and friends in the area generally contributed to lower local spending on all categories of products and services, which could suggest that they are at least in part provided for free by local people (relatives, hired workers, friends) or via informal distribution channels, usually at a lower cost than official prices offered by enterprises.

Higher local spending was also reported by those who had had a second home for a relatively short time (up to 5 years) (1.23 among Finns and 1.41 among Poles), compared for example to those with the longest ownership (over 30 years) (0.86 among Poles and 0.74 among Finns), which is mainly due to a high demand for renovation and construction services and building materials at the early stage in the life cycle of the product (second home) or/and at the early stage of the second-home ownership period, generating very high spending and contributing substantially to the dynamic growth of the overall spending level.

How long people stayed at their second home during the year was also a major factor, and it is no surprise that spending increased gradually with the increasing length of stay. It was similar for those who declared an increasing length of stay (by the number of nights spent) at the second home year-on-year (over the past 3 years) (1.10 for Finns and 1.50 for Poles); this group had a higher level of local spending than people who reported an unchanging or shortening length of stay (0.70 and 0.81 respectively). Declarations as to the future use of the second home were also part of this tendency, as respondents planning to move to their second home for good in the unspecified future reported higher average local spending (1.19 for Finns and 1.82 for Poles) than those who were not considering or rejected such a possibility (0.92 for Finns and 0.73 for Poles), the main factor being high spending on building materials, construction/renovation services and maintenance costs among Poles.

More active forms of leisure time (the number of different leisure practices) were also reflected in the level of spending. The more practices listed, the higher the spending, which could mean that adding to the number of leisure practices requires financial outlays – to buy accessories, pay local fees (e.g. harbour, use of facilities, recreational rentals etc.), use services, and hence the higher average spending for more active respondents.

Higher average local expenses were also incurred by people who took part in local events such as markets, but also by those who showed greater commitment to local community life (through participation in local organisations, community work for the local area, village meetings, consultations), which is important insofar as it indicated the integration of this group of second-home owners into the local community not only in an economic sense but more comprehensively. It may also mean that community activity contributes to greater local economic activity and vice versa, which might at least partly support the idea that second homes (or rather their owners) are a critical/residual resource for reconstructing and revitalising rural/local communities suffering from depopulation and ageing.

There was also a higher level of local spending for respondents with second homes that were bigger and better equipped with media and other facilities. Moreover, in the Finns' case, this was a very strong, linear correlation, since each increase of size and new media/facilities translated into an increased average spending in all the groups of products and services, and most strongly in the construction and infrequent-services categories.

The second-home community/municipality characteristics also played an important role in the level of local spending. The extent to which the village/municipality was covered by retail trade (grocers' and specialist shops) and services (healthcare, catering, etc.). The presence of any such outlet in the second-home locality or nearby (within a 15 km radius from the second home in Finland and within 5–10 km in Poland) contributed significantly to a rising overall expenditure and also spending in a given outlet category (retail shops – spending on basic commodities (food products), bars and restaurants – spending on food away from home). Only for Poles was the proximity of grocers not reflected in an increased overall spending, but only in spending on food and everyday articles, which is not particularly surprising considering that even rural areas are well saturated with family-run grocers.

Furthermore, above-average spending was observed in tourist destinations (in Poland) and typical leisure/holiday-home areas (in Finland), and additionally in Poland in typical tourist regions – on the coast and in the mountains, where seasonal price hikes on goods and services are clearer than in other areas. In non-tourist communities, this is less of a factor because, thanks to a denser network of relationships with local relatives and friends and more intensive integration with the local community, some products are purchased more cheaply or even obtained for free. This is partly confirmed by the motives for choosing the location for a second home, since higher spending was observed in areas/localities with higher prestige, renown and leisure traditions as well as attractive localities where investors treated a second home as an investment.

The distance from the first to the second home also had some influence on the total purchase, though this was much weaker and did not have such a clear/linear effect as in the case of goods and services analysed separately or specific commodities; however, it did show similar generalised tendencies – an increased spending with growing distance to be travelled.

Building one's own leisure living space

Building-material supplies

This category included purchases of building materials from local companies: retailers/wholesalers and, much less often, directly from producers (sawmills, gravel pits). It also included the purchases of minerals/raw materials needed for building/renovating a second home, yard, access road (according to the respondents' accounts), i.e. stone, gravel and sand supplied by the local community (private individuals, as part of informal economic relationships).

These goods were usually purchased by second-home owners when they carried out renovation/construction projects themselves and/or with the help from family and friends, and less often when they used the services of local and/or outside companies. As a rule, construction/renovation orders placed with companies included labour together with the purchase of building materials (including from local shops), the decisive factor being more competitive prices and/or bigger discounts for companies at wholesalers, and companies' wider/easier access to necessary materials. In the present case, the available information only covered materials purchased directly by the respondents, and it is only on this basis that we estimate the demand for goods supplied by the local economy. There were no data on the volume or location of purchases made by local and outside construction companies, so we can assume that local purchases of building materials are underestimated to an unknown degree and in reality are greater than the data set suggests.

Building materials were purchased locally by 42.4% of Finnish and 22.9% of Polish respondents, who spent a total of €176,615 and PLN 596,160 (€143,307) respectively on these goods in the survey year (see Table 4.1.2.2). Individual spending ranged from €20 to €10,000 for Finns and from PLN 20 to PLN 100,000 (from

€5 to €24,039) among Poles, which gave, respectively, the means of €892 and PLN 6,551 (€1,575) per buyer while the median was €300 and PLN 1,000 (€240) per buyer. The share of this spending in total local expenses was 12.4% in the Finnish and 27.3% in the Polish commodity bundle.

As mentioned in the methodology subchapter, the classification tree analysis (CTA) was applied as the main method of identifying factors behind second-home owners' local purchases. Starting from the root node, the multidimensional space of independent variables (employed to explain the dependent variable – here: local purchases) is divided up into subsets/rectangles in order to obtain possibly "pure" or homogenous subsets, i.e. those containing observations/units that belong to just one class or category. Such end subsets that cannot be divided up are the so-called leaf or child nodes. In all the included types of goods and services, a dependent variable has always two classes: "purchase" and "no purchase". Following the subsequent partitions (that are recursive), one may notice to what extent the subsets become more homogenous by checking out the values placed in the right upper corner of the node, where the prevalence of one of two distinct classes is highlighted. The name of the variable selected for splitting up the subsets is always mentioned and supplemented by a strict value, class or type that is the threshold/critical value placed next to each branch of the tree. It is likely that the same independent explanatory variable may appear more than once, albeit with different critical value/threshold. As the following variables explain gradually less of the initial subset, they can be considered as gradually less important factors determining local purchasing among second-home owners.

Among the common/universal factors for both populations, and at the same time those most strongly determining the consumption pattern, one should mention a broadly considered accessibility of building material retailers/wholesalers in time and space (their location in relation to the second home location), 'qualitative' availability of specific building materials (diversity of products available) and cost-related accessibility (prices of the goods) (see Figures 4.1.2.1 & 4.1.2.2). This factor was described by several variables, among which the key ones turned out to be the distance from the permanent home to the second home and the presence (or lack) of a shop selling building materials in the immediate neighbourhood. A relatively short distance (up to 50 km) induced purchases in the buyer's area of residence and the transport of the building materials to the summer home, while a greater distance (over 200 km) created real possibilities for making such purchases locally.

Figure 4.1.2.1 Factors behind Finnish second-home owners' local purchasing of building materials

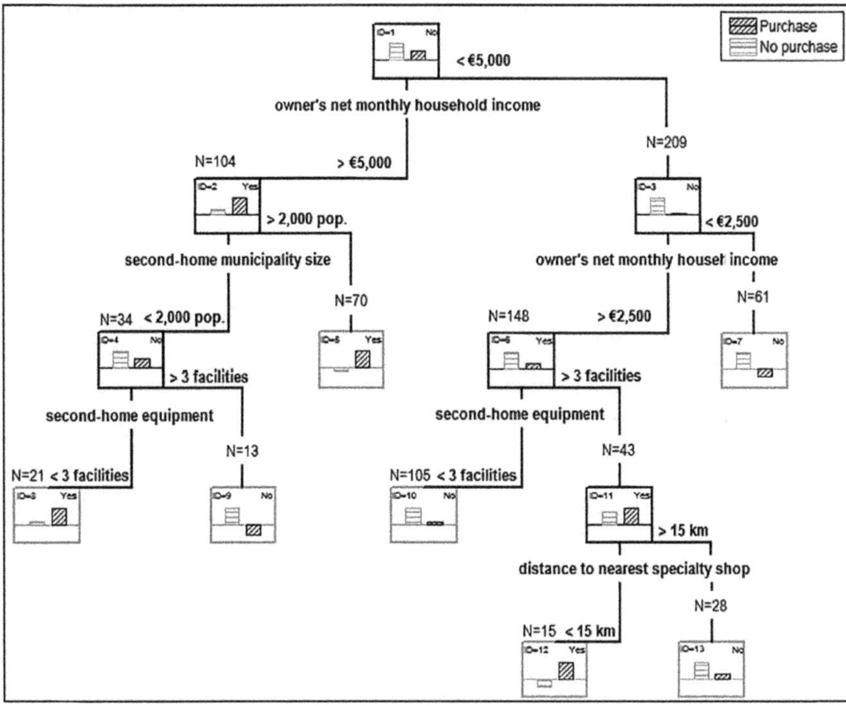

Source: Own study.

An equally important factor in accessibility was whether the locality of a second home or its nearest environs (within the radius of 15 km in Finland and of 5–10 km in Poland) included a specialist shop (the definition of which is unquestionably very general and enigmatic, but definitely includes retailers selling building materials, as the analysis results confirm). In Finland, the accessibility of building-materials shops in this sense is strengthened by the size of the locality: the respondents more often bought building materials in localities whose populations exceeded 2,000, i.e. those that usually have a greater number of retail and service outlets. It was similar for Poland, although the locality size had to be considerably larger, as such purchases were apparently more frequent in small towns (up to 20,000 inhabitants) – second-home municipality – still being important service centres for rural hinterland (especially in 'rural heartland' areas) and hence well-equipped with basic services.

Table 4.1.2.2 Basic data of Finnish and Polish second-home owners' local spending

	Finnish second-home owners						**Polish second-home owners**					
	No of purchasers	Percentage of purchasers	Amount of expenditure (in €)	Share in commodity bundle	Average per 1 purchaser (in €)	Median per 1 purchaser (in €)	No of purchasers	Percentage of purchasers	Amount of expenditure (in PLN)	Share in commodity bundle	Average per 1 purchaser (in PLN)	Median per 1 purchaser (PLN)
Foodstuffs	408	87.4	486,703	34.2	1,193	700	350	87.9	792,151	36.2	2,263	1,145
Foodstuffs & every day-use articles (no fuel)	408	87.4	555,253	39.0	1,361	803	355	89.2	871,450	39.9	2,455	1,300
Building materials	198	42.4	176,615	12.4	892	300	91	22.9	596,160	27.3	6,551	1,000
Construction & renovation services	139	29.8	323,895	22.8	2,330	600	39	9.8	262,400	12.0	6,728	3,000
Maintenance services	282	60.4	150,363	10.6	533	150	77	19.3	117,810	5.4	1,530	600
Infrequent goods (incl. fuel)	316	67.7	153,369	10.8	485	275	170	42.7	186,430	8.5	1,097	400
Infrequent services	275	58.9	63,318	4.4	230	130	172	43.2	152,572	7.0	887	400
Total	429	91.9	1,423,413	100.0	3,318	1,935	371	93.2	2,186,822	100.0	5,894	3,600

Source: Own study.

One particularly useful factor explaining Finnish second-home owners' demand for building materials (which are usually relatively expensive regardless of where they are purchased) was the respondents' wealth/household income. The purchases of the goods in question were mainly made by more affluent owners reporting high and very high net monthly incomes (first and second quintile). In the case of Polish second-home owners, this was partially proved by the respondent's permanent place of residence, with a higher demand for locally provided building materials for those living in Warsaw and other large cities (over 100,000 inhabitants). It is a matter of fact that the majority of wealthy and very wealthy households are located in heavily urbanised areas. However, the other thing is that being aware of usually distant locations of the most attractive leisure destinations, namely on the coast and to some extent in the mountains, second-home owners permanently based in large cities have a long distance to travel and visit less often, thus avoiding importing goods from outside and supplying the necessary inputs locally instead.

Figure 4.1.2.2 Factors behind Polish second-home owners' local purchasing of building materials

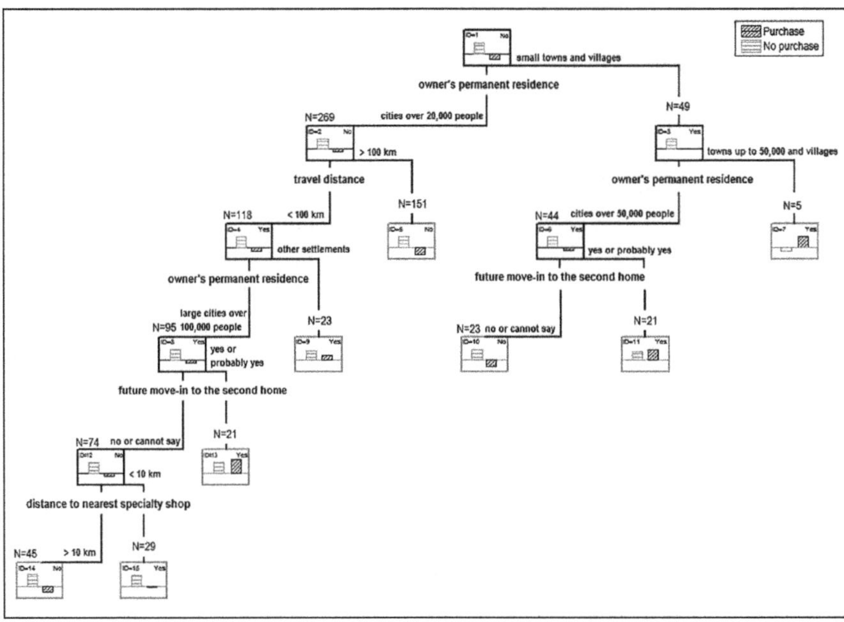

Source: Own study.

From a technical viewpoint, building material purchases (in general, not just locally) were also affected by the size and outfitting of the homes (with a kitchen, bathroom, toilet and garage). Local purchases were more frequent among owners of homes over 100 sq. m as well as those with more amenities (the more facilities, the more frequent the purchases of building materials, as the renovation needs also increased).

On the other hand, the respondents' plans for the future of their second home were not without significance, as those declaring a permanent move to their second home in an unspecified future more often made building material purchases locally. Again, this was closely linked to the mature phase of the second-home ownership and the special strategies of use at this stage, involving either a (gradual) decline in use and leaving the home (selling it or leaving it to family) or preparations (including technical, building and renovation, physical) for the year-round, permanent use of the home.

Purchasing construction/renovation services

Earlier studies (Müller 1999) supported by the results of this analysis unequivocally show that the demand for construction and renovation services is not limited solely to the early/initial stage of using a second home (though naturally it is higher in this case), i.e. soon after the purchase of a piece of real estate when the new owner builds a house, adapts an existing one for seasonal use or modernises it partially or completely. The demand for services of this kind is, after the 'introduction' stage, which is naturally the highest, more or less constant during all stages of using a second home, with some extremes of varying prominence. These are due to natural wear of the materials the home is made of, fulfilling a need to expand the home, changing fashions in home interior decoration, appearance or design, but also essential renovation/replacement due to the detrimental events of the climate/weather or natural disasters. Hence, there is a steady demand for local construction and renovation services which is reduced not so much by jobs being given to outside companies as by second-home owners' widespread practice of doing odd jobs themselves as an element of spending their leisure time at a second home.

In the period in question, 29.8% of Finnish and 9.8% of Polish second-home owners used the construction/renovation services of local companies and private individuals (as part of "informal purchasing"). In addition, Poles included also those (an additional 1%) who engaged local people for such works services, albeit, as they put it, as neighbourly help without incurring any costs. Such distinct disparities between these two populations may here also partly be clarified by the Polish respondents' reluctance to reveal the actual (informal/illegal) origins of most of the construction/renovation services provided by locals (see section 4.1.6). Individually, Finnish consumers' spending ranged from €20 (mostly minor maintenance jobs) to €25,000, reaching a total of €323,895 and the average per customer of €2,330 (median value – €600). Meanwhile, for the Polish respondents' these amounts were respectively from PLN 200 to PLN 40,000 (i.e. from €48 to €9,615), a total of PLN 262,400 (€63,077), and the average per buyer of PLN 6,728 (€1,617), while the median value was PLN 3,000 (€721).

The universal key factors included the respondents' (relatively high) household incomes, which not only made it possible to employ local service providers but created a precondition for such services to be used at all (as they are not cheap, especially in well-known tourist destinations, e.g. on the Polish coast). Income perceptibly split the respondents into two groups: those who used such services (affluent and very affluent second-home owners) and those who did not (those with average, low or very low incomes).

Again, a positive correlation was observed between the purchase of such services and the declared intention to use the second home as a permanent future residence. Thus, a (gradual?) adaptation of homes for permanent future use was observed in the owners' behaviour. For Finns, the size of a second home was another important factor. In the most general terms, the bigger the house, the higher the percentage of owners using construction and renovation services, which can be explained by a greater need for renovation as well as the effect of the most recent home expansion.

Equally important for using local construction and renovation services was the fact of family ties or the respondent's being born where the second home was located. Knowing the local community, having family ties to it and trusting its members and their work undoubtedly created the right conditions for establishing economic relations. Construction and renovation are a serious matter (not only in terms of economic costs but also relevant specialist know-how and qualifications, equipment and technology, as well as being closely linked to user safety), hence the prominent role of trust in the locals.

The length of second-home ownership also had some impact, reflected in a higher percentage of construction and renovation service buyers among relatively "new" owners (up to nine years). Of course, this does not mean that respondents who have owned their second homes for many years do not use such services; on the contrary, they use outside companies or do the jobs by themselves (at least to some extent).

As for the Polish respondents, besides the most crucial income factor, the local consumption of construction/renovation services can also be explained by their educational level, which for Polish second-home owners still generally highly correlates with the household income level. Hence, here one may observe a higher proportion of those acquiring such services among well-educated consumers.

Interestingly, the use of construction/renovation services to some extent also depended upon the 'building environment' of the second-home location, as this was more frequent apparently in a typical 'leisure'/'second home' areas/municipalities. In such locations, due to its growing popularity, 'light' construction as seen in the typical wooden cottages is increasingly prefabricated and assembled by outside companies. In recent years, this has happened quite often in coastal tourist resorts including vast leisure/second-home zones in which, however, the demand for such work/investment has been met seasonally by external companies (even from very distant regions) due to the scarcity of labour for local firms. In addition, this mechanism also works in suburban communities in which the demand for construction/renovation works is often satisfied by (more competitive and usually better experienced/skilled) companies from a nearby town.

Being a second-home owner

Purchasing foodstuffs and everyday articles

Everyday shopping is a category included in the survey questionnaire in order to identify goods with a high recurring purchase rate, but it is arbitrary in that there are no details about what respondents considered as everyday articles. One can only guess that they included basic cosmetics, cleaning agents, chemical products, stationery etc. Moreover, this group did not include medication, fuel and other goods (forming separate categories in the questionnaire), which were treated as examples of infrequently purchased goods (described below), but with the awareness of the fact that they could be seen as everyday goods for some people.

It came as no surprise that foodstuffs and everyday items were purchased locally by the great majority, i.e. 87.4% of Finnish and 89.2% of Polish respondents. There were no surprises in the make-up of products purchased either: food and beverages prevailed in terms of money spent (58.6% and 36.6% respectively). The amount that Finns spent ranged from €6 to €13,000 per year (the average per buyer was €1,361). In total, the Finnish respondents spent €555,253 on these goods during one year, which accounted for 39.0% of their total annual spending related to their second home. Individually, the Polish consumers spent from PLN 20 to PLN 37,050 (from €5 to €8,906), while the average per purchaser was PLN 2,455 (€590) and the median was PLN 1,300 (€313). In total, Polish second-home owners spent PLN 871,450 (€209,483) on food products and every-day goods. It is worth mentioning that, chiefly in the case of unprocessed foodstuffs (agricultural produce), though also others (bread, cheese, meat products), second-home owners satisfied their demand not only through local shops but quite often also through local farmers (either during individual visits or at local markets) as well as through locals who were not officially farmers (did not have the land of at least 1 hectare) but operated small-scale farming on a micro scale (usually for their own needs). In the study, this again was treated as informal purchasing – a separate category of transactions, the so-called informal distribution channels and presented in section 4.1.6, though here it is only an inherent part of the foodstuffs and everyday-articles category.

There is no question (also in accordance with earlier research (Bohlin 1982; Szkup 2003)) that the key factor affecting local purchasing of goods is the distance between the permanent and secondary residence (see Figures 4.1.2.3 & 4.1.2.4). It is the most universal factor explaining goods consumption patterns among second-home residents. Generally speaking, the greater the distance to a second home (in this case, over 100 km), the higher the percentage of people purchasing locally. The shorter the distance, the more frequent the trips to a second home, but for relatively brief stays. This means, firstly, less need to make purchases at all, and secondly, a much higher probability that foodstuffs and everyday articles are purchased at the permanent place of residence and imported to the second home (Müller 1999; Czarnecki 2014). Given that the majority of second-home owners have their permanent homes in cities (usually better supplied with shops than rural areas where second homes are located), when there is no great distance between the two homes, the access to shops increases, which consequently increases the possibility of making better purchases of goods (in terms of price and due to a usually wider range of products).

Interestingly, the next major explanatory factor involves the social relations between the respondents and the local population and other second-home owners. Those who maintained social (neighbourly, friendly) relations with the locals accounted for a higher percentage of those purchasing locally. On the other hand, those who reported lively social contacts exclusively with other second-home owners or lived an isolated life had a significant but negative impact on the economic relations under consideration. One can assume that social relations, besides promoting and increasing the knowledge about local products, build and strengthen trust and confidence between neighbours and at the same time between trade partners, build trust within the local circle or broader community (including seasonal residents), or even build a community (expanding it). Hence, it appears that maintaining social relations as an explanatory variable is applicable not so much to local purchasing as such, or purchasing in shops (as this is often also done without any relations, anonymously), as to purchasing through informal distribution channels (directly from producers – farmers and other residents). Moreover, a diverse group of respondents (60% of Finns and 11.6% of their Polish counterparts) declared rural origins and admitted their second home was in their birthplace or native locality (where close or more distant relatives still lived – 21.6% and 12.8% respectively), which may explain the strong social ties in the locality. Unquestionably, this translated into greater possibilities, demand and willingness to purchase locally, as this often took place directly from relatives. One cannot rule out that the need to shop during a longer stay at a second home in some cases becomes an impulse for or the beginning of closer neighbourly and friendly relations.

Figure 4.1.2.3 Factors behind Finnish second-home owners' local purchasing of basic commodities (food products and everyday-use articles)

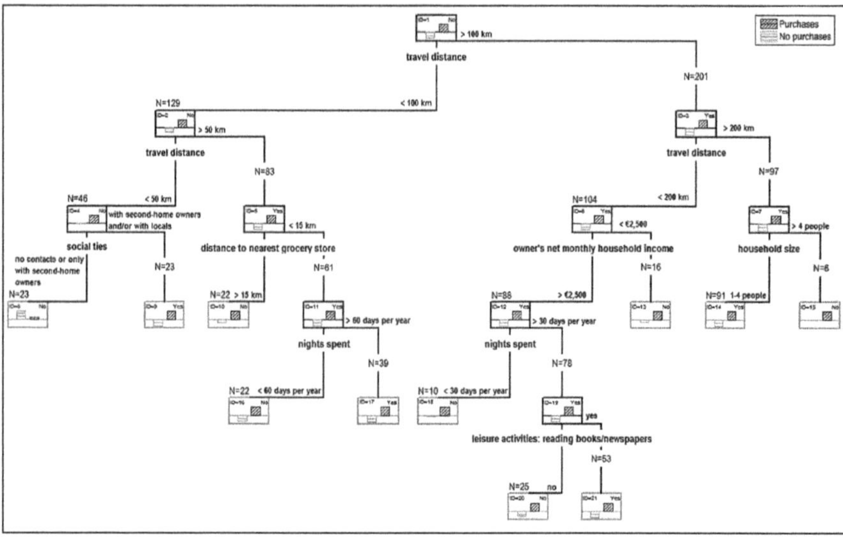

Source: Own study.

Of course another important consideration is the accessibility of retail outlets (namely grocers), i.e. how well the second-home locality or its nearest environs are equipped with such facilities (within the 10–15 km radius of the second home, though one needs to be aware of the large distances to the nearest shop in Lapland municipalities, even up to 50 km according to the respondents). The proximity of grocers means a perceptibly higher percentage of those who buy foodstuffs and everyday articles locally. A greater distance to sources of supplies usually forced second-home owners to buy these goods at their place of permanent residence (if the distance between the primary and secondary residence was small – up to 50 km), or on the way to a second home or in the neighbouring municipality (more accessible) if the distance was greater.

Purchasing locally was also affected by certain characteristics of the respondents' households, primarily size (number of members, including children) and income. In light of the research results, one can accept that from the point of view of purchasing locally, there is an optimal number of household members that results in a higher percentage of such buyers, i.e. a household no larger than three to four people (and for Poles – not smaller than three people). However, household size does not translate in any linear way into the actual fact of shopping locally, though it does affect the amount of spending due to the greater total needs/demand.

Figure 4.1.2.4 Factors behind Polish second-home owners' local purchase of basic commodities (food products and everyday-use articles)

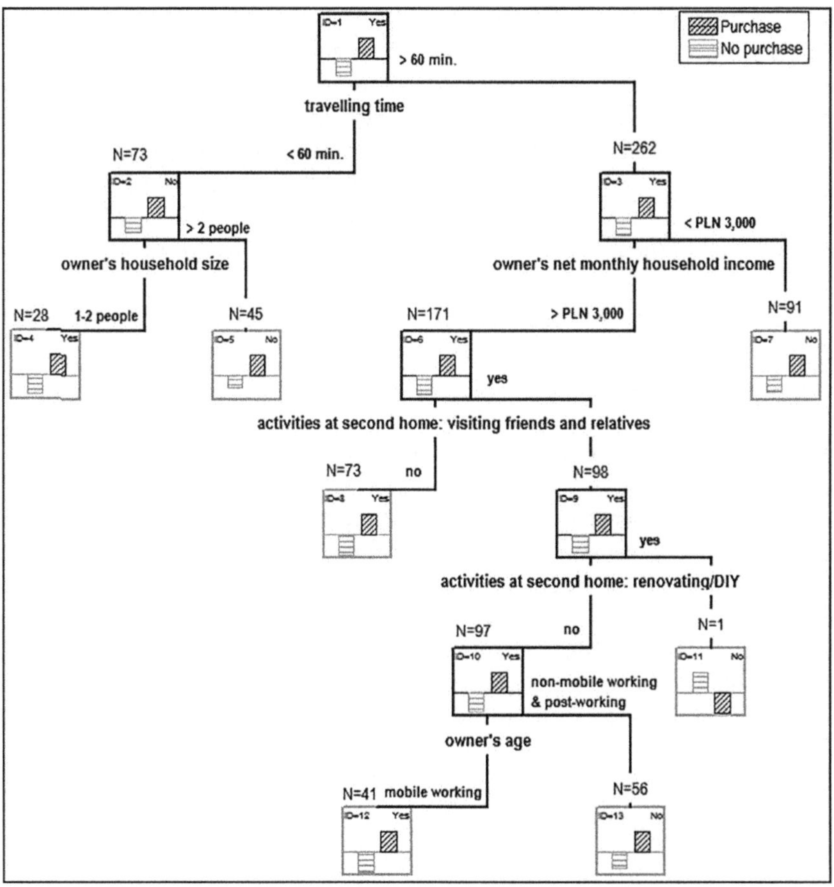

Source: Own study.

As mentioned earlier, a household's financial status also had an impact on purchasing locally. For the respondents from both countries, affluent and very affluent households more frequently purchased foodstuffs and everyday articles locally. In Finnish conditions, however, one cannot offer the simple interpretation according to which higher income means greater purchasing power. In this case, another explanation is more probable, one that takes account of the origins of second-home owners (their permanent place of residence). Assuming that the incomes of second-home owners from large cities (with the population of over 100,000) are on average higher than those of other respondents, and at the same time that big-city residents' second homes are located in the most attractive regions (Finland's lake district, Lapland, the coastal area: Kemiönsaari, Taivassalo), usually further away from the permanent place of residence (there are relatively few big cities and they are scattered irregularly across the country), one can gain a better understanding of why more affluent respondents more often shop locally. This is also partly confirmed by the consumption pattern demonstrated by Polish respondents whose holiday home is in remote locations compared to Warsaw and other large cities in central and southern Poland, namely on the coast. Thus, the decisive factor is the distance between the primary and second home, and is manifested in the respondents' income level and origins (permanent place of residence).

Obviously, the fact of purchasing is also decided to some extent by the length of stay, though to a much lesser degree than the amount spent. For the majority of the respondents, every stay usually meant at least one transaction, though there was also a group of second-home owners (ca. 11–13%) who did not make any purchases locally despite staying longer than one day and visiting more frequently than once a year.

One can also observe a clear influence of the respondents' leisure pastimes on purchasing locally: generally speaking, the more numerous and therefore diverse the pastimes in the second home, the bigger the local demand for foodstuffs and other everyday articles. Moreover, there are certain forms of spending leisure time, such as reading, DIY activities or visiting friends and relatives, that have a much greater impact on local purchases than other activities in the study. This is connected to some extent with the respondents' age, namely, younger owners (of working age) take the advantage of the local purchasing of foodstuffs and everyday articles more often than older respondents (who on average spend their time at the second home in more diverse ways).

Purchasing maintenance services

Being a second-home owner and spending time at a cottage also involves chores that need to be done in order to take the full advantage of a second home. This includes taking care of the property, keeping things in order, cleaning up, minor repairs and maintenance, cutting the grass, snow-ploughing, chopping wood, security and other related tasks which are part of the broader category of 'maintenance services'. This work is to some extent carried out by respondents themselves and partly with the help of local businesses and private individuals. In general terms, these activities constitute important, stable and common objects of transactions carried out by second-home owners everywhere.

They are as significant as the percentage of the respondents using maintenance services provided locally, which accounted for 60.4% for the Finnish respondents and much less – 19.3% – for their Polish counterparts. However, these differences cannot be entirely explained by their leisure patterns, as similar, albeit small, proportions of both respondent groups (15.6% and 14.8% respectively) considered such work (work on the house repairs and small renovations) as a popular way of leisure lifestyle at the summer home. Moreover, climate conditions in Finland, that is snow precipitation and the duration of snow cover, give an opportunity for large demand for snow ploughing services which were of great importance for 46.3% of the Finnish respondents, while in Poland, this proportion was rather marginal – 1%. However, it should be mentioned that in Finland expenses related to snow ploughing of the main roads are covered by the local road tax (*tiemaksu*) while the expenses related to maintaining private driveways and parking areas are incurred additionally by the second-home owner as they hire local individual or a snow ploughing company. Thus, while almost half of the Finnish respondents declared being supplied by the private sector, nearly 2/3 of them admitted to paying the local road tax, which, to sum up, accounted for 77.3% of those using snow ploughing services, i.e. of those combining the two types of provision. A relatively small proportion of Poles who purchase maintenance services is also a result of the popularity of neighbourly help (free of charge) among second-home owners, highly accessible if it is provided by the owner's relatives living in the same village or within the local barter economy.

Obviously, such disparities in demand for maintenance services are reflected in expenditure differences. However, assessing the extent of such impacts becomes problematic in that other 'purely' economic factors may be important, e.g. the size and make-up of second-home owners' demand, the level of supply and the accessibility of service providers, prices, consumer's income and economic power etc. In total, over the 12 months surveyed, Finnish second-home owners spent €150,363 for these purposes, which gives the average of about €533 per purchaser, and the median value of €150. Individually, the amount of expenditure varied greatly, ranging from €10 to €17,100, while the average share in total local expenses related to a second home was 10.6%. For the Polish respondents, expenditure varied individually from PLN 40 to PLN 22,500 (from €10 to €5,409), which gave a total of PLN 117,810 (€28,320), the average of PLN 1,530 (€368) per buyer and the median value of PLN 600 (€144). The average share of spending for such purposes accounted for 5.4% of total local spending.

The length of stay at a cottage and the distribution of stays/nights from month to month (mostly for the Finnish respondents) had a big influence on expenditure patterns for maintenance services for both populations (see Figures 4.1.2.5 & 4.1.2.6). It means that a one-time but relatively long stay (e.g. for the whole summer season), through an intense everyday utilisation of the home itself and its facilities, created the need for maintenance services. On the other hand, frequent but relatively short stays or keeping a second home unused over the year negatively affected the needs in this regard. The growing use of a second home and its amenities causes an increase in demand for repairs, cleaning and maintenance (in general): for snow-ploughing and chopping wood in winter, and for cutting grass and garden work for a longer stay in summer. Another thing is security services, as they are usually negatively correlated with the length of stay: longer periods of absence from a second home generate the need for security. However, for Finns, these were of marginal interest (2.8%) while for Polish second-home owners, they were much more in demand (10.8%), always involving private individuals (not companies) within informal channels. In Poland, security services are often provided by locals as part of neighbourhood help, which means they are free of charge, and this mainly happens in traditional rural communities, remote, isolated villages with few permanent residents.

Figure 4.1.2.5 Factors behind Finnish second-home owners' local purchasing of maintenance services

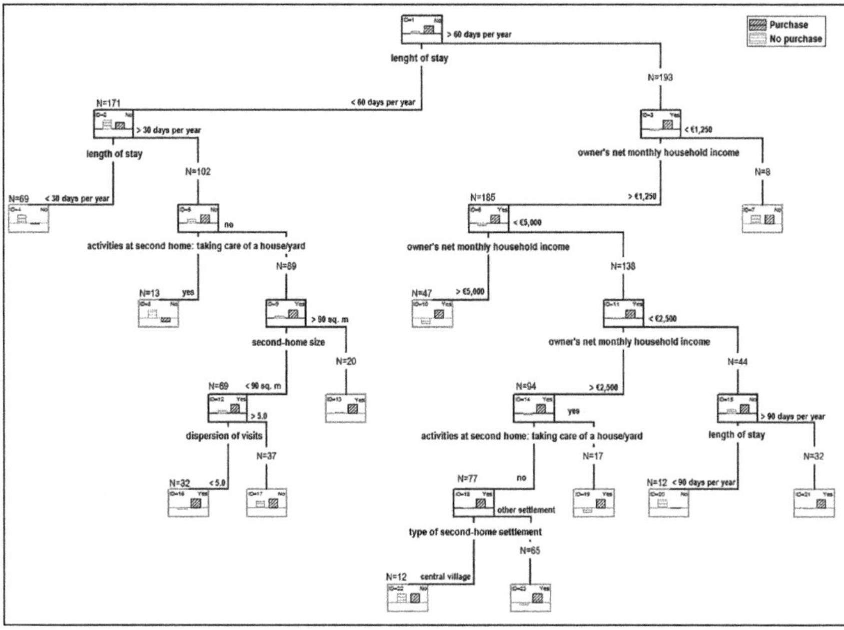

Source: Own study.

Household income also affected local purchasing of maintenance services, since the demand for such services was significantly larger among the respondents who declared high or very high monthly incomes. Thus, we may assume that other income groups are more likely to do at least some basic work themselves rather than engage local or neighbouring companies. An additional explanatory factor is the size of the house. The respondents with properties larger than 100 sq. m usually use local maintenance services more frequently than the owners of relatively small houses, which seems obvious because of the reduced scale of such needs in this regard. As with food purchases, it was very important for the Polish consumers to maintain social ties with local people. As mentioned earlier, for many respondents, this justified using services (e.g. watching the house) provided by relatives and neighbours from the same village or municipality.

The local supply of maintenance services was also influenced, to some extent, by leisure-time patterns at a second home. Among the most popular activities was carrying out minor repairs and renovations, taking care of the yard and home, housework, DIY, chopping wood, grass cutting, raking leaves etc. When at least one of these ways of spending free time was marked on the questionnaire, then it automatically decreased the demand and interest in purchasing maintenance services (including those provided locally).

Figure 4.1.2.6 Factors behind Polish second-home owners' local purchasing of maintenance services

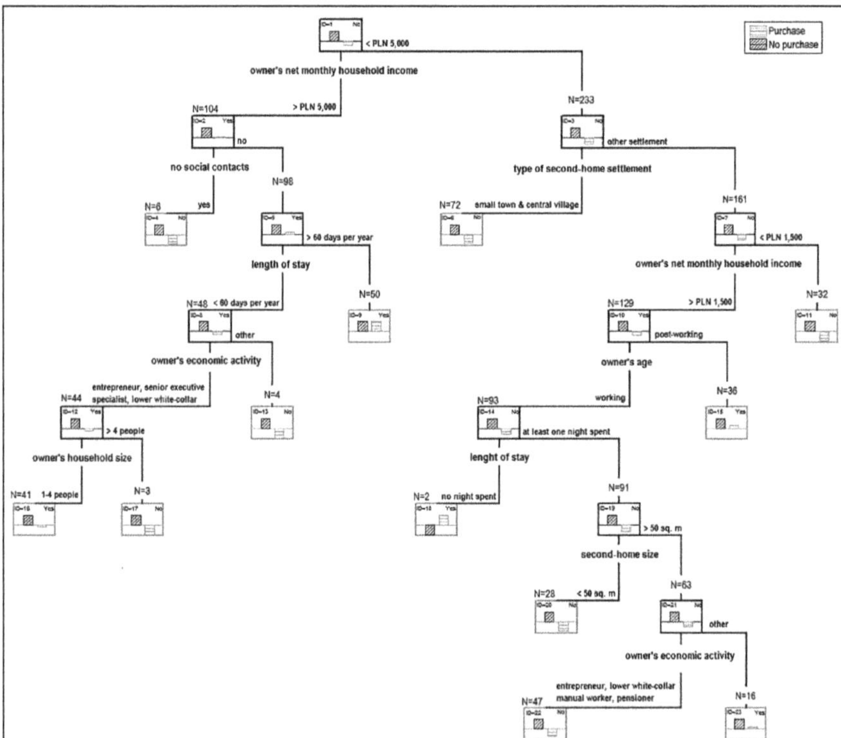

Source: Own study.

It was not surprising that the impact of the distance between the primary and secondary residence on maintenance-service transactions was considerably less important. This relationship, which is very strong for food products and goods purchased, weakens significantly for services, especially for basic, low-cost maintenance work not requiring specific qualifications or specialist knowledge. Hence, the demand for services of such kind can be simply satisfied by the owners' work and not necessarily passed to local companies and experts. Of course, to some extent, the distance between the primary and secondary residence matters, shaping the consumption pattern of maintenance services, but in this case, shorter distance does not so much induce a decrease in the demand for services provided locally as a general decrease and at the same time an increase in doing the work themselves. In both countries, spatial accessibility to services is an influential factor, since most second-home owners engage local businesses and individuals for such work if the cottage is in a small town or a central village rather than in scattered settlements.

The respondent's age and occupation were also quite important when explaining these expenditure patterns for Polish second-home owners. A higher proportion of local-service users among the owners of a post-productive age than in younger generations was observed as well as among non-working (mostly retired people) than among those in paid work or self-employed. Therefore, it seems that, with increasing age, work included in the maintenance services, or at least some of it, is no longer a popular way of spending free time at a summer home and thus may become a troublesome necessity and at the same time an economic opportunity for local businesses or individuals.

Purchasing infrequent goods

'Infrequent goods' is an arbitrary category covering fuel, medications (as separate subcategories in the questionnaire) and 'other' purchases, that is other than foodstuffs, everyday articles and building materials, which actually meant including plants/seedlings, garden soil, organic fertilisers, seeds/sowing material, machinery, home and garden appliances, firewood, clothing, sailing accessories, sports equipment, furniture, bottled gas, books, alcohol, etc. Although incorporating fuel purchases to the category of infrequent goods instead of including them in the group of everyday-use articles may be controversial for some readers, in this analysis, as mentioned above, it follows the ordering/categorisation applied previously to the Müller's study (1999) as well as the author's view that when one is staying at a second home, fuel is often not purchased on the everyday basis.

The majority of the Finnish respondents (67.7%) reported such expenditures, compared to nearly half of their Polish counterparts (42.7%): in total €153,369 and PLN 186,430 (€44,815) respectively. Individually, annual expenditures ranged from €10 to €4,900 for Finns, while the average per buyer was €485 (median value

€275), and the average share of this category in the total expenses accounted for 10.8%. For the Polish respondents, the individual expenditure ranged from PLN 20 to PLN 12,000 (i.e., from €5 to €2,885) with the average value per user of PLN 1,097 (€264), the median value of PLN 400 (€96) and the 8.5% share of the total spending.

In light of the research results, variables influencing local purchasing of infrequent goods could be merged into several broader factors. They represent the wide-ranging issue of spatial accessibility to infrequent goods manifested by the distance between the permanent and the second home, or by the distance to the nearest shops (especially to the 'specialist shops' and pharmacies that offer such goods), or by the permanent place of residence of second-home owners (large city – a village). Of particular importance in explaining these relationships for both populations was the distance between the two houses (as measured by travelling time), which, as in the case of food products and everyday articles, was reflected in an increased percentage of local purchases with an increasing distance. The influence of this factor was corrected by the existence and exact location of specialist shops in the second-home locality or in the neighbourhood. The lack of specialist stores within the 15-km radius from summer home in Finland and within the 10-km radius in Poland significantly reduced the percentage of respondents buying such goods locally.

The origin of the respondents or the urban status (here: considered as a permanent place of living) i.e. cities (over 100,000 inhabitants), as an explanatory variable, strengthened the (critical) significance of the distance between homes. Their secondary residences are usually in the most attractive tourist regions, often 'peripheral' in geographical terms, while their permanent places of residence (i.e. cities) are few and unevenly distributed in the country. At the same time, there are more small towns and their network is geographically denser. Thus, the average distance to a second home is relatively short and as a result infrequent goods are more often purchased at the permanent residence and taken to the summer home.

Local purchasing of infrequent goods was also affected by the length of stay at a secondary residence (including the distribution of stays/nights comparing month to month in a surveyed year) and even more by changes of the length of stay over the previous three years and the number of visits year round. If a longer stay was declared, it would manifest itself in more frequent purchases of otherwise infrequent goods. In addition, these relationships were positively impacted by relatively long stays at a summer home. Both variables can be treated as a fundamental factor in the (natural) occurrence of new needs, i.e. making purchases other than food products and everyday articles. A longer stay is also a critical condition justifying investment in exclusive (recreational) goods such as yachts, when the owner is sure they can be used efficiently (often) when he/she is spending time at a cottage.

Since certain infrequent goods are particularly rare, highly processed and exclusive products (including machinery and appliances), these purchases are highly dependent on the household income. It is also reflected in the study, given that higher percentages of those declaring such transactions were primarily observed among the representatives of wealthy and very wealthy households, and additionally among those of moderate incomes among the Polish respondents.

Furthermore, permanent residence (urban origins) and, consequently, greater distances from the primary to the secondary residence also positively influenced expenditure patterns for infrequent goods through an increased demand for fuel and for buying it locally (to secure fuel for the return trip). Since the majority of the respondents travel to their second homes by car (99.0% of Finns and 95.4% of Poles, including trips in a company car, a hire-car or a neighbour's car), it definitely impacts on local purchasing of fuel and consequently contributes to spending on infrequent goods.

Purchasing infrequent services

This category covered a broad range of services that are common habits in the permanent place of residence (medical/healthcare services, wellness, catering, cultural (incl. libraries), hairdressing, laundry, transport (here served by taxi)) as well as those that are a 'pure' manifestation of leisure, outside the permanent home (sports equipment rentals, recreational facilities). The above characterisation confirms what Müller stressed in his study (1999, p. 169), i.e. that although the use of infrequent services is not restricted to living in a second home, it is certainly more frequent. Thus, second-home living not only implies the relocation of everyday life to a more pleasant environment but also a changed activity pattern.

Buying these services locally was reported by 58.9% of second-home owners surveyed in Finland and 43.2% in Poland (i.e. those incurring expenses on services provided by private sector on site). If one takes into account the frequent use of free services (e.g. medical services covered by health insurance, public libraries, certain recreational facilities and the participation in local summer cultural events), the percentage increased to 64.0% for Finns and to 59.0% for Poles. In total, Finnish second-home owners surveyed spent €63,318 for these purposes while the Polish respondents spent PLN 152,572 (€36,676). For Finns, the annual expenditure ranged individually from €10 to €2,250, while the mean expenditure was €230 per purchaser, and the median was €130 (including only those charged from private sector). For their Polish counterparts, the expenditure ranged from PLN 12 to PLN 6,000 (from €3 to €1,442), while the average was PLN 887 (€213), and the median PLN 400 (€96). The average share of expenditure for infrequent services was the lowest, at 4.4% and 7.0% of the total second-home-related spending respectively.

Figure 4.1.2.7 Factors behind Finnish second-home owners' local purchasing of infrequent services

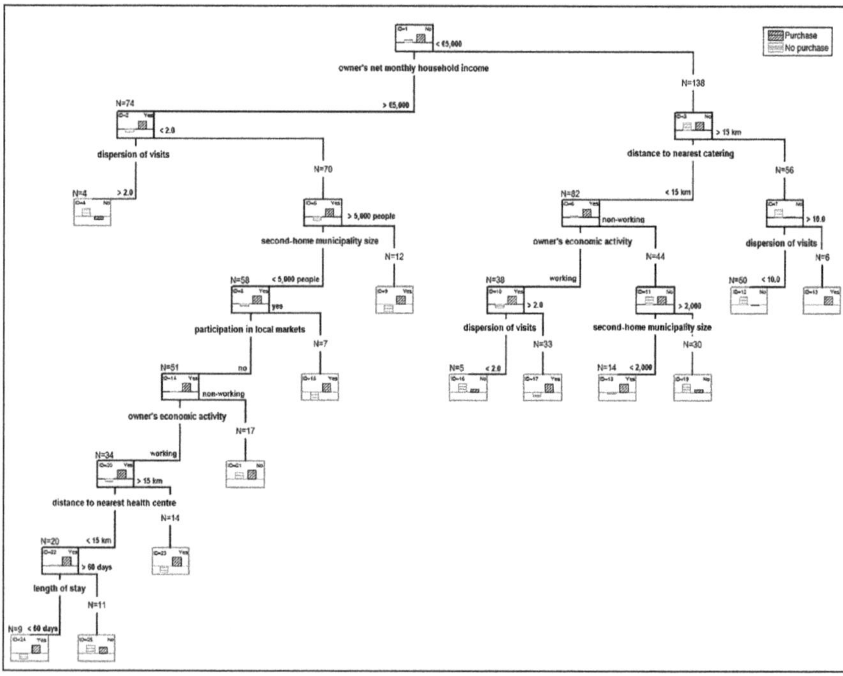

Source: Own study.

On the basis of the classification-tree outcomes, several key determinants influencing local purchasing of infrequent services were identified (see Figures 4.1.2.7 & 4.1.2.8). Spatial and time accessibility to medical, catering and postal services as well as to some recreational facilities at the location of a summer home or in its vicinity (within the radius of 15 km in Finland and 5–10 km in Poland) was one of the most important factors. It was supplemented by the village size, since usually the larger the locality, the better the infrastructure. However, accessibility was considered here broadly, since it was strengthened by the distance between the permanent and the secondary residence. Shorter distances usually cause less demand for the use of infrequent local services (zoning of healthcare services assigned to a permanent place of residence, and the ability to prepare one's own meals at the permanent home, and hence no need for local catering).

Figure 4.1.2.8 Factors behind Polish second-home owners' local purchasing of infrequent services

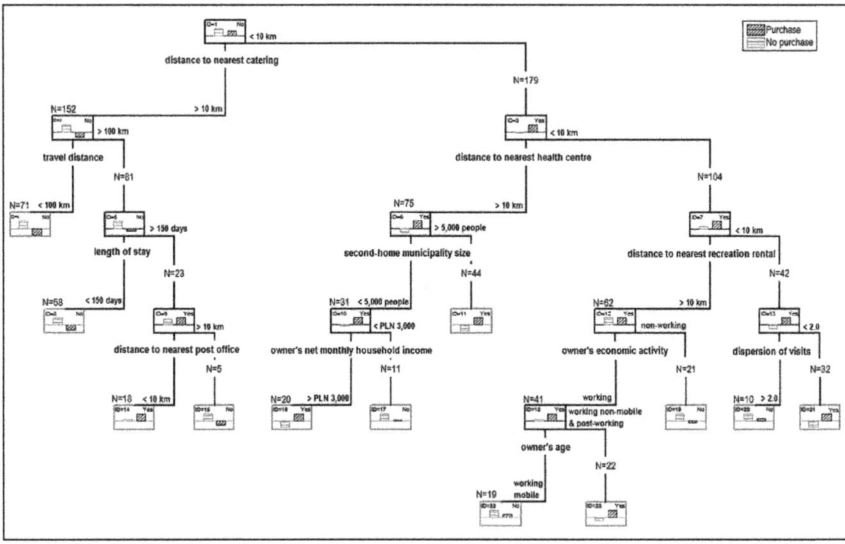

Source: Own study.

Furthermore, the length of stay at a cottage also had an impact on the usage of such services: over 60 days for Finns and 30 for Poles, with a typical distribution of stay during the year (i.e. over the summer season when crucial infrequent services (catering, recreation) are available locally in a large number of offers) and at the same time with no or occasional visits outside the peak season). Then, household wealth (very high, high and medium incomes), household size and the respondent's age (relatively younger generations, i.e. of productive mobile age) formed another important positive factor in the demand and spending patterns for infrequent local services. In addition, in Finland, an active and sociable lifestyle at a cottage, taking part in local festivals, events and summer markets created favourable conditions for the intensive and common use of infrequent local services. In Poland, it was rather the respondent's economic activity that influenced spending on infrequent services, as such expenses were incurred more often by working than non-working second-home owners.

4.1.3 Typology of second-home owners' local consumption patterns (a consumer typology)

A typology of consumption patterns was developed from the cluster analysis of second-home owners' local expenditure structure (commodity bundle). With the use of the k-means clustering method, a few universal consumer types common for Finns and Poles were identified. To be as consistent with other parts of the analysis as possible, the same core categories of locally purchased goods and services were applied, i.e. food products, everyday articles, building materials, construction/renovation services, maintenance services as well as infrequent goods and services. The high internal consistency and reliability of the typology obtained permitted a relatively clear and uncomplicated analysis and interpretation, ensuring a high explanatory value for consumer demand.

As a result, three main universal types of consumers were identified for both Finnish and Polish second-home owners. In type 1, described as minimalist, consumer expenditure was very modest, as the vast majority of the commodity bundle comprised food products, acquired at local groceries stores, and usually unprocessed agricultural produce, bought directly at farms or from farmers' markets. The average consumer spending structure within this type was supplemented by a low proportion of everyday articles and/or maintenance services and/or by a very low proportion of other products provided locally (Figure 4.1.3.1). Against the potentially diversified commodity bundle, the type 1 consumer, with its representatives meeting their basic minimum needs and thus entirely targeting food and elementary services, could here be regarded as minimalist. To learn more about the preconditions, one needs to answer additional questions, still based on the data gathered: who was the minimalist consumer (socio-demographics) and where was this spending pattern most common?

Figure 4.1.3.1 Types of second-home owners' consumption patterns (based on consumer basket). A consumer typology

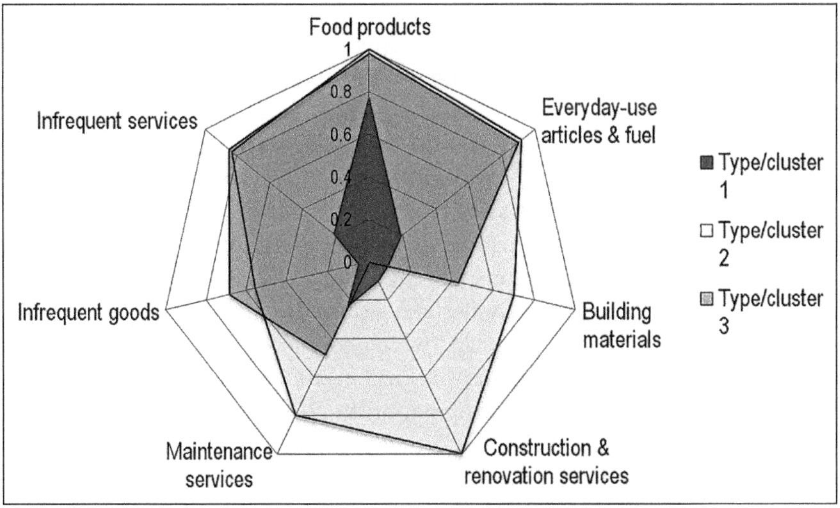

Source: Own study.

Interestingly, the composition of type 1 consumers clearly showed the prevalence of relatively young people (of mobile age), albeit rather less educated (of primary or vocational education level), often non-working (i.e. unemployed and housewives, excepting retirees), while among working people – blue-collar and low-level white-collar workers, and generally low- and very low-income earners (the strongest correlation) proved that consumer/household wealth was a critical factor in the minimalist expenditure pattern (see Table 4.1.3.1). In addition, what seemed to be particularly important was that most of the minimalist consumers lived permanently in medium-size cities, small towns and even rural communities while very rarely in larger cities. Large numbers of medium and small towns and their more even geographical distribution in both countries is therefore reflected in relatively shorter distances between homes (usually up to 100 km and 120 minutes of travelling), easier access to holiday homes and consequently more frequent, albeit short, visits to a second home. This, in turn, influences second-home owners spending more indirectly, as with short stays they do not need more sophisticated, infrequent goods but only basic commodities, if any.

Furthermore, when constructing/renovating a second home, type 1 consumers usually made use of support/help provided by families/relatives and friends, thus not reporting such expenditures and making the pattern less diverse. In general, doing things by themselves (including small-scale farming and thus self-subsistence/'natural consumption') along with a preference towards purchasing things at the permanent residence, too expensive local prices and successively shorter stays at the second home over the years were often reported by minimalist consumers. What is more, the majority stayed at the cottage alone or with few other people (close family), thus limiting the demand for local products.

Interestingly, a minimalist consumer pattern had much in common with a minimalist social and free-time spending pattern, since their representatives reported only a few leisure activities at a second home (up to 5) and did not maintain social contacts with locals (which could be crucial for information on local suppliers). Not taking part in local events and farmers' markets also revealed a low level of social participation in community life. Additionally, they were owners of typical summer cottages, small, unwinterised, and with no special amenities, providing good conditions for short stays mostly in summer. Moreover, this type is often followed by the owners of second homes located in areas with a poor basic services and shopping infrastructure and on the other hand also in semi-urban municipalities in which it is more accessible and convenient (organisationally and economically) to shop in a nearby town, thus by-passing local suppliers.

Although the typology was done jointly for second-home owners of both nations surveyed, statistical tests showed the prevalence of Poles for type I. Thus, for Finns, saving-related minimalism was apparently limited.

Table 4.1.3.1 Factors behind consumer types, %

		Type 1: 'Minimalist'	**Type 2: 'Transitional'**	**Type 3: 'Recreational'**
Gender	F	38.4%	33.9%	**44.2%**
	M	61.6%	**66.1%**	55.8%
Age	Productive mobile	**19.9%**	10.8%	**18.5%**
	Productive non-mobile	46.6%	**54.0%**	47.9%
	Post-productive	33.4%	35.2%	33.5%

		Type 1: 'Minimalist'	Type 2: 'Transitional'	Type 3: 'Recreational'
Permanent place of living	Cities (≥100,000)	49.9%	**55.4%**	50.2%
	Medium-sized towns.1 (50,000–99,999)	**14.3%**	7.3%	9.6%
	Medium-sized towns.2 (20,000–49,999)	12.3%	14.7%	14.4%
	Small towns and villages (<20,000)	**23.0%**	20.9%	**24.9%**
	Abroad	0.0%	1.7%	1.0%
Education	Primary/elementary school	**11.1%**	4.5%	7.1%
	Vocational school/training course	**15.3%**	**17.6%**	12.0%
	High school	34.4%	34.1%	**40.8%**
	University/polytechnics	39.2%	**43.8%**	40.1%
Economic activity	Entrepreneurs	20.7%	21.6%	20.0%
	Senior executives, specialists	12.0%	**22.2%**	16.1%
	Low-level white-collar workers	**11.1%**	9.1%	10.0%
	Manual workers	**9.6%**	5.1%	**9.0%**
	Unemployed	2.0%	0.6%	1.9%
	Retired	39.9%	39.8%	40.3%
Household income	Very wealthy	5.7%	**15.5%**	8.4%
	Wealthy	14.1%	**29.3%**	21.7%
	Middle	38.7%	40.2%	**44.1%**
	Poor	**31.8%**	13.2%	21.4%
	Very poor	**9.6%**	1.7%	4.3%
Travel distance	≤49 km	**25.2%**	9.6%	12.1%
	50–99.9 km	**28.9%**	23.7%	22.7%
	100–199.9 km	32.5%	31.6%	**37.4%**
	200–499.9 km	12.0%	**29.4%**	22.7%
	≥500 km	1.4%	**5.6%**	**5.1%**

		Type 1: 'Minimalist'	Type 2: 'Transitional'	Type 3: 'Recreational'
Nights spent	0	**2.6%**	0.6%	1.0%
	≤29	**12.2%**	8.6%	**11.8%**
	30–59	**24.3%**	21.7%	**22.6%**
	60–89	**22.6%**	**22.9%**	20.3%
	90–149	25.2%	**33.1%**	27.9%
	≥150	13.0%	13.1%	**16.4%**
Home size	≤49.9	**26.9%**	8.0%	19.3%
	50–99.9	45.4%	49.4%	**51.8%**
	100–149.9	17.6%	**24.4%**	21.9%
	≥150	7.3%	**18.2%**	7.1%
Social ties	None	**19.3%**	17.5%	16.9%
	With second-home owners	**17.6%**	10.7%	9.9%
	With locals	16.2%	**29.4%**	16.3%
	With second-home owners and locals	46.8%	42.4%	**56.9%**
Social activity: local event, farmer's markets	Yes	8.1%	**21.5%**	16.0%
	No	**91.9%**	78.5%	84.0%

Source: Own study.

In type 2, described as transitional (between introduction and growth/exploitation phase) the structure of the commodity bundle was highly differentiated, as was the expenditure, with a significant allocation of spending on most of the categories (except infrequent goods – at a moderate level). It appears that such a consumption pattern was demonstrated by the respondents in the initial phase of the second-home ownership which can be confirmed by a particularly high spending on construction/renovation services and building materials (the highest in three consumption types). However, it should be stressed that this is probably not a particularly early phase of house-building, since the work apparently does not influence expenses for other purposes, which still make up a considerable proportion in a way that construction/modernisation and use seem to be simultaneous. Hence, one may argue that renovation work may probably be conducted outside the summer period while in the peak season 'regular' leisure expenditures predominate.

This expenditure pattern was common among the respondents of a working non-mobile age, so it means individuals in transition from work to retirement. This usually overlaps with the introduction phase of the second-home ownership, since many serious decisions regarding future strategies and practices (e.g. dwelling, changing place of residence) are being taken in this specific period of people's lives. As research outcomes have shown, among type 2 consumers, one may find mostly well-educated people, employed at managerial positions or as specialists/senior professionals or entrepreneurs. In general, this type is more prevalent among working people than among the retired, housewives or unemployed, among well-off respondents (reporting high and very high incomes) and among residents of large cities. Given a relatively small number of large cities and their irregular distribution, this factor has a positive effect on local purchasing and spending on various products, because of a relatively greater distance and travel time between the permanent and the second home (over 200 km and 120 minutes).

People in this category hardly ever inherited their second home/property but rather bought a piece of land for a holiday home. In addition, besides these new, 'fresh' owners who were present at the construction stage of their second home, type 2 also included the respondents who had owned a secondary residence for 20 years or longer. It seems that after a certain period of more or less regular use, there is usually a time when renovations/modernisations are needed. These are carried out by local companies or by the owners themselves, with the help of family members and friends, but then their spending patterns show large expenses for building materials. On the other hand, a high proportion of construction/renovation services and building materials resulted from the house characteristics, since these were predominantly large (over 100 or even 150 sq. m) and well-equipped.

Those in consumer type 2 tend to spend a relatively long time at a second home over the year (from 60 to even 150 nights), with the high number of nights suggesting one continuous long stay (e.g. during the peak season) with few or no visits outside the holiday season. This evidently has a positive influence on consumer demand for various types of goods and services, including those of an infrequent nature. The differentiated demand for local goods and services is here a consequence of the respondents' active lifestyle (with a large number of leisure activities while at the second home, varying from 6 to 12), even though at first glance some of them can be seen as an obstacle in local purchasing, namely small repairs, house and garden work done themselves.

Furthermore, these 'transitional' consumers socialise with the locals much more often and are more eager to participate in local (summer) events, thus enhancing various free-time opportunities and consequently exhibiting a more indulgent spending pattern. As their representatives reported that they had increased their length of stay over the years, it may manifest an initial or transitional period of their second-home ownership. Additionally, in type 2, there was a dominating representation of Finns over Poles, confirming the former's closer connections to the local economy not only in terms of spending levels but in terms of an abundant demand for a wide variety of products.

Type 3 was described as typical/traditional leisure/recreational (or even 'in-between', given the moderate characteristics compared to other types) mainly due to a relatively high consumption of food products and everyday articles as well as of infrequent goods and services (which usually exemplify needs other than basic), low spending on building materials and maintenance services and the absence of construction/renovation expenditure. This pattern is more likely at the maturity stage of the second-home ownership, when there is 'regular' typical leisure-related use and no demand for construction/modernisation work. In addition, this type was almost evenly distributed among Finns and Poles.

This type of the consumer was more common among women, relatively young people (of mobile productive age), mid-level of education, manual workers and low-level white collar workers (as in type 1), middle-income earners and members of larger households (five or more), although other relatives or friends were also mentioned as users. Type 3 consumers had more often inherited a second home, more frequently reported rural roots and relatives living in the same community and reported a relatively short length of ownership (up to ten years). They stayed at the cottage from 30 to 90 days a year, spending the whole or extended summer season with no off-season visits, which confirms a typical holiday pattern. In addition, this group engaged in only a few leisure activities (4–6), although on the other hand, they were sociable, maintaining strong social ties with locals and other second-home owners and, importantly, taking part in events and summer festivals but also in collective actions to the advantage of community development.

What was crucial for the 'leisure' pattern was the local accessibility of more specialised retailers and service suppliers (catering, pharmacies, health and well-being centres). Easy access was easily met, at least in the summer season, in localities with good infrastructure, i.e. small towns or tourist localities/resorts, where most type 3 consumers had their holiday homes. In addition, although the consumers mainly came from small urban centres, the greater distance from their primary to secondary residence (usually from 100 to 200 km or over 500 km) together with long travelling time (over 360 minutes) and relatively long stays significantly reinforced such local consumption patterns, which are very advantageous to the local economy. Perhaps, such a 'leisure' type is reflected in the furnishing of second homes with many facilities and appliances, and their larger size (number of rooms), thus ensuring suitable conditions for various leisure activities and a comprehensive recreational type of consumption.

4.1.4 Dynamics of second-home owners' local consumption patterns by Engel's laws/curves and income elasticity of demand

Given that the contribution of second-home tourism to the local economy is highly dependent upon second-home users' consumption behaviour and spending patterns, it was necessary to recognise the commodity bundle. It was logical to refer to Engel's laws, presented in section 3.2.1, and then draw Engel curves for various types of goods and services purchased locally by Finnish and Polish second-home owners. In order to be more comprehensive and informative about second-home owners' local economic activity, Engel's laws and curves were supplemented by the income elasticity of demand index measured for main components of the commodity bundle. Since the income elasticity formula requires data on actual quantity of products demanded, and these were not gathered in the survey, an alternative means of measuring was used, i.e. the average amount of spending per capita (second-home owner's household members) per night spent at a second home, as suggested by researchers dealing with tourist spending (Divisekera & Nguyen 2014). However, it should first be stressed that in light of this study, the length of stay (measured by the number of nights spent) was negatively associated with the second-home owner's household income. This means that the length of stay decreases with the rise in income, which can be explained first by a growing availability of other leisure opportunities for more wealthy consumers, e.g. possession of a second, third holiday home in various locations (also abroad) or regular tourist trips. Naturally, there was, therefore, less time spent at a secondary residence – the object of this survey. One may note that retired people have relatively more time to stay at a holiday home for longer periods but average incomes that are generally lower than of those working – this was particularly relevant in the Polish context. As a result, one needs to bear in mind that consumption patterns for wealthy second-home owners were more fragmented than for low and middle-income earners, thus having a certain influence on the commodity bundle and income elasticity indices.

As far as Engel's first law is concerned – on the decreasing proportion of expenditure on food products (albeit with a slightly increasing amount of overall expenditure) with the household income rise – one may observe the confirmation of this in both populations surveyed. However, for Finns, the negative gradient was much more regular and constant, and the decrease was relatively low, following a linear correlation between the share and the income, while for Poles, the curve was more pronounced and the decrease was higher (Figure 4.1.4.1). For both populations, foodstuffs were indexed as basic commodities (income elasticity of demand accounted for 0.2 for Finns and 0.39 for Poles), which corresponded with the evidence of regular spending (Table 4.1.4.1). As Engel's first law states, at the same time a slight increase in the real expenditure on food products was observed with a rise in income, although this is more dynamic for poor and medium households and more stable for wealthy consumers.

Table 4.1.4.1 Income elasticity of demand for selected goods and services purchased locally by Finnish and Polish second-home owners

	Food products	Food products & EUA (no fuel)	Building materials	Construction services	Maintenance services	Infrequent goods (incl. fuel)	Infrequent services	Home-related payments	Goods. Total	Services. Total
FIN	0.20	0.22	6.64	3.27	0.30	0.06	0.43	0.05	0.23	1.00
POL	0.39	0.37	4.58	2.17	22.98	0.59	5.03	–	0.65	1.02

Source: Own study.

What is worth noting is that household income was more influential in shaping consumption patterns for Poles than for Finns; thus, the differences between the proportions in 'poor' and 'wealthy' households were visibly higher for the former (about 35 pp[3]) than for the latter (about 20 pp). Interestingly, the average proportion of expenditure on food products was basically the same for both populations (36–37% of total spending, not including housing, such as bills for electricity, water supply etc.).

Although public statistics on regular household expenditures show that the average share of foodstuffs for Poles was about 24% (in 2014) (CSO 2015) while for Finns only 15% (including alcoholic beverages and tobacco, in 2012) (Statistics Finland 2013), importantly, in this context, Engel's first law can be statistically

3 Percentage points.

and spatially extended from households to regions and countries. This is due to variations in shares among rich and poor households that can be also observed proportionally in developed and underdeveloped countries. A low proportion of disposable income spent on food products correlates with household/country wealth and high living standards, which is also promising from the economic growth perspective. As previous research has shown, the same economic processes as observed in developed countries still occur in less developed countries but with a certain time lag (Badach 2012), which is known as the analogy rule (Jajuga 1997). Here, the above-mentioned regular expenditure household surveys have shown that there were quite significant disparities in consumption patterns between the two populations. However, this did not apply to seasonal expenditure patterns (demonstrated by second-home owners), which at least with regard to food purchases were more similar between populations than regular ones. Thus, it seems that the seasonal character of stays and spending in specific locations, with no accommodation costs other than bills with high but infrequent expenses for construction services, played a crucial role in these patterns' considerable similarity despite wealth differences and different geographical and cultural contexts (e.g. the second-home phenomenon, origins and ways of spending free time).

Figure 4.1.4.1 Engel's curves for spending on food products

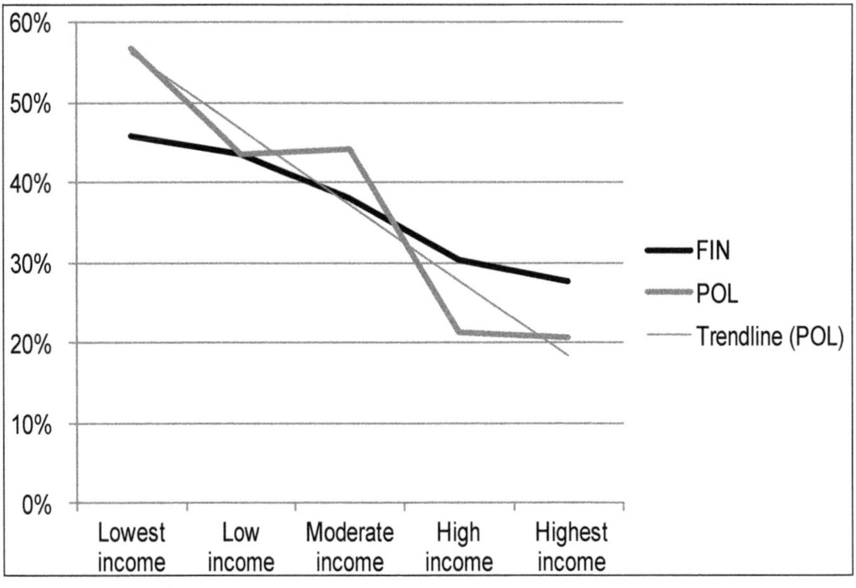

Source: Own study.

The fragmentary nature of the second-home owners' expenditures as only part of total regular spending and performed within certain limited areas was also of great importance in shaping the commodity bundle. While touring or living in a second home, a specific consumption pattern is followed that combines some regular features of the everyday patterns with special characteristics of a seasonal/occasional pattern strictly linked with leisure. As a result, it lacks the range of goods and services that is common in regular consumption (education, some leisure activities not accessible in rural locations) while at the same time including a novelty – certain needs typical of second homes (construction/renovations), leisure and free time. As a consequence, it turned out that the composition was less complex, as the lifestyle was simpler and thus the share of expenditures for food products was larger in second-home owners' consumption patterns than in regular ones. Reflected in a relatively low differentiation of the commodity bundle, this often means a more limited and selective contribution to the local economy both in terms of the number of beneficiary industries and also in terms of money flows – as highly-demanded food products are relatively cheap in comparison to other goods and services. As the data dealt solely with local purchases, another explanation for a relatively simple consumption pattern may be, in some cases, a modest local supply, which was more likely to cater for the main basic needs, while more sophisticated needs forced respondents to import certain products from the outside.

Engel's second law is associated with housing-related expenditure (in this survey including electricity, water supply and wastewater disposal, gas and heating supply, waste service, property tax and property insurance). According to Engel's findings, the proportion of such expenditure increases dramatically with a rise in household income, which means at the same time that an increase in both variables (housing expenditure and household income) is proportional. In this study, Engel's second law was confirmed only for Finnish second-home owners, as such data were not collected for their Polish counterparts. For Finns, even though the leaps and bounds cannot be confirmed since the household income data were not continuous but categorical (5 categories), the tendency observed was diametrically opposite, showing the decreasing of the proportion of housing expenditure (and separately for the property tax) in the total spending with a growing household income.

The downturn in expenditure on housing was very dynamic and accounted for almost 30 pp between 'poor' households and very wealthy ones (see Figure 4.1.4.2). For the former, the proportion was around 55% and for the latter 27%, showing not only large disparities in spending patterns but above all the significance of expenditures that in 'poor' households might definitely be considered as a financial burden influencing the entire consumption pattern, with spending on other goods being subject to serious budget constraints, not to mention its influence on the possibilities of spending time and on the level of satisfaction in having a second home. As a result, it might be confirmed that, along with the high proportion of expenditure for food products, 'poor' households demonstrated a very simple basic consumption pattern, as there are hardly any financial resources left (i.e. less than 25% for this income group) to satisfy higher needs and purchase more refined goods and services.

The differences in the proportion of housing expenditure were explicitly less significant for higher income groups, and thus the curve is more stable and inelastic. This was confirmed by the income elasticity of the demand index, which was 0.05 for the total housing purposes, showing that demand was largely independent of the household income. However, with reference to the budget share dedicated to housing, it still made up a considerable proportion (25–30%) of total spending, thus limiting other spending possibilities. Consequently, it also negatively impacted on the size and structure of a contribution to the local economy, especially as most water, electricity and gas suppliers, but not waste services, were not local companies and thus money was leaking out of the local economy.

Figure 4.1.4.2 Engel's curves for housing-related spending by Finnish second-home owners

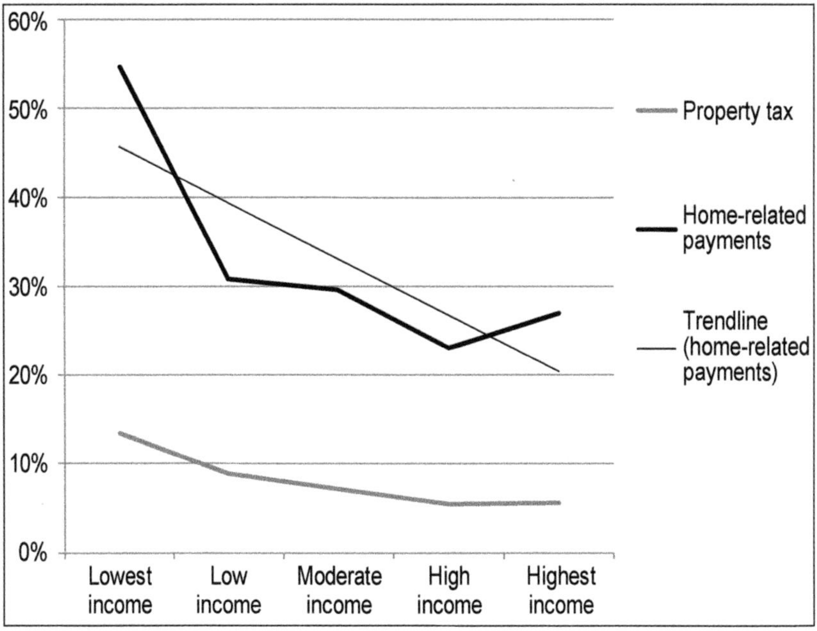

Source: Own study.

The fact that the tendency observed was very different from what was expected (based on Engel's second rule) may result from there being less differentiation between various income groups in second-home living standards than there is in permanent residences, including plot size, home size, number of rooms, technical infrastructure and facilities. It may also confirm that there is less differentiation in the level of households' utilisation of second homes, along with the same local rates for water, waste water supply etc., and that widely varying incomes led to relatively high proportions for 'poor' households and moderate ones for medium and wealthy households.

As far as Engel's third law is concerned, according to which the proportion and real expenditure for luxury goods grow along with a rise in household income, in this study, this rule was applicable to a few of spending categories. First and foremost, these were construction services, for which Engel's curve had a positive gradient towards the X axis, meaning that these were luxury goods (Figure 4.1.4.3). Despite the fact that these were definitely not goods but services, in fact they could be seen as an exemplification of a luxury good, i.e. (the possession) of a secondary residence, even though the expenditure on that category included less construction but more modernisation (incl. minor renovation work). Thus, a holiday home was without a doubt a luxury good, which was confirmed by the income elasticity of demand index for both populations (Finns and Poles) showing values higher than 1, that is, respectively, 3.3 and 2.2. Although for Finns the curve was more regular and showed relatively high dynamics, particularly for lower income groups, and for Poles it was steeper, fluctuated more and confirmed higher dynamics for the most wealthy categories, both trajectories were basically in line with Engel's findings.

Figure 4.1.4.3 Engel's curves for spending on luxury products

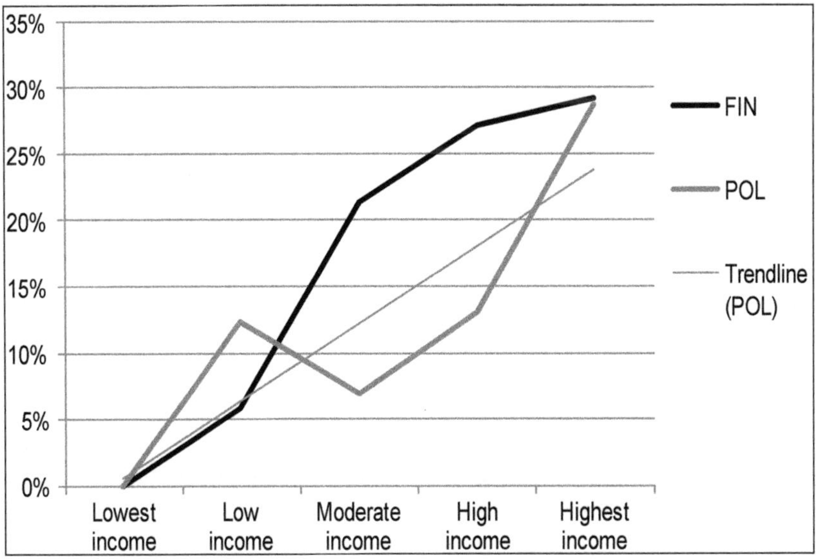

Source: Own study.

Thus, the construction sector was the greatest beneficiary within the local economy, but besides this the high demand (rising with the income) in fact meant not only profits for construction companies but also for others (albeit not necessarily local ones) supplying building materials, tools and machinery as well as home fittings, furnishing and accessories. Therefore, this demand was likely to be more beneficial for the local economy due to large financial flows and significant economic multipliers (given the strong connections with other economic activities) but also in (multi-)functional terms by involving subsequent related industries. What is more, along with construction services, building materials also seem to be an example of luxury goods being a manifestation of possessing a secondary residence. This was confirmed by the income elasticity of demand values, which were estimated as even higher than construction services, i.e. 6.6 for Finns and 4.6 for Poles.

As for other categories of goods and services, maintenance services can be mentioned first, which mainly include simple house, yard and garden work. While for Finns the gradient was negative, for Poles, the curve showed maintenance services rather as necessities or even luxury goods (as it was dynamically bending towards the Y axis) (Figure 4.1.4.4). It was particularly interesting that for the latter group, the dynamics were very high for the wealthiest, showing that maintenance services did really matter for more affluent second-home owners, who might use their time there for other, 'purely' leisure purposes. But it seemed that through the high second-home living standards their wealth was more indirectly influencing the need for maintenance purposes outside the season, which in Poland usually meant the need to provide security services. This was also confirmed by the income elasticity of demand, which differs considerably between the Finnish and Polish consumers (0.3 and 22.3 (!) respectively). The curve for Finns showed little or no difference in demand and in the importance of maintenance services in the make-up of second-home owners' budgets between different income categories (8%-14%) and also no significant dependence on the household income but rather on non-economic factors.

For Poles, who in general live in a less affluent society than Finns, it seemed that not everyone in the survey could afford such services, including not only those from the 'poorest' households but also those from medium and relatively affluent ones (less than 5% of the total spending). Only in the wealthiest category was there a particular demand for these types of services (16%). This also confirmed the previously presented results suggesting that especially for Poles household income was an influential factor shaping the demand for maintenance services. Further explanation can be found in second-home owners' daily practices, lifestyle, ways of spending time, leisure activities etc. as most maintenance services are usually quite simple. They do not generate high costs and such basic work was often done by second-home owners themselves. This is more likely to happen especially with 'poorer' consumers, who tend to spend time at a second home actively involved in work on the house. In terms of benefits for the local economy, it seems that local maintenance-service suppliers may make relatively modest profits unless they served wealthier owners, who (at least in Poland) are concentrated in more well-known tourist areas on the coast (e.g. in apartments).

Figure 4.1.4.4 Engel's curves for spending on maintenance services

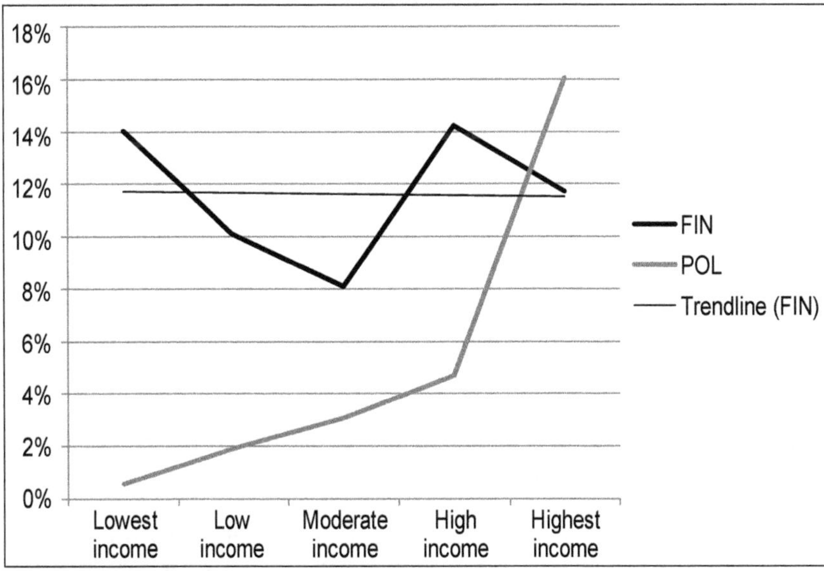

Source: Own study.

Furthermore, what was interesting in the survey data as presented by Engel's curves was the tendency for all types of goods (altogether) to fall in proportion with a rising income while the tendency for all types of services was completely the opposite. On the strength of this, one could consider goods to be inferior whereas services could be seen as luxury items. As for the former, it was a slight surprise, as this category included various types of goods (necessities and luxuries; food products, everyday articles, building materials and infrequent goods), although it meant that high-value ones were in minority and the commodity bundle was dominated by basic commodities that effectively form the 'final' tendency. The average spending pattern both for Finnish and Polish second-home owners was common in this specific aspect, confirming the consumption-determinants analysis (from the previous chapter) suggesting that the significance of goods in their local spending (which varies considerably from 80% for Finns to 92% for Poles) was interestingly less dependent upon household income than on non-economic determinants, e.g. the distance from permanent to secondary residence, accessibility of local shops, and the owners' socio-demographics.

For services, the tendency was basically in line with the extended Engel's first law, known as the Engel-Schwabe-Wright law (Inglot-Brzęk 2010; Zalega 2012), which is based on the argumentation that as household income rises, the proportion of spending on food products decreases, while spending on various types of services increases (e.g. a decline in food purchasing in favour of an increased food consumption away from home). Furthermore, bearing in mind the prevalence (in monetary terms) of construction/renovation services and generally relatively higher costs for providing services than goods (especially those purchased at the second-home location), one can observe that the proportions for both populations surveyed confirmed that locally supplied services were luxuries, or at least normal goods that were highly influenced by household income.

High dependency upon household income was also partly confirmed by the income elasticity of demand, which amounted to 1 for Finns (unitary elasticity) and 1.02 for Poles. Hence, in assessing the role of second-home owners' spending patterns for the local economy, these patterns were apparently more beneficial for the service sector (particularly for construction companies but also for infrequent services such as catering, healthcare, recreational etc. – for which income elasticity among the Polish consumers even amounted to 5.0) than for goods suppliers, no matter what products they provide.

4.1.5 Dynamics of second-home owners' local consumption and satisfaction in light of the owner's life stage and the family life-cycle perspective

As presented in section 3.1.1, the consumer's age along with his/her family current life-cycle stage constitute a solid part of the research framework and a key-determinant vital to understand purchasing habits of the household as described by several variables, i.e. household size, its structure and household members' age. Such a powerful explanatory tool was employed for the analytical part of the study in order to learn more about changes in spending and home utilisation patterns as well as in users' satisfaction levels (utility function) over time. Since the survey does not provide data on consumer's satisfaction levels from the respondents' direct valuations, opinions and insights on this topic, this gap in the analysis was filled by referring to basic alternative indicators of the utility function, i.e. the length of stay at the cottage (number of nights spent), number of leisure activities undertaken on site and number of users – based on the data collected in the study. It was feasible to estimate spending level curves as well as changing commodity bundle charts by structuring the survey data according to the length of ownership, thus tracing expenditure and utilisation patterns as well as partial indicators of the consumers' satisfaction, starting from new (beginners) to more experienced owners. In addition, all the curves were fitted to the data by using the distance-weighted least squares method and, for the same reason (i.e. mainly to ignore extreme values), the observations were calculated for three-year means. This operation has made a curve smoother, more regular and clearly showing the trend line over time, thus making it easier to analyse and interpret. The new owners' initial costs of acquiring the property, based entirely on annual/recurrent local expenses, were excluded from this part of the analysis.

Figure 4.1.5.1 Finnish second-home owners: Changes in total spending over the ownership period

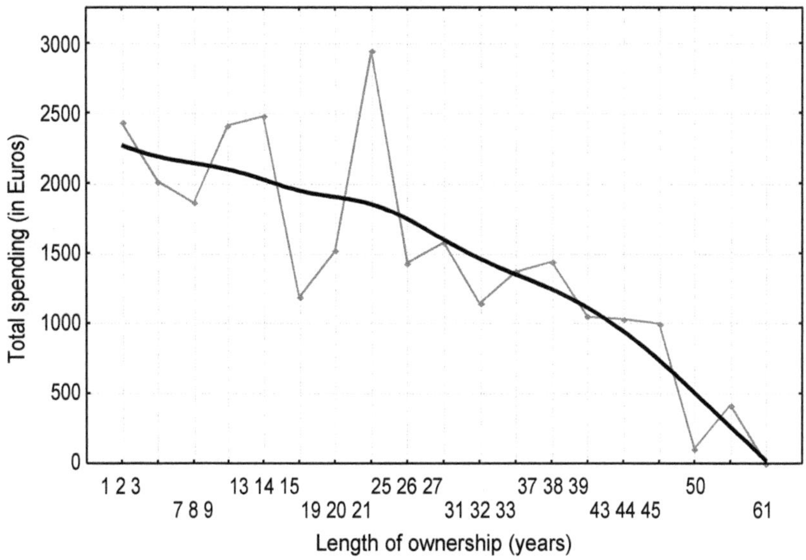

Source: Own study.

The trend line for the total spending by Finnish second-home owners' showed a more or less constant decrease, starting from the peak value for very new owners to no costs for the most experienced (in terms of the length of ownership) owners at the end period (Figure 4.1.5.1). Such a trajectory does not seem to be surprising when one takes into account a gradual reduction of the spending size not only due to the owner's growing age levels but mainly due to the family life-cycle that is a shift from a full-nest to an empty-nest family and consequently to a solitary survivor. Yet, one may assume that the most costly expenditures (on construction/renovation services and building materials) were incurred in the introductory stage and, to a significantly smaller extent, in the maturity stage of the second home ownership, which also reflects in the presented trend line.

This spending pattern was confirmed by the similar curve for construction/renovation services considered as a separate category, although the data revealed inputs falling down even more dynamically (Figure 4.1.5.2). Additionally, the curve for the total spending was also, albeit partly, proved by the trajectory for building-materials expenditure, as the trend line generally showed the decrease of spending over time. Unlike the tendency for construction/renovation services, it showed a climb to a second peak (after the highest one at the introductory stage) in approximately the 20th-25th year of ownership and then declined again. This kind of a bi-modal statistical distribution proved that after a certain period of use second homes need some improvements and modernisation. As it mainly concerns minor renovations that are not as serious as in the initial period, this work is often done by the owners (or with the help of their relatives, friends or neighbours), who supply the building materials, tools and machinery themselves.

Figure 4.1.5.2 Finnish second-home owners: Changes in spending on construction/renovation services over the ownership period

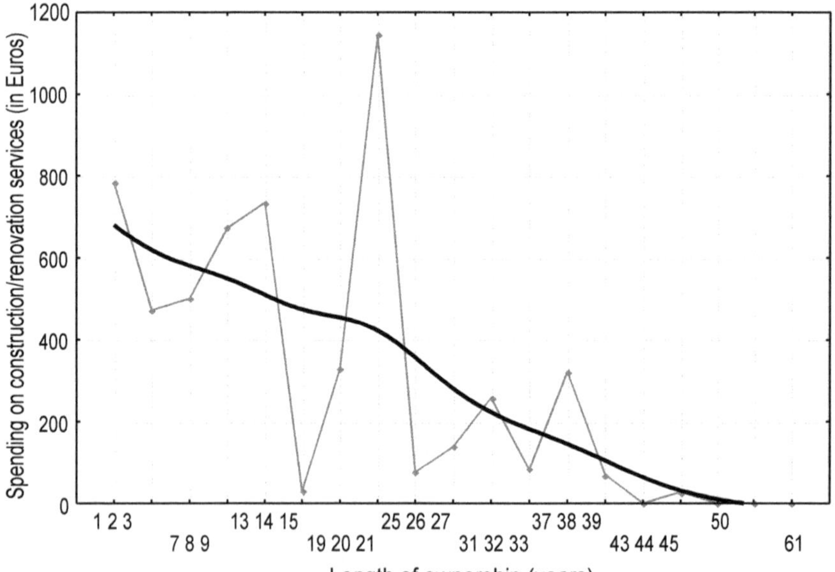

Source: Own study.

Interestingly, the costs for infrequent goods, services (e.g. catering, health care etc.), everyday-use articles and food products purchases were the highest at the introductory and growth stage of the second-home ownership, reflecting similarities to the total expenditure curve (Figure 4.1.5.3). However, with reference to the utilisation patterns (length of stay, number of users) that apart from the ways of spending time are more or less stable over the ownership, the trajectories for foodstuffs, infrequent goods and services are an effect of changing consumption patterns (due to the owner's age and family life-cycle) rather than of a changing duration and intensity of the second home usage.

Figure 4.1.5.3 Finnish second-home owners: Changes of spending on food products over the ownership period

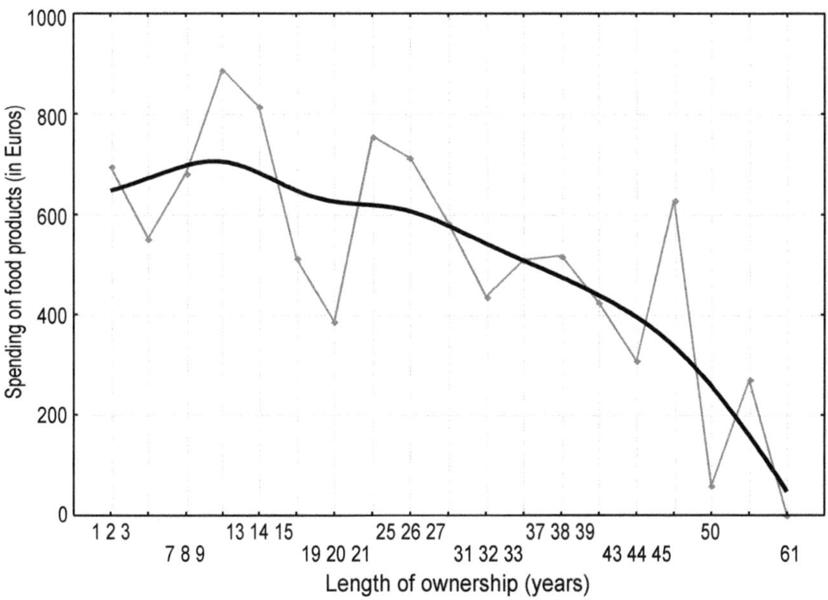

Source: Own study.

Thus, there was no shift in time, as expected. This tendency also shows that Finnish second-home owners started satisfying their leisure-related needs immediately and dynamically as soon as the property was purchased/inherited, but then they began to gradually lose interest, and, consequently, demand to spend time at the summer residence, in about the 20th year of ownership. Thus, in terms of the size of the demand for local goods and services, the first 15–20 years of ownership were particularly dynamic, intense and efficient for second-home owners' expenditure but also beneficial for the local economy. Then, the following periods showed a gradually declining financial input but, interestingly, not necessarily due to changing utility levels.

To better understand such relationships, it is necessary to switch to the consumer's utility function that here was approached through the length of stay. As mentioned earlier, the sample for Finnish respondents was dominated by pre-retired and retired people and by relatively small household size, usually with no children. Hence, these socio-demographic attributes are crucial to explain the spending trajectories for the abovementioned group of owners even though the utilisation patterns, namely the length of stay over the year and the number of users (including individuals from outside of the household surveyed), were favourable, with a clearly growing tendency for the duration of stay (Figure 4.1.5.4), or at least a stable trend line for the intensity of usage (in terms of the number of people visiting the home).

Figure 4.1.5.4 Finnish second-home owners: Changes in time spent at second home over the ownership period (a utility function)

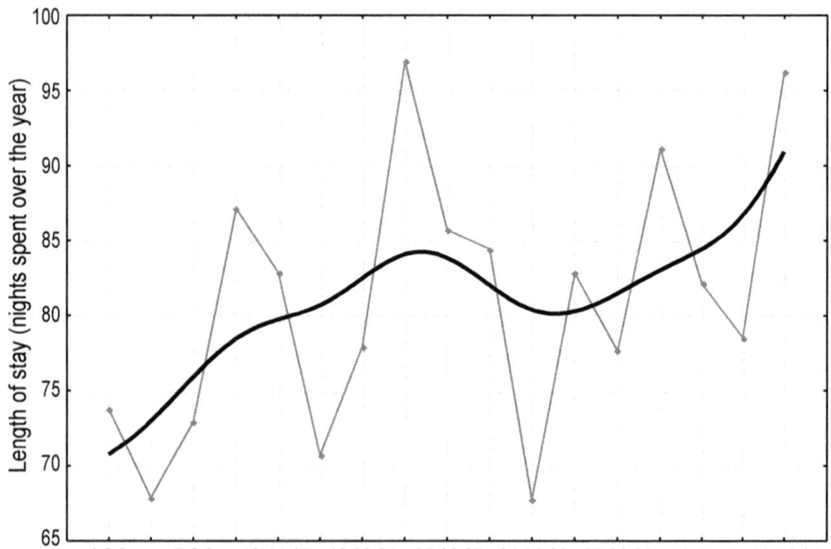

Source: Own study.

For Polish second-home owners, the total expenditure chart showed a slightly different trajectory (Figure 4.1.5.5) compared to the one for Finnish cottagers.

There was a bi-modal distribution with the peak expenditures just at the beginning of the cycle, when most costly purchases (construction works, home equipment and accessories) are usually made. Then, a second, albeit a more moderate, peak occurred some 30 years after the holiday residence was bought/inherited, while further expenditures then gradually decreased. It can be further explained by a reference to the particular types of goods and services purchased by Polish respondents. The highest peak reflects the influence of expenditure for building materials and construction/renovation services, which are always prevalent and excessive in the introductory stage. Then, the curve sloped down quite quickly, mainly due to a declining need for building materials.

Figure 4.1.5.5 Polish second-home owners: Changes in total spending over the ownership period

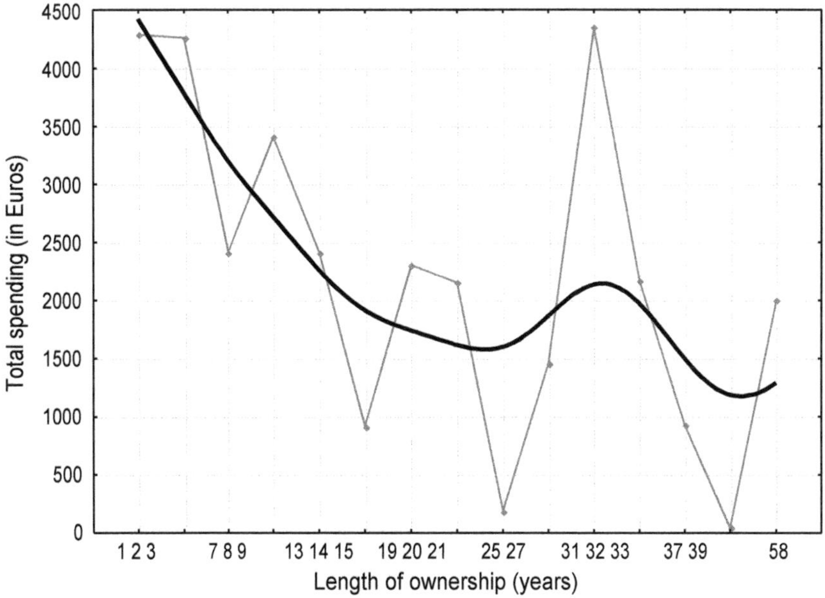

Source: Own study.

Furthermore, the expenditures on food products, everyday articles, maintenance and infrequent services remained stable for almost the entire period, although declining noticeably for the last 12 years of ownership (Figure 4.1.5.6). For each of these items, there was a second peak, approximately in 30th year of ownership, which in the case of Poles can be explained by the overlapping of the end of the owner's working life and the beginning of the retirement (seeing that the Polish respondents were relatively young, with the clear prevalence of the owners in working age, unlike their Finnish counterparts, the majority of whom were in retirement and pre-retirement age), which gives a greater opportunity to spend more time and, consequently, allocate more money to expenditures associated with a secondary residence in the long-term perspective.

Figure 4.1.5.6 Polish second-home owners: Changes in spending on maintenance services over the ownership period

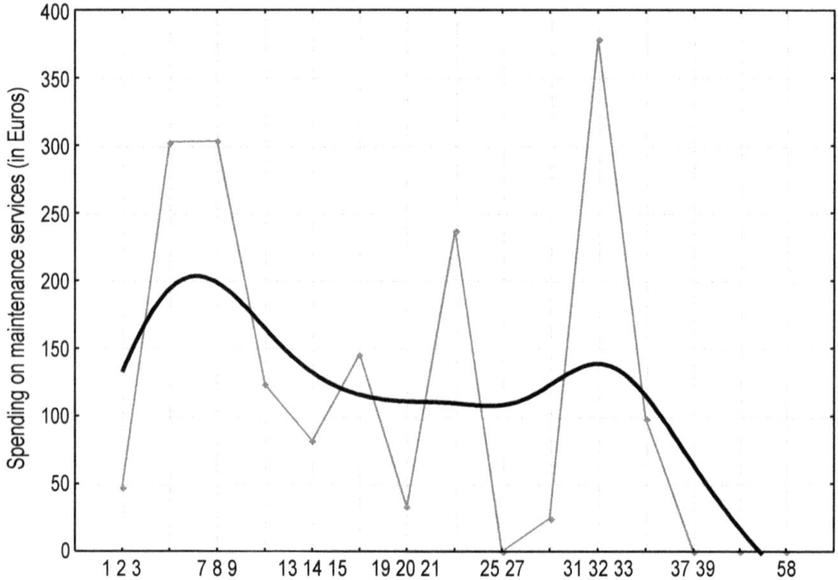

Source: Own study.

Such an opportunity was confirmed by alternative indicators of the utility function: for the Polish respondents, they were the length of stay and the number of leisure activities (Figure 4.1.5.7). These indicators showed a time lag in terms of benefits in that Polish second-home owners do not take the full advantage of investments (occurring at the beginning of the ownership) until the maturity stage, meaning until the owner's retirement. They clearly showed a quite stable and growing demand for actively spending time at the holiday home over the first two stages and then an increase in the maturity stage. It seemed that in this specific aspect, Polish second-home owners, apart from being less efficient in terms of the average flow of financial resources, contributed to the local economy in a very unbalanced manner (through a rapid and considerable decrease in spending, although slightly mitigated, by the second peak of spending in the maturity stage), which can be seen as highly inefficient for the long-term development. Hence, one could argue that Polish second-home owners acted positively mainly for the short-term economic growth, while their Finnish counterparts were more engaged in favour of the middle- and long-term economic and community's development growth as they used their cottages more efficiently, even though their demographic attributes (the owner's age and family life-cycle stage) were definitely more disadvantageous in terms of consumption.

Figure 4.1.5.7 Polish second-home owners: Changes in time spent at second home over the ownership period (a utility function)

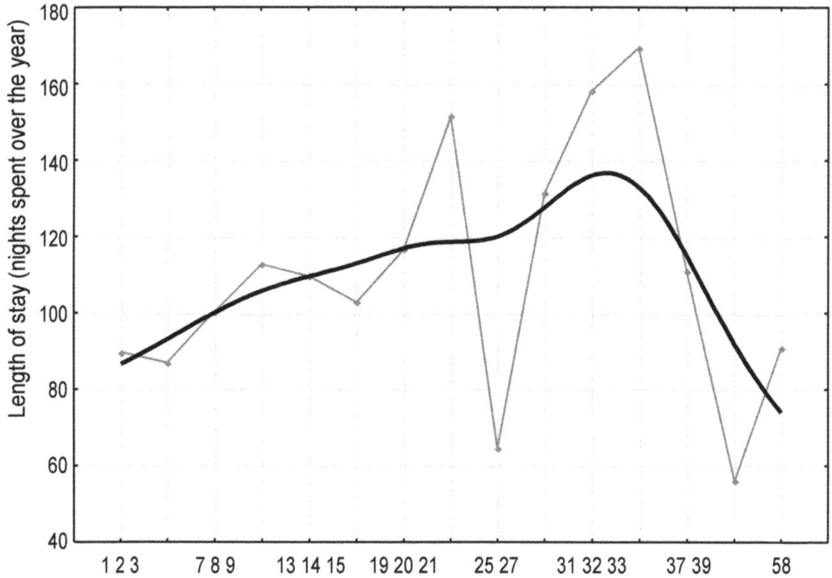

Source: Own study.

Furthermore, seeing how the level of second-home owner's spending changes over time, it is necessary to examine whether and how this change manifests itself in the changing structure of the commodity bundle. Such an analysis may be of help in projecting the dynamics of potential contributions and benefits for local industries, resulting from second-home owners' demand for goods and services. After comparing changes in consumption patterns for Finns and Poles (see Figures 4.1.5.8 & 4.1.5.9), the results clearly showed, respectively, a high and low diversity in the second-home owners' commodity bundle.

Figure 4.1.5.8 Finnish second-home owners: Changes in commodity bundle over the ownership period, %

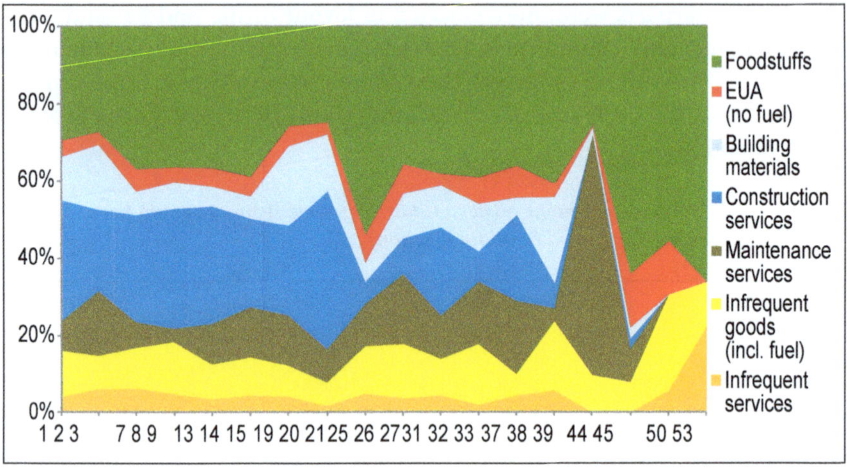

Source: Own study.

Although the amount of local purchases was changing constantly in Finns' case, there was a high level of diversification in the structure over almost the entire ownership period. Obviously, the proportion of construction/renovation services and building materials decreased with time, whereas the proportion of everyday articles, maintenance services, infrequent goods and services remained more or less stable. The proportion of food purchases increased but even in the final period the commodity bundle remained differentiated. The diversification of the commodity bundle is an unquestionable advantage for the local businesses, since differentiation largely contributes to multifunctional development, and thus the community's economy becomes stronger and more resilient. In this sense, the potential impact on the local economy is more sustainable and long-term, as it helps to diversify monofunctional structures that are more vulnerable to external forces. It was very different for Polish second-home owners, although the same tendencies in various local goods and services provision were observed.

Figure 4.1.5.9 Polish second-home owners: Changes in commodity bundle over the ownership period, %

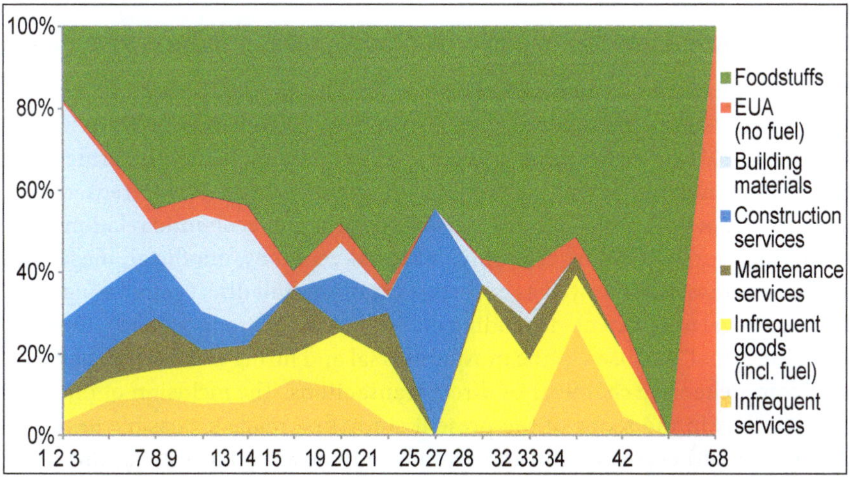

Source: Own study.

In this case, the commodity bundle loses its initial diversity (from the introductory stage) and in a relatively short time becomes monofunctional, comprising solely basic commodities – food products and everyday articles. This lack of diversity can be seen as a serious disadvantage for the local industries, as seeing that Polish respondents were probably using their secondary residence efficiently, most consumers supplied themselves with goods and services (especially highly advanced ones) from outside the locality. Thus, besides the impact of second-home owners' consumption on the local economy being grossly insufficient due to the short-lasting effects, it also did not generate a sufficiently diverse demand for local products, apart from basic commodities. Their positive influence on local businesses was therefore very narrow in functional terms, with detrimental effects for the local economy as well as for the community's retail supply. To sum up, the two first stages ('introduction' and 'growth') were particularly beneficial for the construction/renovation sector and building-materials retailers. In the maturity phase, food products and infrequent goods retailers as well as maintenance and infrequent services providers took a major share of the second-home market supply, although construction services and building-material supply gained growing benefits (due to necessary renovations) after a certain period of insignificance. In the decline phase, the retailing of food and everyday articles predominated, as consumer needs and spending patterns became simpler, although due to ageing and the resulting health issues, the role of maintenance and infrequent services (i.e. healthcare) increased slightly.

4.1.6 Informal purchasing: preconditions, scale, products and effects

After recognising how important informal purchasing could be both for second-home owners and rural communities (Losby *et al.* 2002; Ratner 2000; Heffner & Czarnecki 2015), a separate sub-category of direct transactions with farmers and other local individuals was included in the questionnaire. These transactions, in fact, comprise a broad and heterogeneous group of economic relationships, including 'purely' shadow economy, informal economy, unofficial, illegal and untaxed transactions as well as exchange economy and direct purchasing from farmers (legal to an extent, depending on the volume of products sold). Thus, the term 'informal' was used as the most universal and fitting to describe the broad and comprehensive character of direct transactions. The inclusion of informal transactions in the scope of the present study first made it possible to record specific (often) neglected consumer practices whose significance, as this study showed, was considerable and whose contribution to the local/rural economy had so far been underestimated and therefore underrated. Second, along with the formal business transactions, the inclusion of informal transactions provided solid grounds for a more complex approach to economic relationships between second-home owners and locals (by measuring the scale, economic value and identifying supply structure), and therefore allowed to gain insights into the actual impact of second homes on the local economy. In addition, attention was also paid to non-economic preconditions of the informal channels of distribution, often dependent on the high trust and confidence between players involved as well as strong social ties and local embeddedness. In a broader sense, these attributes are crucial not only for local economic development but also, in a more indirect way, for strong, vital, sustaining and liveable rural communities to overcome negative socio-demographic processes as the main threats to their continuity.

Second-home owners quite often made use of informal distribution channels for local goods and services – this was the case for 73% of Finnish and 47% of Polish respondents (though in fact, the proportions were slightly higher, 78% and 54% respectively, when those reporting informal purchasing but not indicating the amount of money spent are included) (see Table 4.1.6.1). Such expenditures totalled €271,205 among Finns, ranging individually from €4 to €25,650, with the average value of €802 per buyer (the median value was €300) and, for Poles, PLN 438,561 (€105,423), varying from PLN 1 to PLN 52,750 (€0.2 to €12,680), with the mean value of PLN 2,333 (€561) and the median of PLN 500 (€120) per one Polish respondent.

Table 4.1.6.1 Basic data for local informal purchases of Finnish and Polish second-home owners

		Total	**Agricultural produce and raw materials**	**Construction & renovation services**	**Maintenance services**
Finnish second-home owners	No. of purchasers	338	269	91	194
	Share of total purchasers	72.4%	57.6%	19.5%	41.5%
	Amount of spending (in €)	271,205	69,914	151,210	50,081
	Share in informal commodity bundle	100.0%	25.8%	55.8%	18.4%
	Share in each of categories	19.1%	7.9%	46.7%	33.3%
	Average per purchaser (in €)	802	260	1,662	258
	Median per purchaser (in €)	300	150	350	120
Polish second-home owners	No. of purchasers	188	151	38	69
	Share of total purchasers	47.2%	37.9%	9.5%	17.3%
	Amount of spending (in PLN)	438,561	77,571	250,400	110,590
	Share in informal commodity bundle	100.0%	17,7%	57.1%	25.2%
	Share in each category	20.1%	7.3%	95.4%	93.9%
	Average per purchaser (in PLN)	2,333	514	6,590	1,603
	Median per purchaser (in PLN)	500	200	2,500	600

Source: Own study.

Regardless of the evident popularity of informal distribution channels in both populations surveyed, it is argued that, in fact, individually, these channels were more or less important but still only a supplement or, in some situations, a substitute for traditional supply chains, i.e. provided by businesses. In confirmation of this pattern, there were no respondents entirely targeted towards informal distribution channels – among the Finnish buyers, 21% used traditional channels and the rest both forms of provision, while in Poland the proportions were 46% and 64% respectively. In terms of expenditure, informal local purchasing accounted for a similar share of the total local spending for both populations surveyed, i.e. 19%-20%. This relatively small proportion compared to the percentage of players involved in informal transactions shows that either a modest volume of goods and services is purchased in this way, or rather, given the specificity of such goods, that they are of a relatively low value/price in relation to products provided by businesses. Thus, one can argue that informal purchasing is popular or almost common (at least among Finns), although its value and 'purely' economic importance for the rural households is apparently too low to be considered as a main or sole source of income. However, despite its economic/income insignificance, it has other functions that are important in establishing, retaining and strengthening of social relations, and thus building community confidence and contributing to the sense of community. Furthermore, informal distribution channels are more likely to be long-lasting and promising as they are based on trust and strong social contacts. Additionally, direct/informal purchase is a 'pure', bottom-up and spontaneous manifestation of short supply chains between the producer and the consumer, which is particularly desirable as it does not drain the local financial resources, since, at least formally, second-home owners are officially based outside the community. What is more, although informal transactions are of relatively limited economic significance, the simple offer within informal channels of distribution comprised basic unprocessed commodities (raw materials and agricultural produce), and simple services may be a valuable support for the less privileged: unemployed, unskilled, less educated, low-earners, retired and even disabled people (certainly depending on the degree of disability and type of work they provide).

The composition of products and services acquired informally was much less differentiated than the commodity bundle provided by businesses, as for goods it was often limited to unprocessed agricultural produce, and for services to construction, renovation and maintenance work. Other products, usually basic construction materials, e.g. stones, gravel, sand and wood as well as soil, organic fertilisers, plant seedlings, seeds and firewood were already of minor importance.

Most of the food products purchased locally through informal channels were unprocessed agricultural produce, usually provided to second-home owners directly by farmers or other individuals who officially were not farmers and who had a piece of land or home garden and could thus produce and sell basic commodities. In fact, foodstuffs purchased can be categorised into several types: first, those including raw products provided by the farm/garden – vegetables, fruit, meat and honey; second, mixed (processed or unprocessed, taken altogether) – dairy products (milk, eggs and cheese); third, processed – bread (homemade); and fourth, those first collected by sellers in the wild – berries, mushrooms (fresh and dried), fish and others.

The informal purchases of food products were popular among the respondents as they were made by 57.6% of Finnish and 37.9% of Polish respondents. The scale of informal transactions would be even larger if those who did not mention the amount of money spent were taken into account, i.e. 64% and 43%, respectively. In total, Finns spent €69,914 in sums ranging individually from €6 to €4,000, with the mean value of €260 per buyer. For Poles, these values were as follows: total PLN 77,571 (€18,647); individual minimum and maximum PLN 1 and PLN 5,000 (€0.24 and €1,201); average purchase – PLN 514 (€124). It should be noted that among Finnish second-home owners, the majority of buyers combined formal and informal distribution channels (97%). Thus, it seems that informal transactions were a stable, important but supplementary provision with basic commodities from local retail outlets. In contrast, most Polish respondents (58%) bought their food from local stores, while the rest used mixed channels. As a result, the proportion of informal purchases in the total spending on food products was relatively low – 7.9% for Finns and 7.3% for their Polish counterparts. This is not surprising, given the low prices of unprocessed agricultural produce, usually a small volume of goods and mostly incidental purchases. The median value of spending (€150 and PLN 200 (€48) respectively) also confirmed that individual expenditures (on average value per buyer) are relatively low in both cases and significantly well below the average spending.

Figure 4.1.6.1 Factors behind Finnish second-home owners' informal purchasing of food products

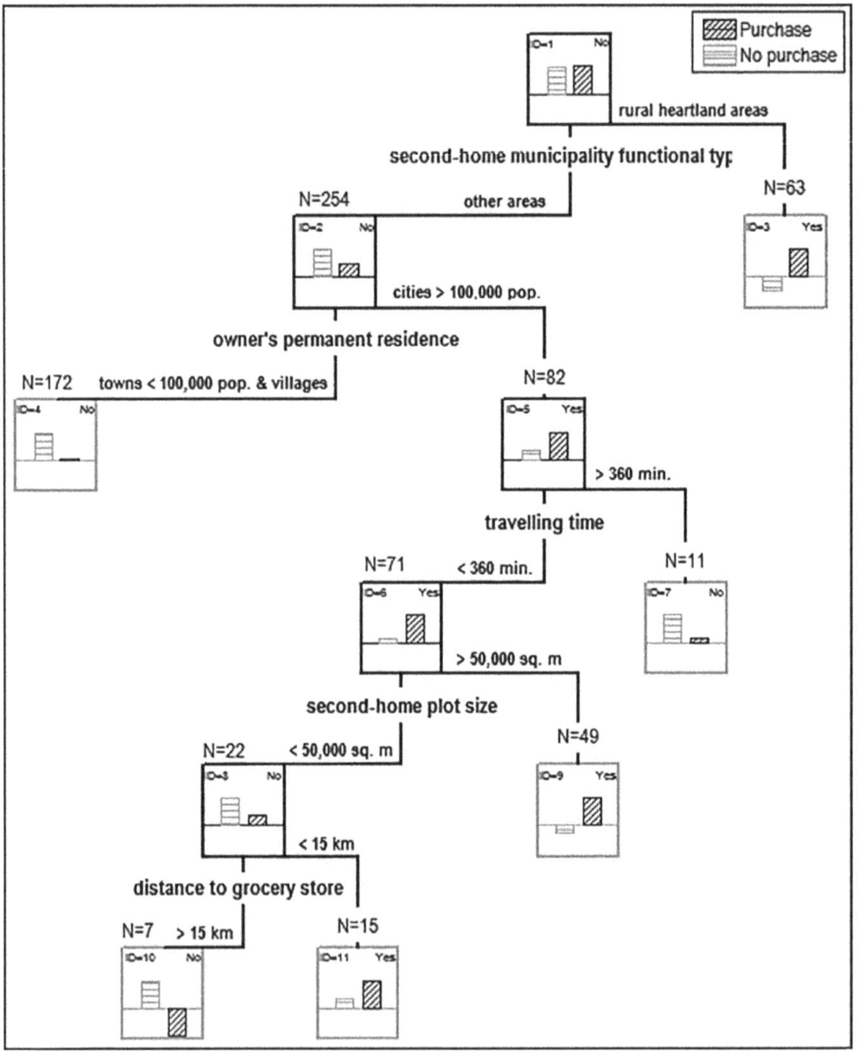

Source: Own study.

When one considers factors and preconditions influencing the informal purchasing of food products, first the functional character of a community/municipality, and consequently equipment in business entities (here: grocery stores) should be mentioned (see Figures 4.1.6.1 & 4.1.6.2). What was common for both populations was that the consumption pattern with strong informal purchasing was far more frequently demonstrated when the economic structure of the municipality (location of the second home) had a highly developed or predominant agricultural sector, which additionally often means more remote and underdeveloped areas. In such communities, as a rule, the level of retail and service infrastructure is relatively poor, so accessibility is very weak. Such specific circumstances successfully induced a shift in supply from remote grocers to much more accessible local farmers, whose offer becomes a natural alternative for meeting basic needs, at least those that can be satisfied by agricultural produce. Thus, a certain, albeit seasonal, market niche opened up to local farmers. This obviously happened more often in traditional agricultural communities with numerous farms, i.e. many potential sources of supply, although, as mentioned above, the provision was also partly from other individuals (non-farmers).

Figure 4.1.6.2 Factors behind Polish second-home owners' informal purchasing of food products

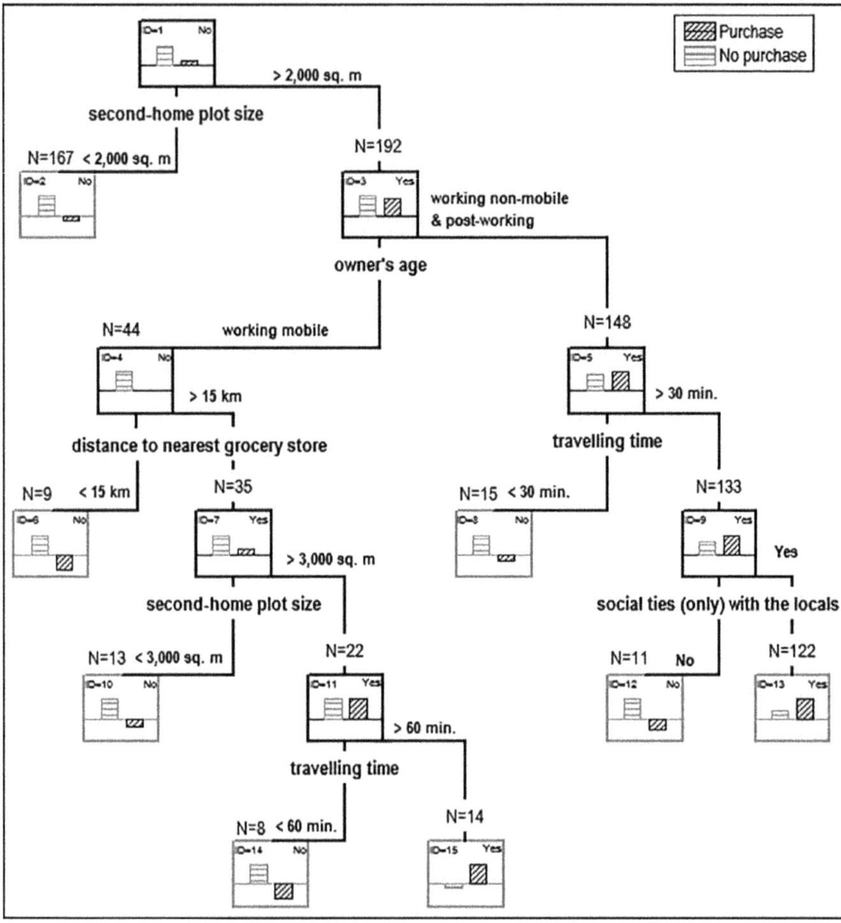

Source: Own study.

Second, the respondents' demographics were an important explanatory factor behind the informal purchasing of foodstuffs. For Finns, it was mainly residents of cities (over 100,000 inhabitants), women, and, interestingly, members of wealthy and very wealthy households. On the other hand, in the case of Poles, the predominant group comprised people of working non-mobile age (45–64 years), the retired and those on low or very low incomes. One may argue, therefore, that for the Finnish respondents such a mode of purchasing was rather a reasonable solution to limited accessibility as well as it probably reflected an inclination towards organic/'natural' food products available directly from farmers or a lifestyle, nutritional habits and preferences in general. Meanwhile, for Poles, informal purchasing was an attempt to tackle limited accessibility but also a solution to rationalising the household budget through the local availability of cheap products (compared to grocers and supermarkets). However, further interpretations regarding fresh, natural products provision may also be logical. Third, the short distance to the permanent home was significant, which, as a universal rule influencing local purchasing regardless of the channels used, limited interest in informally provided food products closer to hand. Fourth, the size of the property negatively influenced informal food purchases, with owners of larger secondary residences being more likely to be self-sufficient through small-scale farming.

Construction/renovation services were important constituents of the informal local supply. However, as opposed to informal food products, here, construction/renovation work by individuals was definitely provided illegally, outside the registration and tax system, and probably not meeting working conditions standards. In light of the research results, these services were used by 19.5% of Finnish and 9.5% of Polish second-home owners, and due to the a number of newly established second homes (within the survey sample), it can be assumed that most were renovation/modernisation services of various scales, as well as technical and organisational requirements, as confirmed by the costs reported in the questionnaire. The Finns surveyed often used construction/renovation services combining different channels of distribution (66% of respondents), which confirmed their complementarity. Given the specificity of the construction work (appropriate skills, knowledge, experience but also physical strength when it comes to heavy work), it is likely that when provided by enterprises, such services involved more sophisticated/advanced work and when provided by individuals, (informally) it was for minor, less complex renovation work. In contrast, the vast majority of Polish respondents (97%) used only informal construction/renovation services. However, besides this distribution channel being popular among Polish second-home owners, this proportion may to some extent have a methodological explanation, as there was no separate category for formal construction/renovation services but only an informal one.

With this in mind, the proportion of informal construction/renovation services in the total expenditure on such purposes was 46.7% for Finnish and 95.4% for Polish respondents (47% and 95%). In total, Finns spent €151,210, with the individual values ranging from €20 to €25,000 and the average value of €1,662 per buyer, while for Poles, it was PLN 250,400 (€60,192), ranging from PLN 200 to PLN 40,000 (from €48 to €9,615), with the average value of PLN 6,590 (€1,584). The relatively low median value (€350 and PLN 2,500 (€601) respectively), together with very low extreme values, seemed to confirm the prevalence of renovation over construction work.

The main factor influencing the consumption pattern of informal provision with construction/renovation services was household income (see Figures 4.1.6.3 & 4.1.6.4). At first glance, one might expect low-earners (low-income households) to be the main customers of informal channels in this case (no taxation – work offered at lower cost); however, it turned out that the highest demand was among wealthy and very wealthy households, which was confirmed for both populations. At the same time, the less well-off households do not carry out such work, or do it rarely/irregularly by using informal channels or even do it themselves, unless they lack time, skills or necessary knowledge. But what are the determinants for the use of illegal renovation services by wealthy and often well-educated respondents?

Figure 4.1.6.3 Factors behind Finnish second-home owners' informal purchasing of construction/renovation services

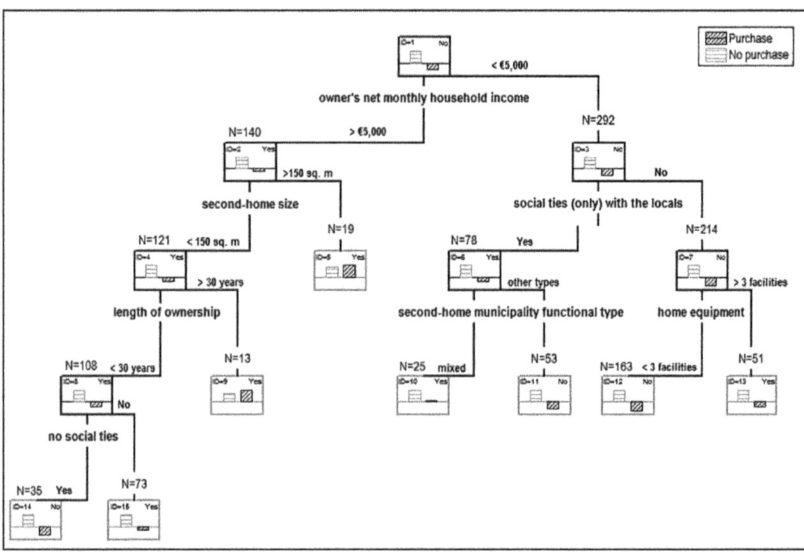

Source: Own study.

As a rule, in the case of informal purchasing, strong social linkages must exist with the locals that enhance confidence between partners needed to find trustworthy and competitive contractors. The home size and furnishings were also important, as an increase in the use of such services was observed with the larger and better standard equipment (kitchen, bathroom, toilet, garage etc.). An additional explanation for Finns was the length of ownership, as with time and more frequent use, some necessary repairs/renovations and modernisations are needed. This was also reflected in the respondent's age, since there was a greater demand for such renovation work among retired second-home owners than among the younger generation. In addition, the Polish respondents used informal renovation work more frequently in smaller and less-urbanised communities, which as such have less access to anything more advanced than basic services. As was the case with food provision, here, too, individuals took advantage of a gap in the supply of construction/renovation services on the part of the formal business sector.

Figure 4.1.6.4 Factors behind Polish second-home owners' informal purchasing of construction/renovation services

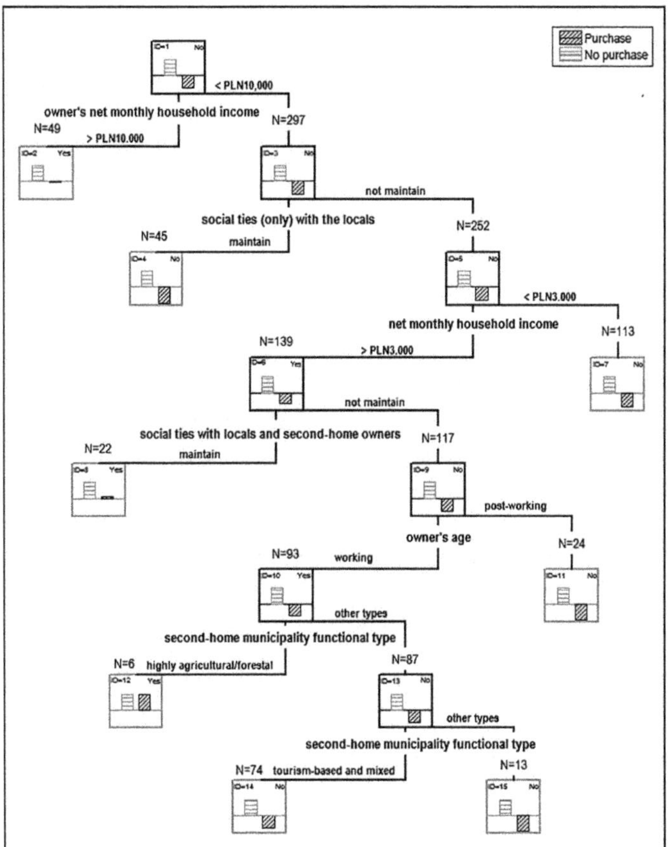

Source: Own study.

Besides food products and construction/renovation services, another category of products often purchased through informal channels was maintenance work. This category covered some basic work done at home, in the back yard or garden/forest (within the property boundaries), i.e. in particular, minor repairs and maintenance work such as cleaning up, lawn-mowing, snow-ploughing, home surveillance/security as well as chopping firewood and felling trees. In general, with some minor exceptions, these include relatively low-cost and simple services, and at the same time not demanding in terms of skills, proper qualifications or high financial input efforts. Typically, they constitute the core and traditional feature of services which locals provide to second-home owners, even, or perhaps especially outside the peak season, when the owners are absent. Obviously, the construction/renovation and maintenance services sometimes have much in common, and hence, may be hard to distinguish for respondents. The main idea was to consider the work done once or very rarely separately from the work of a recurrent nature. However, it seems that more serious and technologically advanced work was classified in the former category while that of a minor, relatively simple character was put in the latter group.

The use of local informal maintenance services was declared by 41.5% of Finnish and 17.3% of Polish respondents (or 19% for the latter group if one takes into account those who did not indicate the amount of money paid). Finnish second-home owners allocated a total of €50,081 for this purpose, with individual expenditure ranging from €4 to €2,900, with the average of €258 per buyer. Spending by their Polish counterparts was considerably lower, with a total of PLN 110,590 (€26,584), while individually it ranged from PLN 40 to PLN 20,000 (€10 to €4,808), with the average of PLN 1,603 (€385). The mean values were obviously lower than in the case of informal construction/renovation services, mainly due to the relatively low prices reflecting the less complex character of work.

It is worth noting that the representatives of both populations surveyed never entirely relied on informal provision of maintenance services, but usually combined the two forms of local supply, which was more evident among Poles (90%) than among Finns (60%). For the Finnish respondents, given the popularity of the second-home phenomenon reflected in spatial terms through vast areas of concentrations of holiday homes, an interest in engaging unregistered individuals was significantly lower. This is because the best part of demand is often satisfied by the so-called *mökkitalkkari* – usually a one-man company (officially registered as a business entity) – from the local community, which supplies the necessary minor renovation and maintenance work on second homes (also outside the summer season). This business entity is particularly popular in localities with a large number of summer cottages, so the activity is economically justified as it does not respond to marginal/singular needs.

However, the role of informal distribution channels in supplying second-home owners with maintenance work can be seen differently with regard to its share in the total expenditure on such services. Here, the proportion was 33% for Finnish consumers and 89% for their Polish counterparts – on the one hand, a sign of the dominance of the formal sector for Finns, and on the other reflecting the marginal role of traditional forms of distribution for Poles. For the latter group, the main supplier for cleaning up, cutting the grass, snow-ploughing and security services has for decades traditionally been local residents. In this context, a relatively low percentage of Poles using informal services proved that the majority of maintenance work was not outsourced to anyone (outside), but more likely carried out by the owners themselves. At the same time, this low figure for the expenditure by the Polish respondents on maintenance work can be assumed as having to be paid by second-home owners in special cases (specific work) requiring the appropriate technology and equipment, and therefore usually provided by qualified companies, or in some locations (seaside resorts with secondary residences in the form of apartments or flats) in which such services are comprehensively provided (based on collective agreements) by authorised companies.

The consumption pattern of informally provided maintenance services was shaped largely by the same factors as those determining the use of such work carried out by companies. Hence, first the length of stay (based on the number of nights spent at a second home), the spread of stay over the survey period and the number of visits should be mentioned. The use of maintenance services increases with the total length of stay and, interestingly, it also increases with a growing frequency/regularity of visits (spread widely over the year). It, therefore, turns out that a one-time stay (e.g. part of the summer vacations) is a critical precondition revealing the highest demand for home care/security services during the owner's absence. A longer presence, on the other hand (e.g. longer than summer holiday), and/or frequent regular visits outside the season, create the conditions for the demand for various maintenance services, since users visiting their second home want to spend time comfortably but do not always have the inclination or skills to perform the work themselves.

Household income plays an important role in the purchase of informal maintenance services, as was proved by the large demand for them by very wealthy and wealthy consumers (1st and 2nd quintiles), although, as mentioned above, such work is not expensive in comparison to construction/renovation services or to maintenance services provided by companies. It was evident that there was little need for such work among less well-off households, as they often did it themselves. This is more likely to happen as for many second-home owners various types of house and garden work are the most common ways of spending time at the cottage.

Supplementary data were collected in order to achieve a greater degree of comparability between the respective Polish and Finnish data sets concerning second-home owners' motivations towards informal channels of distribution and their reasons for non-purchasing. Even though the data pertain to non-usage, it provided some additional information that is important in understanding these specific consumption patterns with a strong inclination to prefer individuals rather than businesses. The research outcomes showed that for the Finnish respondents the main obstacle was that they did most of the work on the house (including small repairs and renovations), the garden and the forest themselves (see Figures 4.1.6.5 and 4.1.6.6). Thus, despite the question being concerned with informal purchasing of goods and services (altogether), in the respondents' answers and opinions, the emphasis was apparently on the latter group. As mentioned above, this relatively simple work, not requiring a significant financial effort, was among the most popular leisure activities undertaken when spending time at the cottage in both populations surveyed.

Figure 4.1.6.5 Finnish second-home owners: Reasons for not using local informal channels of distribution, %

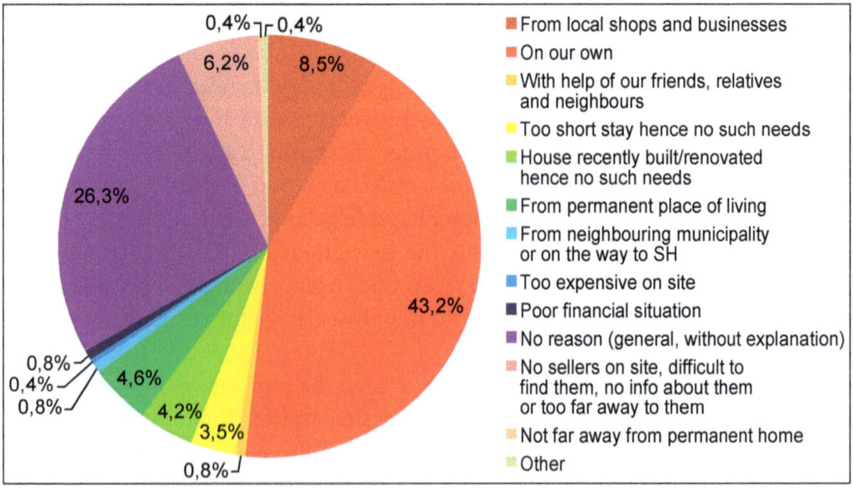

Source: Own study

'No such need' as a very general expression was a very common barrier to the respondents' using informal channels – 26% for Finns and 46% for Poles. However, such a response could not be considered satisfactory, as it did not identify any underlying or specific argument for non-usage. It was too broad and could include many different underlying reasons, which could be classified in any one of the categories provided: e.g. too short a stay, provision at the permanent residence etc.

Furthermore, a preference towards purchases from shops and companies (formal purchasing) was important in negatively influencing the demand for informal channels of distribution, and resulting, in fact, from various underlying reasons which were mostly a subject of speculation, such as too modest an offer of food products on the part of local farms and individuals, low hygiene standards, 'tax honesty', tax relief in the case of purchasing official services, e.g. in the construction sector, etc.

Figure 4.1.6.6 Polish second-home owners: Reasons for not using local informal channels of distribution, %

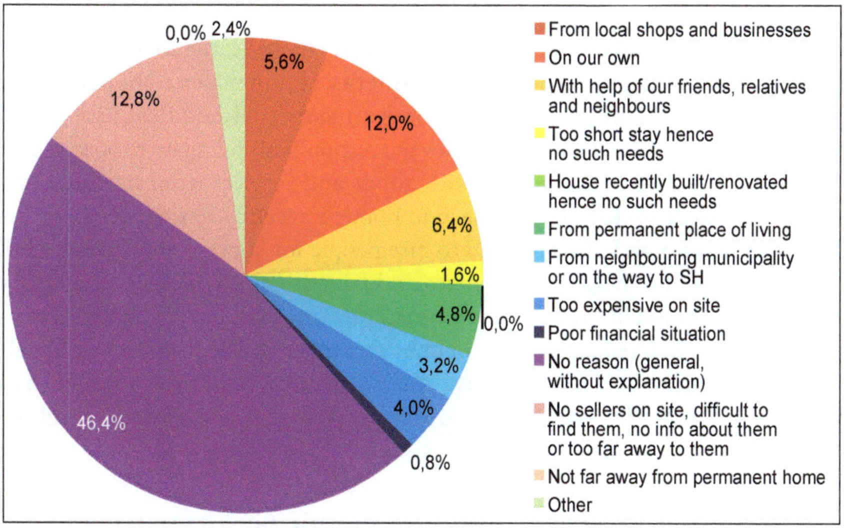

Source: Own study

The opportunity to use informal distribution channels was also generated by the easy access to goods and service providers, and thus, access limitations were highlighted as important obstacles, i.e. 'lack of sellers or service providers on site', 'too far to access them' or 'lack of information on where to find them'/'hard to find them'. Such reasons were much more frequent among the Polish than Finnish respondents and usually, they were associated with the problem of 'no farmers in the village', which happened not only in heavily urbanised regions or tourist localities but also in depopulating areas with declining agriculture. The difficulty of finding sellers and service providers also indicates a certain asymmetry of information among second-home owners in favour of those with rural roots, originating from the second-home locality/community, with relatives still living in the area and those maintaining strong social ties with the locals. While in the case of informal services one can argue about their illegality, at the same time this has also an undoubtedly restrictive potential, limiting circulation of information about them due to lack of confidence, a desire to remain in the shadow economy etc. Those providing informal services do not usually advertise themselves through official channels (preferring word-of-mouth marketing), hence partly contributing to the information asymmetry among potential customers. However, for Finns, a limited access to informal and formal providers can cause real difficulties for some of second-home owners, especially in large-area municipalities in Lapland, where long distances and resulting frequent travelling can be seen as a real burden in using local services.

Among other reasons for not using informal channels, the following should be noted: disadvantageous consumption patterns, i.e. purchases at the permanent place of residence and the import of goods (mainly commodities) to a second home, which is particularly common for the respondents living up to 50 km from a secondary residence; the supply with goods and services from neighbouring municipalities or on the way to a second home; a recently renovated house, resulting in no or a very limited need to hire people for construction/repair work (mostly Finns); the help from relatives and friends (mostly Poles), which may suggest both the aid in the delivery of agricultural produce by neighbouring relatives and friends (farmers), or the help in carrying out the construction/repair and maintenance work; too expensive goods and services (mostly Poles) offered locally and informally, which is somewhat surprising if one bears in mind the lower production costs (excluding taxes, etc.).

4.2 Second-home owner's local economic performance: impact assessment

In order to assess the role of visitors' spending in local economic development, a two-angle approach was applied. First, the local people's viewpoint was considered, according to evidence-based revenues as well as opinions formulated by local suppliers (businesses and individuals). It used local peoples' earnings from providing goods and services to second-home owners and total household incomes as a reference basis to assess the importance of second-home owners' economic contribution. Next, the second-home owners' perspective was adopted, including the evidence-based commodity bundle and the amount of annual, recurrent expenditure on site (excluding one-time expenses such as purchasing a property/land as well as payments for current, home-related bills, i.e. electricity, water supply, wastewater disposal, gas supply and heating, property tax and home insurance).

The rationale for such a combined approach lies in survey and official data limitations as well as reliability constraints resulting from: 1. local people's wrongly addressed mistrust reflected in the common reluctance to respond to survey questions or in untrue answers and unreliable figures, particularly those associated with sales and earnings, and consequently 2. the underestimation of revenues from sales of products and services to second-home owners and underrating the contribution of such revenues to household income, as well as 3. the expression of local people's household incomes on an ordinal scale (in categories) instead of numerical data (i.e. here with no precise income given). Since a considerable proportion of second-home owners in both countries surveyed (73% in Finland and 47% in Poland) used informal distribution channels, i.e. in many cases illegal transactions – mostly of services – the respondents' answers concerning selling things were apparently more difficult and less trustworthy. In light of this and in order to get a clearer, fuller and credible picture of how second-home tourism contributes to the community's economy (including informal economy), the solution was to combine these two perspectives (and in fact two data sets – on expenditures and earnings) so that it would improve the interpretation and assessment opportunities.

The first step to approach the problem that is to measure the impact of second-home tourism on the local economy and then to assess its importance (in economic terms) for community residents (businesses and households), was to make basic calculations entirely grounded in the 'local people' dataset: i.e. based on the number of those declaring themselves as local suppliers, their proportion in the total number of locals surveyed, the revenues/earnings reported by locals as gained from supplying goods and services to second-home owners, and local supplier's (household) total income. As mentioned in section 2.5 'Methodology', in Poland, 392 local residents in the villages where second homes were located were interviewed, while in Finland only 156 local people returned the questionnaires in the postal survey (31.2% response rate).

4.2.1 Basic economic-impact multiplier

Local people's perspective

The proportions of locals selling goods and services to second-home owners were similar in both countries but relatively low (compared for instance to the proportion of second-home owners declaring local purchases), i.e. 19.2% in Finland and 17.0% in Poland. For the Finns, it was clearly more common to sell services (mainly construction/renovation and maintenance: 13.5%) while for their Polish counterparts it was goods (agricultural produce, i.e. raw or home-processed food products: 11.5%). Obviously, these figures can differ considerably from the actual situation, firstly because only a certain number of locals are actual suppliers, since not everyone has the potential and motive to provide people with goods and/or services, so in other words many consumers naturally supply themselves from a few local providers (grocers, construction companies etc.), and secondly, because these figures are more likely to be underrated as a result of the above-mentioned informal economy-related troublesome questions. Thirdly, it will be an underestimate owing to the barter economy – a quite common type of transaction in the countryside between locals and seasonal visitors (such as good-to-good, service-to-service, service-to-good), since these are not translated into monetary values.

As far as the revenues from providing second-home owners with goods and services are concerned, local residents in the municipalities surveyed in Finland admitted to earning a total of €276,482 (over the 12 months surveyed), of which the sales of services accounted for the vast majority, i.e. around 89%, while Poles declared the total earnings of PLN 266,681 (€64,106), where the sales of services similarly accounted for 92%. Individually, the total revenues (including goods and services) differed significantly, from €90 to €201,000 for Finnish locals, with the median value of €525, while for Poles it was far less extreme – from PLN 20 to PLN 60,000 (i.e. from €5 to €14,423) with the median of PLN 450 (€108). As the medians indicate, the majority of revenues in both populations were closer to the lower figure rather than the higher (see Table 4.2.1.1).

One may attempt to assess the importance of revenues from supplying second-home owners, which is in fact about measuring the proportion of the total annual household income gained from these services. Then, as mentioned above, the respondents were not willing to give exact figures on their total incomes and revenues/turnovers (except for those from supplying second-home owners), but they were encouraged to place their incomes among the income categories (five for Finns and four for Poles). Hence, it did not allow to measure the average proportion for the population surveyed but only within the subsequent income categories. In order to do this, the average value of the income for each income category was calculated as a baseline reference to measure the contribution.

Table 4.2.1.1 Sales and earnings of Finnish and Polish local people

	Finnish locals			**Polish locals**		
	Total	Goods	Services	Total	Goods	Services
No. of suppliers	31	16	22	69	46	33
Percentage of suppliers	19.9%	10.3%	14.1%	17.2%	11.5%	8.2%
Earnings (in € and PLN)	276,482	29,190	247,292	266,381	21,380	245,301
Average per supplier (in € and PLN)	8,919	1,824	11,241	3,861	465	7,433
Median per supplier (in € and PLN)	525	250	700	450	200	1,000

Source: Own study.

The research showed that for Finns approximately 86% of the total revenue from supplying second-home owners was earned by local residents in the second quintile, which could be described as wealthy households (with the net annual household income ranging from €60,000 to €120,000), even though this group was very small relative to the population surveyed (only four people). With this in mind, the contribution to the total income per capita was very high for services as well as for goods and services (considered as a unified category), i.e. 81.2% and 66.0% respectively. This means that these earnings were unusual compared not only to other income groups but also to the total income base. Apart from the most affluent household income group of Finns (incomes higher than €120,000), the contribution to local people's incomes varied widely, from moderate (approx. 25%) to very low (3.4%). The situation was slightly different for their Polish counterparts, for whom the revenues were more equally distributed among income categories, with the majority accounting for 36% for a relatively poor third quartile income group (PLN 18,000 to PLN 36,000), although here this group was the largest (32 people). Furthermore, the proportions of the total household income varied significantly, ranging from 3.8% for the wealthiest group to 16.7% for the moderately wealthy group, but being clearly higher for services than for goods.

Given the total declared earnings for supplying goods and services to second-home owners, this was in fact a direct economic impact, as the revenues reported were subject to tax, and the figures included turnover and labour costs. Since there was no data available that would permit an estimate of the indirect impacts by the economic multiplier, such effects were approached by using qualitative data, i.e. based on opinions and descriptive assessments of the potential resulting from second homes, both for supplying their owners with services and for broadly considered community development, e.g. a contribution to community infrastructure improvements.

As far as the direct effects are concerned, the poor quality of data due to the above-mentioned moderate response rate, the low number of locals admitting to selling goods/services and their reluctance to report the exact earnings only made it possible to make a broad-brush impact estimates. These were even more complicated and puzzling since for both populations (untaxed and unregistered) informal economy constituted an important element of their transactions and resulting income. The direct effects include employment, turnover and tax revenues (Scanlon, Sagor & Whitehead 2014); however, in this study, the data collected only made it possible to calculate the two latter components. No data were gathered on employment, business inputs, expenditure and net profits. Employment could only be approached by measuring how many jobs (full-time equivalent and seasonal, given the specificity of the second-home usage – three months during the summer season) could generate the total revenue after taxation based on the average labour cost per job (CSO 2013; Statistics Finland 2013).

For the Finnish suppliers, the total revenue from supplying goods and services to second-home owners – €276,482 – was the basis for further calculations. This turnover was subject to tax at the corporate tax rate of 24.5% at the time of the survey. Thus, the after-tax income would be €189,022. However, as mentioned earlier, some sales were made informally, i.e. goods and/or services were supplied not by local businesses (including farms) but by individuals working as hired workers or not working at all (retired and unemployed people). These earned €19,630 in total, which accounted for 7.1% of the total revenue from second-home owners. This amount has to be deducted from the base figure, which finally gives €256,850 as subject to tax, and subsequently gives €193,922 (after tax) and €17,629 per seller/entrepreneur. If one were to attempt to estimate the number of potential jobs generated by this revenue, it would be necessary to refer to average annual full-time labour costs per job, which stood at €50,600 (Statistics Finland 2012). Given that businesses incur costs other than labour, i.e. input expenditures and other organisational costs (for which there are no detailed data in this study), labour/employment costs usually accounted for 50%-70% depending on the industry (technological advances, duties etc). Since most services to second-home owners were in construction and relatively simple work such as minor renovations and maintenance, it can be assumed that labour costs made up 50% of the total turnover/revenue, which for Finland is €128,425. Breaking down this figure into jobs (taking €50,600 as the annual labour costs for one full-time equivalent job) gives 2.5 full-time equivalent jobs per year or 10.2 seasonal jobs, i.e. three-month full-time equivalent jobs (e.g. for the summer season). This means that supplying goods and services to second-home owners can be the main/only source of income for less than three permanent or ten seasonal workers. Given that there were eleven (registered) local sellers, i.e. business owners who gained this revenue, this means that second homes' contribution to the total income can be considered as only a marginal and at best as an additional/seasonal source of income. This is also reflected in (and reinforced by) the informal transactions between second-home owners and the locals who were paid workers or retired people, and whose main income was from salaries and pension benefits. For locals, selling products to second-home owners was just an additional income, not only due to their main formal source of income but also due to a relatively small amount earned (even though untaxed), which was insignificant with regard to the total household income categories.

For Polish local residents, the same calculation was made from the base amount earned, i.e. PLN 266,681 (€64,106). However, before tax, a large part of that figure (54.9%) was created from informal transactions accounting for PLN 144,970 (€34,849). This untaxed proportion gained by paid workers, retired, unemployed and even disabled people must be deducted from the total income, which in turn gives PLN 119,211 (€28,657) as subject to further taxation. After tax, it gives PLN 91,792 (€22,066) and PLN 3,991 (€959) per seller (entrepreneur/farmer). Considering the job-creation potential comprised by the total revenue, the gross income was reduced by 50% (to estimate the average labour costs as mentioned above) and then divided by the average full-time annual labour costs per job, which in Poland accounted for PLN 47,838 (€11,500) (CSO 2008). Thus, the entire net income could contribute only 1.2 full-time equivalent jobs per year or 5.0 seasonal jobs, i.e. three-months full-time equivalent jobs (e.g. for the summer season). With 23 business owners (including farmers), this impact can thus be regarded as insignificant. Here, for Polish respondents, the contribution to job-creation was largely limited by a very high proportion of informal transactions, which could only generate self-employment. Otherwise, if the total revenue (including from informal transactions) is counted, in both cases (Finns and Poles), the employment estimate will be similar, i.e., respectively, 2.7–2.8 full-time equivalent jobs per year and 10.9–11.1 seasonal jobs (three-month jobs). However, this does not change the marginal importance of income from supplying second-home owners as a job-creation opportunity.

Given the abovementioned data shortages, the broad-brush generalisation provided only a rough indication of the extrapolated number of potential local sellers and consequently, direct effects of second-home tourism on the local economy in the 40 municipalities/communities surveyed. This still focuses on local people's perspective and besides the annual revenue declared by the locals, it also includes the proportion of local sellers and the total number of households (household-dwelling units (CSO 2002; Statistics Finland 2013) in the territorial units surveyed.

For Finland, the number of household-dwelling units in the municipalities varied greatly (from 380 in Luhanka to 3,443 in Kemiönsaari), which was reflected in the subsequent estimates, with a total of 30,515 municipalities surveyed. Given this and other components of the proposed equation, there were 6,064 potential sellers (including the sales of goods and services altogether), ranging from zero in six municipalities to 991 in Savitaipale, while the potential earnings totalled €54,082,360 (of which 10.6% was generated from the sales of goods and 89.4% from the sales of services), ranging from zero in several municipalities to €22,454,100 in Hirvensalmi (Table 4.2.1.2). Further, under the assumption that 92.9% of total original revenue was taxable (obtained by registered enterprises and farms), when applied to potential earnings, this proportion would in effect give €37,933,097 after tax (24.5%). With the use of the same labour costs per year (€50,600) as in the original data from the survey (assuming 50% of the total costs dedicated to employment), this would generate 496.5 full-time equivalent jobs per year or 1,985 seasonal jobs (per the three-month period/over the summer season) in the 20 Finnish municipalities surveyed. With regard to the situation on the local labour market in the municipalities at the time of the survey, a potential number of 496.5 new jobs would increase the existing employment by about 2.3%, which seems quite significant given not only its full-time character but also in view of the fact that rural labour markets are usually weaker and much less efficiently utilised than urban ones. As mentioned, these rough values can be treated only as indicative figures, in reality depending on many different factors and circumstances, which thus do not permit generalisations for other municipalities of a similar socio-economic structure nor extrapolations to the regional or national level. They only provide a broad-brush picture of economic potential derived from the second-home phenomenon for local people (apparently not only business owners).

Table 4.2.1.2 A broad-brush impact estimate for Finnish municipalities based on the survey of local people

	No. of household-dwelling units	No. of potential suppliers			Potential earnings (in €)		
		Goods	Services	Total	Goods	Services	Total
Hartola	1,691	338	169	338	133,589	59,185	192,774
Hirvensalmi	1,227	0	223	223	0	22,454,100	22,454,100
Kemiönsaari	3,443	0	0	0	0	0	0
Kivijärvi	586	0	84	84	0	167,429	167,429
Kuhmoinen	1,321	189	189	377	94,357	377	94,735
Kustavi	452	104	104	139	26,077	297,277	323,354
Luhanka	380	48	143	143	9,500	54,625	64,125
Mäntyharju	3,246	0	0	0	0	0	0
Padasjoki	1,655	497	497	662	3,111,400	3,177,600	6,289,000
Pelkosenniemi	514	0	114	114	0	125,073	125,073
Pertunmaa	957	0	191	191	0	133,980	133,980
Posio	1,685	0	0	0	0	0	0
Puumala	1,197	133	0	133	26,600	0	26,600
Pälkäne	3,101	0	0	0	0	0	0
Savitaipale	1,817	661	496	991	322,105	1,329,714	1,651,818
Siikainen	773	0	0	0	0	0	0
Sulkava	1,416	0	142	142	0	56,640	56,640
Sysmä	2,209	221	0	221	1,325,400	0	1,325,400
Taipalsaari	2,036	0	255	255	0	865,300	865,300
Taivassalo	809	0	0	0	0	0	0
Total	3,0515	3,130	4,303	6,064	5,709,826	4,8372,535	54,082,361

Source: Own study.

This is also the case in Poland, for which the same equation components were included and the same calculations were made. There was a total of 46,899 household-dwelling units in the 20 municipalities surveyed and this number was even more differentiated among these areas than in the Finnish municipalities (from 777 in mountainous Koszarawa to 6,235 in Ziębice). On the basis of these numbers and the proportion of the respondents reporting selling goods and/or services (17.2%), there were 8,070 potential local sellers, ranging from zero in four communities to 1,407 in the densely populated mountainous Stryszawa (Table 4.2.1.3). The potential earnings were estimated at PLN 31,154,651 (€7,489,099), of which 92% were generated by the sales of services and the rest by the sales of goods. The potential earnings were highly uneven and ranged from PLN 0 in four municipalities to PLN 6,690,790 (€1,608,363) in the densely populated and highly-urbanised Mielno on the coast. Given that only 45.1% of the total revenue from supplying second-home owners with goods and services is subject to tax (generated by formal transactions) and taking this as an applicable value to measure the taxable income, this would give PLN 14,050,748 (€3,377,584).

Table 4.2.1.3 A broad-brush impact estimate for Polish municipalities based on the survey of local people

	No. of household-dwelling units	No. of potential suppliers			Potential earnings (in PLN)		
		Goods	Services	Total	Goods	Services	Total
Brenna	3,162	474	632	949	189,720	426,870	616,590
Brok	943	0	94	94	0	707,250	707,250
Dziwnów	1,493	75	0	75	22,395	0	22,395
Goniądz	1,598	0	0	0	0	0	0
Kałuszyn	2,213	443	553	885	38,728	221,300	260,028
Kosów Lacki	2,460	615	123	615	292,740	24,600	317,340
Koszarawa	777	155	194	233	60,218	112,704	172,921
Lądek Zdrój	3,624	181	181	362	543,600	724,800	1,268,400
Mielnik	1,054	474	211	527	316,200	700,910	1,017,110
Mielno	1,695	0	268	268	0	6,690,790	6,690,790
Międzylesie	2,600	260	130	260	84,500	130,000	214,500
Narewka	1,747	262	0	262	165,965	0	165,965
Rajgród	1,613	0	0	0	0	0	0
Rewal	1,174	0	224	224	0	3,628,219	3,628,219
Stryszawa	3,283	1,251	156	1,407	195,417	9,380,000	9,575,417
Ujsoły	1,493	299	75	373	164,230	223,950	388,180
Wolin	4,227	211	211	423	63,405	274,755	274,755
Zgierz	3,779	0	0	0	0	0	0

	No. of household-dwelling units	No. of potential suppliers			Potential earnings (in PLN)		
		Goods	Services	Total	Goods	Services	Total
Ziębice	6,236	312	0	312	93,540	0	93,540
Złoty Stok	1,728	0	0	0	0	0	0
Total	46,899	5,380	3,860	8,070	2,500,495	28,689,114	31,154,651

Source: Own study.

After tax (basic tax rate 23%), potential sellers would receive a net income of PLN 10,819,076 (€2,600,739). Again under the assumption that 50% of the total income covers the labour costs and that PLN 47,838 is needed for one full-time equivalent job per year, the revenue from second-home owners would provide local economies with 294 new full-time permanent jobs or 1,177 new seasonal (three-month) jobs. Furthermore, this number of potential new permanent jobs would contribute to the local labour market by adding 0.7% to the current employment (the most recent data available at municipal level, CSO 2002).

Second-home owners' perspective

In assessing the economic impact, one can measure the flow of financial resources into the community's economy as a result of second-home owners' local expenditures. As mentioned earlier, second-home owners are usually more keen and more accurate in responding to questions, especially if they concern the exact amount of spending and the commodity bundle structure. Thus, the data on expenditure are more complete/sufficient and reliable than the data provided by the locals (especially in the case of informal distribution). The total local expenditure is here considered as a critical component of impact, obviously being subject to reductions due to subsequent financial leakages from the local system (profit-transfer outside the municipality, business and household input supply outside the local system etc.).

Thus, although the estimates and further generalisations are still broad-brush, at the same time they are more precise and trustworthy. Here, as was the case with the locals' earnings, the estimate uses the total number of secondary residences in the municipalities/communities surveyed (provided by Statistics Finland 2013 and CSO 2002), as well as the proportion of second-home owners who admitted to spending money locally and the total amount of their (local) spending, so that the equation is applicable as follows.

As described in the section dedicated to consumer performance (section 4.1), Finnish second-home owners spent a total of €1,423,413 locally (on goods and services). However, the flow of financial resources was unevenly distributed among the municipalities, ranging from €33,636 in Hartola to €115,696 in Sulkava (both located in the Finnish Lakeland). Such inequalities resulted from variations in the response rate, interest in local purchasing and individual/household consumption patterns relating to the size and structure of the commodity bundle. By deconstructing the total gross income into its relevant components, one can obtain the taxable gross income (by removing informal purchasing), which amounted to €1,142,319; then, income tax amounted to €279,868, and finally, labour costs (€571,160), ensuring 11.3 new permanent full-time equivalent jobs or 45.2 new seasonal jobs. Differences were also observed in the proportion of second-home owners spending money locally, from 76.9% in Taipalsaari to 100% in several other municipalities, with the average of 92.3%. Furthermore, although these municipalities had the highest concentration of secondary residences in housing resources, the number varied significantly between areas (from 732 in Pelkosenniemi to 4,794 holiday homes in Mäntyharju), contributing to a total number of 53,064 units. On this basis, a simple and rough estimate of 48,973 potential purchasers was calculated, with the total spending generated by them estimated at €161,842,471, which provided a considerable financial boost to the local economies, although still differentiated among municipalities (see Table 4.2.1.4). Since 80.2% of local purchases were made at formal/registered businesses, the taxable gross income was €129,797,662. Business income tax was €32,044,809, with labour costs (with the same rate per permanent job) covering 50% of this, which in effect provides 1,283 new full-time equivalent permanent jobs or 5,130 seasonal (three-month) jobs.

Table 4.2.1.4 A broad-brush impact estimate for Finnish municipalities based on the survey of second-home owners

	No. of secondary residence	No. of potential purchasers			Potential spending (in €)		
		Goods	Services	Total	Goods	Services	Total
Hartola	2,356	1,832	1,309	1,963	3,822,741	579,838	4,402,579
Hirvensalmi	2,983	2,557	2,450	2,663	4,694,177	3,140,886	7,835,063
Kemiönsaari	4,676	4,676	4,676	4,676	17,888,451	9,662,816	27,551,267
Kivijärvi	751	717	614	717	735,297	589,535	1,324,832
Kuhmoinen	3,040	2,931	2,714	2,931	8,542,400	3,925,943	12,468,343

	No. of secondary residence	No. of potential purchasers			Potential spending (in €)		
		Goods	Services	Total	Goods	Services	Total
Kustavi	3,013	2,882	2,489	2,882	5,304,452	6,177,960	11,482,412
Luhanka	827	700	668	732	897,295	1,793,572	2,690,867
Mäntyharju	4,794	4,586	4,377	4,586	12,588,419	3,678,249	16,266,667
Padasjoki	2,773	2,773	2,329	2,773	5,879,869	2,564,470	8,444,340
Pelkosenniemi	732	666	599	665	1,003,239	484,318	1,487,557
Pertunmaa	1,841	1,688	1,611	1,764	3,142,357	2,564,743	5,707,100
Posio	2,511	2,152	1,794	2,152	6,352,830	4,751,171	11,104,000
Puumala	3,555	3,091	3,246	3,555	5,246,716	2,818,497	8,065,213
Pälkäne	4,179	3,375	3,215	3,536	6,012,134	5,773,449	11,785,584
Savitaipale	2,747	2,622	2,123	2,622	4,385,211	1,263,870	5,649,081
Siikainen	1,049	749	699	899	967,078	986,310	1,953,388
Sulkava	2,116	2,116	1,959	2,116	5,454,499	3,612,639	9,067,138
Sysmä	3,751	3,215	2,679	3,215	11,602,379	2,415,644	14,018,023
Taipalsaari	3,395	2,350	1,959	2,612	4,916,352	3,722,748	8,639,100
Taivassalo	1,975	1,975	1,399	1,975	3,586,600	919,609	4,506,209
Total	53,064	47,496	42,383	48,973	100,730,357	61,113,479	161,843,836

Source: Own study.

Similar calculations were made for their Polish counterparts, who spent a total of PLN 2,186,822 (€525,678), although their expenditures differed significantly among communities, ranging from PLN 18,900 (€4,543) in the heavily urbanised suburban community of Zgierz to PLN 414,410 (€99,618) in the famous mountainous tourism and spa locality of Lądek Zdrój. Since 80% of this amount was received by formal businesses, the taxable gross income was PLN 1,749,458 (€420,543) and the income tax was PLN 402,375 (€96,725). To calculate employment provision, again 50% was estimated for labour costs, which resulted in PLN 874,729 (€210,271) and consequently 18.3 permanent jobs or 73.1 seasonal jobs. Similar variations were also observed in other equation components, i.e. the number of secondary residences (CSO 2002) and the proportion of second-home owners purchasing products and services locally. The number of holiday homes ranged from 40 in the mountainous community of Złoty Stok to as many as 1,609 in Zgierz, with a total figure of 5,519. The percentage of purchasers ranged from 70% in the tourist locality of Rajgród to

100% in six communities of a different functional type. In effect, this would give 5,145 potential consumers, who would generate PLN 30,324,298 (€7,289,495) (Table 4.2.1.5). In order to consider this amount as the basis for further calculations, first, it needs to be reduced to take account of the fact that for Polish second-home owners, as for Finns, 80% of purchases were made officially. Thus, the taxable gross income earned by enterprises and farms was PLN 24,259,438 (€5,831,596), while the business income tax was PLN 5,579,671 (€1,341,267). Under the assumption that 50% of gross income is dedicated to labour costs (PLN 12,129,719, i.e. €2,915,798), this would provide a total of 253.5 new permanent full-equivalent jobs or 1,014.2 seasonal jobs. Relating these rough estimates to the existing local labour markets in the municipalities/communities surveyed would give an increase of 5.9% and 0.6% in new permanent jobs in Finland and Poland respectively.

Table 4.2.1.5 A broad-brush impact estimate for Polish municipalities based on the survey of second-home owners

	No. of secondary residences	**No. of potential purchasers**			**Potential spending (in PLN)**		
		Goods	**Services**	**Total**	**Goods**	**Services**	**Total**
Brenna	911	911	592	911	2,608,193	471,443	3,079,636
Brok	126	126	88	126	424,305	39,060	463,365
Dziwnów	210	158	179	179	777,420	387,660	1,165,080
Goniądz	98	93	69	93	178,458	34,692	213,150
Kałuszyn	163	163	57	163	349,961	25,673	375,634
Kosów Lacki	226	203	79	203	245,323	313,575	558,898
Koszarawa	212	191	53	191	382,766	30,740	413,506
Lądek Zdrój	108	108	81	108	2,091,258	146,556	2,237,814
Mielnik	174	165	87	165	537,573	555,060	1,092,633
Mielno	179	134	161	179	979,130	974,968	1,954,098
Międzylesie	91	87	46	87	415,916	143,484	559,400
Narewka	338	304	152	304	1,164,241	845,000	2,009,241
Rajgród	80	56	44	56	105,840	15,000	120,840
Rewal	76	68	65	68	298,566	116,242	414,808
Stryszawa	381	362	267	362	2,702,052	664,464	3,366,516
Ujsoły	283	241	28	241	393,370	18,395	411,765
Wolin	106	95	84	100	285,915	117,716	403,631

	No. of secondary residences	No. of potential purchasers			Potential spending (in PLN)		
		Goods	Services	Total	Goods	Services	Total
Zgierz	1,609	1529	81	1,529	1,504,415	16,090	1,520,505
Ziębice	108	102	68	108	752,192	160,988	913,180
Złoty Stok	40	38	24	38	245,002	73,760	318,762
Total	5,519	5020	3092	5,145	22,936,298	7,388,000	30,324,298

Source: Own study.

Clear and significant differences can be seen in comparing the total amount of second-home owners' spending and the total earnings that local residents declare as a result of providing second-home owners with goods and services. What are the reasons for this? They can be divided into subject-related arguments of a strictly economic nature and methodological survey-related ones. First, one should consider financial leakages out of the local economy that may significantly reduce the total inflow of local expenditures by second-home owners. Financial leakage is understood as "the return to foreign capital providers in the form of profits, dividends, and interests repatriated to capital originating countries" (Gu 2000, p. 12). This does not include the structural and operational leakages of second-home tourism, including the import of goods and services from outside by their owners, as in the questionnaire they reported only products and services purchased locally.

It is obvious that a certain number of businesses operating in the area of the second homes surveyed are owned and/or credited by individuals/institutions (permanently) located outside the municipality, e.g. in tourism-based or suburban communities as a place of external investment. Consequently, some of the revenues (profits) gained from second-home owners' local expenditures drain away to the owner/creditor/stakeholder's municipality. This is usually not reported in questionnaires, since consumers (including second-home owners) are often not aware of the business owner's origins (permanent residence) and consider spending all expenditures in the municipality to be local. This occurred in both countries, but it seems that this is mainly applicable to Finland. As the supply and distribution of food products is almost entirely in the hands of nationwide chains (K-chain, S-chain) and there are few or no small family shops/grocers, it is very likely that apart from local income tax, capital and property tax, labour costs and part of the input expenditures, the profits are constantly returned to the capital provider/owner. Hence, at least food products and basic commodity supply contribute less to income generation but significantly more to local job-creation.

This explanation applies to the Polish context too, but to a lesser extent, given that besides national or regional chains, there are still numerous small family shops in the countryside (definitely more accessible for second-home owners in more remote locations) for which such financial leakages are non-existent or rare. Besides the food supply sector, similar mechanisms can be observed in various economic sectors (including services) but, compared to Finland, to a lesser extent.

Second, the sample sizes of Finnish second-home owners and locals were different, as questionnaires were mailed to 500 locals compared to 1000 second-home owners. The response rate for second home owners was higher (46.7%) than for locals (31.2%). Third, the locals surveyed included people engaged in varying economic activities, of which entrepreneurs who would mainly profit from supplying second-home owners made up 14.7% in Finland and 17.6% in Poland. Thus, as in both countries only 34%-36% of local sellers (those actually selling products) were business owners (incl. farmers) and most represented the informal/shadow economy, the potential underreporting and consequent underestimation can lead to considerable discrepancies between expenditure/financial inflow and actual earnings/revenues.

4.2.2 Factors influencing local sales

A forward stepwise regression analysis was applied to the study in order to learn more about the preconditions for providing goods and services to second-home owners and distinguish some crucial characteristics of local sellers (incl. their opinions and views as well as characteristics of their residence). Seven variables were identified for local sellers in Finland, which were composed in an explanatory model (see Table 4.2.2.1), i.e. the respondent's age, with one or more children under 18 years of age in the household, the respondent's economic activity, daily commuting to work, the number of secondary residences in the municipality, the respondent's opinion on the attractiveness for tourism of his/her home municipality (here: attractiveness due to historical background) and the respondent's opinion on the influence of the second-home phenomenon on infrastructure improvement (here: wastewater disposal in the village). All these variables were statistically significant, which is described by t-values higher than 0 and p-values lower than 0.05. Given that there were probably some unknown and unobservable factors (not included in the data set) inducing locals to sell things to second home owners, the model explained less than 50% of the total variance, i.e. 41.13% (R^2 was 0.4113). This is acceptable given a large number of variables, observations and the non-linear regression technique applied here. The F-statistics accounted for 4.08 (with $p<0.0004$), which was higher than the average and median of the dependent variables (respectively 0.2 and 1). This proves that the outcome model was statistically significant.

Table 4.2.2.1 Preconditions behind supplying Finnish second-home owners with local goods and services (forward stepwise regression analysis)

	R= .64133003 R2= .41130421 Correct. R2= .31060625 F(13,76)=4.0845 p<0.00004 Standard error: .34712					
	BETA	**Standard error BETA**	**B**	**Standard error B**	**T(76)**	**Statistical significance**
Constant			0.098	0.397	0.248	0.805
Respondent's gender	0.132	0.094	0.111	0.079	1.400	0.165
Respondent's age	**-0.273**	**0.113**	**-0.186**	**0.077**	**-2.413**	**0.018**
Respondent's children	**-0.223**	**0.105**	**-0.108**	**0.051**	**-2.120**	**0.037**
Number of permanent residents	-0.199	0.113	-0.132	0.075	-1.757	0.082
Number of secondary residences	**0.220**	**0.110**	**0.260**	**0.130**	**2.007**	**0.048**
Respondent's economic activity	**-0.904**	**0.218**	**-0.154**	**0.037**	**-4.144**	**0.000**
Respondent's daily commuting	**0.831**	**0.227**	**0.007**	**0.002**	**3.664**	**0.000**
SH location: Close to nature	0.139	0.104	0.120	0.090	1.331	0.187
SH location: Historically significant	**-0.246**	**0.107**	**-0.283**	**0.123**	**-2.306**	**0.024**
SH location: Traditional summer locality	0.133	0.099	0.113	0.084	1.343	0.183
Respondent's sales of recreational land/ property	0.134	0.096	0.209	0.150	1.393	0.168
Respondent's sales of other type of land/ property	-0.134	0.096	-0.243	0.175	-1.392	0.168
Influence of SH on wastewater disposal provision	**0.238**	**0.099**	**0.073**	**0.031**	**2.392**	**0.019**

Source: Own study.

Focusing on subsequent variables (those statistically significant and selected to build up an equation model), one may firmly assume that local sellers were mainly younger people, of productive mobile age, and thus with no children yet, who were at the same time working people (business owners (incl. farmers) and paid workers in the same proportions) and often daily commuters among the latter group. It seems that commuting and living permanently in the countryside (probably even owning a small farm) prompt people to combine different sources of income, here paid work and the 'informal' selling of goods and services to visitors. More local sellers operate in typical leisure/holiday-home municipalities than in typical tourism-based localities (including those mainly attractive to tourists owing to their historical character) with a large number of secondary residences. This indirectly confirms the importance of the size of the demand for local products by second-home owners/users in inducing entrepreneurial initiatives by locals. The regression analysis results confirmed that established economic relationships with second-home owners (namely evidence-based transactions between these two populations) become stronger along with the locals' positive opinions on the role of second-home tourism in improving living standards (here by influencing improvements in the municipalities infrastructure (e.g. wastewater disposal system)). As the next step of the regression analysis, a model equation was formulated as follows:

$$\hat{Y}=0.098417+-0.186052*x_1+-0.108411*x_2+0.260407*x_3+-0.153931*x_4+0.007086*x_5+-0.282642*x_6+0.073260*x_7$$

Thus, considering the most positive scenario for selling goods and services among locals, the equation model will produce the following formula:

$$\hat{Y}=0.098417+-0.186052*1+-0.108411*0+0.260407*3+-0.153931*1+0.007086*1+-0.282642*0+0.073260*5=0.91$$

This leads to the conclusion that if the necessary criteria are met, the final result will at most be close to 1, which means selling goods and services to second-home owners but it needs to be remembered that the rest of the variance – approx. 40% – is explained by other factors, including those not observed here. Based on the equation model, selling goods is carried out by younger people who are employed (daily commuters) or self-employed, live in a typical leisure municipality and see second homes as a community development opportunity.

On the other hand, the most negative scenario is based on the following equation:

$$\hat{Y}=0.098417+-0.186052*3+-0.108411*3+0.260407*1+-0.153931*7+0.007086*2+-0.282642*1+0.073260*0=-1.87$$

Despite the Ŷ-value being lower than the range for no sales ('0'), it in fact means the same. Not selling goods and services to second home owners is the case among older locals (but still with children in the household), retired or unemployed people who live in a municipality other than of a leisure character (suburban or peripheral) and who have more negative opinions on the role of second-home tourism in improving the municipality's infrastructure.

The intention of applying the same regression analysis to identify the main factors influencing the selling activity by local Polish people to second-home owners was thwarted by too low a value of the determination coefficient, which was 0.19. In other words, the regression model explained only 19% of the total variance and, even if a large number of variables and observations, and thus a possibly complex structure of considered relationships are taken into account, this was regarded as insufficient. Hence, the solution was to use the Kruskal-Wallis test (based on median instead of mean values) as an appropriate technique to approach data on the ordinal scale (as in this case it considered both dependent and independent variables) and combine its results with cross-tabulation outcomes.

Interestingly, in the results of the Kruskal-Wallis test, only nine of the almost 40 explanatory variables were statistically significant (with p-value lower than 0.05) and none of these represented the respondent's socio-demographics. Instead, they were mainly second-home municipality landscape/physiographic and functional characteristics, locality characteristics and the respondent's views on the positive and negative sides of second-home tourism (see Table 4.2.2.2). The lack of strict respondent characteristics was probably a manifestation of the intricate and complex structure analysed and consequently the low explanatory value of the regression model initially proposed.

Table 4.2.2.2 Preconditions behind supplying Polish second-home owners with local goods and services (Kruskal-Wallis test)

	Selling goods and services to second-home owners	
	H-value	p-value
Community functional type	**15.744**	**0.0076**
Community landscape type	**30.392**	**0.0000**
Community administrative status (urban, rural, semi-urban)	**6.119**	**0.0134**
Type of settlement	**11.782**	**0.0028**
Influence of SH on wastewater disposal provision	**11.878**	**0.0365**

	Selling goods and services to second-home owners	
	H-value	p-value
Influence of SH on cleanliness in the village	**10.828**	**0.0549**
Social contacts with SH owners	**13.396**	**0.0199**
SH owner's behaviour	**12.885**	**0.0245**
Vandalism/hooliganism	**3.972**	**0.0463**

Source: Own study.

Let us start with statistically significant municipal characteristics: it is worthwhile first to pay attention to the functional type with a large proportion of locals who sell goods to second-home owners in mixed/multifunctional and tourism-based communities. These are especially those located in eastern Poland, usually of a transitional nature and facing serious demographic and economic problems such as depopulation, ageing, brain drain and agricultural decline. Hence, being aware of this, local people take advantage of various opportunities that occur locally by engaging in entrepreneurial initiatives (including supplying visitors with local goods and services) just to raise their extremely insufficient incomes. According to the research results, this takes place more often in rural communities, in large villages rather than in small villages and scattered settlements. Furthermore, what is important and basically in line with the second-home owners study outcomes is that social contacts/ties between locals and seasonal immigrants play a considerable role in establishing economic relationships, but it may also be true that initially purely economic contacts develop into strong social relationships. This is corroborated by the opinions on social contacts with second-home owners and their behaviour (in fact daily practices) expressed by the locals. Selling them goods is more likely to happen for those local residents who have assessed social contacts as at least average but stronger if they are considered 'good' or 'very good'. In addition, more sellers were identified among those locals who noticed a positive influence of second-home owners on the environmental cleanliness of the village and general environmental awareness with regard to local development. On the other hand, the negative opinions strictly related to second-home owners' vandalism and hooliganism (though only a few of them) and did not in any sense affect the provision of necessary local products to second-home owners.

4.2.3 Economic-related impacts

As an integral (albeit more descriptive) part of the impact assessment, in addition to evidence-based revenues, local residents were asked to express their opinions on the opportunities to supply second-home owners with goods and services. The answers ranged from 0 (no opportunities) to 5 (very good opportunities). For Finns, there was the prevalence of negative views, since two-thirds rated them as lacking or very weak possibilities (0 & 1) while only 16.0% found them to be good (4) or very good (5). For their Polish counterparts, the distribution of answers was significantly different, with 43.3% considering such economic opportunities to be non-existent or very weak while 35.2% saw them as good and very good. Hence, comparing those two populations, one can find a generally negative assessment among Finns while Poles' views are more diverse and polarised. The factors behind the respondents' characteristics and attitudes to second homes' potential contribution to the local economy need to be identified in order to learn more about the reasons that can consequently help interpret the findings.

By using a forward stepwise regression analysis, an explanatory model was selected that best suited the dataset variance. It included several valid explanatory variables extracted as the main factors influencing the respondents' views and opinions. For Finnish locals, the value of coefficient of determination (R^2) was 0.5456, i.e. the proportion of the total variance explained by the model was 54.56%, which was quite high given how difficult it is to predict human behaviour (Lancaster 1975; Zarębski 2015). The F-test statistics value was 11.41 ($p < 0.05$), confirming that the outcome of the analysis was statistically significant, since it explained the greater variance of the dependent variable than its mean and median –1.4 and 1 respectively. As shown in Table 4.2.3.1, four variables were included in the model, i.e. those with a statistically significant beta coefficient (i.e. with a significant t-value – higher than 0) and the p-value of less than 0.05: evidence-based sales of goods and services to second-home owners, the respondent's opinions on social relationships with second-home owners, the respondent's gender and the respondent's opinions on the influence of the second-home phenomenon on infrastructure improvement.

Table 4.2.3.1 Explanatory factors behind the locals' opinions on opportunities to supply Finnish second-home owners with local goods and services (forward stepwise regression analysis)

	R= .73869251 R2= .54566663 Correct. R2= .49784206 F(6,57)=11.410 p<0.00000 Standard error: .97571					
	BETA	**Standard error BETA**	**B**	**Standard error B**	**T(76)**	**Statistical significance**
Constant			1.793	0.515	3.478	0.001
Respondent's sales goods & services	**0.363**	**0.133**	**1.104**	**0.404**	**2.730**	**0.008**
Influence of second homes on local roads	**0.265**	**0.097**	**0.289**	**0.106**	**2.729**	**0.008**
Importance of second homes for social contacts	**0.231**	**0.095**	**0.237**	**0.097**	**2.446**	**0.018**
Respondent's gender	**-0.232**	**0.092**	**-0.638**	**0.254**	**-2.510**	**0.015**
Respondent's education	-0.147	0.092	-0.198	0.123	-1.601	0.115
Respondent's sales of goods	0.208	0.131	0.752	0.475	1.584	0.119

Source: Own study.

Despite the fact that regression analysis cannot indicate the direction of cause-effect relationships but only identify the linkage itself, in some cases, the direction seems to be quite obvious. Thus, it is very likely that the respondents' opinions on the economic opportunities resulting from second homes are highly dependent upon facts and actual actions, i.e. sales to second-home owners. The higher the rate of social contact with second-home owners, the higher the evaluation of economic opportunities, which in fact confirms what was found in the second-home owners' data set, i.e. that social relationships with the locals overlapped with the economic relationships (transactions) with them. Furthermore, the respondent's gender was influential, showing more positive views on economic opportunities among local women and then linking those views with the opinions on the impact of second-home tourism on the infrastructure improvements in the municipality (namely roads).

The next step is to formulate a regression equation, which in this case is described as follows:

$$\hat{Y}=1.79+1.103956*x_1+0.288684*x_2+0.236736*x_3+-0.637630*x_4$$

Thus, one can consider the most positive scenario by predicting how locals assess second homes as an economic opportunity if they sell goods and services, have well-established and valued social contacts, are female and are most positive assessing the influence of second homes on the local infrastructure. Following that model:

$\hat{Y}$=1.79+1.103956*1+0.288684*5+0.236736*5+-0.637630*1=4.88

Here, the value close to the highest range ('5') indicates very good economic opportunities for locals supplying second-home owners.

On the other hand, if there are no sales, non-existent social ties, the respondent is male and has a negative opinion on second homes' influence on the infrastructure, the following equation was calculated:

$\hat{Y}$=1.79+1.103956*0+0.288684*0+0.236736*0+-0.637630*2=0.51

Here, the conditions are not fulfilled at all and the predicted value of assessment will be between 'non-existent' and 'very weak'.

The same was measured for Polish locals, for whom the value of the coefficient of determination (R^2) was 0.5644, i.e. in this case, the proportion of the total variance explained by the model was 56.44% higher than for their Finnish counterparts. The F-test statistics was 23.05 (while $p < 0.05$), confirming the statistical significance of the outcome as it explained more variance of the dependent variable than its mean and median –3.2 and 3 respectively. This time, eight statistically significant variables (with a t-value higher than 0 and p-value lower than 0.05) were included in the regression model (see Table 4.2.3.2), i.e. opinions on the influence of second homes on the community development (in general) and on the infrastructure improvement (roads), the size and type of the locality, the respondent's household size, the number of permanent residents in the municipality, the area of the farm (where the respondent was a farmer), the respondent's economic activity and the leisure traditions of the locality (essentially the time when the first holiday homes were set up there).

Table 4.2.3.2 Explanatory factors behind the locals' opinions on opportunities to supply Polish second-home owners with local goods and services (forward stepwise regression analysis)

	R= .75129158 R2= .56443904 Correct. R2= .53994967 F(14,249)=23.048 p<0.0000 Standard error: 1.0444					
	BETA	**Standard error BETA**	**B**	**Standard error B**	**T(76)**	**Statistical significance**
Constant			**3.416**	**0.595**	**5.740**	**0.000**
Community development opportunities resulting from second homes	**0.365**	**0.045**	**0.364**	**0.045**	**8.021**	**0.000**
Type of settlement	**-0.289**	**0.048**	**-0.573**	**0.095**	**-6.029**	**0.000**
Traditional second-home area	**-0.185**	**0.044**	**-0.200**	**0.048**	**-4.190**	**0.000**
Number of permanent residences	**0.129**	**0.043**	**0.254**	**0.085**	**2.987**	**0.003**
Respondent's household size	**0.105**	**0.047**	**0.168**	**0.076**	**2.219**	**0.027**
Respondent's farm area	**-0.180**	**0.051**	**-0.268**	**0.076**	**-3.516**	**0.001**
Respondent's economic activity	**-0.112**	**0.053**	**-0.114**	**0.054**	**-2.093**	**0.037**
Influence of second homes on local roads	**-0.090**	**0.044**	**-0.116**	**0.057**	**-2.049**	**0.042**
Respondent's education	0.066	0.046	0.094	0.065	1.435	0.152
Respondent's job position	-0.077	0.047	-0.062	0.038	-1.632	0.104
Respondent's sales of services	-0.042	0.044	-0.185	0.191	-0.969	0.333
Respondent's household income	0.061	0.047	0.127	0.099	1.286	0.200
Influence of second homes on recreational facilities	-0.056	0.045	-0.062	0.050	-1.235	0.218
Second homes negative effects	0.049	0.043	0.202	0.176	1.147	0.252

Source: Own study.

On the basis of the value of b coefficients, it can be said that the respondent's views on the importance of second homes for community development, infrastructure improvements and economic opportunities resulting from second homes overlapped to a large extent (in most cases). The larger the locality (small town or central village) and the larger the municipality (based on the number of inhabitants), the more positive were the opinions expressed by the respondents on economic opportunities. Representatives of larger households (two-three people or more) and/or the owners of small farms and/or working people (especially entrepreneurs) were more likely to find second homes an income opportunity.

Finally, the longer the leisure tradition of the village, the higher the evaluation of the average level of economic opportunities.

As a consequence, a regression equation was formulated as follows:

$$\hat{Y}=3.416257+0.364458*x_1+-0.572637*x_2+-0.200020*x_3+0.253921*x_4+0.168031*x_5+-0.268235*x_6+-0.113770*x_7+-0.115794*x_8$$

Thus, considering the most positive scenario/model predicting how the locals assess second homes as an economic opportunity, if they express very good opinions on second homes in community's development and infrastructure improvements, they are members of a four-person or and larger household, they are small farmers, working people (self-employed), live in a small town or central village, or in a relatively large municipality with a long leisure tradition. Following this model:

$$\hat{Y}=3.416257+0.364458*5+-0.572637*1+-0.200020*1+0.253921*3+0.168031*4+-0.268235*1+-0.113770*1+-0.115794*5=4.94$$

Here, the outcome value was slightly lower than the highest value within the range of the actual assessment and it confirmed that, by meeting the above criteria, the economic opportunities will be evaluated as nearest to '5' – very good. On the other hand, for members of single households, small farmers, those living in a small village, with negative opinions on the influence on community development and indicating various negative effects of second homes, the formula will be as follows:

$$\hat{Y}=3.416257+0.364458*0+-0.572637*3+-0.200020*4+0.253921*1+0.168031*1+-0.268235*3+-0.113770*7+-0.115794*0=-0.28$$

Thus, if the conditions are not fulfilled, the predicted value of the respondent's opinion on economic opportunities will be non-existent.

In addition to economic/income opportunities for a rural community resulting from second-home tourism, local people rated its influence on infrastructure and social development/improvements. This included a general view and a view of its components, i.e. infrastructure (roads, sidewalks, bicycle paths, water supply and wastewater disposal systems), tourism facilities (incl. cultural events in the peak season), security level and environmental cleanliness. The impact of second homes was ranked from negative – 1 (very weak) to the most positive – 5 (very high/significant).

After comparing Finns' and Poles' opinions, it was clear that for the former group negative and very negative views predominated, while the latter had more positive attitudes towards the effects of second homes on the local community (Figure 4.2.3.1). The Finnish respondents had a slightly negative view on most aspects except the influence on culture (in fact local summer events) and tourism facilities (mainly accessible and well-equipped harbours and local markets). Their Polish counterparts had a positive or moderately positive (although in some cases evenly distributed) perception of most components, i.e. the influence of second-home tourism on the quality of roads, the water supply and wastewater disposal systems, improving environmental cleanliness and awareness, security, tourist facilities and cultural events. Thus, second homes in Finland were not considered as an important but rather additional community development tool, while in Poland they were more likely to be seen as an indubitable asset for other objective development preconditions such as transport accessibility, proximity to a large city and highly rated natural/environmental amenities. This is all the more interesting in that the scale of the second-home phenomenon differs significantly between the two countries in favour of Finland. Hence, it confirms that even in Finnish municipalities with a large number and concentration of holiday homes (predominantly a considerable number of permanent homes) and with local authorities considering this phenomenon as critical development direction (e.g. Hirvensalmi, Kivijärvi, Kustavi, Kemiönsaari, Mäntyharju, Padasjoki, Pelkosenniemi, Savitaipale, Siikainen, Sulkava and Sysmä, based on HOBO Project results) the perceived non-strictly economic influence is limited.

In Poland, on the other hand, with a relatively low number of secondary residences, even where there are few of them in the municipality, they are treated as a potential and actual advantage with respect to the positive (although small) changes that have occurred in the villages/localities in which they are located. As second-home owners are considered a powerful and influential social group in the countryside, they are often decisive in convincing local authorities to build a new road, a sewage system, improve tourist facilities or organise summer events. This is particularly important where more remote, depopulated and traditionally rural Polish communities are often infrastructurally underdeveloped compared to urbanised areas. This is not the case in Finland, where the infrastructure is well developed in rural areas, and thus, second homes may only be an influential factor with regard to social development, hence the positive opinions on summer cultural events or tourist facilities that seem unlikely to be provided without the demand from tourists and other visitors.

Figure 4.2.3.1 Local people's opinions about influence of second homes on: A. Local roads; B. Water supply system; C. Wastewater disposal system; D. Environmental cleanliness; E. Security level; F. Culture (cultural events) and G. Tourism and recreational facilities, %

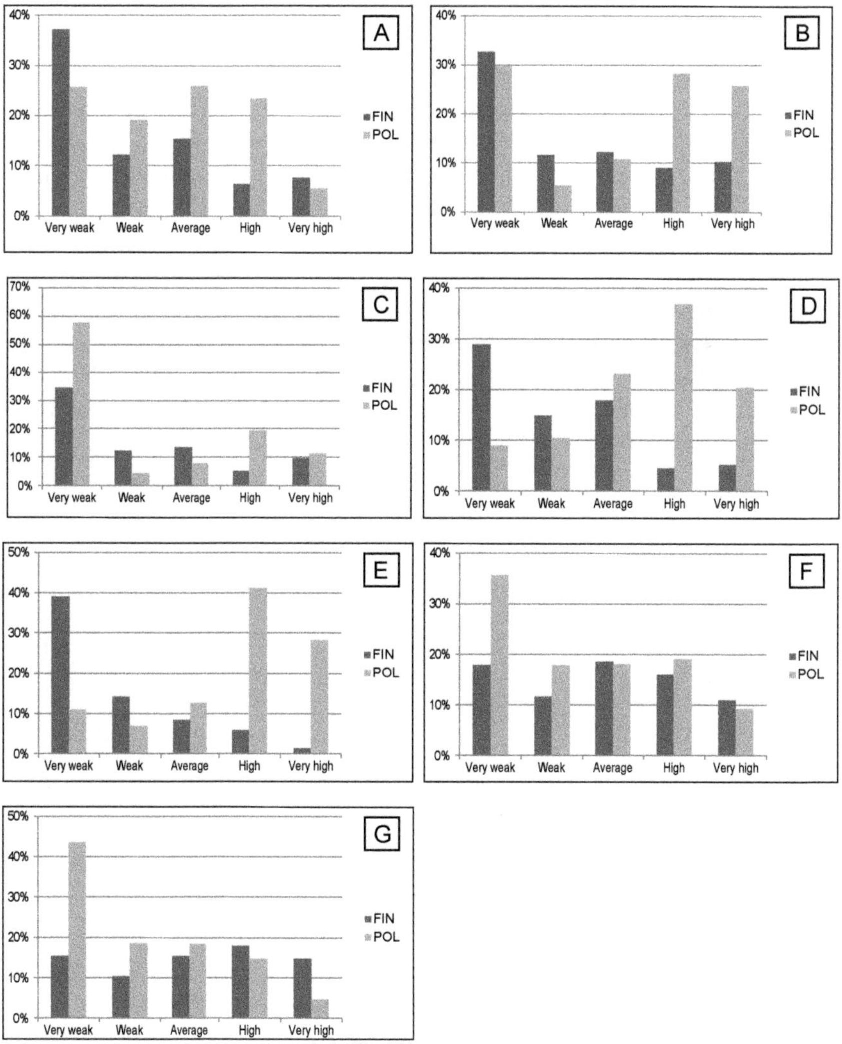

Source: Own study.

This tendency is confirmed by the fact that the perception of the advantageous influence of second homes was more common among the respondents living in less developed Lapland communities, with highly-rated natural amenities and sparsely populated areas, as well as in small villages, where certain development problems (even those related to infrastructure) are more common and similar to those in remote areas of Poland. This view was certainly enhanced by the opinions on social contacts with second-home owners, since the stronger the social relations, the more positive the views on the influential aspect of this phenomenon, and this is more likely as social ties are more easily established in small communities. This explanation is also logical for the Polish respondents who had a more positive general view of the influence of second homes, since they mainly represented small villages in eastern Poland, which is more traditional and less economically developed. They are often low-income earners or retired people living in depopulated villages affected by a dramatic ageing process. Hence, they are more likely to see second homes and their owners as new, more affluent, well-educated and relatively young people, inducing small but positive changes in everyday rural life, and in a broader sense in community development or maintaining the community's viability.

5. Discussion

5.1 Determinants behind second-home owners' local purchasing

At first glance, and in the most general sense, this study has apparently provided a very positive outcome, showing that there is a large demand and interest from Finns and Poles in buying local goods and services (sometimes simply out of necessity). Thus, in terms of the scale measured by the number of players involved in local transactions, there is no doubt that second-home owners are strongly linked to local (mostly rural) economies. This is slightly surprising in light of certain differences between both populations with regard to second-home owners' characteristics and leisure practices, but also between the origins and drivers of the second-home phenomenon and the peculiarities of the two countries.

As regards the total local spending incurred by second-home owners, it was proved that household wealth (mostly measured by household disposable income) was a crucial stimulus, and, at the same time, a core element of the internal (consumer-related) group of economic factors of consumer behaviour. Since there is a gap in the second-home studies dealing with income elasticity for the commodity bundle, the significance of household wealth in shaping purchasing patterns was confirmed by some researchers' findings in the field of tourism economics. These findings have shown the household disposable income to be a key consumption driver through a highly income-elastic demand for tourism activities (Song, Romilly & Liu 2000; Wang & Davidson 2010), but, at the same time, these studies have dealt with 1. traditional forms of tourism, and 2. general demand for tourism, not distinguishing shopping expenditures as a core element of this. Bull (1995) has stressed that traditional forms of tourism are highly income-elastic especially in developing countries (Middleton & Clarke 2001), while for instance VFR tourism is apparently less income-elastic. However, in light of the research findings, despite certain similarities with VFR (no accommodation costs such as in the case of traditional forms of tourism), second-home tourism, in contrast, is clearly more income-elastic. It includes some specific demands, such as construction/renovation, maintenance services and building materials as well as home-related payments, not to mention coming into possession of the cottage (apart from the property inheritance), which are often extremely income elastic.

If one focuses solely on tourist shopping performance, the findings of this study are basically in line with other researchers' views (Lehto *et al.* 2004; Dougan 2007) on disposable household income as a statistically significant factor in consumer behaviour. In this research, it was particularly felt in the course of examining the demand for high-priced products such as building materials and construction services, infrequent goods, which are often luxuries (furnishing, home appliances, leisure and tourist accessories), and services that are relatively expensive compared to other components of the seasonal (but also regular) commodity bundle. Additionally, this factor was important for Poles with regard to the utilisation of maintenance services, seeing that with relatively lower incomes and wealth levels (compared to Finns) they more often used substitutively informal services or even did simple work by themselves, thus employing a common money-saving strategy with regard to home maintenance.

Unsurprisingly, this research did not confirm the slightly unexpected conclusions of the most recent Norwegian study on the low importance of second home owners' household income for local spending (Velvin *et al.* 2013). However, as the general view on the central role of disposable incomes in regular household expenditure (Cage 1989; Solomon, Russell-Bennett & Previte 2013; Gutkowska & Piekut 2014) is still in line with these research outcomes, one may assume, on the basis of the study outcomes, that generally second home-related expenditure incurred locally and outside (and then imported to the second home) may be highly dependent upon household income. Therefore, the study at the same time suggests that the demand for local provision is highly income-elastic, although there are clear and sometimes considerable discrepancies as regards demand among specific categories of goods and services within the commodity bundle. Obviously, household income is less important as an explanatory variable when it deals with necessities (e.g. food and everyday articles) that are less dependent upon income, and hence low-income elastic. Additionally, the consumer's age and family life-cycle stage, which are strictly demographic but at the same time important factors for the consumption level and the commodity bundle, in this case play a great explanatory role.

Then, the frequently mentioned distance between the permanent and second home was proved to be very important in explaining second-home owners' local purchasing (Bohlin 1982; Müller 1999; Nicolau & Más 2005), albeit with significant variations among product categories. It is admittedly a decisive factor in re-constructing patterns of the consumption of commodities such as food, everyday articles, building materials and infrequent goods, as was confirmed by this study. However, it is not necessarily relevant for service purchases, e.g. those provided by construction/renovation companies. Interestingly, the respondent's urban status, which usually and indirectly reflects household wealth, proved the role of travel distance, with the following to be borne in mind: 1. the majority of second-home owners are urban or city dwellers, 2. large cities in both surveyed countries are located far from the main second home concentration areas, which naturally reflect in longer distances between both residences and, in economic terms, in more common local purchasing. On the other hand, the insignificance of distance was most clearly seen in the case of making use of maintenance services. It was due to the simplicity of such services, with no need to engage local or even non-local suppliers as in the case of construction works, for example – and consequently, no need to use highly qualified external providers, since no specific qualifications are needed for basic maintenance works, so the demand is more directed towards locals, but, as mentioned, they are individuals within the informal economy rather than companies.

Hence, the hypothesis "Household wealth vs. accessibility" H_1: *Second-home owners' household income, as a crucial explanatory factor of consumer behaviour, declines in importance in favour of trip-related variables, namely the distance between permanent and secondary residence* was verified positively. In terms of the total spending, household income having the highest influence on the second-home owners' local spending proved to be statistically significant. This relationship, however, was considerably moderated by the travel distance to the holiday home, which was confirmed to be among the key-drivers of second-home owners' consumer behaviour, along with the household income and the length of stay at the cottage.

Furthermore, in the context of the fact that the purchasing determinants are highly-dependent upon the product acquired, this hypothesis was additionally confirmed for each of the product categories separately. Thus, for building materials, the more important explanatory factor for Finns was household income while for Poles it was travel distance; for construction services, it was household income in both populations; for food products, it was travel distance/time for both Finns and Poles; for maintenance services, again, it was household income for both groups; for infrequent goods, it was travel distance for both groups; for infrequent services, it was household income for Finns and travel distance for Poles. In general, this research has shown that household wealth/income declined in its importance in favour of trip-related factors for purchases of goods while the opposite tendency was observed for service transactions.

Furthermore, the research results also confirmed the findings from previous studies in the field on the considerable role of other demographic attributes in shaping regular and seasonal spending patterns, such as the consumer's/household head's age (Agarwal & Yochum 2000), education level (Schiffman, Kanuk & Hansen 2008), occupation (Bihagen 1999; Gorczyca 2005) and urban status (Lázaro, Molto & Sanchez 2000; Turczak & Zwiech 2013). However, taking a closer look, one can note that certain respondent's characteristics, particularly being well-educated, young employees (especially with high-status jobs), reflect in his/her urban status, and altogether are a manifestation of a wealth status. Despite the blurring rural-urban dichotomy and the increasing heterogeneity of the social composition of the countryside, resembling rural-urban socio-demographics and lifestyles (Węgleński 1992; Champion 1998; Scott, Gilbert & Gelan 2007; Pitkänen, Adamiak & Halseth 2014), this study showed that the respondent's urban status can be an important explanatory factor of second-home owner's spending in rural locations. It seems that various consumer's social characteristics (education, wealth, economic activity, occupation, job position and first and foremost social class) are manifested through the urban or rural status (here identified by permanent place of living), and hence, it may be treated as a universal predictor incorporating at least the abovementioned partial variables. The hypothesis "Urban influence" H_2: *Having an urban status predetermines second-home owners to purchase goods and services locally* was thus considered to be true, seeing that consumers giving proof of their urban origins (especially representing large cities over 100,000 inhabitants) spend clearly more in total through local purchases (Finns) and, in particular, significantly more on building materials (Poles).

Longer stays at a second home naturally increase the needs and interest in local purchasing (Agarwal & Yochum 1999; Downward & Lumsdon 2003; Pouta, Neuvonen & Sievänen 2006), which was also found in this study, especially as far as spending on basic commodities is concerned, e.g. food, rather than building materials or construction services. This relationship was also confirmed for the usage of maintenance services, but here it was additionally moderated by the spread of visits over the year, with a particular positive influence of relatively long, uninterrupted periods (e.g. summer holidays) and a negative one for numerous but short, i.e. day or weekend, visits. The significance of the dispersion of the nights spent was clearly visible in the case of the purchasing of infrequent goods and services. Longer stays induce occasional and irregular needs, so sooner or later during the stay the owners will have such an expenditure. Infrequent goods and services is a specific category within the commodity bundle, being an inseparable part of regular spending but at the same time being more common during stays at the second home when it is a part of a leisure lifestyle and specific consumption pattern, in line with Müller's findings (1999). Additionally, the influence of second-home owners' leisure life and daily practices on expenditure patterns was confirmed, seeing that the demand and spending for a variety of goods, e.g. food, increase with the number of leisure activities undertaken while at the cottage.

Access to retailers and services in the second-home municipality turned out to be an important factor of consumer behaviour (confirming the role of basic services and facilities in attracting visitors and buyers (Alward, Workman, & Maki 1992; Wall 1997; Zawadzka & Zieliński 2013)). As a result, the hypothesis labelled "Social amenities" H3: *Second-home owners are more likely to purchase locally and spend larger amounts of money in municipalities where the distance to local shops and services is short* was confirmed to be true. The following relation was proved to be statistically significant: the amount of spending by Finnish and Polish second-home owners was larger in those municipalities in which spatial accessibility to shops and basic services was clearly higher. Furthermore, this factor was particularly influential in shaping local purchases on food products, everyday-use articles, building materials and infrequent services made by representatives of both nations. This was especially true for Finns, given the relatively extensive municipalities (particularly in Lapland), but also the usual concentration of retailers and service suppliers in the central village/local service centre and the scattered pattern of secondary residences, thus contributing to longer (on average) distances between holiday homes and local good and service providers. The critical question of distance and transportation accessibility to local suppliers is rather not the case for Poland, due to a high saturation of basic grocery shops, and thus quite easy access to them, even in more remote villages and settlements.

5.2 Second-home owners' consumption patterns as a manifestation of (dis)integration with local economy

A similar demand for local purchasing for Finnish and Polish second-home owners, regarded here in terms of the number of players involved, was confirmed in this study. There was an almost equal demand in both populations for goods and services considered totally as well as for necessities – food and everyday articles. However, there were considerable differences for the rest of shopping categories, usually with Finnish consumers having clearly more diverse commodity bundle compared to their Polish counterparts. As mentioned above, the respondent's (household) wealth was very helpful in explaining Poles' lack of interest in buying non-basic commodities. Thus, with the Polish consumers' relatively low purchasing power compared to Finns (World Bank 2016), relatively uncompetitive prices, a limited range and often poor quality of products offered by local retailers and service providers compared to easily accessible urban markets (at the permanent place of living, on the way to the holiday home or in the neighbouring municipalities), Poles bought significantly fewer products on site. For Finns, the high demand and variety of products purchased, despite greater distances for the access to basic services (Nieminen 2010), rather demonstrates their deep and comprehensive integration into the local economy. This research shows that the accessibility problem was not in fact a particular obstacle, as demand and spending are driven first by consumer income, then by acceptable prices and further by the range and quality of products, which the main Finnish chains keep at the same level all over the country, regardless of the location (rural or urban), at least in the case of food products and other necessities (FGT 2014).

As a consequence, one can argue that the Finnish national supply system together with the level of the development of the whole country, regardless of the objectively more unfavourable factors (natural conditions, scattered settlement, longer distances), is a critical resource to induce second-home owners to buy locally and to establish strong bonds with local suppliers, and is thus successful in terms of the actual contribution to the community's economy. In this respect, it is more efficient and beneficial for the locals than in Poland, where even favourable spatial conditions (n terms of accessibility and density of service providers) are insufficient and play a surprisingly insignificant role compared to purely economic factors. As a result, there are two distribution models: 1. More dispersed spatially and relatively inaccessible, due to centralisation (Rantanen 2014), although fairer in terms of availability – equal prices, quality and range of products, and 2. Highly accessible for transportation but, at the same time, failing in terms of the competitive offer compared to urban markets (Smolarek & Dzieńdziora 2010, Cyrek 2013). The former unquestionably provides suitable economic conditions at the beginning of the process ('inputs', demand size) for common and efficient local purchasing.

Despite clear similarities in demand for basic commodities in both populations (proved by income elasticity of demand), Engel's curves again confirmed the more significant role of household income/wealth in shaping Polish consumer behaviour towards food products compared to consumers from other European countries (in line with previous research, e.g. Badach 2012; Piekut 2014; CSO 2016). This suggests that other non-economic factors are important for Finns, such as lifestyle and accessibility – given that for Finnish second-home owners the average distance to a grocery was 11 km, as stressed by Nieminen (2010). While the tendency described by Engel's curve was in line with regular spending, at the permanent place of living, the average proportions of second-home spending on food apparently showed that second-home owners have a specific lifestyle and consumption pattern (as argued by Müller (1999, p. 169) on 'changed activity patterns'). In this context, two hypotheses were verified, first – "Income effect"

H_4 *Engel's laws for food, home fees/charges and luxury products prove to apply in the same way as for regular household spending.* It was confirmed that for basic commodities (food products) and luxuries the shape of Engel's curves was similar to those for regular spending, while for housing-related costs including recurrent fees and charges, data inconsistency (lack of continuous data on household income) meant it was not possible to verify any sudden rises, by leaps and bounds, in the curve. However, despite that, the overall tendency in this category of goods was surprisingly proved to be the opposite to that known for regular household spending, that is a decreasing proportion of expenses dedicated to home fees and charges with the household income rise. It seems that there was a relatively low differentiation in second-home living standards among various household income groups than there was in the standards of permanent residences, including plot and home size, the number of rooms, technical infrastructure and facilities; hence, the observed tendency revealed contrasting characteristics. It may also be said that there was less diversity in the utilisation intensity of holiday homes, along with the same level of local rates for water supply, wastewater disposal etc., and that widely varying incomes led to relatively high proportions for 'poor' households and moderate ones for medium and wealthy households.

Then comes the hypothesis labelled "Commodity bundle" H_5: *The proportion of basic commodities and home-related expenses in the total local expenditure is equal for regular and seasonal (second-home) consumption.* However, the hypothesis was proved to be false as it was not confirmed that the proportion of basic commodities (food products) and home-related expenses in the commodity bundle was equal for seasonal and regular spending. Thus, the findings contradicted the results widely known from public statistics on consumer behaviour and the commodity bundle (Statistics Finland 2013; CSO 2015). Instead, the findings proved that the amount of purchase for both categories accounted for far higher percentages in the total seasonal spending than in regular spending (i.e. made at the permanent place of residence) that reflected similarly in shopping structures of Finns and Poles. Thus, it can be additionally argued that for seasonal spending the structure of purchase clearly demonstrated the unifying role of leisure time for spending on basic commodities, at least for this specific context of local consumption.

The contrasting characteristics of second-home owners' expenditure compared to a regular pattern are partly due to the specificity of seasonal spending and stays, as they provide only an incomplete picture of the total (year-round) spending pattern. What is more, it is not only fragmental but refers to very specific spatial and time conditions, in which such expenditures occur, i.e. with no accommodation costs as in the case of traditional forms of tourism, except home-related bills, but with other important, albeit irregular, expenses such as building materials and construction services that are not incurred by traditional tourists (Long, Perdue & Venturoni 2012). In the course of touring, there is a specific consumption pattern demonstrated, combining some everyday patterns with peculiarities strictly linked with seasonal leisure activities (Müller 1999). As a consequence, it turned out that the commodity bundle was less complex, as the lifestyle was simpler (than the regular one, i.e. performed in the permanent place of living), and hence, the share of expenditure on food products was higher in second-home owners' consumption than in regular spending.

Furthermore, a low differentiation in the commodity bundle often means a more limited and selective contribution to the local economy (Roszkowska-Mądra 2009), both in terms of the number of industries benefiting and the flows of money – seeing that food products in high demand are relatively cheap in comparison to other goods and services. To some extent, besides the crucial factor of income, this can be influenced by the modest range of products offered locally, which is a direct obstacle to visitor spending (Ross 1994), and which makes it possible only to fulfil basic needs, while visitors are forced to import more sophisticated goods from the outside.

Interestingly, besides a very low income elasticity, which confirmed the general independence of home-related payments from household incomes, this study contradicted Engel's second law with regard to seasonal housing. Unlike regular home-related household spending, seasonal spending surprisingly proved to fall in proportion to the rise in household income. Such a divergence between household incomes and the second home-related payments is bizarre and unusual, given the extremely high costs for (regular) housing rental in Finland (the highest in EU) but also obviously compared to Poland (Eurostat 2014). This puzzling tendency is even enhanced by a high dynamic rate between income groups and a relatively high proportion of poorer households. Thus, for those less well-off, it probably constitutes a real burden, effectively reducing spending for other purposes and consequently limiting leisure activity and the general utility level of a holiday home. It seems to be caused by the low variety of home standards or by low differences in the intensity of home usage (the latter explanation being more plausible), which are reflected in the level of bills, especially associated with electricity, as also confirmed by Nieminen (2010). Here, this means that despite various types of summer homes and home facilities, the utilisation level is more or less similar, creating comparable expenses but certainly felt more heavily by lower-income earners. A certain proportion of total expenditures on home-related bills definitely leaks out of the local economy, as some suppliers (electricity, insurance) are based outside the municipality. Additionally, the building materials and construction/renovation services were found to be luxury goods given their high income elasticity. This was also confirmed by Engel's curve, since it in fact concerns the possession or coming into possession of a second home, which is always seen as a luxury (Perdue 2004; CSO 2006, 2010; Paris 2010; Lipkina 2013; Czapiński & Panek 2014).

The application of the individual and family life-cycle concept and the life course perspective in the consumer spending context made it possible to interpret second-home owners' consumption patterns changing in time. This revealed certain differences between Finns and Poles in consumption trajectories over the ownership period. It was confirmed that the amount of spending on local products decreases over the length of ownership, although it was more constant for Finns while more fluctuating in time and unbalanced for Poles. At the same time, the study proved that the commodity bundle becomes less diverse over the ownership period for both populations surveyed, although it is far more drastic for Poles while gradual and steady disappearance of subsequent types of goods and services is the case for Finns. Hence, the hypothesis "Family life-cycle and life-course perspective" H_6: *Spending levels for local produce decrease while the commodity bundle becomes less diverse with subsequent family life-cycle stages and the owner's life-course* was proved to be true in those two aspects under examination. Furthermore, the situation in Finnish municipalities thus confirmed to be advantageous for various local industries and, in a broader sense, particularly contribuitive to multifunctional development that makes the community's economy stronger and more resilient in a long-term perspective and sustainable manner (Imbs & Wacziarg 2003; Bogdanov & Vasiljević 2011; Siciliano 2012; Raczyk & Majkowska 2015). Conversely, consumption tendencies in Polish municipalities proved to be greatly inefficient in terms of local economic development due to the short-lasting effects and very limited in functional terms.

It was found that changes in local consumption over the ownership period were highly dependent upon the owner's age and the stage of family life-cycle, which confirms the results from previous studies (Gourinchas & Parker 1997; Antonides & van Raaij 1998; Du & Kamakura 2006) as well as the findings on the changing motives and needs over the owner's life course (Lundmark & Marjavaara 2013; Lagerqvist, Strandin Pers & Nordin 2014; Rantanen 2014). The survey samples (Finns and Poles) were significantly different in terms of the respondents' age structures – with the prevalence of pre-retired and retired people in the Finnish sample and the domination of relatively young people (working mobile) in the Polish population surveyed – and these differences reflected directly in the consumption pattern but also in a more indirect way through the family life-cycle, i.e. basically household size and its structure (presence or absence of children). However, interestingly, an importance of the owner's age and the stage the of family life-cycle in recognising and explaining the changing consumer behaviour over time was significantly moderated by the length of stay at a second home: hence, there obtains the abovementioned favourable consumption pattern among Finns (in terms of a stable and diverse commodity bundle as well as in terms of a non-drastic constant decrease of demand), even despite the disadvantageous age structure and related features, e.g. small household size with no children at home. At the same time, the role of the length of stay as one of the crucial factors shaping consumption in tourism (proved by numerous studies, e.g. (Martinez-Garcia & Raya 2008; Barros & Machado 2010) among Finns can be explained at least partly by cultural factors and lifestyle associated with second homes that trigger their owners to utilise it significantly longer over the year even for elderly people. This is not that common among Polish owners, who apparently have more possibilities to visit the cottage, given that almost 50% lived permanently up to 100 km from a secondary residence (according to the sample).

Including informal purchasing in the analysis provided an opportunity to learn more about this particular (often neglected) aspect of the local economy and, at the same time, to take a broader look at economic relationships. It also provided ground for more comprehensive and complete grasp of the impact of second homes on the local economy, which has often been approached too narrowly, i.e. was limited to the formal economies. Two hypotheses were verified with this regard: 1. "Demand for informal purchasing" H_7: *Informal purchasing is less common among Finnish than Polish second-home owners* and "Logic of informal purchasing" H_8: *Formal economy's failure, in terms of spatial accessibility and product availability, prompts second-home owners to make use of informal distribution channels.* The former hypothesis was rejected, as Finnish second-home owners used informal distribution channels more often than their Polish counterparts in terms of scale, i.e. measured by the proportion of consumers acquiring goods and services informally. Moreover, informal purchases accounted for almost equal shares of the total expenditures allocated by both populations of second-home owners in local economies. As the research showed, informal channels of distribution were used by the majority of second-home owners in Finland and almost half of their Polish counterparts. It was less important but still valuable in terms of spending in both cases, since informal spending accounted for a fifth of the total expenditure incurred locally. However, the popularity of informal purchasing, especially among Finnish second-home owners, and consequently, little to no significant difference in expenditure share compared to Poles, slightly contradicted the general view on the relatively modest role of the informal economy in Nordic countries (based on GDP share and percentage of undeclared work) in contrast to post-socialist/transition countries provided by previous international comparisons, at least with regard to second-home owners (Hazans 2011; Schneider 2011, 2013). This can be partly explained by the fact that this study included also direct purchases of food/agricultural produce from farms (which is not illegal in either country) in the category of the informal economy.

As far as the latter hypothesis is concerned, it was proven to be true that in terms of spatial accessibility measured by the average distance to selected local services (e.g. grocers, specialty shops, catering within the same municipality) as well as by the travel distance from the permanent to secondary residence, local formal economy failure was a significant factor influencing informal purchasing, especially with regard to basic commodities, namely food supply, enhanced, at the same time, by proximity and accessibility to local, mainly self-subsistent, farmers.

Thus, informal transactions were found to be a substitute form of provision, as no respondents used only informal distribution channels, which slightly contradicts the previous research findings on the minor importance of formal economy failure as a motive inducing informal purchasing (Sassen 1998; Williams & Martínez-Pérez 2014; Williams & Horodnic 2016). Consequently, local informal provision was less diverse and comprised mostly basic commodities and simple services, because they can be easily provided informally by farmers and individuals. Despite its economic insignificance for rural residents (on average), as the amount of expenditure was largely dispersed among the local providers, it has other functions that are important in establishing, retaining and strengthening social relations, and thus building confidence between stakeholders and contributing to the sense of community (Duncan 1992; Losby *et al.* 2002). This is mainly due to the origins of and motivations behind informal economy, heavily based in the confidence between players, frequent local embeddedness of both sides of transactions, and social interdependence of community members (Toennis 1957), here including second-home owners, but also due to strong family connections (Williams & Martínez-Pérez 2014). The study found that rural roots (the owner's place of birth in the municipality of the second-home location) as well as having relatives and friends in the local community were critical for establishing informal transactions. Hence, informal channels of distribution are more likely to be long-lasting and promising (at least if they are not illegal) as they are based on trust and strong social contacts and networks (Fernández-Kelly & Schefner 2006).

Hypothesis H_8 was confirmed in that the most important motive driving informal food purchases was accessibility, i.e. wide access to farmers (in typical agricultural communities) and, at the same time, low access to local grocers, formal retailers and service providers (for a third of Finns, the average distance to the nearest grocery was more than 15 km), which suggests a great role of the formal economy failure in inducing informal transactions (Bajada 2002; Williams & Martínez-Pérez 2014). In such circumstances, farmers and individuals somehow naturally bridge the gap of inaccessible/non-existent good and service providers so that at least basic needs are met by alternative supply channels (a kind of 'survival or 'coping' strategy on the part of consumers). Hence, the satisfaction of demand shifts from formal (non-existent or inaccessible) to informal (nearest and most accessible) suppliers, unless there is an asymmetry of information on where to find local (informal) suppliers in favour of the community members.

5.3 Second-home owners' spending and its impact on the local economy

Based on the survey among the local community members, in terms of revenues, the median values confirmed that local sellers from both countries did not earn much on average, compared to their total household incomes. Thus, the hypothesis "Income creation" H_9: *The contribution of second homes to local household income rise proves its significance as an important/main source of income* was proven to be false, since the research findings confirmed varying contribution of second-home tourism to the local people's household incomes from moderate (for Finns) to only marginal (for Poles), where at best it can be considered as an additional and seasonal source of income.

In Finland, the revenues from supplying second-home owners were gained rather by the representatives of relatively wealthy local households, while in Poland it was more by members of middle- and lower-income groups. As most local Polish sellers had permanent jobs elsewhere or another major source of income (pensions), it confirms that supplying second-home owners constituted only a secondary source of funding. In addition, combining two or more sources of income in practice meant very often selling goods and services informally as part of a 'survival' strategy by struggling (low-income) households, as argued by some researchers (Berger & Buvinić 1989; Leonard 1998). Thus, the contribution to the community's economy was very limited, with marginal extra income for local households and with no contribution to municipal budgets (through evading tax payments). In contrast, in Finland, with wealthy households being the main beneficiaries of supplying second-home owners, it was confirmed that their members were mainly entrepreneurs with official businesses and possibly focusing on catering for second-home owners. In turn, they contributed to the local economy more comprehensively through income rise and tax revenues to the local council budgets.

Then, in terms of the contribution to the local labour market, the following hypothesis was verified: "Jobs creation" H_{10}: *The contribution of second homes to local labour market proves its significance as a job-maintaining rather than a job-creation factor*. This hypothesis was confirmed to be true when measured through revenues gained by local people, since Finnish second-home owners' contribution to local job creation was higher than for Poles, albeit marginal in both cases. In light of that, the picture for Finland partly supports the positive assessment of the influence found in previous studies (Nielsen *et al.* 2009; Guisan & Aguayo 2010; Scanlon, Sagor & Whitehead 2014; Oliveira, Roca & Roca 2015), seeing the importance of second-home tourism as an income and employment opportunity for rural households. The results for Poles are basically in line with a discouraging view according to which the contribution is of minor importance, usually with many limitations with regard to working conditions and the quality of jobs (Marcouiller 1997; Gallent, Mace & Tewdwr-Jones 2002; Müller 2002b; Wallace *et al.* 2005).

The survey sample, data shortages, moderate informal purchasing and locals' reluctance to give exact figures for earnings permitted only a broad-brush estimate of the potential impact on the local economy of the communities surveyed. The potential earnings for the municipalities surveyed in Finland, still based on the data provided by the locals, totalled €54,082,360, or €37,933,097 after tax. This would generate 497 full-time equivalent jobs per year or 1,985 seasonal jobs. In relation to the current employment situation in the municipalities surveyed, this translates into a potential increase in existing employment of about 2.3%, which seems to be a not significant but visible proportion, given that rural labour markets are usually weaker and monofunctional, with low-paid work, and are much less efficiently utilised than urban ones. Potential earnings for Polish municipalities surveyed were estimated at PLN 31,154,651 (€7,489,099), which would provide potential sellers with a net after-tax income of PLN 10,819,076 (€2,600,739). The revenue would provide local economies with 294 new full-time permanent jobs (adding 0.7% to the current employment rate) or 1,177 seasonal jobs, thus rather maintaining existing jobs than creating new ones.

Then, it is worth noting that the situation is significantly better when one attempts to make the impact assessment based on second-home owners' spending, i.e. the in-flow of money into local economies. The Finnish second-home owners surveyed spent €1,423,413 locally, but the financial flow was unevenly distributed among municipalities. This was due to variations in the response rate, interest in local purchasing and household consumption patterns with regard to the size and structure of the commodity bundle. After taxation, the inflow amounted to €1,142,319, while the remaining share potentially ensured 11 new permanent full-time equivalent jobs or 45 seasonal jobs. Furthermore, based on this, a simple and rough estimate of potential purchasers was calculated as 48,973 owners, while the total spending they generated was estimated at €161,842,471, providing a considerable financial boost to the local economies. In relation to a potential contribution to the local labour market, this would in effect cover 1,283 new full-time equivalent permanent jobs or 5,130 seasonal jobs.

Poles spent a total of PLN 2,186,822 (€525,678), although their expenditures differed significantly between municipalities. After taxation, the income was PLN 402,375 (€96,725), ensuring 18 permanent jobs or 73 seasonal jobs. In effect, this would give 5,145 potential consumers, who would generate PLN 30,324,298 (€7,289,495), providing 254 new permanent full-equivalent jobs or 1,014 seasonal jobs after taxation and other input expenses. If these rough estimates are related to existing local labour market in the municipalities surveyed, the contribution to new permanent jobs would differ significantly, giving 5.9% in Finland and 0.6% in Poland.

What is important in understanding the differences in the impact assessment between the locals' viewpoint and second-home owners perspective is that the local expenditure is subject to reductions due to various financial leakages from the local system, e.g. profit transfer outside the municipality, business and household input supply from the outside etc. (Swarbrooke 1999). The fact that second-home owners buy goods and services locally does not mean that it is always from local (or locally-based) providers. For consumers, it is often not possible to distinguish between local and external suppliers, hence the declared amount of expenditure, although spent locally, usually does not remain in full in the community's economy, which is one of the reasons for the disparities between the size of inflow and the earnings reported by locals.

To be more accurate with discrepancies between second-home owners' spending and local people's earnings, first, financial leakages out of the local economy that may significantly reduce the total inflow of expenditure should be mentioned. Because in the tourism sector such leakages are the highest in weak economies (Meyer 2007), it is more likely that they were more significant in Polish than in Finnish municipalities, as well as in more remote, monofunctional economies than in those with high levels of functional diversity. This does not include the structural and operational leakages of second-home tourism, including owners importing goods and services from the outside (as confirmed by many researchers: Müller 2002b; Müller, Hall & Keen 2004; Marjavaara 2008; Nordin 2011)), as in the questionnaire they reported only goods and services purchased locally. Some of the businesses operating in the area are owned and/or invested in by individuals and companies from outside the municipality, e.g. through an external investment in tourism-based or suburban municipalities. Consequently, some of the profits from second-home owners' local expenditures drain away to these investors' municipalities. This is usually not reported in questionnaires, since consumers are often not aware of the business owner's origins and consider all expenditures made locally to be a local spending. This occurred in both countries; however, it seems that it mainly applies to Finland: food supply and distribution is almost entirely in the hands of nationwide chains (K-Chain, S-Chain) and there are no small, family shops (FGT 2014). It is very likely that, apart from local income, capital and property tax, labour costs and some of the input expenditures, the profits are continuously returned to the external investor/owner. Hence, at least food products and basic commodity supplies contribute less to income generation but significantly more to local job creation, since mainly the local community members are engaged as workers in retails chains. This explanation is applicable to the Polish context to a rather smaller extent, given that besides national or regional sales networks there are still numerous small family shops in the countryside (definitely more accessible for second-home owners in more remote locations), for which such financial leakages are rare or non-existent. Besides the food-supply sector, similar mechanisms can be observed in various other sectors (including services) but to a lesser extent when compared to Finland. Second (in more methodological terms), the sample sizes and response rates of Finnish second-home owners and locals were different. Third, the survey sample of locals included people with different economic activities. The entrepreneurs who should mainly profit from supplying second-home owners accounted only for 14.7% in the Finnish survey and 17.6% in the Polish one. Thus, as in both countries only a third of local sellers (incl. farmers) were business owners, most represented the informal/shadow economy and the potential under-reporting and consequent underestimation can cause considerable discrepancies between financial inflow and actual revenues.

The analysis of the views on the impact of the second-home phenomenon on the local infrastructure enabled to verify the hypothesis "Developmental impact" H_{11}: *Second-home tourism, in the local people's opinions, is less significant in strictly economic terms (income and source of employment) but more appreciated in broad developmental terms (infrastructure and service provision) for the local community.* As mentioned earlier, the findings of this study proved that second-home tourism, at least measured by the revenues to the local household budgets, was rather insignificant in economic terms, providing only supplementary and often marginal incomes and contributing to the local labour market rather by maintaining the existing level of employment than by creating new jobs. However, with regard to more general development goals, it was found that in local people's opinions the impact of second homes on infrastructure and service provision was assessed as significant by Poles and as insignificant by Finns (apart from their positive view on the influence on local culture and community's tourism facilities).

In this regard, locals in Finland did not consider second homes to be an important but rather a supplementary community development tool. In Poland, on the other hand, they were seen as an unquestionable asset, similarly to other objective development preconditions such as good transport access, proximity to a large city and highly rated environmental amenities. This is all the more interesting as the scale of the second-home phenomenon between the two countries differs significantly in favour of Finland. Hence, this confirms that even in Finnish municipalities with large concentrations of holiday homes, where the phenomenon may be a critical development resource for local authorities, the economic effect is perceived as very limited. In Poland, with a relatively low number of secondary residences, they are nevertheless seen as a potential and actual advantage (especially in remote communities), given the positive, although limited, changes in villages in which they are located. In light of that, the hypothesis was considered to be true for Poles while false for Finns.

Since second-home owners are considered as a powerful and influential social group in rural locations, they are often decisive in convincing local authorities to build a new road, a sewage system, improve the tourist facilities or organise summer events (Pammer *et al.* 2008, Farstad & Rye 2013). This is particularly important for more remote, depopulated and traditionally rural communities, which are often infrastructurally underdeveloped compared to urban areas (Overvåg & Berg 2011). This is not the case in Finland, where the infrastructure is well developed even in peripheral rural areas, and thus, second homes may only be an influential factor with regard to social development. This explains the positive opinions on summer cultural events or tourist facilities, which seem unlikely to be provided without the demand from tourists and visitors. This is confirmed by the fact that the perception of the beneficial influence of second homes was more prevalent in less developed Lapland communities with highly-rated natural amenities and sparsely populated areas, as well as in small villages, where certain development problems (even related to infrastructure) are more common and similar to those in remote areas of Poland.

This view was influenced positively by the opinions on social contacts with second-home owners, which are more likely to be maintained in small communities with few local people. This is also logical for the Polish respondents, who had a more positive general view on the role of second homes, since they mainly represented small villages in eastern Poland, a region which is more traditional and less economically developed. They are often low-income earners and retired people living in depopulated villages, and hence, it is to be expected that second-home owners, as new, more affluent, well-educated and relatively young people, will be seen as inducing positive changes in locals' everyday life and in a broader sense as maintaining the community's viability.

6. Conclusions

In previous chapters of this book, second-home owners' consumer behaviour, spending patterns as well as the resulting inflow of money and its impacts on the local economy were discussed. The research objectives were met by: assessing the level of integration of second-home owners with the community's economy in Finland and Poland, identifying factors of local purchasing, depicting consumption patterns and attempting to estimate the contribution and importance of second-home tourism for the economic development of rural communities.

The research findings led to the general conclusion, being at the same time a confirmation that the introductory *Consumption convergence* thesis was correctly stated, that despite contrasting cultural, social and economic backgrounds as well as clear differences in the second home functioning, Finnish and Polish second-home owners are similar in terms of consumer behaviour. The converging role of the second-home possession reflects explicitly through a variety of consumer behaviour constituents. Therefore, as a result of this study, one may find strong evidence-based arguments behind the similarities among both consumer groups in terms of: 1. Proportion of purchasers; 2. Structure of commodity bundle; 3. Income elasticity for basic commodities and other types of goods and services; 4. Engel's curves for necessities and luxury goods; 5. Popularity of direct and informal purchasing; 6. Various determinants of consumer behaviour; 7. Beneficiary industries taking advantage of second-home owners' demand for local produce – retail and construction/renovation sectors; and 8. Local people's assessment of the role of second homes in their income creation. That unifying ability/role of (local) consumption can be consequently seen as a universal aspect of second-home living and, at the same time, a valuable contribution to the common understanding of this specific consumer behaviour applied in international comparisons.

The two populations surveyed differ, sometimes significantly, in terms of the drivers and developments of the second-home phenomenon as well as in the macro-scale/national context. At the same time, however, they resemble each other in terms of consumer behaviour, which appears to be an argument for its universality, i.e. applicability to studies of other populations/nations (although possibly to be confirmed case-by-case). Consequently, under such assumptions, the research findings could be considered as universal and applicable to other contexts, thus proving substantial – and locally even significant – impact of second-home tourism on the rural economy, including the rise of household incomes, the creation or at least maintenance of job places, an impulse for local people's retraining by learning new skills and starting an economic activity, but in a broader context also in terms of social development increase of social contacts, social inclusion, vitality, social revitalisation especially of declining communities.

The study apparently showed that despite certain distinctive differences (e.g. in purchasing power, financial situation and lifestyles), leisure time and seasonal stays at a second home unify their owners' consumption patterns, at least in this narrow sense, thus showing the specificity of second-home owners' demand, needs, preferences, motivations and access to such goods. What is essential in terms of the specificity of the second-home phenomenon is that it reflects various attributes, resources and actions such as return and retirement migrations, second-home owners' rural roots and previous experiences in spending time/visiting the countryside, the recurrence of visits and stays at a second home (year to year), an increase in the likelihood of converting a second home into a permanent one, and a visibly longer season (compared to traditional tourism). Those can form a critical potential for meeting social and economic development objectives of rural communities, as they provide diversity, strengthen the local social fabric (often weakened by intense out-migration and depopulation), and foster the vitality of the community.

In addition, due to the fact that root and return migration partly reflect through second-home ownership, the social and economic integration with the local community is clearly stronger than in the case of other seasonal residents not having (previous) family ties with local people. Consequently, more coherent visions and representations of the rural among second-home owners and local residents are more likely to endure. There is usually a greater interest in the development of local territory on the part of seasonal residents, not just the home and its close surrounding, and hence, local embeddedness, rootedness, bonds with community members, local participation and involvement are truly strong, creating a valuable opportunity for rural development. As the local society often offers to second-home owners relatively small community size, the friendliness of people, closeness to family and friends as well as more spare time possibilities to undertake certain actions, these altogether provide the owners with an actual opportunity to actively take part in the social life of the community through social participation, self-reliance, self-confidence and conviction of being more agent (acting more independently, on one's will and having influence on the local community decisions) and empowered. Then, through second homes, the owners offer to the community a strong sense of place, local belonging, embeddedness and awareness stronger than among traditional tourists or urban residents in their permanent place of living.

Importantly, the starting point for these considerations, that is the specificity of second-home tourism, means in fact that consumption patterns of second-home owners over a leisure stay at the cottage are in general far more contextual than regular spending, as they occur in a specific place, at a specific time, and usually with additional psychological features (in a birth place, with a strong sense of place, and enhanced by a deliberate choice of the second home location). This is indeed worth emphasising due to the fact that second-home owners unquestionably provide rural communities with social power but simultaneously with social responsibility, at least to a higher extent than traditional tourists do (with weak place attachment, anonymity, no promise to re-visit) or than new ex-urban dwellers, e.g. in a suburban area, who usually express a low level of sense of place, albeit with a greater social and political power (due to his/her wealth and social position) to influence the local community's life. For second-home owners, social power is often not negative and goes hand in hand with social responsibility, which is crucial in avoiding excessive exploitation and also in striving towards a more balanced and sustainable use of diverse local resources resulting in maintaining the local community liveable.

At this point, in the case of second homes, the institution of ownership plays a great role when compared, for instance, to traditional forms of tourism (regular tourists), since the latter offers stronger, broader in scope, more comprehensive and long-term local impacts. What is more, that role is manifested through more conscious and responsive willingness/interest in local resources. Thus, the demand is less consumptionist and less propelled by the pure, hedonistic utilisation of local resources, resulting in such inattentive attitude to the close neighbourhood. At the same time, it is more conscious and mindful, with more attention, concern and responsibility expressed not only to the property itself but also to the local resources in the immediate surrounding area; home possession is more deeply rooted locally, with a stronger place attachment, denser and stronger social ties with locals, and familiarity with the nearest context, and hence, it is potentially more positive and beneficial with regard to the community development.

In addition to the significance of ownership, another universal factor crucial for local purchasing was household wealth/income. Therefore, if it is not up to the local suppliers to increase consumer income (as it is in this case), the priority should be shifted to other pull forces making local goods and services more attractive and thus reducing the role of income, i.e. such that are dedicated to product features/distinctiveness and price competitiveness. The focus should be on other elements underlying consumer motivations and preferences, with attention paid to quality, range, localism (local products), diversity, uniqueness, freshness, accessibility, availability, proximity, individualised goods and services and competitive prices. These attributes can be ensured even by small, family-based enterprises with apparently limited resources, as local and direct purchasing is based on confidence, trust and social interaction, so there is the absence of anonymity and a direct contact with the customer/supplier and short supply chains, thus creating suitable conditions to adjust what is on offer to individual consumers' demands and preferences. Links between the demand and supply sides can be strengthened more indirectly through certain marketing activities, as well as those that weaken information asymmetry, such as marking, signs and adverts to supplement the word-of-mouth marketing, which is common for local, direct and informal purchasing. These can easily improve accessibility, as can other indirect actions, e.g. the prolongation the season.

Additionally, the demand for locally produced goods was also confirmed by a considerable interest in informal and direct purchasing on the part of tourists and seasonal dwellers, thus revealing another local market niche segment as a (potential) beneficiary of providing basic commodities to second-home owners, e.g. the local food production system. It is clear that for various reasons consumers are particularly keen on such products, confirming and manifesting close relationships between alternative agriculture and distribution channels (short supply, local food production, civic agriculture and farmer's market) and tourism and leisure activities. Hence, in a broader sense, local, direct and partly informal purchases are a pure manifestation of contemporary consumption/consumerism, whose representative is the aware consumer, interested in improving his/her knowledge about the provenience of products, the way of their processing, but also about how these characteristics are important for other aspects of his/her lives (concerns about natural environment, health, social issues, local development etc.). For second-home owners, local suppliers are usually better recognised, less enigmatic and less anonymous, since maintaining closer social ties to them makes a real difference compared to such relationships in urban locations, where critical attributes (advantages) for the savvy consumer cannot be easily found and identified. What is more, some alternative agricultures do not have an economic focus (short-term profit maximisation) but the emphasis is more on social-, health- and well-being-related matters, thus additionally contributing not only to local household wealth but also to their members' quality of life.

As many second-home owners purchase local goods and services (mostly food, construction/renovation and maintenance) informally, and their spending makes up a fifth of the total local purchasing, this irrefutably demonstrates that there is an economic and social potential that could be formalised and utilised to the advantage of the whole community. Obviously, here it is not clear whether formalisation would not hamper economic relationships and foster the rejection of this activity (e.g. due to unacceptable tax and registration burdens). However, in terms of community's own good, fairness and legality (although not all informal transactions are illegal), this should be required. At the same time, a large demand for informally provided goods suggests that this is a reaction to the failure of the formal economy in terms of accessibility, prices, quality, range and consumer approach, and also an expression of the need for social contacts. This last attribute is definitely one that the local economy certainly has and naturally provides (as this is one of the inherent characteristics of small-scale supply systems). In order to formalise it without losing these crucial features and without losing economic rationality – given the tax and input expenditure burden as well as relatively low and seasonal-dependent incomes – the most logical solution would be to initiate and develop more community-based initiatives such as cooperatives, social enterprises (e.g. in maintenance and renovation service sector) as well as local food-production systems, farmer's markets and alternative agricultures. The informal economy is certainly a segment of local economy that includes a valuable, and certainly not inconsiderable part of expenditures, incomes and relationships that have not been examined by previous research in the context of second homes.

Apart from its monetary importance, informal economy has an important social value, given how strongly these informal linkages are anchored in social relations, close contacts, neighbourhood, closeness, community attachment and mutual help, and how significant these linkages can be in contributing to social inclusion, community and place attachment, the enhancement of social networks, community development and contributing to the vitality of the community. The analysis of both groups surveyed (locals and second-home owners) has shown the importance of non-economic motivations, needs, determinants and their effects. Societal impact proves to be an equally important aspect of economic transactions. It often further translates into social cohesion, community vitality, resilience and the strengthening of human and social capital. These help to incorporate other people into community life, giving opportunities to economically, socially, and physically 'disabled' people or even fostering more balanced, sustainable local development. In addition, this study has confirmed the active role of second-home owners in the community's life, their local participation, local embeddedness and community attachment, which are crucial for building new communities and, in turn, influence purchasing patterns, e.g. towards ethnocentricity and localism. Conversely, local purchasing transactions may in themselves help build social ties and, consequently, strengthen the community spirit.

Specifically, as this research has shown, the economic significance for the local community due to the large inflow of expenditures incurred on site by second-home owners (excluding spending related to the original purchase and home-related payments) is a noticeable contribution both to local people's income as well as to local job creation. However, at the same time, from the local people's perspective, this influence on local financial and labour resources is considerably weaker. Thus, there is a sort of inconsistency, which in part derives from the methodological issues of the survey, but is also a result of revenues leaking out of the local economy (mainly by being transferred to owners and companies' head offices based outside the municipality). Thus, the size of local spending is often inefficiently 'processed' to the advantage of the local economy, as a considerable portion of it is filtered out by various financial leakages. Consequently, these are the main issues to be improved for the sake of community benefits and success. This is all the more important as one can easily see that the potential significance and multidirectional impact could contribute far more to the wealth of local people (who often struggle with the disadvantages of rural life, i.e. limited accessibility, local labour market shortages, a weak local economy, a monofunctional economy and the long-term structural effects of heavy and sustained emigration). In this context, this is an untapped and missed opportunity that represents a hidden 'giant'.

The high proportion of local purchases among second-home owners along with their high levels of spending have proven the existence of strong linkages and an apparently close integration of Finnish and Polish second-home owners into the local economies. However, considerable differences were found for the commodity bundle, which was slightly disadvantageous, with the prevalence of basic commodities (food) and simple services, the contribution of which is often economically limited, especially compared to construction/renovation and infrequent services. Thus, with a relatively low purchasing power of Polish consumers, uncompetitive prices, the limited range and more often a poor quality of rural retailers' products, they bought significantly fewer products on site. For Finns, the high demand for a variety of local products, despite poorer access to basic services, manifested their deep and comprehensive integration into the local economy. As a consequence, Finland and Poland display two different provision models: 1. (Finland) More spatially dispersed and relatively inaccessible in terms of transport (e.g. due to centralisation) but fairer in terms of equal prices and quality as well as availability, and 2. (Poland) Easily accessible but at the same time failing in terms of availability of various goods and services. The first model unquestionably provides more suitable economic conditions for local purchasing at the beginning of the process (inputs, demand size). However, given the nationwide character of Finnish retail chains based outside the municipalities, this model is undoubtedly less supportive of the local economy due to a greater potential for financial leakages, since the headquarters of nationwide sale chains are based in large cities. At the same time, it is more supportive with regard to the labour market, ensuring job creation for locals. On the other hand, the Polish model contributes more to (informal) local business and household incomes, thus improving their wealth and living conditions. However, it is less important in terms of employment, as the revenues are usually sufficient for self-employment and the maintenance of existing jobs, seeing that the revenues are too insignificant to generate new employment.

Then, unlike external markets which are generally unknown, anonymous, difficult to enter, highly demanding for promotions and marketing, and often with significant transport costs for rural producers, the market comprising second-home owners/users is pretty more accessible, as here customers come themselves to local suppliers, and thus, it offers more suitable conditions for instance in terms of transportation (no significant transport costs, no agents/intermediaries), being a pure exemplification of short-supply chains, while in societal dimension it generates a significantly smaller ecological footprint. What is more, second-home owners' needs for a wide variety of goods and services, in economically monofunctional areas, create unique development opportunities for individuals – retraining, increasing skill levels, improving knowledge, gaining experience as well as rising incomes and the quality of life of local people but also, in a more collective sense, such a large and diversified demand provides actual opportunities for functional diversification (through enriching monofunctionality), and consequently, strengthens resilience, viability and sustainability of rural systems.

Obviously, it should be remembered that, similarly to other social phenomena, second homes bring not only positive implications to the community development but could also entail negative or at least non-positive side effects, which has been confirmed by numerous studies in the field. These manifest themselves in various aspects of second-home functioning, typically in the form of local spatial conflicts or those associated with the degree and way of the utilisation of local resources. Additionally, they may also reflect in controversies through ambiguous or negative impact of the second-home tourism on certain industries (traditional tourism sector, forestry, farming etc.) or second-home owners' influence on local authorities' decisions that altogether could be generalised as divergences in the visions and future developments of the rural between various stakeholders (including second-home owners and locals on what the rural will be and for whom it will be). It is necessary to be aware of those negative tendencies, but this study has confirmed that a key-factor crucial for vitality of the countryside is to provide income and employment to the local people. This opportunity can be ensured by second homes, albeit under certain conditions (optimal scale/concentration of the phenomenon, strong linkages between supply and demand side, localism in purchasing, reduced leakages out of the local economy, availability of labour force, valuable endogenous resources etc.).

Therefore, the final positive effect depends on regulation, policies, their enforcement and generally on governance so as to capitalise on the economic and social potential to the advantage of a community's development, and, at the same time, to reduce various pressures and unrestrained utilisation of local resources in order to be the least excessive but possibly sustainable and long-lasting. These should be implemented starting from local spatial planning, the access to and the use of local assets, also in terms of good and service provision to second-home owners by local suppliers and producers. Achieving a local success is possible if the role that second homes can play in contributing to local incomes and employment is acknowledged among the community leaders and, at the same time, translated into more formal language, i.e. by incorporating the second-home phenomenon into the vision and strategic planning for local development at the local and regional territorial scale. Then, only the active (targeted) role of second homes in local development can be planned to maximise the community's benefits with no harm to and for the good of the locals and their territory. In other words, second homes cannot be treated as (the only) remedy for all the difficulties occurring in rural communities but, at the same time, they can be considered as a valuable and useful alternative and a supplementary development tool that, along with other measures and supportive instruments, can provide the locals with the positive effect: the vitality of the community or, in particular conditions, its social and economic regeneration.

To conclude, the current situation is that second homes are a stable and increasingly common reality in rural areas. This means that for various types of areas (in terms of economic functions) and their residents a new quality will be occurring and challenging the communities' development. This research proves that capitalising on this phenomenon is possible and may bring substantial tangible economic and social benefits to rural areas. It seems, however, that despite second home's importance, seriousness and unquestionable usefulness for future development of the countryside, some aspects still remain a 'terra incognita', or invisible and untapped potential. This is what often happens, with the economic potential of second homes being considered important by researchers and proved by the evidence, but largely neglected or unrecognised by regional policy-makers, local authorities and finally local people, who concentrate more on the contribution of traditional tourism, and thus, lose sight of a long-term development opportunity provided by second-home tourism. What is more, when one seeks (alternative) development directions, it is common to look for and apply external solutions and ignore the existing, well-grounded, locally nested actual responses. Thus, second homes along with their owners, despite constituting a considerable potential, are often overlooked and their potential is underrated by local authorities and businesses. Hence, this book aims to raise awareness among various stakeholders, pointing to the fact that second homes may have a significant, quantifiable potential to be utilised successfully to the advantage of the community development. This study stresses the importance of the problem, noting that the issue of second homes is worth exploring not only for cognitive but also practical reasons.

References

Ackerman, J.M., Griskevicius, V. & Li, N.P. (2011). Let's get serious: Communicating commitment in romantic relationships. *Journal of Personality and Social Psychology*, 100(6), 1079–1094.

Ackerman, J.M., Becker, D.V., Mortensen, C.R., Sasaki, T., Neuberg, S.L. & Kenrick, D.T. (2009). A pox on the mind: Disjunction of attention and memory in the processing of physical disfigurement. *Journal of Experimental Social Psychology*, 45, 478–485.

Adamiak, C. (2012). Miejsce drugich domów w zagospodarowaniu obszarów wiejskich województwa kujawsko-pomorskiego. *Studia Obszarów Wiejskich*, 29, 175–191.

Adamiak, C., Pitkänen, K. & Lehtonen, O. (2016). Seasonal residence and counterurbanization: The role of second homes in population redistribution in Finland, *GeoJournal*, ?, 1–16.

Adamowicz, M. & Zwolińska-Ligaj, M. (2009). Koncepcja wielofunkcyjności jako element zrównoważonego rozwoju obszarów wiejskich. *Zeszyty Naukowe SGGW, Polityki Europejskie, Finanse i Marketing*, 2(51), 11–38.

Agarwal, V.B. & Yochum, G.R. (1999). Tourist spending and race of visitors. *Journal of Travel Research*, 38(2), 173–176.

Agarwal, V.B. & Yochum, G.R. (2000). Determinants of tourist spending. In: A.G. Woodside, G.I. Crouch, J.A. Mazanec, M. Oppermann, & M.Y. Sakai (Eds.), *Consumer psychology of tourism, hospitality and leisure*, (pp. 311–330). CABI Publishing: Wallingford.

Aguglia, L. & Salvioni, C. (2010). Direct selling in Italy: A marketing strategy to promote localized agro-food systems. Paper presented at 9th European IFSA Symposium on "Localised sustainable agri-food systems in times of rural changes", 4th-7th July 2010, Vienna http://ifsa.boku.ac.at/cms/fileadmin/Proceeding2010/2010_WS4.2_Aguglia.pdf

Ahmad, A. & Thyagaraj, K.S. (2015). Consumer's intention to purchase green brands: The roles of environmental concern, environmental knowledge and self expressive benefits. *Current World Environment*, 10(3), 879–889.

Allanson, P. & Whitby, M. (1996). Rural policy and the British countryside (pp. 1–16). University of Newcastle upon Tyne, Centre for Rural Economy, Earthscan Publications Ltd.: London.

Almstedt, Å. (2013). Post-productivism in rural areas: A contested concept. In: L. Lundmark & C. Sandström (Eds.), *Natural resources and regional develop-*

ment theory, (pp. 8–22). Institutionen för geografi och ekonomisk historia, Umeå universitet. GERUM Kulturgeografisk arbetsrapport: Umeå.

Alward, G.S., Workman, W.G. & Maki, W.R. (1992). Regional economic impact analysis for Alaskan wildlife resources. In: G.L. Peterson, C.S. Swanson, D.W. McCollum & M.H. Thomas (Eds.), *Valuing wildlife resources in Alaska*, (pp. 61–86). Westview Press: Boulder.

Amilien, V. (2005). About local foods: An introduction. *Anthropology of food*, 4, 1–13.

Anderson, W. (2011). Enclave tourism and its socio-economic impact in emerging destinations. *Anatolia*, 22(3), 361–377.

Andersson, K. & Lehtola, M. (2009). Farmers, businessmen or green entrepreneurs: Producers of new rural goods and services in rural areas under urban pressure. *Journal of Environmental Policy & Planning*, 11(1), 29–43.

Angowski, M. & Lipowski, M. (2014). Uwarunkowania wyboru produktów żywnościowych i miejsc ich zakupu. *Marketing i Rynek*, 6, 2–16.

Antonides, G. & van Raaij, W.F. (1998). *Consumer behaviour: A European perspective*. John Wiley and Sons: Chichester.

Armah, M. & Teensma, T. (2012). *Estimates of categories of personal consumption expenditures adjusted for net foreign travel spending*, Research Spotlight, April 2012.

Armstrong, G., Harker, M., Kotler, P. & Brennan, R. (2009). *Marketing: An introduction*. Financial Times Prentice Hall: Harlow.

Auruskeviciene, V., Vianelli, D. & Reardon, J. (2012). Comparison of consumer ethnocentrism behavioural patterns in transitional economies. *Transformations in Business and Economics*, 11(2), 20–35.

Babin, B.J., Darden, W.R. & Griffin, M. (1994). Work and/or fun: Measuring hedonic and utilitarian shopping value. *Journal of Consumer Research*, 20, 644–656.

Backhouse, R.E. & Middleton, R. (2000). Exemplary economists, Vol. 1, North America, Vol. 2, Europe, Asia and Australasia, Edward Elgar: Aldershot.

Backlund, E.A. & Williams, D.R. (2003). *A quantitative synthesis of place attachment research: Investigating past experience and place attachment*. Proceedings of the 2003 Northeastern Recreation Research Symposium.

Badach, E. (2012). Zastosowanie metod statystycznej analizy wielowymiarowej do badania struktury wydatków gospodarstw domowych. *Metody Ilościowe w Badaniach Ekonomicznych*, 13(1), 29–35.

Bae, M. (1992). *Analysis of Household Spending Patterns. Dissertation*. Ohio State University: Columbus.

Bajada, C. (2002). *Australia's cash economy: A troubling issue for policymakers*. Ashgate: Aldershot.

Baker, M.J., Graham, P. & Harker D. (1998). *Marketing: Managerial foundations*. Macmillan Education: Melbourne.

Balázs, B. (2012). Local food system development in Hungary. *International Journal of Sociology of Agriculture and Food*, 19(3), 403–421.

Bański, J. (2009). *Typy obszarów funkcjonalnych w Polsce*. Instytut Gegografii i Przestrzennego Zagospodarowania PAN: Warsaw, (expert assessment), http://www.igipz.pan.pl/tl_files/igipz/ZGWiRL/Projekty/Ekspertyza_typologia.pdf

Bański, J. (2015). Rozwój przedsiębiorczości na terenach wiejskich: Diagnoza i wyzwania. In: Heffner, K. & Klemens, B. (Eds.), *Obszary wiejskie: Wielofunkcyjność, migracje, nowe wizje rozwoju*, (pp. 274–284), Studia KPZK PAN, 167. Komitet Przestrzennego Zagospodarowania Kraju PAN: Warsaw.

Baranowska, M. (2007). Miasta-ogrody, utopia a rzeczywistość. *Acta Universitatis Lodziensis, Folia Geographica Socio-Oeconomica*, 8, 15–38.

Barraket, J. & Anderson, H. (2010). *Developing strong social enterprises: A documentary approach*. Working Paper CPNS 52. The Australian Centre for Philanthropy and Nonprofit Studies, Queensland University of Technology: Brisbane.

Barrantes, M.R. (2004). *Feed Your City: Berkeley field guide to planning for food*. City of Berkeley Food Policy Council: Berkeley.

Barros, C.P. & Machado, L.P. (2010). The length of stay in tourism. *Annals of Tourism Research*, 37(3), 692–706.

Batkoska, L. & Koseska, E. (2012). The impact of cognitive learning on consumer behaviour. *Procedia - Social and Behavioral Sciences*, 44, 70–77.

Batra, R. & Ahtola, O.T. (1991). Measuring the hedonic and utilitarian sources of consumer attitudes. *Marketing Letters*, 2(2), 159–170.

Bearden, W. & Etzel, M.J. (1982). Reference group influence on product and brand purchase decisions. *Journal of Consumer Research*, 9(2), 183–194.

Becker, G.S. (1965). A theory of the allocation of time. *The Economic Journal*, 75(299), 493–517.

Becker, G.S. (1974). A theory of social interactions. *Journal of Political Economy*, 82(6), 1063–1093.

Becker, G.S. (1981). *A treatise on the family*. Harvard University Press: Cambridge.

Becker, K. (2004). *The informal economy: Fact finding study*. SIDA: Stockholm.

Bell, M. & Ward, G. (2000). Comparing temporary mobility with permanent migration. *Tourism Geographies*, 2(1), 87–107.

Belsky, E.S., Di, Z.X. & McCue, D. (2006). *Multiple-home ownership and the income elasticity of housing demand.* W06-5. Joint Center for Housing Studies, Harvard University: Cambridge.

Berger, M. & Buvincić, M. (Eds.) (1989). *Women´s ventures: Assistance to the informal sector in Latin America.* Kumarian Press: Hartford.

Bevan, M. & Rhodes, D. (2005). *The impact of second homes and holiday homes in rural Scotland.* Precis, 70, Communities Scotland.

Bianchi, M. (2006). *The active consumer: Novelty and surprise in consumer choice.* Routledge: London and New York, (Series: Routledge Frontiers of Political Economy).

Bihagen, E. (1999). How do classes make use of their incomes?. *Social Indicators Research*, 47, 119–151.

Bizzarri, C. & Querini, G. (2006). *Economia del turismo sostenibile: Analisi teorica e casi studio.* Franco Angeli: Milano.

Black, A. & Hughes, P. (2001). *The identification and analysis of indicators of community strength and outcomes.* Occasional Paper 3. Department of Family and Community Services, Commonwealth of Australia: Canberra.

Blank, U. (1989). *The community tourism imperative: The necessity, the opportunities, its potential.* Venture Publishing: State College.

Block, L. & Williams, P. (2007). Consumer behavior. *Encyclopedia of business and finance*, (2nd edition). Thomson Gale: Farmington Hills.

Bobonis, G.J. (2009). Is the allocation of resources within the household efficient? New evidence from a randomized experiment. *Journal of Political Economy*, 117(3), 453–503.

Boedeker, M. (1997). *Recreational shopping: The role of the basic emotional dimensions of personality.* Publications of Turku School of Economics and Business Administration: Turku (Series A–9,1997): Turku.

Bogdanov, N. & Vasiljević, Z. (2011). Role of agriculture and multifunctional rural development in Serbia. *APSTRACT: Applied Studies in Agribusiness and Commerce*, 5, 47–55.

Bohlin, M. (1982). *Fritidsboendet i den regional ekonomin: vart fritidshusägarnas pengar tar vägen.* Geografiska Regionstudier, 14: Uppsala.

Bojanic, D.C. (1992). A look at modernized family life cycle and overseas travel. *Journal of Travel and Tourism Marketing*, 61–79.

Bojanic, D.C. (2011). The impact of age and family life experiences on Mexican visitor shopping expenditures. *Tourism Management*, 32, 406–414.

Boman, M., Fredman, P., Lundmark, L.J.T. & Ericsson, G. (2013). Outdoor recreation – A necessity or a luxury? Estimation of Engel curves for Sweden. *Journal of Outdoor Recreation amd Tourism*, 3–4, 49–56.

Bonilla, A. & Mordt, M. (2008). *Turismo y conflictos territoriales en el Pacífico de Nicaragua: El caso de Tola, más allá de los titulares*. PRISMA (Programa Salvadoreño de Investigación sobre Desarrollo y Medio Ambiente/Salvadoran Research Program on Development and Environment).

Borzaga, C. & Solari, L. (2001). Management challenges for social enterprises. In: C. Borzaga & J. Defourny (Eds.), *The emergence of social enterprise*, (pp. 333–349). Routledge: Aledrshot.

Botazzi, G. (2003). Sull'economia informale: Temi e problemi di ricerca. In: F. Lazzari & A. Merler (Eds.), *La sociologia delle solidarietá: Scritti di onore di Giuliano Giorio*, (pp. 353–366). Franco Angeli: Milano.

Bourdonnec, F. (2010). *Identity, nostalgia and leisure: Technology use in second homes*. Dissertations and Theses. Paper, 143. Portland State University: Portland.

Bowbrick, P. (2014). *The economics of quality, grades and brands* (Routledge Revivals). Routledge: Abingdon, Oxon.

Bowen, D. & Clarke, J. (2009). *Contemporary tourist behaviour: Yourself and others as tourists*. CABI Publishing: Wallingford.

Bowen, S. & Mutersbaugh, T. (2014). Local or localized? Exploring the contributions of Franco-Mediterranean agrifood theory to alternative food research. *Agriculture and Human Values*, 31, 201–213.

Bowie, D. & Buttle, F. (2004). *Hospitality marketing: An introduction*. Elsevier: Oxford.

Boyle, P.J. & Halfacree, K.H. (1998). *Migration into rural areas: Theories and issues*. John Wiley & Sons: Chichester.

Breuer, T. (2005). Retirement migration or rather second-home tourism? German senior citizens on the Canary Islands. *Die Erde*, 136(30), 313–333.

Brida, J.G., Osti, L. & Santifaller, E. (2011). Second homes and the need for policy planning. *Tourismos: An International Multidisciplinary Journal of Tourism*, 6(1), 141–63.

Briones Alonso, E. (2015). *The impact of culture, religion and traditional knowledge on food and nutrition security in developing countries*. FOODSECURE, Working paper, 30, March 2015.

Brocato, E.D. (2006). *Place attachment: An investigation of environments and outcomes in service context*. Doctoral Thesis. The University of Texas: Arlington.

Brocato, E.D., Baker, J. & Voorhees, C.M. (2015). Creating consumer attachment to retail service firms through sense of place. *Journal of the Academy of Marketing Science*, 43, 200–220.

Brunetti, M. & Torricelli, C. (2014). *Second homes: Households' life dream or (wrong) investment?*. EFMA Annual Meeting: Rome.

Bryła, P. (2013). Znaczenie odwołań do tradycji w marketingu żywności. *Zeszyty Naukowe Uniwersytetu Szczecińskiego, Problemy Zarządzania Finansów i Marketingu*, 30, 173–188.

Budruk, M., Thomas, H. & Tyrrell, T. (2009). Urban green spaces: A study of place attachment and environment attitudes in India. *Society and Natural Resources*, 22(9), 824–839.

Bukraba-Rylska, I. (1991). Szanse i bariery aktywizacji obszarów wiejskich przez turystykę. In: K. Duczkowska-Małysz (Ed.), *Przedsiębiorczość na obszarach wiejskich: W stronę wsi wielofunkcyjnej*, (pp. 75–84). Instytut Rozwoju Wsi i Rolnictwa, Polska Akademia Nauk: Warsaw.

Bull, A. (1995). *The economics of travel and tourism*, (2nd edition). Longman: Melbourne.

Buller, H. & Hoggart, K. (1994). *International counter-urbanization: British migrants in rural France*. Aldershot: Avebury.

Burchardt, J. (2002). *Paradise lost: Rural idyll and social change since 1800*. I.B. Tauris: London, New York.

Burchardt, T., Le Grand, J. & Piachaud, D. (2002). Degrees of exclusion: Developing a dynamic, multidimensional measure. In: J. Hills, J. Le Grand & D. Piachaud (Eds.), *Understanding social exclusion*, (pp. 30–43). Oxford University Press: Oxford.

Burton, R.J.F. & Wilson, G.A. (2006). Injecting social psychology theory into conceptualisations of agricultural agency: Towards a post-productivist farmer self-identity?. *Journal of Rural Studies*, 22, 95–115.

Bylok, F. (2005). *Konsumpcja w Polsce i jej przemiany w okresie transformacji*. Wydawnictwo Politechniki Częstochowskiej, Monografie nr 1008: Częstochowa.

Bywalec, C. (2007). *Konsumpcja w teorii i praktyce gospodarowania*. Państwowe Wydanictwo Naukowe: Warsaw.

Bywalec, C. & Rudnicki, L. (2002). *Konsumpcja*. Polskie Wydawnictwo Ekonomiczne: Warsaw.

Cabinet Office of the Third Sector. (2006). *Social enterprise action plan: Scaling new heights*. Office of the Third Sector: London.

Cage, R. (1989). Spending Differences across Occupational Fields. *Monthly Labour Review*, December 1989, 33–42.

Cahuc, P. & Zylberberg, A. (2004). *Labor economics*. MIT Press: Cambridge.

Cai, L.A., Hong, G. & Morrison, A.M. (1995). Household expenditure patterns for tourism products and services. *Journal of Travel & Tourism Marketing*, 4(4), 15–40.

Carlin, W., Fries, S., Schaffer, M. & Seabright, P. (2000). *Barter and non-monetary transactions in transition countries: Evidence from a cross-country survey*, Centre for Economic Reform and Transformation, Discussion Paper, 2000/04.

Cassett, M. (1999). Le vocabulaire des résidences « secondaires » des archevêques et évêques normand au Moyen Âge: une image du bâti?. *Aux marches du palais... Le Mans-Mayenne* 9th-11th September 1999, 163–177.

Cassidy, F. (2005). A credibility gap for marketers. *McKinsey Quarterly*, 2, 9–10.

Cătoiu, I. & Teodorescu, N. (1997). *Comportamentul consumatorului: Teorie şi practică*, Editura Economică: Bucureşti.

CBOS, (2013). *Jak i gdzie kupujemy żywność?* BS/94/2013, Komunikat z badań. Akademia Leona Koźmińskiego, Centrum Badania Opinii Społecznej: Warsaw.

Champion, T. (1998). Studying counterurbanisation and the rural population turnaround. In: P. Boyle & K. Halfacree (Eds.), *Migration into rural areas: Theories and issues*, (pp. 21–40). John Wiley & Sons: Chichester.

Chang, T.-Z. & Wildt, A.R. (1994). Price, product information, and purchase intention: An empirical study. *Journal of The Academy of Marketing Science*, 22(1), 16–27.

Cheng L.W. & Zhen, X.C. (2004). Consumer ethnocentrism and willingness to buy domestic products in a developing country setting: Testing moderating effects. *Journal of Consumer Marketing*, 21(6), 391–400.

Chiappori, P.-A. & Lewbel, A. (2015). Becker's a theory of the allocation of time. *The Economic Journal*, 125, 410–442.

Chiou, W.-B., Wan, C.-S. & Lee, H.-Y. (2008). Virtual experience vs. brochures in the advertisement of scenic spots: How cognitive preferences and order effects influence advertising effects on consumers. *Tourism Management*, 29(1), 146–150.

Chhabra, D., Sills, E. & Rea, P. (2002). Tourist expenditures at heritage festivals. *Event Management*, 7(4), 221–230.

Christodoulides, G., Michaelidou, N. & Li, H.C. (2008). Measuring perceived brand luxury: An evaluation of the BLI scale. *Brand Management*, 16, 5/6, 395–405.

Chuang, S.C. (2007). The effects of emotions on the purchase of tour commodities. *Journal of Travel & Tourism Marketing*, 22(1), 1–13.

Cieloch, G., Kuczyński, J. & Rogoziński, K. (1992). *Czas wolny – czasem konsumpcji?* Polskie Wydawnictwo Ekonomiczne: Warsaw.

Cloke, P. (1989). Rural geography and political economy. In: R. Peet & N. Thrift (Eds.), *New models of geography: The political economy perspective*, (pp. 164–197). Unwin Hyman: London.

Clout, H.D. (1969). Second homes in France. *Journal of the Town Planning Institute*, 55, 440–443.

Cohen, S.A., Prayag, G. & Moital, M. (2014). Consumer behaviour in tourism: Concepts, influences and opportunities. *Current Issues in Tourism*, 17(10), 872–909.

Coleman, R. (1982). Second homes in North Norfolk. In: M.J. Moseley (Ed.), *Power, planning and people in rural East Anglia*. Centre for East Anglian, Studies, University of East Anglia: Norwich.

Commons, J. & Page, S. (2001). Managing seasonality in peripheral tourism regions: The case of Northland, New Zealand. In: T. Baum & S. Lundtrop (Eds.), *Seasonality in tourism*, (pp. 153–172). Pergamon: New York, Amsterdam.

Consoli, D. (2009). Emotions that influence purchase decisions and their electronic processing. *Annales Universitatis Apulensis Series Oeconomica*, 11(2), 996–1008.

Copper, C., Fletcher, J., Fyall, A., Gilbert, D. & Wanhill, S. (2008). *Tourism: principles and practice*, (4th edition). Prentice Hall, Financial Times: Harlow.

Coppock, J.T. (1977). *Second homes: Curse or blessing?* Pergamon Press: Oxford.

Cosenza, R.M. & Davis, D.L. (1981). Family vacation decision-making over the family life cycle: A decision and influence structure analysis. *Journal of Travel Research*, 20(2), 17–23.

Cowell, D.K. & Green, G.P. (1994). Community attachment and spending location: The importance of place in household consumption. *Social Science Quarterly*, 75, 637–655.

Cox, G., Lowe, P. & Winter, M. (1989). The farm crisis in Britian. In: D. Goodman (Ed.), *The international farm crisis*, (pp. 113–134). Palgrave Macmillan: London.

Croes, R.R. & Vanegas-Sr., M. (2005). An econometric study of tourist arrivals in Aruba and its implications. *Tourism Management*, 26, 879–890.

Crowley, E. (2006). *Land matters: Power struggles in rural Ireland*. The Lillyput Press: Dublin.

CSO, (2001). *Instrukcja metodologiczna do Narodowego Spisu Powszechnego Ludności i Mieszkań w 2002 roku*. CSO: Warsaw.

CSO, (2003). *Narodowy Spis Powszechny Ludności i Mieszkań 2002. Mieszkania zamieszkane*. CSO: Warsaw.

CSO, (2006). *Turystyka i wypoczynek w gospodarstwach domowych w 2005 roku*. CSO: Warsaw.

CSO, (2010). *Turystyka i wypoczynek w gospodarstwach domowych w 2009 roku*. Informacje i opracowania statystyczne. CSO: Warsaw.

CSO, (2011). *Metodologia badania budżetów gospodarstw domowych*. Zeszyt metodologiczny zaopiniowany przez Komisję Metodologiczną GUS. CSO: Warsaw.

CSO, (2013). *Sytuacja społeczno-ekonomiczna gospodarstw domowych w latach 2000–2011: Zróżnicowanie miasto-wieś*. Informacje i Opracowania Statystyczne. CSO: Warsaw.

CSO, (2015). *Budżety gospodarstw domowych w 2014 roku*. Informacje i Opracowania Statystyczne. CSO: Warsaw.

CSO, (2016). *Dochody i warunki życia ludności Polski (raport z badania EU-SILC 2014)*. CSO: Warsaw.

Csordás, L. (1999). Second homes in Hungary. In A. Duró (Ed.), *Spatial research in support of the European integration* (pp. 145–160). Discussion Papers. Special Issue. Centre for Regional Studies: Pécs.

Cyran, K. (2013). Preferencje konsumentów w zakresie miejsc zakupów żywności jako wyznacznik możliwości rozwoju handlu na targowiskach i bazarach. *Polityki Europejskie, Finanse i Marketing*, 10(59), 142–155.

Cyrek, P. (2013). Dysproporcje w poziomie oferty handlowej w województwie podkarpackim. *Handel Wewnętrzny*, 1(348), 48–59.

Czapiński, J. & Panek, T. (Eds.). (2013). *Diagnoza społeczna: Warunki i jakość życia Polaków*, Contemporary Economics, 7, Special Issue, Quarterly of University of Finance and Management in Warsaw: Warsaw.

Czapiński, J. & Panek, T. (Eds.). (2014). *Diagnoza społeczna 2013: Warunki i jakość życia Polaków*, Raport. Ministerstwo Pracy i Polityki Społecznej and Centrum Rozwoju Zasobów Ludzkich: Warsaw.

Czarnecki, A. (2009). *Rola urbanizacji w wielofunkcyjnym rozwoju obszarów wiejskich*. Instytut Rozwoju Wsi i Rolnictwa PAN: Warsaw.

Czarnecki, A. (2014). Economically detached? Second home owners and the local community in Poland. *Tourism Review International*, 18(3), 153–166.

Czarnecki, A. & Frenkel, I. (2015). Counting the 'invisible': second homes in Polish statistical data collections. *Journal of Policy Research in Tourism, Leisure and Events*, 7(1), 15–31.

Czarnecki, A. & Heffner, K. (2008). „Drugie domy" a rozwój obszarów wiejskich. *Wieś i Rolnictwo*, 4, 29–46.

Czech, A. (2012). Metodologiczne aspekty badań konsumpcji w ujęciu bezpośrednim. *Economics and Management*, 4, 7–17.

Człapka-Matyasik, M., Fejfer, M. & Homan-Helenius, P. (2014). Analiza oraz porównanie zachowań konsumenckich i wyborów żywieniowych osób powyżej 55. roku życia z Polski i Finlandii. *Marketing i Rynek*, 6, 121–132.

Dale, A. & Onyx, J. (2005). *A dynamic balance: Social capital and sustainable community development*. USB Press: Vancouver.

Dávila, V.R., Asgary, N., de los Santos, G. & Vincent, V. (1999). The effects of governmental restrictions on outbound tourists expenditures. *Journal of Travel Research*, 37(3), 285–290.

Deaton, A.S. (1986). Long-term projections of consumer demand in the United Kingdom. In: T.S. Khachaturov (Ed.), *Methods of long-term planning and forecasting: Proceedings of a Conference held by the International Economic Association at Moscow* (pp. 368–381). International Economic Association Conference Volumes, Stockton Press: New York.

Deaton, A.S., Ruiz-Castillo, J. & Thomas, D. (1985). *The influence of household composition on household expenditure patterns: Theory and Spanish evidence*. Woodrow Wilson School, Princeton University: New Jersey.

Debenedetti, A. & Oppewal, H. (2009). *Place Attachment and the Consumption of Servicescapes*, Australian and New Zealand Marketing Academy Conference (ANZMAC), 30th November-2nd December 2009 in Melbourne, Australia.

De Miras, C. (1990). État de l'informel: Informel et état: Illustrations sud-américaines. *Revue Tiers-Monde*, 31(122), 377–391.

Derek, M. (2008). *Funkcja turystyczna jako czynnik rozwoju lokalnego w Polsce*. Rozprawa doktorska. Wydział Geografii i Studiów Regionalnych, Uniwersytet Warszawski: Warsaw.

Devine, D.G. & Marion, B.W. (1979). The influence of consumer price information on retail pricing and consumer behaviour. *American Journal of Agricultural Economics*, 61(2), 228–237.

De Soto, H. (1989). *The other path: The invisibly revolution in the Third World*. Harper and Row: New York.

de Vries, J. (2008). *The industrious revolution: Consumer behavior and the household economy, 1650 to the present*. Cambridge University Press: New York.

Deželan, S. (2001). *Essays on consumer search and interlocking directorates.* Rozenberg Publishers: Amsterdam.

Dijst, M. & Vermuelen, B. (1999). *The second home as a challenge for spatial policy? A study into compensation hypothesis.* Colloquium Vervoersplanalogisch Speurwerk: Delft.

Dijst, M., Lanzendorf, M., Barendregt, A. & Smit, L. (2005). Second homes in Germany and the Netherlands: ownership and travel impact explained. *Tidschrift voor Economische en Sociale Geografie*, 96(2), 139–152.

Dikčius, V., Armenakyan, A., Urbonavičius, S., Jonynienė, & Gineikienė, G. (2014). The influence of children on family purchasing in Lithuania and Azerbaijan. *Organizations and Markets in Emerging Economies*, 5(2), 79–96.

Din, B.H., Habibullah, M.S., Baharom, A.H. & Saari, M.D. (2016). Are shadow economy and tourism related? International evidence. 7th International Economics & Business Management Conference (IEBMC 2015), 5th-6th October 2015 in Kuantan, Pahang, Malaysia. *Procedia Economics and Finance*, 35, 173–178.

Dirksmeier, P. (2008). Strife in the rural idyll? The relationship between autochthons and in-migrants in scenic regions of South Bavaria. *Erdkunde*, 62(2), 159–171.

Divisekera, S. & Deegan, J. (2010). An analysis of consumption behaviour of foreign tourists in Ireland. *Applied Economics*, 42(13), 1681–1697.

Divisekera, S. & Nguyen, V. (2014). *Regional variations in tourist consumption patterns: A model of demand for domestic tourism in Australia.* Nara Tourism Statistics Week: 13th Global Forum on Tourism Statistics, 17th-21st November 2014, Nara, Japan.

Dougan, J.W. (2007). Analysis of Japanese tourist demand to Guam. *Asia Pacific Journal of Tourism Research*, 12(2), 79–88.

Dougherty, M., Brown, L.E. & Green, G.P. (2013) The social architecture of local food tourism: Challenges and opportunities for community economic development. *Journal of Rural Social Sciences*, 28(2), 1–27.

Douglas, E.J. & Morris, R.J. (2007). *Time and intensity trade-offs at work, at leisure, and in life*, http://www.anzam.org/wp-content/uploads/pdf-manager/1823_DOUGLASEVAN_289.pdf

Downward, P.M. & Lumsdon, L. (2000). The demand for day-visits: An analysis of visitor spending. *Tourism Economics*, 6(3), 251–261.

Downward, P.M. & Lumsdon, L. (2003). Beyond the demand for day visits, an analysis of visitor spending. *Tourism Economics*, 9(1), 67–76.

Du, R.Y. & Kamakura, W.A. (2006). Household life cycles and lifestyles in the United States. *Journal of Marketing Research*, 43 (February), 121–132.

Duncan, C. (Ed.) (1992). *Persistent poverty in America*. Auburn House: New York.

Duniam, M. & Eversole, R. (2013). *Social enterprises and local government: A scoping study*. Australian Centre of Excellence for Local Government: Sydney.

Durmay, Y., Çelik, M. & Oruc, R. (2011). The impact of cultural factors on the consumer buying behaviours examined through an empirical study. *International Journal of Business and Social Science*, 2(5), 105–110, http://www.ijbssnet.com/journals/Vol._2_No._5_[Special_Issue__March_2011]/13.pdf

Dwyer, L., Forsyth, P. & Dwyer, W. (2010). *Tourism economics and policy*. Channel View Publications: Bristol.

Dybczak, K., Tóth, P. & Voňka, D. (2014). Effects of price shocks on consumer demand: Estimating the QUAIDS demand system on Czech household budget survey data. *Czech Journal of Economics and Finance (Finance a uver)*, 64(6), 476–500.

Dziegieć, E. (1987). Przemiany osadnictwa wiejskiego pod wpływem turystyki i wypoczynku w świetle literatury. *Acta Universitatis Lodziensis, Turyzm* 3, 7–31.

Dziekański, P. (2012). Informacja jako dobro ekonomiczne będące źródłem przewagi konkurencyjnej. *Nierówności społeczne a wzrost gospodarczy*, 24, 387–403.

Dziennik Ustaw, (1997). No 137, Pos. 926. Ustawa z dnia 29 sierpnia 1997 roku – Ordynacja podatkowa. Kancelaria Sejmu: Warsaw.

Dziennik Ustaw, (1998). No 144, Pos. 930. Ustawa z dnia 20 listopada 1998 roku o zryczałtowanym podatku dochodowym od niektórych przychodów osiąganych przez osoby fizyczne. Kancelaria Sejmu: Warsaw.

Dziennik Ustaw, (2004). No 167, Pos. 1758. Ustawa o nabywaniu nieruchomości przez cudzoziemców, Art. 1, § 5, Art. 8, § 2, § 2a. Kancelaria Sejmu: Warsaw.

Dziennik Ustaw, (2012). Pos. 729. Rozporządzenie Ministra Spraw Wewnętrznych z dnia 20 czerwca 2012 roku w sprawie szczegółowych informacji oraz rodzajów dokumentów, jakie jest obowiązany przedstawić cudzoziemiec ubiegający się o wydanie zezwolenia na nabycie nieruchomości. Kancelaria Sejmu: Warsaw.

Dziennik Ustaw, (2014). Pos. 1380. Obwieszczenie Marszałka Sejmu Rzeczypospolitej Polskiej z dnia 4 września 2014 roku w sprawie ogłoszenia jednolitego tekstu ustawy o nabywaniu nieruchomości przez cudzoziemców. Kancelaria Sekmu: Warsaw.

Dziennik Ustaw, (2015). Pos. 605. Ustawa z dnia 9 kwietnia 2015 roku o zmianie ustawy o podatku dochodowym od osób fizycznych oraz niektórych innych ustaw regulującej opodatkowanie sprzedaży bezpośredniej. Kancelaria Sejmu: Warsaw.

Emmery, R. (2009). Looking past the rural idyll: "De Kat", or televising the post-productivist countryside. *Revue Belge de Philologie et d'Histoire*, 87(3), 793–809.

Eppli, M. & Benjamin, J.D. (1994). The evolution of shopping centre research: A review and analysis. *Journal of Real Estate Research*, 9(1), 5–32.

EC, (1988). *The future of rural society*. Bulletin of the European Communities Supplement, 4/88. Office for Official Publications of the European Communities: Luxembourg.

EC, (1997). *Towards a common agricultural and rural policy for Europe* (Buckwell Report). Convened by Commission of European Communities, Directorate General VI/A1, European Commission: Brussels.

Eurostat, (2014). *Living conditions in Europe – 2014 Edition*. European Commission: Brussels.

Evans, N., Morris, C. & Winter, M. (2002). Conceptualizing agriculture: A critique of post-productivism as the new orthodoxy. *Progress in Human Geography*, 26(3), 313–332.

Evers, A. (2001). The significance of social capital in the multiple goal and resource structure of social enterprise. In: C. Borzaga & J. Defourny (Eds.), *The emergence of social enterprise*, (pp. 296–311). Routledge: New York.

Falkowski, A., Rożnowski, B. & Witkowski, T.W. (1996). Etnocentryzm konsumencki: Nowe wyzwanie dla marketingu. *Marketing i Rynek*, 3–4.

Fanzo, J., Hunter, D., Borelli, T. & Mattei, F. (Eds.) (2013). *Diversifying food and diets: using agricultural biodiversity to improve nutrition and health*. Earthscan: London.

FAO, (2008). *Potato world*. FAOSTAT. FAO: Rome.

FAO, (2010). *A living from livestock pro-poor livestock policy initiative: Status and prospects for smallholder milk production: A Global Perspective*. FAO: Rome.

Farmer, J., Steinerowski, A. & Jack, S. (2008). Starting social enterprises in remote and rural Scotland: Best or worse of circumstances?. *International Journal of Entrepreneurship and Small Business*, 6(3), 450–464.

Farstad, M. & Rye. J.F. (2013). Second home owners, locals and their perspectives on rural development. *Journal of Rural Studies*, 30, 41–51.

Feige, E. (1979). How big is the irregular economy?. *Challenge*, 12, 5–13.

Ferguson, C.E. & Gould, J.P. (1975). *Micro economic theory*. Richard D. Irwin: Homewood.

Fernández-Kelly, P. & Shefner, J. (Eds.) (2006). *Out of the shadows: Political action and the informal economy in Latin America*. Penn State University Press: University Park.

FGT, (2014). *Finnish Grocery Trade 2014*. Finnish Grocery Trade Association, Erweko Oy: Oulu.

Fields, K. (2002). Demand for the gastronomy tourism product: Motivational factors. In: A. Hjalager, & G. Richards (Eds.), *Tourism and gastronomy*, (pp. 37–50). Routledge: London.

Figiel, A. (2004). *Etnocentryzm konsumencki. Produkty krajowe czy zagraniczne*. Polskie Wydawnictwo Ekonomiczne: Warsaw.

FitzGerald, J.D. (2005). The Irish housing stock: Growth in number of vacant dwellings. *Quarterly Economic Commentary: Special Articles*, 1, 1–22.

Flagestad, A. & Hope, C.A. (2001). "Scandinavian Winter": Antecedents, concepts and empirical observations underlying destination umbrella branding model. *Tourism Review*, 56(1–2), 5–12.

Flemsæter, F. (2009). The role of home in property enactment on Norwegian smallholdings. *Norsk geografisk tidsskrift*, 63, 204–214.

Flognfeldt, T. (2002). Second home ownership: A sustainable semi-migration. In: C.M. Hall & A.M. Williams (Eds.), *Tourism and migration: New relationships between production and consumption*, (pp. 187–203). Kluwer Academic Publishers: Dordrecht.

Fluitman, L.P. (1973). The necessity of an industrial product mix analysis. *Industrial Marketing Management*, 2, 345–352.

Foellmi, R. & Zweimüller, J. (2008). Structural change, Engel's consumption cycles and Kaldor's facts of economic growth. *Journal of Monetary Economics*, 55, 1317–1328.

Foglio, A. (2008). *Marketing relazionale e consumatori alleati: Come realizzare un'alleanza vincente e duratura con il consumatore-cliente*. Franco Angeli: Milano.

Forssell, S. & Lankoski, L. (2014). The sustainability promise of alternative food networks: An examination through 'alternative' characteristics. *Agriculture and Human Values*, 32(1), 63–75.

Fraisse, L. (2008). France. In: J. Defourny & M. Nyssens (Eds.), *Social enterprise in Europe: Recent trends and developments*, (pp. 20–21), Working Paper 08/01. EMES European Research Network: Liège.

Fratu, D. (2011). Factors of influence and changes in the tourism consumer behaviour. *Bulletin of the Transilvania University of Braşov, Series V: Economic Sciences*, 4(1), 119–126.

Friedland, W.H. (2008). "Chasms" in agrifood systems: rethinking how we can contribute. *Agriculture and Human Values*, 25(2), 197–201.

Frisvoll, S. (2014). *Beyond the idyll: Contested spaces of rural tourism*. Thesis for the degree for Philosophiae Doctor. Norwegian University of Science and Technology, Faculty of Social Sciences and Technology Management, Department of Geography, NTNU: Trondheim.

Frost, W. & Lawrence, M. (2006). Commentary: Taxes and host-tourist tensions in Australian coastal resorts. *Current Issues in Tourism*, 9(2), 152–156.

Fuguitt, G.V., Brown, D.L. & Beale, C.L. (1989). *Rural and small town America*. Russell Sage Foundation: New York.

Funk, D.C. (2008). *Consumer behaviour in sport and events: Marketing action*. Elsevier Butterworth-Heinemann: Amsterdam.

Gallent, N. (2014). The social value of second homes in rural communities. *Housing, Theory and Society*, 31(2), 174–191.

Gallent, N. & Tewdwr-Jones, M. (2000). *Rural second homes in Europe: Examining housing supply and planning control*. Ashgate: Aldershot.

Gallent, N., Mace, A. & Tewdwr-Jones, M. (2002). *Second homes in rural areas of England*. The Countryside Agency: Wetherby.

Garrod, G. & Willis, K. (1992). Valuing goods' characteristics: An application of the Hedonic Price Method to environmental attributes. *Journal of Environmental Management*, 34(1), 59–76.

Gaś, M. (1996/7, printed 1999). „Drugie domy", jako element zagospodarowania turystycznego wsi w strefie podmiejskiej Krakowa. *Folia Geographica, Seria Geogr.-Oecon.*, 29/30, 91–108.

Gaughan, J. & Fermand, L. (1987). Toward an understanding of the informal economy. *The Annals of the American Academy of Political and Social Sciences*, 493, 15–25.

Gąsiorowski, P. & Kuszewski, T. (2004). Modelowanie preferencji konsumenta w symulacyjnych modelach stosowanej równowagi ogólnej. *Prace Naukowe Instytutu Organizacji i Zarządzania Politechniki Wrocławskiej, Studia i Materiały*, 75(17), 99–113.

Gergelyova, M. (2007). *An investigation of the potential of genealogy tourism as a catalyst for regional development in county Galway*. Thesis submitted in fulfilment of the requirements for the Master of Arts (by Research) degree in Heritage Studies. Galway-Mayo Institute of Technology: Galway.

Giambelluca, R., Julien, C., Khanal, B., Laskai, S., Pavlikova, K., Piekar, P., Bulakh, E., Malinen, H. & Oppong, C.O. (2014). *Phenomena of second homes in Finland: Case of South Savo and Mäntyharju*. University of Eastern Finland: Joensuu.

Gill, I.S., Izvorski, I., van Eeghen, W. & De Rosa, D. (2014). *Diversified development: Making the most of natural resources in Eurasia*. ECA Regional Flagship Report. World Bank: Washington.

Giuliani, M.V. (1991). Towards an analysis of mental representations of attachment to the home. *The Journal of Architectural and Planning Research*, 8(2), 133–146.

Goodman, A.C. & Kawai, M. (1982). Permanent income, hedonic prices, and housing demand: New evidence. *Journal of Urban Economics*, 12, 214–237.

Gordon, B. (1986). The souvenir: Messenger of the extraordinary. *Journal of Popular Culture*, 20(3), 135–151.

Gorczyca, M. (2005). Zróżnicowanie poziomu, struktury i realnej dynamiki wydatków i dochodów polskich gospodarstw domowych. *Nierówności Społeczne a Wzrost Gospodarczy*, 7, 55–73.

Gourinchas, P.-O. & Parker, J.A. (1997). Consumption over the life cycle. *Econometrica*, 70(1), 47–89.

Gómez-Limón, J.A., Vera-Toscano, E. & Rico-González, M. (2012). Measuring individual preferences for rural multifunctionality: The importance of demographic and residential heterogeneity. *Journal of Agricultural Economics*, 63(1), 1–24.

Graham, H., Mason, R. & Newman, A. (2009). *Literature review: historic environment, sense of place, and social capital*. English Heritage: London.

Grano, J.G. (1952). Settlement of the country Suomi: A general handbook on the geography of Finland. *Fennia*, 72, 340–380.

Gross, M.J. & Brown, G. (2008). An empirical structural model of tourists and places: Progressing Involvement and place attachment into tourism. *Tourism Management*, 29, 1141–1151.

Gu, Z. (2000). Strategies for minimising tourist leakage in Indo-Chinese development countries. *Asia Pacific Journal of Tourism Research*, 5(2), 11–20.

Guisan, M.C. & Aguayo, E. (2010). Second homes in the Spanish regions: Evolution in 2001–2007 and impact on tourism, GDP and employment. *Regional and Sectoral Economic Studies*, 10(2), 83–104.

Gutiérrez-Romero, R. (2010). The dynamics of the informal economy. CSAE WPS/2010-07. Department for International Development, Oxford University: Oxford.

Gutkowska, K. & Piekut, M. (2014). Konsumpcja w wiejskich gospodarstwach domowych. *Wieś i Rolnictwo*, 4, 159–178.

Halamska, M. (2001). Wieś popegeerowska między adaptacją a marginalizacją. In: I. Bukraba-Rylska & A. Rosner (Eds.), *Wieś i rolnictwo na przełomie wieków*, (pp. 197–219). Instytut Rozwoju Wsi i Rolnictwa, Polska Akademia Nauk: Warsaw.

Halamska, M. (2011). Wieś jako przedmiot badań naukowych. In: M. Halamska (Ed.), *Wieś jako przedmiot badań naukowych*, (pp. 225–240). Scholar Publishing: Warsaw.

Halfacree, K. (1997). Contrasting roles for the post-productivist countryside: a postmodern perspective on counterurbanisation. In: P. Cloke & J. Little (Eds.), *Contested countryside cultures: Otherness, marginalisation and rurality*, (pp. 70–93). Routledge: London.

Halfacree, K. (2008). To revitalise counterurbanisation research? Recognising an international and fuller picture. *Population, Space and Place*, 14, 479–495.

Halfacree, K. (2012). Heterolocal identities? Counter-urbanisation, second homes and rural consumption in the era of mobilities. *Population, Space and Place*, 18, 209–224.

Hall, C.M. (2005). *Tourism: Rethinking the social science of mobility*. Pearson Education Ltd.: Harlow.

Hall, C.M. (2014). *Mobile second homes or cheap permanent homes? The problematic fluidity of caravans and motor homes as second homes*. Paper presented at the conference "New Perspectives on Second Homes", 9th-11th June 2014 in Stockholm, Sweden. Available online: https://www.academia.edu/7312722/Mobile_second_homes_or_cheap_permanent_homes_The_problematic_fluidity_of_caravans_and_motor_homes_as_second_homes

Hall, C.M. & Gossling, S. (Eds.) (2013). *Sustainable culinary systems: Local foods, innovation, tourism and hospitality*. Routledge: London and New York.

Hall, C.M. & Müller, D.K. (2004). Introduction: Second homes, curse or blessing? Revisited. In: C.M. Hall & D.K. Müller (Eds.), *Tourism, mobility and second homes: Between elite landscape and common ground*, (pp. 3–32). Channel View Publications: Clevedon.

Hall, C.M. & Müller, D.K. (2012). Second homes. In: A.T. Carswell (Ed.), *The encyclopedia of housing*, (2nd edition). Sage: Thousand Oaks.

Hall, C.M., Müller, D.K. & Saarinen. J (2009). *Nordic tourism: Issues and cases*. Channel View Publications: Bristol, Buffalo and Toronto (Series: Aspects of tourism).

Hall, C.M. & Williams, A.M. (Eds.) (2002). *Tourism and migration: New relationships between production and consumption*. Kluwer Academic Publishers: Dordrecht.

Hardill, I., Graham, D.T. & Kofman, E. (2001). *Human geography of the UK: An introduction*. Routledge: London.

Hathaway, J.T. & Hughes, J.C. (2000). Factory outlet malls: The example of Prime Outlets at Grove City. In: K.J. Patrick & J.L. Scarpaci (Eds.), *A geographic perspective of Pittsburgh and the Alleghenies: From precambrian to post-industrial*, (pp. 189–195). Association of American Geographers: Washington.

Hawk, W. (2013). Consumer Expenditure Program, "Expenditures of urban and rural households in 2011, *Beyond the Numbers: Prices & Spending*, 2(5), (U.S. Bureau of Labor Statistics, February 2013), http://www.bls.gov/opub/btn/volume-2/expenditures-of-urban-and-rural-households-in-2011.htm

Hawkins, D.I., Best, R.J. & Coney, K.A. (2001). *Consumer behaviour: building marketing strategy*. Irwin/McGraw Hill: Boston.

Hawks, L.K. & Ackerman, N.M. (1990). Family life cycle differences for shopping styles, information use, and decision-making. *Journal of Family and Economic Issues*, 11(2), 199–219.

Hazans, M. (2011). *Informal workers across Europe: Evidence from 30 European countries*. Background paper for "In from the Shadow: Integrating Europe's Informal Labor". World Bank: Washington.

Heckman, J. (2014). *Introduction to a theory of the allocation of time by Gary Becker*. Discussion Paper Series, IZA DP, 8424. Institute for the Study of Labor: Bonn.

Hediger, W. & Lehmann, B. (2003). *Multifunctional agriculture and the preservation of environmental benefits*. Proceedings of the 25th IAAE, 16th-22nd August 2003, Durban, South Africa.

Heffner, K. (2000). Kreacja ośrodków wielofunkcyjnego rozwoju na obszarach wiejskich. *Wieś i Rolnictwo*, 2, 4–59.

Heffner, K. (2011a). Wielofunkcyjność obszarów wiejskich w Polsce – rzeczywistość czy mit? Ewolucja zagospodarowania przestrzeni wiejskiej. In: W. Kamińska & K. Heffner (Eds.), *Obszary wiejskie: Wielofunkcyjność, migracje, nowe wizje rozwoju*, (pp. 8–26). Studia KPZK PAN, 133.

Heffner, K. (2011b). Zakres i zróżnicowanie przestrzenne zjawiska drugich domów. In: K. Heffner & A. Czarnecki (Eds.), *Drugie domy w rozwoju obszarów wiejskich*, (pp. 69–88). Instytut Rozwoju Wsi Rolnictwa PAN: Warsaw, (Series: Problemy rozwoju wsi i rolnictwa).

Heffner, K. & Czarnecki, A. (2011). Wpływ zjawiska drugich domów na rozwój obszarów wiejskich. In: K. Heffner & A. Czarnecki (Eds.), *Drugie domy w rozwoju obszarów wiejskich*, (pp. 131–162). Instytut Rozwoju Wsi Rolnictwa PAN: Warsaw, (Series: Problemy rozwoju wsi i rolnictwa).

Heffner, K. & Czarnecki, A. (2015). Linking locally: Second home owners and economic development of the rural community. In: P. Dannenberg & E. Kulke (Eds.), *Economic development in rural areas: Functional and multifunctional approaches*, (pp. 185–210). Ashgate Publishing: Farnham, (Series: The dynamics of economic spaces).

Heitmann, S. (2011). Tourist behaviour and tourism motivation. In: P. Robinson, S. Heitmann & P.U.C. Dieke (Eds.), *Research themes for tourism*, (pp. 31–44). CABI Publishing: Wallingford.

Henthorne, T.L. (2000). An analysis of expenditures by cruise ship passengers in Jamaica. *Journal of Travel Research*, 38(3), 246–250.

Hernández, B., Hidalgo, M.C., Salazar-Laplace, M.E. & Hess, S. (2007). Place attachment and place identity in natives and non-natives. *Journal of Environmental Psychology*, 27, 310–319.

Hess, D.J. (2009). *Localist movements in a global economy: Sustainability, justice, and urban development in the United States*. MIT Press: Cambridge, London.

Hetemäki, L. & Hänninen, R. (2009). *Arvio Suomen puunjalostuksen tuotannosta ja puunkäytöstä vuosina 2015 ja 2020*. Metla Working Papers of the Finnish Forest Research Institute, 122. METLA: Vantaa.

Hidalgo, M.C. & Hernandez, B. (2002). Attachment to the physical dimension of places. *Psychological Reports*, 91(3 f.), 1177–1182.

Higley, S.R. (1995). *The geography of the American upper class*. Rowman & Littlefield: Lanham.

Hiltunen, M.J. (2004). *Second housing in Finland: Perspective of mobility*. Paper presented at the 13th Nordic Symposium in Tourism and Hospitality, 4th-7th November 2004 in Aalborg.

Hiltunen, M.J. (2007). Environmental impacts of rural second home tourism – case Lake District in Finland. *Scandinavian Journal of Hospitality and Tourism*, 7(3), 243–265.

Hiltunen, M.J., Pitkänen, K., Vepsäläinen, M. & Hall, C.M. (2013). Second home tourism in Finland: Current trends and eco-social impacts. In: Z. Roca (Ed.), Second home tourism in Europe: Lifestyle issues and policy responses, (pp. 165–198). Ashgate: Farnham.

Hiltunen, M.J. & Rehunen, A. (2014). Second home mobility in Finland: Patterns, practices and relations of leisure oriented mobile lifestyle. *Fennia* 192(1), 1–22.

HM Treasury, (1999). *Enterprise and social exclusion*. HM Treasury National Strategy for Neighbourhood Renewal Policy Action Team 3: London.

Holbrook, M.B. & Hirschman, E.C. (1982). The experiential aspects of consumption: consumer fantasies, feelings, and fun. *Journal of consumer research*, 9(2), 132–140.

Holloway, J.C. (2012). *The business of tourism*, Longman: Essex.

Holmes, K., Hughes, M., Mair, J. & Carlsen, J. (2015). *Events and sustainability*. Routledge: Abingdon, Oxon.

Honkanen, A. & Mustonen, P. (2007). Tourism consumption revisited – an empirical study of Finnish consumers. *Research on Finnish Society*, 1, 43–58.

Hoogendoorn, G. (2010). *Second homes and local economic impacts in the South African post-productivist countryside*. A dissertation submitted in fulfilment of the requirement for a Philosophiae Doctor in Geography. Faculty of Humanities, University of the Free State: Bloemfontein.

Hoogendoorn, G., Mellett, R. & Visser, G. (2005). Second homes tourism in Africa: Reflections on the South African experience. *Urban Forum*, 16(2–3), 112–154.

Hoogendoorn, G., Mellett, R. & Visser, G. (2007). Festival tourism in urban Africa: The case of South Africa. In: C.M. Rogerson & G. Visser (Eds.), *Urban tourism in the developing world: The South African experience*, (pp. 127–166). Transaction Publishers: New Brunswick.

Hooghe, M. (2008). *Ethnocentrism. International Encyclopedia of the Social Sciences*. MacMillan Reference: Philadelphia.

Horáková, H. (2010). Post-communist transformation of tourism in Czech rural areas: New dilemmas. *Anthropological Notebooks*, 16(1), 59–77.

Hosany, S. & Gilbert, D. (2009). *Dimensions of tourists' emotional experiences towards hedonic holiday destinations*. Working Paper Series, 7, (pp. 1–34). School of Management, Royal Holloway University of London: London.

Houthakker, H.S. & Taylor, L.D. (1970). *Consumer demand in the U.S.* Cambridge University Press: Cambridge.

Hörnström, L., Perjo, L. & Johnsen, I.H.G. (2015). *Nordic ways of dealing with depopulation and ageing in rural and peripheral areas*. Nordregio Policy Brief 2015, 8. http://www.nordregio.se/en/Publications/Publications-2015/Nordic-ways-of-dealing-with-depopulation-and-ageing--in-rural-and-peripheral-areas

Høst, J. (2014). Living in the niche: Self-employment and the cultural turn. In: T. Thomassen & M. Villa (Eds.) *Book of abstracts*, (p. 45), 3rd Nordic Conference for Rural Research "Nordic Ruralities – Thriving and Declining Communities", 8th-10th September 2014 in Trondheim, Norway.

Hsieh, S., Lang, C.-T. & O'leary, J.T. (1997). Modeling the determinants of expenditure for travelers from France, Germany, Japan and the United Kingdom to Canada. *Journal of International Hospitality, Leisure & Tourism Management*, 1(1), 67–78.

Hudson, S. (2008). *Tourism and hospitality marketing: A global perspective*. Sage Publications Ltd.: London.

Hummon, D.M. (1992). Community attachment: Local sentiment and sense of place. In: I. Altman & S.M. Low (Eds.), *Place attachment*, (pp. 253–278), Plenum Press: New York.

Huotari, T. (2008). Työllistämisen uudet politiikat. In: T. Huotari, M. Pyykkönen & P. Pättiniemi (Eds.), *Sosiaalisen ja taloudellisen välimaastossa: Tutkimusnäkökulmia suomalaiseen sosiaaliseen yritykseen*, (pp. 16–33). Sosiaali- ja terveysturvan keskusliitto: Helsinki.

Hurrelmann, K. (1996). The social world of adolescents: A sociological perspective. In: K. Hurrelmann & S.F. Hamilton (Eds.), *Social problems and social contexts in adolescence: Perspectives across boundaries*, (pp. 3–24). Aldine De Gruyter: New York.

Huylenbroeck, G. van (2003). *Multifunctional agriculture: How to provide incentives to farmers?* 13th International Farm Management Congress (IFMA), 10th-15th August 2003 in Perth, Australia.

Hwan, Y.M. & Lee, K.C. (2015). How does consumers' emotion affect visual attention patterns in online shopping environments? – Emphasis on eye-tracking approach. In: J. Strouhal (Ed.), *Recent advances on finance science and management*, (pp. 51–55). Business and Economic Series, 20. WSEAS Press.

Ilmakunnas, I. (2014). Societal change and poverty in Finland 1971–2011: The roles of distribution of market income, redistribution and demographic change. *Research on Finnish Society*, 7, 37–49.

ILO, (2002). *Decent work and the informal economy.* Report of the Director-General, International Labour Conference, 90th Session, 3rd-20th June 2002, Report 6, ILO: Geneva.

ILO, (2003). *Household income and expenditure statistics*, Report II, Seventeenth International Conference of Labour Statisticians, 24th November-3rd December 2003, Geneva. ICLS/17/2003/2, ILO: Geneva.

ILO, (2014). *Transitioning from the informal to the informal economy.* Report, 5(1), International Labour Conference, 103rd Session, 28th May-12th June 2014, ILO: Geneva.

Imbs, J. & Wacziarg, R. (2003). Stages of diversification. *American Economic Review*, 93(1), 63–86.

Inglot-Brzęk, E. (2010). Społeczno-ekonomiczne procesy modernizacji gospodarstw domowych w Polsce w okresie transformacji systemowej. *Nierówności Społeczne a Wzrost Gospodarczy*, 17, 265–277.

Irwin, E.G. (2002). The effects of open space on residential property values. *Land Economics*, 78(4), 465–480.

Ishengoma, E.K. & Kappel, R. (2006). *Economic growth and poverty: Does formalisation of informal enterprises matter?* German Institute of Global and Area Studies (GIGA): Hamburg.

Izard, C.E. (1977). *Human emotions*. Plenum Press: New York.

Jaakson, R. (1986). Second-home domestic tourism. *Annals of Tourism Research*, 13(3), 367–391.

Jachnis, A. (2007). *Psychologia konsumenta: Psychologiczne i socjologiczne uwarunkowania zachowań konsumenckich*. Branta Publishing: Bydgoszcz-Warsaw.

Jajuga, K. (1997). Metody statystycznej analizy wielowymiarowej w projekcji ścieżek rozwojowych. *Prace Naukowe Akademii Ekonomicznej we Wrocławiu, Informatyka i Ekonometria*, 743(2), 75–80.

Jang, S., Bai, B., Hong, G. & O'Leary, J. (2004). Understanding travel expenditure patterns: A study of Japanese pleasure travellers to the United States by income level. *Tourism Management*, 25, 331–341.

Jarlöv, L. (1999). Leisure lots and summer cottages as places for people´s own creative work. In: D. Crouch (Ed.), *Leisure/tourism geographies: practices and geographical knowledge*, (pp. 231–237). Routledge: London.

Jean-Vasile, A. (2013). Multifunctional agriculture and the green economy. In: A. Jean-Vasile, A. Turek, J. Subić & D. Dusmanescu (Eds.), *Sustainable technologies, policies and constraints in the green economy*, (pp. 290–311). IGI Global: Hershey.

Johnstone, M.-L. & Conroy, D.M. (2008). Place attachment: the social dimensions of the retail environment and the need for further exploration, In: A.Y. Lee & D. Soman (Eds.), *Advances in Consumer Research*, (pp. 381–386). Association for Consumer Research: Duluth.

Jokinen, P. Järvelä, M. & Puupponen, A. (2009). Local food systems and rural sustainability initiatives by small scale rural entrepreneurs in Finland. *Maaseudun Uusi Aika*, 2, 5–20.

Jolibert, A., Mühlbacher, H., Flores, L. & Dubois, P.-L. (2012). *Marketing management: A value-creation process*. Palgrave Macmillan: New York.

Jorgensen, B.S. & Stedman, R.C. (2001). Sense of place as an attitude: Lakeshore owners attitudes toward their properties. *Journal of Environmental Psychology*, 21(3), 233–248.

Jumppanen, A., Lee, Y-J., Koyata, F. & Suutari, T. (2013). Social enterprises as tools for employment and social policies in Japanese and Finnish rural regions. *Finnish Social Enterprise Research Network*, 1, 111–119.

Jung, B. (1987). *O czasie wolnym: Kultura i rekreacja w procesach rozwoju społeczno-ekonomicznego*. Szkoła Główna Planowania i Statystyki: Warsaw.

Jurek, J. (1996). Różnicowanie wiejskiego rynku pracy. In: J. Falkowski & E. Rydz (Eds.), *Wielofunkcyjna gospodarka na obszarach wiejskich (ze szczególnym uwzględnieniem Pomorza Środkowego)*, (pp. 141–149). Materiały XIII Ogólnopolskiego Seminarium Geograficzno-Rolniczego oraz 45 Zjazdu Polskiego Towarzystwa Geograficznego. Polskie Towarzystwo Gegoraficzne i Wyższa Szkoła Pedagogiczna w Słupsku: Słupsk.

Kachniewska, M. (2011). Funkcja turystyczna jako determinanta jakości życia na wsi. *Folia Pomeranae Universitatis Technologiae Stetinensis, Oeconomica*, 288(64), 53–72.

Kahneman, D. & Tversky, A. (1979). Prospect Theory: An analysis of decision under risk. *Econometrica*, 47(2), 263–292.

Kaltenborn, B.P. (1997). Nature of place attachment: A study among recreation homeowners in Southern Norway. *Leisure Sciences: An Interdisciplinary Journal*, 19(3), 175–189.

Kankaanranta, J. (2011). *Finnish second homes: From father to son? Finnish second home phenomenon in the 21st Century*. Master of Social Science Thesis. Department of Service Management, Hospitality and Tourism, University of Lund: Helsingborg.

Kasprzyk, B. & Leszczyńska, M. (2012). Dochody i wydatki jako determinanty dobrobytu ekonomicznego gospodarstw domowych w Polsce: Ujęcie regionalne. *Nierówności społeczne a wzrost gospodarczy*, 28, 263–273.

Katz-Gerro, T. & Talmud, I. (2005). A structural analysis of consumption-based stratification: Relational proximity of household expenditures. *Social Indicators Research*, 73(1), 109–132.

Kauppila, P. (2010). Resorts, second home owners and distance: A case study in northern Finland. *Fennia*, 188(2), 163–178.

Kauppinen, E.-L. (1991). Herrasväen huviloista vapaa-ajan asuntoihin: Lomaasumisen vaiheita Saimaalla. In: T. Jaatinen (Ed.), *Saimaa-kirja*, (pp. 143–145). Tammi: Helsinki.

Kelly, G. & Hosking, K. (2008). Nonpermanent residents, place attachment, and "sea change" communities. *Environment and Behavior*, 40(4), 575–594.

Kernot, C. & McNeill, J. (2011). *Australian stories of social enterprise*. The University of New South Wales: Sydney.

Keynes, J.M. (1964). *The general theory of employment, interest and money*. Harcourt, Brace & Wald, Inc.: New York, Chicago, Burlingame.

Khan, H., Chou, F.S. & Wong, K.C. (1990). Tourism multiplier effects on Singapore. *Annals of Tourism Research*, 17(3), 408–418.

Kieżel, E. (1995). *Konsumpcja i gospodarstwo domowe w gospodarce rynkowej*. Zeszyty Naukowe AE, 136: Akademia Ekonomiczna w Katowicach: Katowice.

Kim, S. & Littrell, M.A. (2001). Souvenir buying intentions for self versus others. *Annals of Tourism Research*, 28(3), 638–657.

Kim, Y.G., Eves, A. & Scarles, C. (2009). Building a model of local food consumption on trips and holidays: A grounded theory approach. *International Journal of Hospitality Management*, 28, 423–431.

King, D. & Ilacqua, J.A. (2014). *Analyzing the state of local business & organizational purchasing in Rhode Island. Regional competitiveness: The state of local business & organizational purchasing in Rhode Island*. Brown University and Bryant University: Providence and Smithfield.

Kinley, T.R., Josiam, B.M. & Kim, Y. (2003). Why and where tourists shop: Motivations of tourist-shoppers and their preferred shopping center attributes. *Journal of Shopping Center Research*, 10, 7–28.

Kirwan, J. (2004). Alternative strategies in the UK agro-food system: Interrogating the alterity of farmer's market. *Sociologia Ruralis*, 44, 395–415.

Kleinc, S.S. & Baker, S.M. (2004). An integrative review of material possession attachment. *Academy or Marketing Science Review*, 1, 1–29.

Kłodziński, M. (1992). Wielofunkcyjny rozwój terenów wiejskich w Wielkiej Brytanii. *Wieś i Rolnictwo*, 3–4, 67–77.

Kłodziński, M. (1996). Wielofunkcyjność warunkiem aktywizacji gospodarczo-społecznej obszarów wiejskich. In: M. Kozakiewicz (Ed.), *Wieś i rolnictwo w badaniach społeczno-ekonomicznych: Księga Jubileuszowa*, (pp. 154–168). Instytut Rozwoju Wsi i Rolnictwa PAN: Warsaw.

Kłodziński, M. (1997). Istota wielofunkcyjnego rozwoju terenów wiejskich. In: M. Kłodziński & A. Rosner (Eds.), *Ekonomiczne i społeczne uwarunkowania i możliwości wielofunkcyjnego rozwoju wsi w Polsce*, (pp. 41–67). Szkoła Główna Gospodarstwa Wiejskiego: Warsaw.

Kłodziński, M. (1999). *Aktywizacja gospodarcza obszarów wiejskich*. Instytut Rozwoju Wsi i Rolnictwa PAN, Centrum Naukowo-Wdrożeniowe SGGW: Warsaw.

Kolny, B. (2004). Czynniki kształtujące zachowania w czasie wolnym. *Zeszyty Naukowe Polskiego Towarzystwa Ekonomicznego*, 2, 303–322.

Kondracki, J.A. (2002). *Geografia regionalna Polski*. Państwowe Wydawnictwo Naukowe: Warsaw.

Konishi, H. (2005). Concentration of competing retail stores. *Journal of Urban Economics*, 58(3), 488–512.

Kotler, P. (1994). *Marketing: Analiza, planowanie, wdrażanie i kontrola*. Gebethner i Ska: Warsaw.

Kotler, P. & Keller, K.L. (2015). *Marketing management*, (15th edition). Pearson Education limited: Harlow.

Kowalczyk, A. (1994). *Geograficzno-społeczne aspekty zjawiska drugich domów*. Uniwersytet Warszawski: Warsaw.

Kowalczyk, A. (1995). Second homes in Poland. *Acta Universitatis Carolinae, Geographica*, 2, 37–45.

Kozak, M. (2001). An analysis of tourist spending and its determinants. *Anatolia*, 12(2), 196–202.

Kurland, N.B., McCaffrey, S.J. & Hill, D.H. (2012). The localism movement: Shared and emergent values. *Journal of Environmental Sustainability*, 2(2), 45–57.

Kusińska, A. (2009). Zmiany w sektorze konsumpcji i ich uwarunkowania w latach 1989–2009. *Handel Wewnętrzny*, 4–5, 33–43.

Kuś, G. (2011). *Decyzje zakupowe konsumentów a systemy komunikowania*. Novea Res, Innovative Publishing: Gdynia.

Kuśmierczyk, K. (2002). *Regionalne zróżnicowanie konsumpcji indywidualnej*. Instytut Rynku Wewnętrznego i Konsumpcji: Warsaw.

Kyle, G.T., Absher, J.D. & Graefe, A.R. (2003). The moderating role of place attachment on the relationship between attitudes toward fees and spending preferences. *Leisure Sciences*, 25(1), 33–50.

Kyle, G.T., Graefe, A.R. & Manning, R. (2005). Testing the dimensionality of place attachment in recreational settings. *Environment and Behavior*, 37(2), 153–177.

Labrecque, J. & Ricard, L (2001). Children's influence on family decision-making: A restaurant study. *Journal of Business Research*, 54(2), 173–176.

Laesser, C. & Crouch, G.I. (2006). Segmenting markets by travel expenditure patterns: The case of international visitors to Australia. *Journal of Travel Research*, 44(4), 397–406.

Lagerqvist, M., Pers, A.S. & Nordin, U. (2014). The more, the merrier? Experiences of shared usage and generational intersections at second homes in Sweden. *Tourism, Leisure and Global Change*, 1, pp. 14.

Laitamäki, J. & Järvinen, R. (2013). The impact of the 2008 financial crises on Finnish and American households. *LTA*, 1(13), 41–65.

Landefeld, S.J., Moulton, B.R., Platt, J.D. & Villones, S.M. (2010). GDP and beyond: Measuring economic progress and sustainability, *Survey of Current Business*, April 2010.

Lancaster, K.J. (1966). A new approach to consumer theory. *Journal of Political Economy*, 74, 132–157.

Lancaster, K.J. (1971). *Consumer demand: A new approach*. Columbia University Press: New York.

Lancaster, K.J. (1975). The theory of household behaviour: Some foundations. *Annals of Economic and Social Measurement*, 4(1), 5–21.

Lancaster, K.J. (1979). *Variety, equity and efficiency*. Columbia studies in Economics, 10. Columbia University Press: New York and Guildford.

Lazear, E.P. & Michael, R.T. (1988). *Allocation of income within the household*. University of Chicago Press: Chicago and London.

Lázaro, N., Moltó, M.L. & Sánchez, R. (2000). Unemployment and consumption patterns. *Applied Economics*, 32, 367–379.

Lähteenoja, S., Lettenmeier, M., Kauppinen, T., Luoto, L., Moisio, T., Salo, M., Tamminen, P. & Veuro, S. (2007). *Natural resource consumption caused by Finnish households*. Proceedings of the Nordic Policy Research Conference, 3rd-5th October 2007 in Helsinki. Part III, 15 Sustainable consumption. http://www.consumer2007.info/?p=38>

Le Cotty, T. & Voituriez, T. (2003). *Multifunctionality and non-agricultural supply of public goods*. Proceedings of the 25th IAAE, 16th-22nd August 2003, Durban, South Africa: Durban.

Lee, H.-C. (2001). Determinants of recreational boater expenditures on trips. *Tourism Management*, 22(6), 659–667.

Lee, S.J. & Jeong, M. (2009). *Tourists' emotional experiences with an event and their consequences*. Hospitality & Tourism Management International CHRIE Conference – Refereed Track.

Lee, J.S., Lee, C.K. & Choi, Y. (2011). Examining the role of emotional and functional values in festival evaluation. *Journal of Travel Research*, 50(6), 685–696.

Lehto, X.Y., Cai, L.A., O'Leary, J.T. & Huan, T.-C. (2004). Tourist shopping preferences and expenditure behaviours: The case of the Taiwanese outbound market. *Journal of Vacation Marketing*, 10(4), 320–332.

Lehtonen, O., Tykkyläinen, M. & Voutilainen, O. (2012). Root causes of rural decline in economic well-being in Finland. *European Countryside*, 4(3), 217–239.

Leonard, M. (1998). *Invisible work, invisible workers: The informal economy in Europe and the U.S.* St. Martin's Press, Inc.: New York.

Leones, J., Colby, B. & Crandall, K. (1998). Tracking expenditures of the elusive nature tourists of Southeastern Arizona. *Journal of Travel Research*, 36(3), 56–64.

Leppänen, J. (2003). *Finlands Skärgårdsprogram och fritidshusboende 2003–2006*. Paper presented at second home ownership and shore line protection: Seminar on regional development in the Kvarken Region, Umeå, Sweden, 25th June 2003, Skärgårdsdelegationen: Helsinki.

Leś, E. (2008). Gospodarka społeczna i przedsiębiorstwo społeczne. Przegląd koncepcji i dobrych praktyk. In: E. Leś (Ed.), *Gospodarka społeczna i przedsiębiorstwo społeczne: Wprowadzenie do problematyki*, (pp. 37–55). Uniwersytet Warszawski: Warsaw.

Levitan, L. & Feldman, S. (1991). For love or money: Nonmonetary economic arrangements among rural households in central New York. In: D. Clay & H. Schwarzwller (Eds.), *Research in rural sociology and development*, (pp. 149–172). JAI Press: Greenwich.

Lewicka, M. (2011). Place attachment: How far have we come in the last 40 years?. *Journal of Environmental Psychology*, 31(3), 207–230.

Lewis, R., Hunt, P. & Carson, D. (2006). *Social enterprise and community-based care: Is there a future for mutually owned organisations in community and primary care?* Working Paper, April 2006. King's Fund: London.

Linehan, M. (2008). *Consumer behaviour: Irish patterns and perspectives.* Gill & Macmillan Ltd.: Dublin.

Lipkina, O. (2013). Motives for Russian second home ownership in Finland. *Scandinavian Journal of Hospitality and Tourism*, 13(4), 299–316.

Lipsey, R.G., Steiner, P.O. & Purvis, D.D. (1987). *Economics*, (8th edition). Harper & Row, Publishers: New York.

Lisowski, A. (2005). Janusowe oblicze suburbanizacji. In: I. Jażdżewska (Ed.), *Współczesne procesy urbanizacji i ich skutki: XVIII Konwersatorium Wiedzy o Mieście*, (pp. 91–100). Uniwersytet Łódzki: Łódź.

Lisowski, A. (2007). The centralisation and decentralisation processes in the Warsaw Metropolitan Area in the years 1950-2002. In: J. E. Klausen & P. Swianiewicz (Eds.), *Cities in city regions: Governing the diversity*, (pp. 15–38). University of Warsaw: Warsaw.

Littrell, M.A., Baizerman, S., Kean, R., Gahring, S., Niemeyer, S., Reilly, R. & Stout, J.A. (1994). Souvenirs and tourism styles. *Journal of Travel Research*, 33(1), 3–11.

Long, C. (1958). *The labor force under changing income and employment*, (Gen. Ser. 65). National Bureau of Economic Research (distr. Princeton University Press): New York.

Long, P., Perdue, R. & Venturoni, L. (2012). Home away from home: A research agenda for examining the resort community second home industry in Colorado. In: Hsu, C.H.C. & Gartner, W.C. (Eds.), *The Routledge handbook of tourism research*, (pp. 145–156). Routledge Taylor and Francis Group: New York.

Losby, J.L., Else, J.F., Kingslow, M.E., Edgcomb, E.L., Malm, E.T. & Kao, V. (2002). *Informal economy literature review*. Institute for Social and Economic Development (ISED) Consulting and Research, the Aspen Institute: Newark, Washington.

Losby, J.L., Kingslow, M.E. & Else, J.F. (2003). *The informal economy: Experiences of African Americans*. Institute for Social and Economic Development (ISED) Solutions, Aspen Institute: Washington.

Low, S.M. & Altman, I. (1992). Place attachment: A conceptual inquiry. In: I. Altman & S.M. Low (Eds.), *Place Attachment*, (pp. 1–12). Plenum Press: New York.

Lötter, M.J., Geldenhuys, S. & Potgeiter, M. (2013). Profiling adventure tourists in Pretoria: A comparative analysis. In: Taylor, S., Varley, P. & Johnston, T. (Eds.), *Adventure tourism: Meanings, experience and learning*, (pp. 85–98). Series: Contemporary geographies of leisure, tourism and mobility. Routledge: Abingdon, Oxon.

LUKE, (2013). *Preliminary balance sheet for food commodities 2012: What was eaten in Finland in 2012?*, Published 20.09.2013.

Luloff, A.E., Bridger, J.C., Graefe, A.R., Saylor, M., Martin, K. & Gitelson, R. (1994). Assessing rural tourism efforts in the United States. *Annals of Tourism Research*, 21, 46–64.

Lundmark, L. & Marjavaara, R. (2013). Second home ownership: A blessing for all? *Scandinavian Journal of Hospitality and Tourism*, 13(4), 281–298.

Łapczyński, M. (2003). *Drzewa klasyfikacyjne w badaniach satysfakcji i lojalności klientów*. StatSoft Polska: Cracow.

Łapiński, K., Peterlik, M. & Wyżnikiewicz, B. (2015). *Szara strefa w polskiej gospodarce w 2015 roku*. Instytut Badań nad Gospodarką Rynkową: Warsaw.

MacDonald, D., Crabtree, J.R., Wiesinger, G., Dax, T., Stamou, N., Fleury, P., Gutierrez, L. & Gibon, A. (2000). Agricultural abandonment in mountain areas of Europe: Environmental consequences and policy responses. *Journal of Environmental Management*, 59, 47–69.

Mahika, E.C. (2011). Current trends in tourist motivation. *Cactus Tourism Journal*, 2(2), 15–24.

Mair, J. & Noboa. E. (2003). *The emergence of social enterprise and their place in the new organisational landscape*. Working Paper, 523. IESE Business School, University of Navarra: Barcelona.

Mak, J. (2004). *Tourism and the economy: Understanding the economics of tourism*. University of Hawaii Press: Honolulu.

Mandel, M. (2007). Censoring and truncation: Highlighting the differences. *The American Statistician*, 61(4), 321–324.

Marcelli, E.A., Pastor, Jr, M. & Joassart, P.M. (1999). Estimating the effects of informal economic activity: evidence from Los Angeles County. *Journal of Economic Issues*, 33, 579–607.

Marcouiller, D.W. (1997). Toward integrative tourism planning in rural America. *Journal of Planning Literature*, 11/3, 337–357.

Marcouiller, D.W., Gartner, W.F. & Chraca, A. (2013). *Recreational homes and planning in gateway communities: A review of the planning and public policy literature*, http://expeng.anr.msu.edu/uploads/files/133/Marcouiller%20Publication%20Document.pdf

Marjavaara, R. (2008). *Second home tourism: The root to displacement in Sweden?* Gerum 2008:1, Umeå University, Department of Social and Economic Geography: Umeå.

Marsden, T. & Sonnino, R. (2008). Rural development and the regional state: Denying multifunctional agriculture in the UK. *Journal of Rural Studies*, 24, 422–431.

Marsden, T., Banks, J. & Bristow, G. (2000). Food supply chain approaches: Exploring their role in rural development. *Sociologia Ruralis*, 40(4), 424–438.

Marshall, A. (1920). *The distribution of the national income*. Macmillan & Co., Ltd.: London.

Martinez-Garcia, E. & Raya, J.M. (2008). Length of stay for low-cost tourism. *Tourism Management*, 29(6), 1064–1075.

Maslow, A.H. (1943). A theory of human motivation. *Psychological Review*, 50, 370–396.

Matczak, A. (1986). Budownictwo letniskowe w strefie podmiejskiej Łodzi. *Acta Universitatis Lodziensis, Folia Geographica*, 7, 137–166.

Mather A.S., Hill G. & Nijnik, M. (2006). Post-productivism and rural land use: Cul de sac or challenge for theorization? *Journal of Rural Studies*, 22, 441–455.

Mathieson, A. & Wall, G. (1982). *Tourism: economic, physical and social impacts*. Longman Ltd: New York.

Matteucci, X., Lund-Durlacher, D. & Beye, R.M. (2008). The socio-economic and environmental impacts of second home tourism: the South Pacific coast of Nicaragua example. In: P. Keller & T. Bieger (Eds.), *Real estate and destination development in tourism*, (pp. 149–164). Erich Schmidt Verlag: Berlin.

Maye, D. & Kirwan, J. (2010). Alternative food networks. *Sage – ISA: Sociopedia*.

Mazón, T. (2007). *El turismo residencial en el Mediterráneo Español*. Fecha de Consulta, 15th January 2008, Pensando Turismo, http://pensandoturismo.com/template.php?archivo=Tomas_Mazon.htm

Mazón, T., Huete, R. & Mantecón, A. (2010). Il turismo residenziale in Spagna nella prospettiva sociológica. In: T. Romita (Ed.), *Il turismo residenziale: Nuovi stili di vita e di residenzialitá, governance del territorio e sviluppo sostenibile del turismo in Europa*, (pp. 67–93). Franco Angeli: Milano.

McIntosh, A.J. & Siggs, A. (2005). An exploration of the experiential nature of boutique accommodation. *Journal of Travel Research*, 44(1), 74–81.

McIntosh, R., Goeldner, C. & Ritchie, J. (1995). *Tourism principles, practices, philosophies*, (7th edition). John Wiley and Sons: New York.

McIntyre, N. & Pavlovich, K. (2006). Changing places: amenity coastal communities in transition. In: N. McIntyre, D.R. Williams & K.E. McHugh (Eds.), *Multiple dwelling and tourism: Negotiating place, home and identity*. CABI Publishing: Wallingford.

McIntyre, N., Williams, D. & McHugh, K. (Eds.) (2006). *Multiple dwelling and tourism: Negotiating place, home and identity*. CABI Publishing: Wallingford.

McKenzie, F., Martin, J. & Paris, C. (2008). Fiscal policy and mobility: The impact of multiple residences on the provision of place-based service funding. *Australasian Journal of Regional Studies*, 14(1), 53–72.

McLuhan, M. & Nevitt, B. (1972). *Take today: The executive as dropout*. B.J. Harcourt: Boston.

Mehmetoglu, M. (2007). Nature-based tourists: The relationship between their trip expenditures and activities. *Journal of Sustainable Tourism*, 15(2), 200–215.

Mettepenningen, E., Messely, L., Schuermans, N., Cappon, R., Vandermeulen, V., Van Huylenbroeck, G., Dessein, J., Van Hecke, E., Leinfelder, H., Bourgeois, M., Laurijssen, T., Bryon, J., Lauwers, L., Allaert, G. & Jourez, M. (2011). *Multifunctionality and local identity as paradigms for a sustainable and competitive agriculture*. CONTACTFORUM, Koninklijke Vlaamse Academie van Belgievoor Wetenschappen en Kunsten: Brussels.

Meyer, D. (2007). Pro-poor tourism: From leakages to linkages. A conceptual framework for creating linkages between the accommodation sector and 'poor' neighbouring communities. *Current Issues in Tourism*, 10, 558–583.

Michael, R.T. (1975). Education and consumption. In: F.T. Juster (Ed.), *Education, income, and human behaviour*, (pp. 233–252). National Bureau of Economic Research: New York.

Michael, R.T. & Becker, G.S. (1973). On the new theory of consumer behaviour. *Swedish Journal of Economics*, 75(4), 378–396.

Middleton, V.T.C. & Clarke, J. (2001). *Marketing in travel and tourism*, (3rd edition). Butterworth-Heinemann: Oxford.

Mika, M. (1997). Drugie domy w Beskidzie Śląskim. *Turyzm*, 7(1), 25–42.

Mills, G. (2002). *Retail pricing strategies and market power*. Melbourne University Publishing: Melbourne.

Mincer, J. (1962). Labor force participation of married women: A study of labor supply. In: H.G. Lewis (Ed.), *Aspects of labor economics*, (pp. 63–97). Princeton University Press: Princeton, New Jersey.

Miškolci, S. (2008). Multifunctional agriculture: Evaluation of non-production benefits using the Analytical Hierarchy Process. *Agricultural Economics (AGRICECON)*, 54(7), 322–332.

Modenes, J.-A. & Lopez-Colas, J. (2007). Second homes and compact cities in Spain: Two elements of the same system? *Tijdschrift Voor Economische En Sociale Geografie*, 98, 325–335.

Modigliani, F. & Ando, A.K. (1957). Tests of the life cycle hypothesis of savings. *Bulletin of the Oxford Institute of Statistics*, 19, 99–124.

Moorman, C. (1990). The effects of stimulus and consumer characteristics on the utilization of nutrition information. *Journal of Consumer Research*, 17, 362–374.

Moorthy, S., Ratchford, B.T. & Talukdar, D. (1997). Consumer information search revisited: Theory and empirical analysis. *Journal of Consumer Research*, 23(4), 263–277.

Moreno, I.L. & Ploeg, J.D. van der (2011). *Local food governance and territorial development: The case of the Wadden Goud*. XXIV Congress of the European Society of Rural Sociology "Inequality and Diversity in European Rural Areas", 22nd-25th August 2011 in Chania, Greece.

Morgan, P. (2010). Towards a developmental theory of place attachment. *Journal of Environmental Psychology*, 30, 11–22.

Morley, C.L. (1998). A dynamic international demand model. *Annals of Tourism Research*, 25, 70–84.

Mottiar, Z. (2006). Holiday home owners, a route to sustainable tourism development? An economic analysis of tourist expenditure data. *Journal of Sustainable Tourism*, 14(6), 582–599.

Mottiar, Z. & Quinn, B. (2003). Shaping leisure/tourism places – the role of holiday home owners: A case study of Courtown, Co Wexford, Ireland. *Leisure Studies*, 22, 109–127.

Moutinho, L. (1987). Consumer behaviour in tourism. *European Journal of Marketing*, 21(10), 5–44.

Mowen, J.C. (1995). *Consumer behaviour*, (4th edition). Prentice Hall International: New Jersey.

Mruk, H. & Rutkowski, I.P. (1994). *Strategia produktu*. Polskie Wydawnictwo Ekonomiczne: Warsaw.

Muilu, T. & Rusanen, J. (2004). Changes in population and industries in the rural areas of Finland: from analysis of administrative regions to a GIS based approach In: J. Bański (Ed.), *Changing functions of rural areas in the Baltic Sea Region*, (pp. 109–118), Series: Rural areas and development, 2. IERiGŻ, ERDN, IGiPZ PAN: Warsaw.

Muñoz, T.G. (2007). German demand for tourism in Spain, *Tourism Management*, 28, 12–22.

Murdoch, J. & Marsden, T. (1994). *Reconstituting rurality: Class, community and power in the development process*. University College London Press: London.

Murphey, P.E. & Staples, W.A. (1979). A modernized family life cycle. *Journal of Consumer Research*, 5 (June), 12–22.

Musiał, W. (2007). Dezagraryzacja polskiej wsi: Problemy ekonomiczne, ekologiczne i społeczne. *Wieś i Rolnictwo*, 3, 29–44.

Mutombo, E. & Bauler, T. (2009). *Scenarios as strategizing and learning tool?*, Paper presented at 9th Nordic Environmental Social Science Conference "Knowledge: Learning and action for sustainability", 10th-12th June 2009 in London, UK.

Müller, D.K. (1999). *German second home owners in the Swedish countryside*. Gerum kulturgeografi 1999:2. Department of Social and Economic Geography, Umeå University: Umeå.

Müller, D.K. (2002a). Second homes ownership and sustainable development in Northern Sweden. *Tourism and Hospitality Research*, 3, 343–355.

Müller, D.K. (2002b). German second homeowners in Sweden: Some remarks on the Tourism – Migration – Nexus. *Revue européenne des migrations internationals*, 18(1), 67–86.

Müller, D. & Hall, C.M. (2004). The future of second homes. In: C.M. Hall & D.K. Müller (Eds.), *Tourism, mobility and second homes*, (pp. 273–278). Channel View: Clevedon.

Müller, D.K., Hall, C.M. & Keen, D. (2004). Second home tourism: Impact, management and planning issues. In: C.M. Hall & D.K. Müller (Eds.), *Tourism, mobility and second homes: Between elite landscape and common ground*, (pp. 15–32). Channel View Publications: Clevedon, Buffalo, Toronto.

Naukkarinen, A., Rusanen, J. & Colpaert, A. (1993). The future of rural settlement structure in Finland. *Geography Research Forum*, 13, 61–70.

Neal, C., Quester, P. & Hawkins, D.I. (2004). Consumer behaviour: Implications for marketing strategy, (4th edition). McGraw-Hill Australia: Sydney.

Newby, H. (1988). *The countryside in question*. Century Hutchinson: London.

Newland, K. & Taylor, C. (2010). *Heritage tourism and nostalgia trade: A diaspora niche in the development landscape*. Migration Policy Institute: Washington.

Nicolau, J.L. & Más, F.J. (2005). Heckit modelling of tourist expenditure: Evidence from Spain. *International Journal of Service Industry Management*, 16(3), 271–293.

Nielsen, N.C., Salling Kromann, D., Kjeldsen, Ch. & Just, F. (2009). *Second homes: A possible pathway to rural development?* Paper presented to the WorkGroup on Multifunctional Landscapes at the ESRS Conference, 17th-20th August 2009 in Vaasa. http://www.academia.edu/189780/Second_homes_a_possible_pathway_to_rural_development

Nielsen, T.K. (2014). *Emotional place attachment to a holiday destination: An explorative research on place attachment and displays on Instagram with focus on emotional and functional dimensions that could amplify attachment*. Master Thesis. Aalborg Universitet: Aalborg.

Nieminen, M. (2010). *Kesämökkibarometri 2009*. Työja elinkeinoministeriö, Alueiden kehittäminen, 12, http://www.tem.fi/files/27185/tem_12_2010_web.pdf

Niezgoda, A., Kachniewska, M., Nawrocka, E. & Pawlicz, A. (2012). *Rynek turystyczny: Ekonomiczne zagadnienia turystyki*. Wolters Kluwer Polska: Warsaw.

Nivalainen, S. (2003). *Who move to rural areas? Micro evidence from Finland*. Paper presented in ERSA 2003, Jyväskylä.

Nordell, P.O. & Rydberg, H. (1959). From the plains of Middle Sweden to the high mountains. *Geografiska Annaler*, 41(2), 170–193.

Nordin, U. (1993). Fritidshusbebyggelse. In: H. Aldskogius (Ed.), *Kulturliv, rekreation och turism*, (pp. 72–79). SNA: Stockholm.

Nordin, U. (2011). Den Stationära Mobiliteten: Fritidsboende i Informationssamhället. *Geografiska Notiser*, 69(1), 6–12.

Norris, M. & Winston, N. (2007). *Second homes in scenic rural areas of Ireland: Preliminary results from a study of social, economic and environmental impacts*. Paper presented at European Network for Housing Research Conference, 25th-28th June 2007 in Rotterdam.

Norris, M. & Winston, N. (2009). Social, economic and environmental impacts of second homes in Ireland. In: S. Tsenkova (Ed.), *Planning sustainable communities: Diversity of approaches and implementational challenges*, (pp. 149–168). University of Calgary Press: Calgary.

Norris, M. & Winston, N. (2010). Second-home owners: Escaping, investing or retiring? *Tourism Geographies*, 12, 546–567.

Nouza, M., Ólafsdóttir, R. & Müller, D.K. (2013). A new approach to spatial–temporal development of second homes: Case study from Iceland. *Scandinavian Journal of Hospitality and Tourism*, 13(1), 20–37.

Nowak, S., Herbuś, A. & Szczerbowski, M. (2012). Zjawisko szarej strefy w gospodarce turystycznej. In: S. Nowak (Ed.), *Regionalne i lokalne strategie rozwoju turystyki: Materiały i studia*, (pp. 189–198). Akademia Wychowania Fizycznego w Katowicach: Katowice.

Nyssens, M. (Ed.). (2006). *Social enterprise: At the crossroads of market, public policies and civil society*. Routledge: London and New York.

Obach, B.K. (2015). *Organic struggle: The movement for sustainable agriculture in the United States*. MIT Press: Cambridge, London.

O'Connor, R., Elson, P., Hall, P. & Reimer, B. (2012). *Measuring the size, scope and scale of the social enterprise sector in Manitoba.* http://www.mtroyal.ca/wcm/groups/public/documents/pdf/ins-mbsurvey.pdf

OECD, (2000). *Agricultural policies in OECD countries: Monitoring and evaluation 2000: Glossary of agricultural policy terms*. OECD Publishing: Paris.

OECD, (2001). *Multifunctionality: Towards an analytical framework*. OECD Publishing: Paris.

OECD, (2008). *Environmental performance of agriculture in OECD countries since 1990*. OECD Publishing: Paris.

OECD, (2011a). *ISIC REV. 3 technology intensity definition: Classification of manufacturing industries into categories based on R&D intensities*. OECD Directorate for Science, Technology and Industry, Economic Analysis and Statistics Division. OECD Publishing: Paris.

OECD, (2011b). *Politique agricoles: Suivi et evaluation 2011*. OECD Publishing: Paris.

OECD, (2013a). Measuring household wealth through surveys. In: *OECD guidelines for micro statistics on household wealth*. OECD Publishing: Paris.

OECD, (2013b). *National accounts of OECD countries*. OECD Publishing; Paris.

Ogloblin, C. & Brock, G. (2006). Household income and the role of household plots in rural Russia. *Applied Econometrics and International Development*, 6(1), 59–76.

Oliveira, J.A., Roca, M.N.O. & Roca, Z. (2015). Economic effects of second homes: a case study in Portugal. *Economics and Sociology*, 8 (3), 183–196.

Ollikainen, M. & Lankoski, J. (2005). *Multifunctional agriculture: The effect of non-public goods on socially optimal policies*. Paper prepared for presentation at XI EAAE Congress "The Future of Rural Europe in Global Agri-Food System", 24th-27th August 2005 in Copenhagen, Denmark.

Osborne, S.P. (1998). *Voluntary organisations and innovation in public services.* Routledge: London.

O'Shaughnessy, N. (2012). The death and life of propaganda. *Journal of Public Affairs*, 12(1), 29–38.

Overvåg, K. & Berg, N.G. (2011). Second homes, rurality and contested space in Eastern Norway. *Tourism Geographies*, 13(3), 417–442.

Owen, J.D. (1969). *The price of leisure: An economic analysis of the demand for leisure time.* Rotterdam University Press: Rotterdam.

Paajanen, M. (1994). *The economic interaction between tourists and tourism enterprises.* School of Economics: Helsinki.

Pahl, R.E. (1984). *Divisions of labour.* Blackwell: Oxford.

Palmer, A. & Bejou, D. (1995). Tourism destination marketing alliances. *Annals of Tourism Research*, 22(3), 616–629.

Pammer, W.J., Cohen, E., Weyer, J.M., Jacksy, H., Mall, J. & Kiyan, J.R. (2008). *Second home owner study: Assessing attitudes, consumer behavior, and housing tenure in Sullivan County.* Division of Planning & Environmental Management: Sullivan County.

Panek, E. (2000). *Ekonomia matematyczna.* Akademia Ekonomiczna w Poznaniu: Poznań.

Pardała, W. (2015). Problemy funkcjonalne, techniczne i społeczne drewnianej architektury letniskowej okolic Łodzi. *Budownictwo i Architektura*, 14(3), 59–72.

Paris, C. (2009). Re-positioning second homes within housing studies: Household investment, gentrification, multiple residence, mobility and hyper-consumption. *Housing, Theory and Society*, 26(4), 292–310.

Paris, C. (2010). *Affluence, mobility and second home ownership.* Routledge: London and New York.

Park, C.W. & MacInnis, D.J. (2006). What's in and what's out: Questions on the boundaries of the attitude construct. *Journal of Consumer Research*, 33(1), 16–18.

Paterson, M. (2006). *Consumption and everyday life.* Routledge: London and New York.

Patmore, J.A. (1970). *Land and leisure.* David & Charles: Newton Abbott (Pelican Books 1972).

Pättiniemi, P. (2006). *Social enterprises as labour market measure.* Publications E. Social Sciences, 130. Kuopio University: Kuopio.

Pearce, P.L. (1982). *The social psychology of tourist behaviour.* Pergamon: Oxford.

Pearce, P.L. (1988). *The Ulysses factor: evaluating visitors in tourist settings.* Springer-Verlag: New York.

Perdue, R.R. (2004). Sustainable tourism and stakeholder groups: A case study of Colorado ski resort communities. In: G.I. Crouch, R.R. Perdue, H.J.P. Timmermans & M. Uysal (Eds.), *Consumer psychology of tourism, hospitality and leisure*, (pp. 253–264). CABI Publishing: Wallingford.

Perkins, H.C. (2006). Commodification: re-resourcing rural areas. In: P. Clarke, T. Marsden & P.H. Mooney (Eds.), *Handbook of rural studies*, (pp. 243–257). Sage Publications Ltd.: London.

Perrels, A. & Berghäll, E. (2010). Mökkikannan kehitys. In: A. Rytkönen & A.-M. Kirkkari (Eds.), *Vapaa-ajan asumisen ekotehokkuus*, (pp. 10–15). Suomen ympäristö 6. Ympäristöministeriö: Helsinki.

Peter, J.P. & Olson, J.C. (2010). *Consumer behavior & marketing strategy*, (9th edition). McGraw-Hill Irwin: New York.

Philipson, J.B. (1937). *Consumption standards and housing.* Annals of American Academy of Political and Social Science, 190. Current Developments in Housing: New York.

Piekut, M. (2014). Wydatki Europejczyków na wyposażenie i prowadzenie gospodarstwa domowego. *Konsumpcja i Rozwój*, 2(7), 50–59.

Pinchot, A. (2014). *The economics of local food systems: A literature review of the production, distribution, and consumption of local food.* Extension Center for Community Vitality, University of Minnesota: Duluth.

Pitkänen, K. (2008). Second-home landscape: The meaning(s) of landscape for second-home tourism in Finnish Lakeland. *Tourism Geographies*, 10(2), 169–192.

Pitkänen, K. & Puhakka, R. (2012). *ATTREG – Alueiden vetovoiman tarkastelua matkailun ja muuttoliikkeen näkökulmasta. Nordia Tiedonantoja*, 1, 9–26.

Pitkänen, K., Puhakka, R. & Sawatzky, M. (2011). The role of nature in the place meanings and practices of cottage owners in northern environments. *Norsk Geografisk Tidsskrift – Norwegian Journal of Geography*, 65(3), 175–187.

Pitkänen, K. & Vepsäläinen, M. (2008). Foreseeing the future of second home tourism: The case of Finnish media and policy discourse. *Scandinavian Journal of Hospitality and Tourism*, 8(1), 1–24.

Pitkänen, K., Adamiak, C. & Halseth, G. (2014). Leisure activities and rural community change: Valuation and use of rural space among permanent residents and second home owners. *Sociologia Ruralis*, 54(2), 143–166.

Ploeg, J.D. van der & Roep, D. (2003). Multifunctionality and rural development: The actual situation in Europe. In: G. van Huylenbroeck & G. Durand (Eds.),

Multifunctional agriculture: A new paradigm for European agriculture and rural development, (pp. 37–54). Ashgate: Aldershot.

Plutchik, R. (1980). *Emotion: A psychoevolutionary synthesis.* Harper & Row: New York.

Polinsky, M.A. & Ellwood, D.T. (1979). An empirical reconciliation of micro and grouped estimates of the demand for housing. *The Review of Economics and Statistics*, 61, 199–205.

Pouta, E., Neuvonen, M. & Sievänen, T. (2006). Determinants of nature trip expenditures in Southern Finland – Implications for nature tourism development. *Scandinavian Journal of Hospitality and Tourism*, 6(2), 118–135.

Powers, J.E. & Cooper, R.B. (1976). *Waupaca Chain-O-Lakes second home owners: Expenditures, perceptions, characteristics, and economic impact.* Recreation Resource Center, University of Wisconsin-Extension: Madison.

Prasad, T.G.C. (2012). *Unusual people do things differently.* Penguin Books India Ltd.: New Delhi.

Prayag, G. & Ryan, C. (2012). Antecedents of tourists' loyalty to Mauritius: The role and influence of destination image, place attachment, personal involvement, and satisfaction. *Journal of Travel Research*, 51(3), 342–356.

Prazić, I.T., Devcić, K. & Jergović, I. (2014). Analysis of consumers' local purchasing in Osijek-Baranya county. *Economy of Eastern Croatia, Yesterday, Today, Tomorrow*, 3, 427–434.

Preissing, J., Marcouiller, D.W., Green, G.P., Deller, S.C & Sumathi, N.R. (1996). *Recreational homeowners and regional development: A comparison of two Northern Wisconsin counties*, Staff Paper 96.4. Center for Community Economic Development, University of Wisconsin-Extension: Madison.

Pretty, G.H., Chipuer, H.M. & Bramston, P. (2003). Sense of place amongst adolescents and adults in two rural Australian towns: the discriminating features of place attachment, sense of community and place dependence in relation to place identity. *Journal of Environmental Psychology*, 23(3), 273–287.

Pronovost, G. (2007). *L'univers du temps libre et des valeures chez les jeunes.* Presses de l'Universite du Quebec: Quebec.

Puupponen, A., Kortetmäki, T., Paloviita, A. & Järvelä, M. (2015). Social acceptance of climate change adaptation in farms and food enterprises: A case study in Finland. *International Journal of Sociology of Agriculture and Food*, 22(2), 105–123.

Raczyk, A. & Majkowska, I. (2015). Problemy identyfikacji gmin o zdominowanej strukturze gospodarki. In: R. Brol, A. Raszkowski & A. Sztando (Eds.), *Gospodarka lokalna w teorii i praktyce*, (pp. 62–70), Prace Naukowe Uniwersytetu Ekonomicznego we Wrocławiu, 391. Uniwersytet Ekonomiczny we Wrocławiu: Wrocław.

Rantanen, M. (2014). Palvelujen kysyntään vaikuttavat mökkeilytyylien muutokset: Aiemmin oli Pakko Kaikkien Osallistua, enää ei ole Työleiriä. In: M. Rantanen (Ed.), *Modernisoituvat mökkeilytyylit: Paikallisten palveluympäristöjen muutosvoima*, (pp. 37–48). Raportteja No. 123. Helsinki University, Ruralia Institute: Helsinki.

Rantanen, M. & Hyyryläinen, T. (2012). Vapaajan asukkaat paikallisia palveluympäristöjä muovaamassa. *Maaseudun Uusi Aika*, 2, 59–67.

Ratner, S. (2000). *The informal economy in rural community economic development*. Tennessee Valley Authority Rural Studies (now University of Kentucky Rural Studies Programe), http://www.rural.org/publications/Ratner00-03.pdf

Rausch, S., Metcalf, G.E. & Reilly, J.M. (2011). Distributional impacts of carbon pricing: A general equilibrium approach with micro-data for households. *Energy Economics*, 33, 20–33.

Rebollo, J. & Baidal, J. (2003). Measuring sustainability in a mass tourist destination: Pressures, perceptions and policy responses in Torrevieja, Spain. *Journal of Sustainable Tourism*, 11, 181–203

Rehunen, A., Rantanen, M., Lehtola, I. & Hiltunen, M.J. (Eds.) (2012). *Palvelujen saavutettavuus muutoksessa: Maaseudun vakituisten ja vapaa-ajan asukkaiden palveluympäristön kehityssuunnat ja uudet mahdollisuudet*, Reports 88. Ruralia Institute, University of Helsinki: Mikkeli.

Renting, H., Marsden, T.K. & Banks, J. (2003). Understanding alternative food networks: Exploring the role of short food supply chains in rural development. *Environment and Planning A*, 35(3), 393–411.

Rich, S.U. & Jain, S.C. (1968). Social class and life cycle as predictors of shopping behaviour. *Journal of Marketing Research*, 5 (February), 41–49.

Riihelä, M., Vaittinen, R. & Vanne, R. (2011). *Changing patterns of intergenerational resource allocation in Finland*. Finnish Centre for Pension Reports, 2011, 1.

Rinne, P & Saastamoinen, O. (2005). Local economic role of nature-based tourism in Kuhmo municipality, Eastern Finland. *Scandinavian Journal of Hospitality and Tourism*, 5(2), 89–101.

Rizzo, F. (2016). Approaching multifunctionality by a 'normative view': Finnish farmers' visions on contemporary agriculture. *European Countryside*, 1, 16–32.

Roberts, K. (1999). *Leisure in contemporary society*. CABI Publishing: Wallingford, Oxon.

Roep, D. & Oostindie, H. (2005). Multifunctional agriculture in perspective: Conceptualisations and debate in Dutch policy and research. *Roczniki Akademii Rolniczej w Poznaniu - Ekon.*, 4, 105–111.

Rojek, C. (2000). *Leisure and culture*. Palgrave Macmillan: London.

Romesburg, H.C. (2004). *Cluster analysis for researchers*. Lulu Press: North Carolina.

Romita, T. (2010). Il turismo residenziale in Italia: Un fenomeno sociale diffuso e "fai da te". In: T. Romita (Ed.), *Il turismo residenziale: Nuovi stili do vita e di residenzialitá, governance del territorio e sviluppo sostenibile del turismo in Europa*, (pp. 35–66), Collana: Turismo, consumi, tempo libero. FrancoAngeli: Milano.

Ross, G.F. (1994). *The psychology of tourism*. Hospitality Press: Melbourne.

Roszkowska-Mądra, B. (2009). Koncepcje rozwoju europejskiego rolnictwa i obszarów wiejskich. *Gospodarka Narodowa*, 10, 83–102.

Rudnicki, L. (2010). *Zachowania konsumentów na rynku turystycznym*. Proksenia Publishing: Cracow.

Rudnicki, L. (2012). *Zachowania konsumentów na rynku*. Polskie Wydawnictwo Ekonomiczne: Warsaw.

Russell, H., Watson, D. & McGuinnity, F. (2013). Unemployment and subjective well-being. In: D. Gallie (Ed.), *Economic crisis, quality of work and social integration: The European experience*, (pp. 229–255). Oxford University Press: Oxford.

Rusu, S. (2011). Tourism multiplier effect. *Journal of Economics and Business Research*, 17(1), 70–76.

Ryan, M.M. (2009). Mixed methodology approach to place attachment and consumption behaviour: A rural town perspective. *Electronic Journal of Business Research Methods*, 7, 107–116.

Ryan, B., Bloms, J., Hovland, J. & Scheler, D. (1999). *Tourism retail development: Attracting tourists to local businesses*. University of Wisconsin - Extension, Center for Community Economic Development: Madison.

Rădan-Gorska, M.M. (2013). Destinations without regulations: Informal practices in Romanian rural tourism. *Journal of Comparative Research in Anthropology and Sociology*, 4(2), 195–225.

Sabates-Wheeler, R., Devereux, S., Mitchell, T., Tanner, T., Davies, M. & Leavy, J. (2008). *Rural disaster risk: Poverty interface*, Prepared for global assessment report on disaster reduction. University of Sussex, Institute of Development Studies: Brighton.

Samli, A.C. (1995). *International consumer behaviour: Its impact on marketing strategy development*. Quorum Books: Westport.

Santos, V., Ramos, P. & Almeida, N. (2014). Consumer behaviour in tourism: A content analysis of relationship between involvement and emotions. *Journal of Tourism Research*, 9(B), 28–64.

Sassen, S. (1998). *Globalization and its discontents. Essays on the new mobility of people and money*. New York: New Press.

Savani, K., Markus, H.R. & Conner, A.L. (2008). Let your preference be your guide? Preferences and choices are more tightly linked for North Americans than for Indians. *Journal of Personality and Social Psychology*, 95(4), 861–876.

Scanlon, K., Sagor, E. & Whitehead, C. (2014). *The economic impact of holiday rentals in the UK*, A project for HomeAway, Final report, November 2014. London School Economics: London.

Scannell, L. & Gifford, R. (2010). Defining place attachment: a tripartite organizing framework. *Journal of Environmental Psychology*, 30, 1–10.

Schiffman, L.G., Kanuk, L.L. & Hansen, H. (2008). *Consumer behaviour: A European outlook*. Prentice Hall: Essex.

Schmit, T.M., Jablonski, B.B.R. & Mansury, Y. (2013*). Impacts of local food system activities by small direct – to – consumer producers in a regional economy: A case study from upstate NY*. Working Paper, WP 2013–16. Charles H. Dyson School of Applied Economics and Management, Cornell University: New York.

Schneider, F. (2011). *Size and development of the shadow economy from 2003 to 2012: Some new facts*. Johannes Kepler Universität Linz: Linz. www.ecom.jku.at/members/schneider/files2011

Schneider, F. (2013). *The shadow economy in Europe, 2013*. ATKearney, Johannes Kepler Universität Linz: Linz.

Schneider, F. & Williams, C.C. (2013). *The shadow economy*. The Institute of Economic Affairs: London.

Schoepfle, G., Perez-Lopez, J. & Griego, E. (1992). *The underground economy in the United States*. Occasional Paper No 2. Cooperative Work Programme on the Informal Sector, US Department of Labour: Washington.

Scott, A., Gilbert, A. & Gelan, A. (2007). *The urban-rural divide: Myth or reality?* Socio-Economic Research Group (SERG), 2. Macaulay Institute: Aberdeen.

Scrinis, G. (2007). From techno-corporate food to alternative agri-food movements. *Local-Global*, 4, 112–140.

Selwood, J. (2006). Second homes Russian/Ukrainian style. In: B.C. Hallman, J. Gardiner & D. Blair (Eds.), *Prairie perspectives: Geographical essays*, (pp. 118–142). University of Manitoba: Winnipeg.

Shaw, G. & Williams, A.M. (2004). *Tourism and tourism spaces*. Sage: London.

Sherry, J.R. (1998). *Servicescapes*. American Marketing Association: Chicago.

Shimp, T.A. (1984). Consumer ethnocentrism: The concept and a preliminary empirical test. In: T.C. Kinnear (Eds.), *NA - Advances in Consumer Research*, 11, (pp. 285–290). Association for Consumer Research: Provo.

Shimp, T.A. & Sharma, S. (1987). Consumer ethnocentrism: Construction and validation of the CETSCALE. *Journal of Marketing Research*, 24(3), 280–289.

Short, J.R. (1996). *The urban order*. Blackwell: Oxford.

Siciliano, G. (2012). Urbanization strategies, rural development and land use changes in China: A multiple-level integrated assessment. *Land Use Policy*, 29(1), 165–178.

Sidali, K.L., Kastenholz, E. & Bianchi, R. (2013). Food tourism, niche markets and products in rural tourism: Combining the intimacy model and the experience economy as a rural development strategy. *Journal of Sustainable Tourism*, 1–19.

Sikorska, J. (1988). *Konsumpcja: Warunki, zróżnicowania, strategie*. Instytut Filozofii i Socjologii PAN: Warsaw.

Sikorska-Wolak, I. (2007). Społeczno-ekonomiczne przesłanki kształtowania funkcji turystycznych obszarów wiejskich. In: I. Sikorska-Wolak (Ed.), *Turystyka w rozwoju obszarów wiejskich*, (pp. 13–28). Warsaw University of Life Sciences: Warsaw.

Similä, M., Taskinen, O., Männistö, S., Lahti-Koski, M., Karvonen, M., Laatikainen, T. & Valsta, L. (2005). *Terveyttä edistävä ruokavalio, lihavuus ja seerumin kolesteroli karttoina*. Publications of the National Public Health Institute, B20/2005, Kansanterveyslaitos (KTL): Helsinki.

Simpson, J.A. & Weiner, E.S.C. (1989). *The Oxford English Dictionary*. Oxford University Press: New York.

Sims, R. (2009). Food, place and authenticity: Local food and the sustainable tourism experience. *Journal of Sustainable Tourism*, 17(3), 321–336.

Sireni, M. (2006). Paikallinen ruoka: Marginaalinen ilmiö vai tulevaisuuden trendi?. *Alue ja Ympäristö*, 35, 50–57.

Skak, M. (2004). Restricting ownership of vacation homes. *Tourism Economics*, 10(4), 435–447.

Skawińska, E. (1994). *Wielofunkcyjny rozwój obszarów wiejskich w regionie toruńskim*. Uniwersytet Mikołaja Kopernika: Toruń.

Slee, R.W. (2005). Centenary review. From countrysides of production to countrysides of consumption?. *Journal of Agricultural Science*, 143, 255–265.

Smallwood, D. & Blaylock, J. (1982). *Impact of household size and income on food spending patterns*, National Economics Division, Economics and Statistics Service, Technical Bulletin No 1650. U.S. Dept. of Agriculture: Washington.

Smolarek, M. & Dzieńdziora, J. (2010). Uwarunkowania rozwoju małych przedsiębiorstw na terenach wiejskich. In: Pangsy-Kania, S. & Szczodrowski, G. (Eds.), *Gospodarka polska po 20 latach transformacji: Osiągnięcia, problemy i wyzwania* (pp. 253–266). Instytut Wiedzy i Innowacji: Warsaw.

Smuga, T., Burzyński, W., Karpińska-Mizielińska, W., Marzec, A., Niemczyk, J., Ważniewski, P. & Pucek, A. (2005). *Metodologia badań szarej strefy na rynku usług turystycznych*. Instytut Koniunktur i Cen Handlu Zagranicznego: Warsaw.

Solomon, M.R. (1996). *Consumer behaviour*, (3rd edition). Prentice Hall, Englewood Cliffs: New York.

Solomon, M.R. (2006). *Zachowania i zwyczaje konsumentów*. HELION Publishing: Gliwice.

Solomon, M.R., Bamossy, G. & Askegaard, S. (1999). *Consumer behaviour: A European perspective*, (4th edition). Prentice Hall Inc.: New Jersey.

Solomon, M.R., Russell-Bennett, R. & Previte, J. (2013). *Consumer behaviour*. Pearson Education Australia: French Forests.

Song, H., Dwyer, L., Li, G. & Cao, Z. (2012). Tourism economics research: A review and assessment. *Annals of Tourism Research*, 39(3), 1653–1682.

Song, H., Romilly, P. & Liu, X. (2000). Empirical study of outbound tourism demand in the UK. *Applied Economics*, 32(5), 611–624.

Song, Y.J., Joung, H., Engelhardt, K., Yoo, S.Y. & Paik, H.Y. (2005). Traditional v. modified dietary patterns and their influence on adolescents' nutritional profile. *The British Journal of Nutrition*, 93, 943–949.

Sousa, B. & Simões, C. (2014). An approach on place attachment, involvement and behavioural intentions in cross-border tourist regions. *Revista Turismo e Desenvolvimento*, 21/22, 159–160.

Soutar, G.N. & Sweeney, J.C. (2001). Consumer perceived value: The development of a multiple item scale. *Journal of Retailing*, 77, 203–220.

Stabler, M.J., Papatheodorou, A. & Sinclair, M.T. (2009). *The economics of tourism*, (2nd edition). Routledge: London and New York.

Stanny, M. (2012). Dynamika zmian demograficznych ludności wiejskiej i jej zasobów pracy. *Polityka Społeczna*, 7, 1–9.

Statistics Finland, (2013). *Households' consumption 2012*. Statistics Finland: Helsinki.

Stebbins, R. (2009). *Leisure and consumption: Common ground/separate worlds*. Palgrave Macmillan: New York.

Stedman, R.C. (2002). Toward a social psychology of place: Predicting behaviour from place-based cognitions, attitude, and identity. *Environment and Behavior*, 34(5), 561–581.

Stedman, R.C. (2006). Understanding place attachment among second home owners. *American Behavioral Scientist*, October 2006, 50(2), 187–205.

Steenkamp, J.-B. & Baumgartner, H. (1992). The role of Optimum Stimulation Level in exploratory consumer behaviour. *Journal of Consumer Research*, 19, 434–448.

Steinicke, E., Čede, P. & Cirasuolo, L. (2011). Amentity migration e nuove tendenze demografiche nelle aree tradizionali di spopolamento in Italia. *Bollettino della Societa Geografica Italiana*, 3/2, 273–293.

Steinmetz, R. (2010). *Food, tourism and destination: Differentiation: The case of Rotorua, New Zealand.* http://aut.researchgateway.ac.nz/bitstream/handle/10292/1090/SteinmetzR.pdf?sequence=3

Stephenson, K., Speir, C., Shabman, L. & Bosch, D. (2001). *The influence of residential development patterns on local government costs and revenues.* Department of Agricultural and Applied Economics, Virginia Polytechnic Institute and State University: Blacksburg.

Stewart, S.I. & Stynes, D.J. (2006). Second homes in the Upper Midwest. In: N. McIntyre, D.R. Williams & K. McHugh (Eds.), *Multiple dwelling and tourism: Negotiating place, home and identity*, (pp. 180–193). CABI Publishing: Wallingford.

Strandell, A. & Hall, C.M. (2015). Impact of the residential environment on second home use in Finland: Testing the compensation hypothesis. *Landscape and Urban Planning*, 133, 12–23.

Stryjakiewicz, T. (Ed.) (2004). *Wpływ inwestorów zagranicznych na rozwój regionalny i lokalny na przykładzie GlaxoSmithKline Pharmaceuticals S.A. w Poznaniu.* Bogucki Wydawnictwo Naukowe: Poznań.

Stryjakiewicz, T. (2007). Konsekwencje globalizacji w skali regionalnej i lokalnej jako przedmiot badań geografii ekonomicznej. In: W. Maik, K. Rembowska & A. Suliborski (Eds.), *Geografia a przemiany współczesnego świata*, (pp. 151–163). Wyższa Szkoła Gospodarki: Bydgoszcz.

Stynes, D.J. (1997). *Economic impacts of tourism.* Illinois Bureau of Tourism, Department of Commerce and Community Affairs: Chicago.

Stynes, D.J. (1999). *Approaches to estimating the economic impacts of tourism: Some examples.* Michigan State University: East Lansing.

Suhartanto, D., Ruhadi, N. & Triyuni, N.N. (2015). *Revealing the domestic tourist shopping motivation on fashion product.* Conference paper, https://www.researchgate.net/publication/283726026_Revealing_the_Domestic_Tourist_Shopping_Motivation_on_Fashion_Product

Swagemakers, P. (2003). Novelty production: New directions for the activities and role of farming. In: G. Durand & G. Van Huylenbroeck (Eds.), *Multifunctional agriculture: A new paradigm for European agriculture and rural development*, (pp. 189–207). Ashgate: Aldershot.

Swanson, K.K. (2004). Tourists' and retailers' perceptions of souvenirs. *Journal of Vacation Marketing*, 10(4), 363–377.

Swarbrooke, J. (1999). *Sustainable tourism management*. CABI Publishing: London.

Swarbrooke, J. & Horner, S. (2005). *Consumer behaviour in tourism*, (1st edition). Elsevier Butterworth-Heineman: Burlington.

Szczepański, J. (1970). *Elementarne pojęcia socjologii*. Państwowe Wydawnictwo Naukowe: Warsaw.

Szkup, R. (2003). *Kształtowanie podmiejskiej przestrzeni wypoczynkowej: Przykład zachodniego sektora strefy podmiejskiej Łodzi*. University of Łódź: Łódź.

Szromnik, A. (1998). Etnocentryzm konsumencki jako zjawisko społeczne i problem badawczy. In: Z. Kędzior (Eds.), *Konsument – Przedsiębiorstwo – Przestrzeń*, (pp. 238–245). Akademia Ekonomiczna w Katowicach: Katowice.

Szromnik, A. & Wolanin-Jarosz. E. (2013). Diagnoza poziomu etnocentryzmu konsumenckiego Polaków z wykorzystaniem metody CETSCALE. *Konsumpcja i rozwój*, 1(4), 98–111.

Sztompka, P. (2002). *Socjologia: Analiza społeczeństwa*. Znak: Cracow.

Szul, E. (2013). Prosumpcja jako aktywność współczesnych konsumentów: Uwarunkowania i przejawy. *Nierówności Społeczne a Wzrost Gospodarczy*, 31, 347–358.

Szulce, H. (2013). Przemiany zachowań konsumentów w zmieniającej się gospodarce. *Handel Wewnętrzny*, 1–3, 32–37.

Szymusiak, T. (2015). *Prosument – Prosumpcja – Prosumeryzm: Ekonomiczne oraz społeczne korzyści prosumpcji na przykładzie Polski oraz Niemiec (podejście naukowe)*. Bezkresy Wiedzy: Saarbrücken.

Światowy, G. (2006). *Zachowania konsumentów: Determinanty oraz metody poznania i kształtowania*. Polskie Wydawnictwo Ekonomiczne: Warsaw.

Tamer-Görer, N., Erdoğanaras, F., Güzey, Ö. & Yüksel, Ü. (2006). *Effects of Second Home Development by Foreign Retirement Migration in Turkey*. Paper presented at the 42nd ISoCaRP Congress, 14th-18th September 2006 in Istanbul, Turkey.

Tanasă, L. (2014). Benefits of short food supply chains for the development of rural tourism in Romania as emergent country during crisis. *Agricultural Economics and Rural Development, New Series*, 2, 181–193.

Tapscott, D. & Williams, A.D. (2006). *Wikinomics*. Penguin Books: London.

Tauber, E.M. (1972), Why do people shop?. *Journal of Marketing*, 36, 46–49.

Taylor, D.T., Fletcher, R.R. & Clabaugh, T. (1993). A comparison of characteristics, regional expenditures, and economic impact of visitors to historical sites with other recreational visitors. *Journal of Travel Research*, 32(1), 30–35.

Teasdale, S. (2009). *Can social enterprise address social exclusion? Evidence from an inner city community*. TSRC Working Papers, 3. Third Sector Research Centre: Birmingham.

Tewdwr-Jones, M., Gallent, N. & Mace, A. (2002). *Second homes and holiday homes and the land use planning system*. Welsh Assembly: Cardiff.

Thrane, C. (2002). Jazz festival visitors and their expenditures: Linking spending patterns to musical interest. *Journal of Travel Research*, 40(3), 281–286.

Timothy, D. (2005). *Shopping tourism, retailing, and leisure*. Channel View Publications: Clevedon, Buffalo and Toronto, (Series: Aspects of tourism).

Tobin, J. (1958). Estimation of relationships for limited dependent variables. *Econometrica*, 26, 24–36.

Toennis, F. (1957). *Community and society* (1887). Harper Torchbooks: New York.

Toffler, A. (1980). *The third wave*. William Collins Sons & Co. Ltd.: New York.

Torres, R. (2002). Toward a better understanding of tourism and agriculture linkages in the Yucatan: Tourist food consumption and preferences. *Tourism Geographies*, 4(3), 282–306.

Torres, E. & Domínguez-Menchero, S.J. (2006). The impact of second homes on local taxes. *Fiscal Studies*, 27/2, 231–250.

Toyama, M. & Yamada, Y. (2012). The relationships among tourist: Novelty, familiarity, satisfaction and destination loyalty: Beyond the novelty-familiarity continuum. *International Journal of Marketing Studies*, 4(6), 10–18.

Tress, G. (2002). Development of second home tourism in Denmark. *Scandinavian Journal of Hospitality and Tourism*, 2(2), 109–121.

Tribe, K. (2015). *The economy of the world: Language, history, and economics*. Oxford University Press: Oxford.

Turczak, A. & Zwiech, P. (2013). Czynniki wpływające na strukturę wydatków konsumpcyjnych gospodarstw domowych w Polsce. In: B. Kryk & H. Nakonieczna-Kisiel (Eds.), *Gospodarka regionalna i międzynarodowa* (pp. 189–207), Studia i Prace Wydziału Nauk Ekonomicznych i Zarządzania, 33. Uniwersytet Szczeciński: Szczecin.

Tuorila, H. (2006). *Täällä maalla on hyvä asua. Kokemukset maaseudusta uutena asuinympäristönä*. Kuluttajatutkimuskeskus, julkaisuja, 4. Savion Kirjapaino Oy: Kerava.

Tuulentie, S. (2006). Tourists making themselves at home: Second homes as a part of tourist careers. In: D. McIntyre, R. Williams & K. E. McHugh (Eds.), *Multiple Dwelling and Tourism: Negotiating Place, Home and Identity*, (pp. 145–157). CABI International: Wallingford.

Tyagi, C.L. & Kumar, A. (2004). *Consumer behaviour*. Atlantic Publishers and Distributors: New Delhi.

Tversky, A. & Kahneman, D. (1992). Advances in prospect theory: Cumulative representation of uncertainty. *Journal of Risk and Uncertainty*, 5(4), 297–323.

Ujang, N. (2010). Place attachment and continuity of urban place identity, Proceedings of the 1st National Conference on Environment-Behaviour Studies, 1nCEBS, FAPS, UiTM, 14th-15th November 2009 in Shah Alam, Malaysia. *Procedia – Social and Behavioral Sciences*, 49, 156–167.

Ujang, N. & Dola, K. (2007). Linking activity and place attachment dimensions in enhancing the sense of place. *International Journal on Sustainable Tropical Design Research & Practice*, 2(1), 59–67.

UN, (1998). *Central Product Classification (CPC)*. Version 1.0., Series M, No. 77, Ver. United Nations: New York.

Urban, S. & Michałowska, M. (2013). Czynniki wpływające na zachowania konsumentów w zakresie wyboru targowisk jako miejsca zakupu produktów konsumpcyjnych na przykładzie województwa lubuskiego. *Roczniki Ekonomii Rolnictwa i Rozwoju Obszarów Wiejskich*, 100(2), 108–118.

Utzig, M. (2013). Regionalne zróżnicowanie konsumpcji i dochodów gospodarstw domowych w Polsce. *Roczniki Naukowe Stowarzyszenia Ekonomistów Rolnictwa i Agrobiznesu*, 15(2), 361–366.

Uusitalo, L. (1980). Identification of consumption style segments on the basis of household budget allocation. *Advances in Consumer Research*, 7, 451–459.

Vanhove, N. (2012). *The economics of tourism destinations*. Elsevier Butterworth-Heinemann: Oxford, Burlington.

Vanslembrouck, I., Van Huylenbreock, G. & Van Meensel, J. (2005). Impact of agriculture on rural tourism: A Hedonic Pricing approach. *Journal of Agricultural Economics*, 56(1), 17–30.

Veal, A.J. (2006). *Research methods for leisure and tourism: A practical guide*, (3rd edition). Prentice Hall, Financial Times: Harlow.

Veal, A.J. (2009a). *Leisure and the concept of need*, U-Plan Project Paper 4. School of Leisure, Sport and Tourism, Working Paper 14. University of Technology: Sydney.

Veal, A.J. (2009b). *The elusive leisure society*, (3rd edition). School of Leisure, Sport and Tourism, Working Paper 9. University of Technology: Sydney.

Velvin, J., Kvikstad, T.M., Drag, E. & Krogh, E. (2013). The impact of second home tourism on local economic development in rural areas in Norway. *Tourism Economics*, 19(3), 689–705.

Vepsäläinen, M. & Pitkänen, K. (2010). Second home countryside. Representations of the rural in Finnish popular discourses. *Journal of Rural Studies*, 26, 194–204.

Vepsäläinen, M. & Rehunen, A. (2009). Lomalla kylän lomassa? Kylämökkeilyn rajaaminen, nykytila ja muutokset. *Matkailututkimus*, 5(2), 43–56.

Vermeulen, F. (2002). Collective household models: Principles and main results. *Journal of Economic Surveys*, 16(4), 533–564.

Vickers, J.S. & Renand, F. (2003). The marketing of luxury goods: An exploratory study – Three conceptual dimensions. *The Marketing Review*, 3, 461–474.

Vihinen, H., Tapio-Biström, M.-L. & Voutilainen, O. (2005). *Rural marginalisation and multifunctional land use in Finland*. Rural Studies, Agrifood Research Working Papers, 103. MTT Agrifood Research Finland: Helsinki.

Vittersø, G. & Amilien, V. (2011). From tourist product to ordinary food? The role of rural tourism in development of local food and food heritage in Norway. In: L. Tibère and J. Bessière (Eds.), *Food heritage*. Series: Anthropology of Food, 8. INRA: Toulouse.

Vuoristo, K.V. (2002). Regional and structural patterns of tourism in Finland. *Fennia*, 180(1–2), 251–259.

Vágner, J., Müller, D.K. & Fialová, D. (2011). Second home tourism in light of the historical-political and socio-geographical development of Czechia and Sweden. *Geografie*, 116(2), 191–210.

Wagner, J. & Sherman, H. (1983). The effectiveness of family life cycle variables in consumer expenditure research. *Journal of Consumer Research*, 10 (December), 281–291

Wall, G. (1997), Scale effects on tourism multipliers. *Annals of Tourism Research*, 24, 446–450.

Wallace, A., Bevan, M., Croucher, K., Jackson, K., O'Malley, L. & Orton, V. (2005). *The impact of empty, second and holiday homes on the sustainability of rural communities: A systematic literature review*. Centre for Housing Policy: York.

Wang, X. (2006). *Second home phenomenon in Haikou, China*. A thesis presented to the University of Waterloo in fulfilment of the thesis requirement for the degree of Master of Arts in Planning. University of Waterloo: Waterloo.

Wang, S.-T. & Lee, Y.-S. (2011). Expenditure differences among conference and regular tourists in Taiwan: The role of situational factors. *Journal of Convention & Event Tourism*, 12(4), 290–312.

Wang, Y. & Davidson, M.C.G. (2010). A review of micro-analyses of tourist expenditure. *Current Issues in Tourism*, 13(6), 507–524.

Wang, Y. & Pizam, A. (2011). *Destination marketing and management: Theories and applications*. CABI Publishing: Wallingford.

Wang, Y., Rompf, P., Severt, D. & Peerapatdit, N. (2006). Examining and identifying the determinants of travel expenditure patterns. *International Journal of Tourism Research*, 8(5), 333–346.

Wanninayake, B.W.M.C. (2014). Consumer decision-making styles and local brand biasness: Exploration in the Czech Republic. *Journal of Competitiveness*, 6(1), 3–17.

Watson, J.J. & Wright, K. (2000). Consumer ethnocentrism and attitudes toward domestic and foreign products. *European Journal of Marketing*, 34(9), 1149–1166.

Wątorski, J. (1987). *Mieszkanie i domowe dobra trwałe w konsumpcji rodzin miejskich*. Wrocław Academy of Economics Publishing: Wrocław.

Węgleński, J. (1992). *Urbanizacja bez modernizacji?* Uniwersytet Warszawski: Warsaw.

White, C. & Scandale, S. (2005). The role of emotions in destination visitation intentions: a cross-cultural perspective. *Journal of Hospitality and Tourism Management*, 12(2), 168–178.

Wierenga, B. (1984). Empirical test of the Lancaster characteristics model. *International Journal of Research in Marketing*, 263–293.

Wilkin, J. (2008). Wielofunkcyjność rolnictwa i obszarów wiejskich. In: M. Kłodziński (Ed.), *Wyzwania przed obszarami wiejskimi i rolnictwem w perspektywie lat 2014–2020*, (pp. 9–20). Instytut Rozwoju Wsi i Rolnictwa PAN: Warsaw.

Wilkin, J. (2010). Wielofunkcyjność rolnictwa: Nowe ujęcie roli rolnictwa w gospodarce i społeczeństwie. In: J. Wilkin (Ed.), *Wielofunkcyjność rolnictwa: Kierunki badań, podstawy metodologiczne i implikacje praktyczne*, (pp. 17–41). Instytut Rozwoju Wsi i Rolnictwa PAN: Warsaw.

Wilkin, J. (2011). Jak zapewnić rozwój wsi w warunkach zmniejszającej się roli rolnictwa. In: M. Halamska (Ed.), *Wieś jako przedmiot badań demograficznych*, (pp. 117–137). Scholar Publishing, EUROREG, Uniwersytet Warszawski: Warsaw.

Wilkins, H. (2009). *Souvenirs: What and why we buy?* Department of Tourism, Leisure, Hotel & Sport Management, Griffith University: Gold Coast.

Williams, A.M. & Hall, C.M. (2000). Tourism and migration: New relationship between production and consumption. *Tourism Geographies*, 2(1), 5–27.

Williams, C.C. (2002). *Consumer services and economic development.* Routledge: London and New York.

Williams, C.C. (2007). Socio-spatial variations in the nature of entrepreneurship. *Journal of Enterprising Communities*, 1(1), 27–37.

Williams, C.C. & Horodnic, I.A. (2016). Evaluating the multifarious motives for acquiring goods and services from the informal sector in Central and Eastern Europe. *Journal of Contemporary Central and Eastern Europe*, 24(3), 321–338.

Williams, C.C. & Martínez-Pérez, A. (2014). Entrepreneurship in the informal economy: A product of too much or too little state intervention?. *International Journal of Entrepreneurship and Innovation*, 15(4), 227–237.

Williams, D.R., Patterson, M.E., Roggenbuch, J.W. & Watson, A.E. (1992). Beyond the commodity metaphor: Examining emotional and symbolic attachment to place. *Leisure Science*, 14, 29–46.

Wilson, G.A. (2001). From productivism to post-productivism … and back again? Exploring the (un)changed natural and mental landscapes of European agriculture. *Transactions of the Institute of British Geographers*, NS(26), 77–102.

Wilson, G.A. (2007). *Multifunctional agriculture: A transition theory perspective.* CABI Publishing: Wallingford, Oxon.

Wilson, G.A. (2009). The spatiality of multifunctional agriculture: A human geography perspective. *Geoforum*, 40, 269–280.

Wilson, G.A. & Rigg, J. (2003). 'Post-productivist' agricultural regimes and the South: Discordant concepts?. *Progress in Human Geography*, 27, 681–707.

Wilson, R.M.S. & Gilligan, C. (2005). *Strategic marketing management: Planning, Implementation & Control*, (3rd edition). Prentice-Hall, Inc.: New Jersey.

Wippler, R. (1968). Sociale *determinanten van het vrijetijdsgedrag.* Van Gorcum: Assen.

Wiśniewska, A. (2005). *Czynniki decydujące o wrażliwości konsumentów na markę.* Wyższa Szkoła Promocji: Warsaw.

Witt, U. (2001). Learning to consume: A theory of wants and the growth of demand. *Joural of Evolutionary Economics*, 11, 23–36.

Witt, C. & Wright, P. (1992). Tourist motivation: Life after Maslow. In: P. Johnson & B. Thomas (Eds.), *Choice and demand in tourism*, (pp. 33–55). Mansell: London.

Wojewodzic, T. (2014). Dezagraryzacja produkcyjno-ekonomiczna gospodarstw rolnych w Polsce: Próba pomiaru zjawiska. *Journal of Agribusiness and Rural Development*, 4(34), 213–223.

Woods, M. (2005). *Rural Geography.* Sage: London.

World Bank, (2015). *World Development Indicators database*. World Bank: Washington.

World Bank, (2016). *World Development Indicators database*. World Bank: Washington.

Woroniecka-Leciejewicz, I. & Terwińska, M. (2008). Preferencje konsumpcyjne a struktura wydatków gospodarstw domowych w Polsce. *Współczesne Problemy Zarządzania*, 1, 29–58.

Wright, R. (2006). *Consumer behaviour.* Thomson Publishing: London.

Wyrębek, H. (2010). Znaczenie kredytu w finansowaniu zakup nieruchomości mieszkaniowych w Polsce na przykładzie banku PKO BP. *Europejskie Finanse i Marketing*, 4(53), 196–203.

Yazdani, M. (2007). *An investigation on influencing factors on tourists shopping; Attitude of Iranian handmade carpet in Isfahan*. Master's thesis. Luleå University of Technology: Department of Business Administration and Social Sciences: Luleå. epubl.ltu.se/1653…/LTU-PB-EX-08020-SE.pdf4

Yang, J. (2001). Some thoughts and analysis on second homes (in Chinese). *Land Economics*, 6(19).

Yuksel, A., Yuksel, F. & Bilim, Y. (2010). Destination attachment: Effects on customer satisfaction and cognitive, affective and cognative loyalty. *Tourism Management*, 31(2), 274–284.

Zalega, T. (2008). Human needs and their hierarchy vs. the contemporary theories of consumption. In: A.Z. Nowak, B. Glinka & P. Hensel (Eds.), *Business environment in Poland: The selected managerial and economic aspects and their interconnections* (pp. 132–149). Uniwersytet Warszawski: Warsaw.

Zalega, T. (2012). *Konsumpcja: Determinanty, teorie, modele*. Polskie Wydawnictwo Ekonomiczne: Warsaw.

Zarębski, P. (2015). Typy obszarów wiejskich w Polsce ze względu na poziom rozwoju społeczno-gospodarczego i dynamikę przedsiębiorstw. *Wieś i Rolnictwo*, 3, 63–77.

Zawadzka, A. & Ferenz, K. (1998). *Społeczne aspekty wypoczynku młodych kobiet*. Uniwersytet Wrocławski: Wrocław.

Zawadzka, L. & Zieliński, G. (2013). Kluczowe determinanty łańcucha wartości w kreowaniu sukcesu usług turystycznych. *Zarządzanie i Finanse*, 11(4), 2, 413–424.

Zepeda, L. & Leviten-Reid, C. (2004). Consumers views on local food. *Journal of Food Distribution Research*, 35(3), 1–6.

Appendix

Appendix 1.1

University of Eastern Finland, Karelian Institute, Aurora, Yliopistokatu 2 B, Joensuu, tel.: +359 13 251 111, http://www.uef.fi/fi/ktl/etusivu

Second homes: an opportunity for rural economy?

Questionnaire for second-home owners

Questionnaire no .....

....

PART I: Background and housing conditions

1. Household members. Please include all the people living in the household
Gender: ☐ F ☐ M Year of birth: ....
Spouse's year of birth: ....
How many adults are in the household? ....
How many children (less than 18 yo) are in the household? ....

2. Place of permanent residence (ZIP-code, locality and municipality)
....
....

3. Native language
☐ Finnish
☐ Other, what? ....

4. Education (please, mark the highest level obtained)
☐ Primary/elementary school
☐ Vocational school/course
☐ High school
☐ Vocational high school
☐ University/polytechnics (Bachelor's degree)
☐ University/polytechnics (Master's degree)

5. Main occupation
☐ Entrepreneur (business owner)
☐ Senior officer or specialist (e.g. in management, teaching, research or design)
☐ Lower white-collar (e.g. in management, office sales, public administration)
☐ Manual worker (e.g. in services, agriculture, manufacturing, construction)
☐ Unemployed
☐ Student
☐ Retired
☐ Housewife, family career
☐ Other, what? ....

6. Place of work (locality and municipality)

……………………………………………

……………………………………………

7. Place of work (economic sector)

- ☐ Agriculture, forestry and fishing
- ☐ Mining and excavations
- ☐ Manufacturing
- ☐ Electricity-, water-, gas- and heating delivery; waste and wastewater disposal management
- ☐ Construction
- ☐ Wholesale and retail trade; auto repairs
- ☐ Transportation and storage
- ☐ Tourism and hospitality (accommodation and catering)
- ☐ Public administration and defence
- ☐ Education
- ☐ Health and social services
- ☐ Real estate management
- ☐ Other services, what? …………………..

8. Net monthly household income

- ☐ €10,001 and more
- ☐ €7,501–€10,000
- ☐ €5,001–€7,500
- ☐ €2,501–€5,000
- ☐ €1,251–€2,500
- ☐ Up to €750

9. Housing type

- ☐ Detached house
- ☐ Apartment (in a block of flats)
- ☐ Semi-detached house
- ☐ Other, what? ……………………………

10. Size of the house living area

…………… m^2

11. Did you in your childhood or youth
(please, mark all that apply)

- ☐ Live in the countryside
- ☐ Spend time at cottage in the countryside
- ☐ Spend holidays or free time in the countryside
- ☐ Have no experience of childhood or youth in the countryside

Part II: SECOND-HOME LIVING

12. Second-home location, country (if abroad), municipality

……………………………………………

13. Second-home location (town or village, ZIP-code)

……………………………………………

……………………………………………

14. Second-home location built environment (please, mark all that apply)

- ☐ Town
- ☐ Large or central village
- ☐ Sparsely populated rural area
- ☐ Tourist centre (downhill skiing, Nordic skiing, golf, wellness/spa)
- ☐ Leisure or cottage-area
- ☐ Other, what? ....

....

15. Distance from permanent to to second home:

.... km

16. How much time does usually take to reach your second home from your permanent residence?

.... hours .... minutes

17. How do you usually travel to your second home? (please, mark all that apply)

- ☐ Own car
- ☐ Company car
- ☐ Rented auto
- ☐ Relatives' or friends' car
- ☐ Taxi
- ☐ Bus/Long-distance bus
- ☐ Train
- ☐ Plane
- ☐ Motorboat
- ☐ Boat
- ☐ Bicycle
- ☐ Other means of transportation, what?

....

18. How did you come into possession of your second home?

- ☐ Inherited or gifted
- ☐ Purchased
- ☐ Partly inherited and partly purchased
- ☐ Self-built on inherited/gifted piece of land
- ☐ Self-built on purchased piece of land
- ☐ Other way

19. How long have you owned your second home?

.... years

20. Motives for the second-home location:
(please, mark max. 3 options)
- ☐ Relatives/friends in the area
- ☐ Sukujuuret ovat paikkakunnalla
- ☐ Place of birth
- ☐ Previous positive experience as a tourist in the area
- ☐ Pleasant natural environment
- ☐ Tranquility and closeness to nature
- ☐ Good infrastructure and services
- ☐ Good sport activity opportunities
- ☐ Child-friendly place
- ☐ Easy access (close to permanent home, workplace)
- ☐ Image or reputation of the place
- ☐ Traditional leisure locality
- ☐ Price-quality ration and home equipment
- ☐ Investment
- ☐ Other reasons, what?

....

21. How did you build your second home or converted acquired property into second home?
- ☐ By myself
- ☐ With help of my relatives and friends
- ☐ By local company (including companies from neighbouring municipalities)
- ☐ By other company (from outside)

22. Size of land (plot of land) associated to second home:
.... ha

23. Please, estimate how often did you visit and how many nights did you spend your second home over past 12 months?
January: .... visits, ... nights
February: .... visits, ... nights
March: .... visits, ... nights
April: .... visits, ... nights
May: .... visits, ... nights
June: .... visits, ... nights
July: .... visits, ... nights
August: .... visits, ... nights
September: .... visits, ... nights
October: .... visits, ... nights
November: .... visits, ... nights
December: .... visits, ... nights

24. How much do you spend on travel to second home (fuel, tickets)
.... €

25. Who usually uses your second home?
- ☐ Own family
- ☐ Other relatives
- ☐ Friends
- ☐ Other, (who?)

....

26. Do you rent out your second home to people from outside?

☐ Yes, often
☐ Yes, from time to time
☐ No

27. How many people (including you and your close family) did use your second home over past 12 months?

………………

28. Size of living area of the second home (including sauna, bower)

……… m^2

29. Second home equipment

☐ Kitchen
☐ Bathroom ☐ Shower
☐ WC
☐ Electric sauna
☐ Wooden-heated sauna
☐ Terrace, veranda, balcony
☐ Cold cellar
☐ Garage

Electricity

☐ Network ☐ Solar panel
☐ Wind turbine ☐ Other

Heating

☐ Oven- ☐ Fireplace ☐ Iron stove
☐ Electric-
☐ Water- or air-
☐ Other, what? ……………………………

Water-supply

☐ Own or neighbour's well
☐ Imported in containers from elsewhere
☐ Water-supply network
☐ Other way

Wastewater disposal

☐ To the yard or forest
☐ Onsite wastewater treatment system
☐ Septic tank
☐ Wastewater disposal network
☐ Other way

Home equipment

☐ Television
☐ Washing machine
☐ Dishwasher
☐ Fridge
☐ Telephone (land-line)
☐ Internet
☐ Boat

30. Where did you purchase building materials used to construct or renovate second home?

☐ In the second-home village (sawmill, brickyard, etc.)
☐ In the second-home municipality
☐ In other places/locations

31. Distance to the nearest:

☐ Local council office ………… km
☐ Health centre ………… km
☐ Vet ………… km
☐ Pharmacy ………… km
☐ Grocery store ………… km
☐ Specialty store ………… km
☐ Post office ………… km
☐ Police station ………… km
☐ Fire brigades ………… km
☐ Church ………… km
☐ Bus stop ………… km
☐ Train station ………… km
☐ Taxi ………… km
☐ Catering ………… km
☐ Playground ………… km
☐ Swimming pool ………… km
☐ Public beach ………… km
☐ Other, what? ………………… …… km

32. How do you usually spend time at your second home?

☐ Walking ☐ Cycling ☐ Swimming
☐ Sailing ☐ Fishing ☐ Hunting
☐ Other sports, what?
……………………………
☐ Picking up mushrooms and berries
☐ Cooking
☐ Barbecuing ☐ Meeting friends
☐ Sauna
☐ Reading ☐ Watching TV
☐ Doing nothing ☐ Other, what
…………………………………………….

33. Social relations and networks

☐ I socialize only with my family members and friends at second home
☐ I socialize only with other second-home owners
☐ I socialize with local residents
☐ I take part in local events (social, religious, sport etc.)
☐ I do not take part in local events

34. Which of these products below did you and your family members buy from <u>local farmers and other residents (individuals)</u> over past 12 months?

☐ Dairy products
☐ Bread (pastry)
☐ Vegetable
☐ Berries
☐ Fruits
☐ Meat
☐ Flowers
☐ Honey
☐ Fresh and dried mushrooms
☐ Firewood
☐ Stones
☐ Other, what? ………………………….
……………………………………………
……………………………………………

35. How much did you and your household members spend on these products provided by local farmers and other residents (individuals) over past 12 months?

…………… €

36. How much did you and your household members spend on the following services provided by local farmers and other residents (individuals; no companies) over past 12. months?

Construction and renovations ………… €
Repairs …………… €
Security/watching the house …………… €
Cleaning up ………….. €
Grass cutting …………… €
Snow ploughing …………… €
Tree felling/chopping the wood … €
Other, what? ………………………….
……………………………… …….. €

37. In the case you did not purchase any of these goods or services, please give explanations why?

……………………………………………
……………………………………………

38. How much did you and your household members spend on these products and services provided by <u>local businesses</u> over past 12 months?

Food and drinks .... €
Other every day-use articles .... €
Medicines .... €
Fuel .... €
Building materials .... €
Other goods, what? ....
....
.... €
Health care: ☐ free of charge or .... €
Library: ☐ free of charge or .... €
Cultural events: free of charge or .... €
Restaurant, coffee bar .... €
Recreational services: ☐ free of charge or ..... €
Construction and renovation services ... €
Repairs .... €
Security/watching the house .... €
Cleaning-up .... €
Grass cutting .... €
Snow ploughing .... €
Tree felling/chopping the wood .... €
Hairdresser .... €
Laundry .... €
Taxi .... €
Other services, what? ....
....
.... €

39. In the case you did not purchase any of these goods or services, please give explanations why?

....
....
....

40. How much do you spend yearly on the following second home-related fees and charges?

Waste collection fees .... €
Electricity fees .... €
Water-/wastewater disposal fees .... €
Heating fees .... €
Road fees .... €
Property tax .... €
Other, what? .... €

41. Where do you buy daily commodities (food, drinks and household goods) for longer stays at the second home?

Second-home municipality shops and companies .... %
Permanent home municipality shops and businesses .... %
On the way to the second home .... %
Other places, where? <u>....... %</u>
100%

42. Where do you buy other commodities (clothing, cosmetics) for longer stays at the second home?

Second-home municipality shops and companies ...... %
Permanent home municipality shops and businesses .... %
On the way to the second home .... %
Other places, where? .... %
100%

43. Where do you purchase services for longer stays at second home?

Second-home municipality shops and companies ...... %
Permanent home municipality shops and businesses .... %
Other places, where? .... %
100%

44. Has the usage of your second home over the past three years (e.g. in terms of length of stay, number of users)

- ☐ Increased a lot
- ☐ Increased slightly
- ☐ Remained the same
- ☐ Decreased slightly
- ☐ Decreased significantly
- ☐ Cannot say

45. Will the usage of your second home in the next three years (e.g. in terms of length of stay, number users)

- ☐ Increase a lot
- ☐ Increase slightly
- ☐ Remain the same
- ☐ Decrease slightly
- ☐ Decrease a lot
- ☐ Cannot say

46. Do you or your household members plan to move permanently to the second home location (holiday home or another dwelling) in the next three years?

- ☐ Yes
- ☐ Possibly
- ☐ No
- ☐ Cannot say

47. Do you or your household plan to move permanently to the second home location (holiday home or another dwelling) later in the future?

- ☐ Yes
- ☐ Possibly
- ☐ No
- ☐ Cannot say

48. Do you or your household members possess other holiday homes?

- ☐ Yes, where? ....

....

- ☐ No

Thank you for answering this questionnaire!

Appendix 1.2

Institute of Rural and Agricultural Development, Polish Academy of Sciences, Department of Rural Economy, Nowy Świat 72, 00–330 Warsaw, tel.: (+48 22 826 94 36), www.irwirpan.waw.pl

Significance of second homes in rural development

Questionnaire for second-home owners

Questionnaire no …..

………………………………………………………………………………

PART I: Background

Questionnaire no ………. Date of interview ………..
Interviewer's telephone number ……..……………..

1. Respondent's socio-demographics

1.1 Gender ………
1.2 Year of birth ………
1.3 Marital status
☐ Single
☐ Married
☐ Divorced
☐ Widow/widower
1.4 Number of household members ………
incl. underage ……….
1.5 Economic activity
☐ Entrepreneur/farmer
☐ Senior executive and specialist
☐ Low white-collar
☐ Manual worker
☐ Unemployed
☐ Housewife
1.6 Net monthly household income
☐ 10,001 and more
☐ 5,001–10,000 PLN
☐ 3,001–5,000 PLN
☐ 1,501–3,000 PLN
☐ Up to 1,500 PLN

1.7 Education
☐ Primary school
☐ Vocational school/training
☐ High school
☐ Vocational high school
☐ University/polytechnic
1.8 Permanent place of living
Locality …………………………………………
Municipality ……………………………………
Region …………………………………………..
1.9 Place of work
Own farm, (area of land) ………….. ha
Other (location/industry) …………………
……………………………………………………

PART II: Second home

2. Location of the second home in the settlement:

☐ In the village
☐ "Isolated" location (outside the village)
☐ In the second-home settlement

3. Travel from permanent residence to second home (one way)

Distance (in km) ………………..
Time (in minutes) ………………..

4. How do you usually travel to your second home? (means of transportation)

....

5. When did you:

Buy the land (plot of land) .... (year)
Build your second home .... (year)
Buy your second home .... (year)

6. Motives for the second home location (please mark max. 3 options, then choose the most important one)

- ☐ Municipality of birth
- ☐ Family roots
- ☐ Social environment (relatives and friends in the area)
- ☐ Previous positive experience as a tourist in this area
- ☐ Naturally attractive place
- ☐ Tranquility and closeness to nature
- ☐ Close to permanent residence, workplace
- ☐ Child-friendly place
- ☐ Good transportation accessibility
- ☐ Well-equipped municipality (technical infrastructure, services)
- ☐ Close to leisure services and/or facilities
- ☐ Image/reputation of the place
- ☐ Traditional leisure locality
- ☐ Investment
- ☐ Price-quality ratio
- ☐ Adverts
- ☐ Other, (what?) ....

7. How have you become the second home owner? (origins of second home)

- ☐ Purchase of the property, then renovation of the old house
- ☐ Purchase of the property, then demolition the old house and construction of the new one
- ☐ Inheritance of the property, then renovation of the old house
- ☐ Inheritance of the property, then demolition of the old house and construction of the new one
- ☐ Purchase of the piece of land where the house has been moved from elsewhere
- ☐ Purchase of the piece of land, then construction of the second home
- ☐ Purchase of the leisure property (second home)

8. Please, estimate the value of the property:

Land, at the moment of purchase:
.... PLN
Land, current value: .... PLN
House, at the moment of purchase or construction:
.... PLN
House, current value .... PLN
Property (land + house), at the moment of purchase:
.... PLN
Property (land+ house), current value:
.... PLN

9. How did you build your second home or converted acquired property into second home?

- ☐ By myself
- ☐ With help from my family and friends
- ☐ By local company (including companies from neighbouring municipalities)
- ☐ By other company (from outside)

10. Size of land (plot of land):
- ☐ 3,001 m^2 and more
- ☐ 2,001–3,000 m^2
- ☐ 1,001–2,000 m^2
- ☐ 501–1,000 m^2
- ☐ Up to 500 m^2

11. What was your pattern of using your second home over past 12 months (from September 2008 to August 2009)?
- ☐ Occasionally – a few times
- ☐ Weekends and (public, religious) holidays
- ☐ Summer and/or winter holidays
- ☐ Other, what? ....

....

12. How many nights did you spend at your second home monthly over past 12 months (from September 2008 to August 2009)?

September 2008 ...... March ....
October .... April ....
November .... May ....
December .... June ....
January 2009 ...... July ....
February .... August ....

13. Who usually uses your second home?
- ☐ Owner and his/her close family
- ☐ Other relatives
- ☐ Friends

13. Do you rent out your second home?
- ☐ Yes, often
- ☐ Yes, occasionally
- ☐ No

14. Size of living area and number of rooms in the second home?
- ☐ 151 m^2 and more
- ☐ 100–150 m^2
- ☐ 50–100
- ☐ Up to 50 m^2

Number of rooms ....

15. Second home equipment

☐ Kitchen ☐ Bathroom ☐ Toilet
☐ Terrace ☐ Veranda ☐ Balcony
☐ Fireplace ☐ Garage ☐ Shed
☐ Electricity ☐ Water-supply network
☐ Well ☐ Wastewater disposal system
☐ Septic tank ☐ Gas supply system
☐ Gas cylinder ☐ Central heating system
☐ Television ☐ Washing machine
☐ Telephone (land-line)
☐ Internet

Is your home winterised?
☐ Yes ☐ No

16. Plot equipment

Plants:
☐ Lawn ☐ Flowers
☐ Fruit bushes ☐ Ornamental bushes
☐ Fruit trees ☐ Ornamental trees
☐ Vegetables ☐ Ground fruits
☐ Greenhouse ☐ Plastic/low tunnel
☐ Other, what? ....

....

Recreational facilities:
☐ Garden furniture ☐ Swing
☐ Swimming pool ☐ Tennis court
☐ Other, what? ....

....

Fencing:
☐ Wire netting ☐ Wooden fence
☐ Metal fence ☐ Wall ☐ Hedge
☐ Other, what? ....
....
☐ Unequipped plot of land

17. Building materials used to construct the house

Walls:
☐ Wood ☐ Brick
☐ Other, what? ....
....

Type of the roof:
☐ Flat ☐ Sloped

Roof:
☐ Tile ☐ Shake ☐ Old thatching
☐ New thatching ☐ Tar paper ☐ Eternit
☐ Sheet metal ☐ Other, what? ....
....

18. Where did you purchase building materials used to construct or renovate the house?

☐ In the second-home village (sawmill, brickyard)
☐ In the second-home municipality
☐ In other places/locations

19. Facilities/services in the second home location and its immediate surroundings

☐ Physician ☐ Vet ☐ Pharmacy
☐ Grocery store ☐ Specialty shop
☐ Catering
☐ Post office ☐ Police station ☐ Fire brigade
☐ Church ☐ Entertainment
☐ Bus stop ☐ Train station
☐ Playground ☐ Beach ☐ Pitch
☐ Recreational equipment rental
☐ Swimming pool ☐ Other, what?
....

20. How do you perceive the second-home village with regard to: (1 – very poor/low to 5 – very good/high)

Roads ...... Sidewalks ......
Water-supply system ......
Wastewater disposal system ......
Gas-supply system ....
Waste collection ......
Public transportation (frequency and number of connections ....
Tranquility ...... Cleanliness ......
Safety ......
Activities of local authorities supporting local development ......

21. Leisure activities and practices at second home:

☐ Sports, what? ....

....

☐ Walking ☐ Cycling ☐ Gardening

☐ Picking up mushrooms and berries

☐ Social contacts ☐ Reading books, newspapers

☐ Watching TV ☐ Doing nothing

☐ Other, what? ....

....

22. Social ties and local participation

☐ I socialize only with other second-home owners

☐ I socialize only with local people

☐ I socialize with both groups

☐ I take part in the local community activities (please, give examples)

....

☐ I take part in the local community religious activities (please, give examples)

....

....

23. Please, mark goods and services you purchased from local people (individuals) and farmers over past 12 months then estimate approximate expenditures:

Food:

Dairy products .... PLN;

Bread (pastry) .... PLN;

Vegetables .... PLN;

Fruits .... PLN; Meat .... PLN;

Flowers .... PLN; Honey .... PLN;

Fresh and dried mushrooms .... PLN;

Berries .... PLN;

Other, what? .... PLN

Services:

House construction/renovation ...... PLN;

Repairs ..... PLN; Moving the lawn ... PLN;

Snow ploughing .... PLN;

Watching the house .... PLN;

Watching the children .... PLN;

Other, what? .... PLN

24. In the case you did not make any purchase from local residents nor farmers, please give explanation why?

....

....

....

....

25. Please, mark goods and services you purchased from local enterprises over past 12 months then estimate approximate expenditures:

Goods:
Food and drinks ……… PLN;
Other every day-use articles ……… PLN;
Medicines ……… PLN;
Fuel (gas station) ……… PLN;
Building materials ……… PLN;

Services:
Health care Free of charge or ……… PLN;
Catering ……… PLN;
Recreational equipment rental ……… PLN;
Recreational facilities (charged) …… PLN;
Hairdresser …… PLN; Repairs …… PLN;
Laundry ……… PLN; Other (what?) ……..
……………………………………… PLN;

26. In the case you did not make any purchase from local companies, please give explanations why?

……………………………………………
……………………………………………
……………………………………………
……………………………………………

27. Do you plan to move-in to your second home on a permanent basis in the future?

☐ Yes
☐ No
☐ Cannot say

28. Has your stay at your second home, from year to year, become:

☐ Longer
☐ Shorter
☐ Steady

Thank you for answering this questionnaire!

Appendix 2.1

University of Eastern Finland, Karelian Institute, Aurora, Yliopistokatu 2 B, Joensuu, tel.: +359 13 251 111, http://www.uef.fi/fi/ktl/etusivu

Second homes: an opportunity for rural economy?

Questionnaire for permanent residents

……………………………………………………………… Questionnaire no

………………………………………………………………………………………………

PART I: Background and housing conditions

1. **Household members.** Please include all the people living in the household
Gender: ☐ F ☐ M Year of birth: ……………
Spouse's year of birth: ……………
How many adults are in the household? ……
How many children (less than 18 yo) are in the household? ……

2. **Place of permanent residence (ZIP-code, locality and municipality)**
……………………………………………
……………………………………………

3. **Native language**
☐ Finnish
☐ Other, what?……………………………

4. **Education (please, mark the highest level obtained)**
☐ Primary/elementary school
☐ Vocational school/course
☐ High school
☐ Vocational high school
☐ University/polytechnics (Bachelor's degree)
☐ University/polytechnics (Master's degree)

5. **Main occupation**
☐ Entrepreneur (business owner)
☐ Senior officer or specialist (e.g. in management, teaching, research or design)
☐ Lower white-collar (e.g. in management, office sales, public administration)
☐ Manual worker (e.g. in services, agriculture, manufacturing, construction)
☐ Unemployed
☐ Student
☐ Retired
☐ Housewife, family career
☐ Other, what? ………………………………

6. **Place of work (locality and municipality)**
……………………………………………

7. **Place of work (economic sector)**
☐ Agriculture, forestry and fishing
☐ Mining and excavations
☐ Manufacturing
☐ Electricity-, water-, gas- and heating delivery; waste and wastewater disposal management
☐ Construction

☐ Wholesale and retail trade; Auto repairs
☐ Transportation and storage
☐ Tourism and hospitality (accommodation and catering)
☐ Public administration and defence
☐ Education
☐ Health and social services
☐ Real estate management
☐ Other services, what? …………………

8. Net monthly household income

☐ €10,001 and more
☐ €7,501–€10,000
☐ €5,001–€7,500
☐ €2,501–€5,000
☐ €1,251–€2,500
☐ Up to €750

9. Housing type

☐ Detached house
☐ Apartment (in a block of flats)
☐ Semi-detached house
☐ Other, what? ……………………………

10. Size of the house living area

……………………… m²

PART II: RELATIONSHIPS WITH SECOND-HOME OWNERS

11. How long have you lived in your current permanent residence?

……… years

12. Where did you have live before you moved in to your current place of residence?

Locality……….………………………….
Municipality ………………………………

13. Do you think your current place of living is an attractive place for leisure stays and tourism activities?

Yes, due to
☐ Beautiful scenery
☐ Place close to nature
☐ Lake/waterway is attractive
☐ Historical sites in the area
☐ Traditional leisure/cottage area
☐ Other, what? …………………………
……………………………………………
No, please give the reason for that? ……….
……………………………………………
……………………………………………

14. Have you ever:

☐ Sold land and/or buildings to second-home owners (the real estate sales) in your current residence?
☐ Sold land and/or buildings to other customers than second-home owners in your current residence?

15. If you have sold land or buildings to second-home owners, when did this happen?

Year: ………..

16. If you sold land or buildings to second-home owners, what was the size of the land sold?

……………………… m²

17. What was the value of the sold real estate?

Land .... €

Land and buildings .... €

18. Do you or any of your household members sell agricultural produce or services to second-home owners?

☐ Yes

☐ No

19. If you sell products (over past 12 months), what are they?

☐ Dairy products

☐ Home-made bread

☐ Vegetables

☐ Berries

☐ Fruits

☐ Meat

☐ Flowers

☐ Honey

☐ Fresh or dried mushrooms

☐ Wood

☐ Stones

☐ Other, what? ....

....

....

20. How much did you/your household earn from the aforementioned sales over past 12 months?

.... €

21. What services did you provide to second-home owners and how much did you earn from that source over the past 12 months?

☐ Construction and renovations .... €

☐ Repairs .... €

☐ Security/watching the house .... €

☐ Cleaning .... €

☐ Grass cutting .... €

☐ Snow ploughing .... €

☐ Tree felling/chopping the wood .... €

☐ Other, what? ....

....

....

.... €

22. How do you assess the importance of second-home owners for your household in the following matters (1= very little importance, 5= very high importance)

Social contacts ....

New ideas and innovative stimulation ....

Economic opportunities (e.g. selling goods and services) ....

Economic benefits of the municipality (e.g. taxes, infrastructure etc.) ....

23. Have you ever noticed any negative influence of second-home owners on the local community?

☐ No
☐ Yes:
☐ Environmental deterioration
☐ Degradation of natural habitats (plants, animals)
☐ Noise
☐ Crime
☐ Too densely built-up area, excessive dwelling
☐ Other, what? ....
....
....

24. In your opinion, have second-home owners (second homes) had an impact on developing the local infrastructure the municipality (1= very little impact 5= very high impact)

Roads ......
Bike and walking paths ......
Water supply ......
Wastewater disposal ......
Other infrastructure, what? ....
....
Cleanliness ......
Security ......
Cultural events ......
Tourism and recreational facilities ......
Other, what? ....
....

25. Do you have your own second home?

☐ Yes
☐ No

26. Location of your second home (locality, municipality, country if abroad)

....
....

Thank you for answering this questionnaire!

Appendix 2.2

Institute of Rural and Agricultural Development, Polish Academy of Sciences, Department of Rural Economy, Nowy Świat 72, 00–330 Warsaw, tel.: (+48 22 826 94 36), www.irwirpan.waw.pl

Significance of second homes in rural development

Questionnaire for permanent residents

....

PART I: Background

Questionnaire no .... Date of interview ....

Interviewer's telephone number ……..……………..

1. Respondent's socio-demographics

Gender ....

Year of birth ....

Marital status

☐ Single

☐ Married

☐ Divorced

☐ Widow/widower

Number of household members ....

Economic activity

Entrepreneur/farmer

☐ Senior executive and specialist

☐ Low white-collar

☐ Manual worker

☐ Unemployed

☐ Housewife

Net monthly household income

☐ 5,001 PLN and more

☐ 3,001–5,000 PLN

☐ 1,501–3,000 PLN

☐ Up to 1,500 PLN

Education

☐ Primary school

☐ Vocational school/training

☐ High school

☐ Vocational high school

☐ University/polytechnic

Permanent place of living

Locality……………………………………..

Municipality………………………………..

Region ……………………………………..

Place of work

Own farm, (area of land) ………….. ha

Other (location/industry) …………………

....

2. How many years have you lived in your current address?

....

3. Your previous permanent place of living was in (locality, municipality, region):

....

....

....

4. Is, in your opinion, your locality attractive for tourists and for recreational purposes?

YES, because of:

- ☐ Environmental attractiveness
- ☐ Vicinity of forests
- ☐ Vicinity of rivers and lakes
- ☐ Historical sites in the area
- ☐ Being a traditional tourist locality
- ☐ Other reasons, (what?) ....

....

NO, because of: ....

....

....

5. When did second homes appear for the first time in the locality?

.... (year)

6. Have you or your household member ever (please mark proper option/ options):

- ☐ Sold a property (a piece of land + house) to people from outside the community
- ☐ Sold a house to be relocated away from the community
- ☐ Sold a piece of land to people from outside the community
- ☐ Sold a piece of land (agricultural land, meadow, forest) belonging to your own property to people from outside the community
- ☐ Sold a second/vacation home property to people from outside: (if so, how many?) ....

7. If the sale occurred, when did this happen?

.... (year)

8. If the sale(s) occurred, what was the size of total area sold?

- ☐ 3,001 m^2 and more
- ☐ 2,001–3,000 m^2
- ☐ 1,001–2,000 m^2
- ☐ 501–1,000 m^2
- ☐ Up to 500 m^2

9. What was the amount of money obtained from those transactions?

Land .... PLN

House to be moved away .... PLN

Property (piece of land + house) ....

.... PLN

10. Have you or your household member ever (please mark proper option/ options):

☐ Granted land/property to someone from your family living outside the locality

☐ Sold land, house or property to someone from your family living outside the locality?

11. Have you or your household member sold agricultural, forest produce or services to second-home owners over past 12 months? (please mark types of products and services offered and estimate your earnings)

Goods:
Dairy products .... PLN
Bread (pastry) .... PLN
Vegetables .... PLN
Fruits ....PLN
Meat .... PLN
Flowers .... PLN
Honey .... PLN
Fresh and dried mushrooms .... PLN
Berries .... PLN
Other, (what?) .... PLN

Services:
House construction & renovations .... PLN
Repairs .... PLN
Moving the lawn .... PLN
Snow ploughing .... PLN
Watching the house .... PLN
Watching the children .... PLN
Catering .... PLN
Recreational equipment rental .... PLN
Other, (what?) .... PLN

12. How do you perceive second home owners and their stay (ranging from 1 – very bad to 5 – very good)?

Social interactions (visiting, spending free time together etc.) ....
Lifestyle (behaviour) ....
Influence on standard of equipment of your house/household ....
Opportunities to supply them with products and services (opportunities to earn money) ....
Opportunities for local development ....

13. Have you noticed any disadvantages resulting from second homes and their owners/users in the locality?

☐ NO

YES, due to:

☐ Environmental pollution
☐ Devastation of natural habitats
☐ Noise
☐ Demoralization
☐ Criminality
☐ Hooliganism
☐ Limitations in the access to public space
☐ Decrease in agricultural and forest area
☐ Other, (what?) ....

14. **How do you perceive performance of local authorities with regard to local development (technical infrastructure, social facilities improvements) (ranging from 1 – very poor to 5 – very high)?**

General opinion …………..
Roads …………..
Sidewalks …………..
Bridges …………..
Water-supply network …………..
Wastewater disposal system ……………..
Gas supply system …………..
Other infrastructures (what?) ………….
……………………………………….. ……
Cleanliness …………
Safety …………..
Cultural events …………..
Tourist and recreational facilities
…………..
Applying for external funds and attracting investors …………..
Other, (what?) ……………………………
…………………………………….. ……..

Thank you for answering this questionnaire!

Polish Studies in Economics

Edited by Ryszard Kokoszczyński

Volume 1 Wojciech Grabowski: Employee Stock Options, Payout Policy, and Stock Returns. Shareholders and Option Holders in Large U.S. Technology Corporations. 2012.

Volume 2 Jan Jakub Michałek / Michał Brzozowski / Andrzej Cieślik (eds.): The Relationship between Human Development, Exports and Foreign Direct Investments in Emerging Europe. 2013.

Volume 3 Tomasz Żylicz: The Economics of International Environmental Cooperation. 2015.

Volume 4 Juliusz Jabłecki / Ryszard Kokoszczyński / Paweł Sakowski / Robert Ślepaczuk / Piotr Wójcik: Volatility as an Asset Class. Obvious Benefits and Hidden Risks. 2015.

Volume 5 Janusz Kudła / Konrad Walczyk / Robert Kruszewski / Katarzyna Kopczewska / Agata Kocia: Modeling Fiscal Policy in the European Union. 2015.

Volume 6 Andrzej Cieślik / Jan Jakub Michałek (eds.): Liberalization of Transportation Services in the EU: the Polish Perspective. 2015.

Volume 7 Katarzyna Metelska-Szaniawska: Economic Effects of Post-Socialist Constitutions 25 Years from the Outset of Transition. The Constitutional Political Economy Approach. 2016.

Volume 8 Elżbieta Czarny / Andżelika Kuźnar / Jerzy Menkes (eds.): The Impact of the Transatlantic Trade and Investment Partnership on International Cooperation. 2017.

Volume 9 Adam Czarnecki: Going Local? Linking and Integrating Second-Home Owners with the Community's Economy. A Comparative Study between Finnish and Polish Second-Home Owners. 2017.

www.peterlang.com

www.ingramcontent.com/pod-product-compliance
Ingram Content Group UK Ltd.
Pitfield, Milton Keynes, MK11 3LW, UK
UKHW021829100926
8556IPUK00004B/233

9 783631 729014